BEDFORDSHIRE
HISTORICAL RECORD
SOCIETY
1999

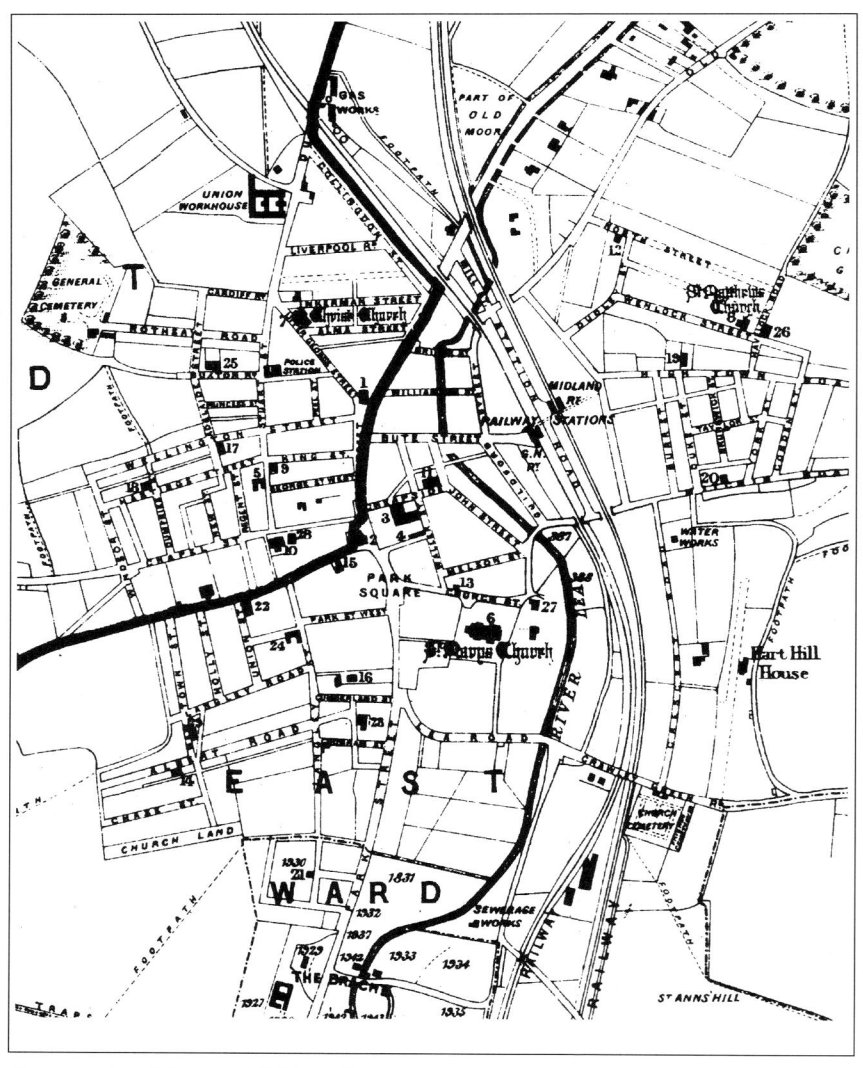

From a map of Luton of 1876 (LM).

THE PUBLICATIONS OF THE BEDFORDSHIRE
HISTORICAL RECORD SOCIETY
VOLUME 78

STRAWOPOLIS

Luton Transformed 1840–1876

by

Stephen Bunker

PUBLISHED BY THE SOCIETY   1999

©
THE BEDFORDSHIRE
HISTORICAL RECORD
SOCIETY
AND
STEPHEN BUNKER 1999

ISBN 0 85155 062 2
First published in 1999 by the Society

All rights reserved. Except as permitted under current legislation, no part of this work may be photocopied, stored in a retrieval system, published, performed in public, adapted, broadcast, transmitted, recorded or reproduced in any form or by any means without the prior permission in writing of the copyright owners.

This volume has been published with the help of grants from Bedford Borough Council, Mid-Beds. District Council, Luton Borough Council and the University of Luton.

Cover design by Ian Davies, Park Farm Studios Ltd.,
Riseley Road, Bletsoe, Bedford MK44 1QU

Printed and bound by
Stephen Austin and Sons Ltd., Hertford

For Mum and Dad.

CONTENTS

List of Illustrations	viii
Acknowledgements	ix
Abbreviations	x
Introduction	1
Chapter One. Hats, Land and Houses	18
1. A Distinctive Local Economy	19
2. Vendors and Builders	25
3. Property and the Hat Trade	40
Appendices	74
Chapter Two. The Board of Health	84
Chapter Three. Society: Belief and Behaviour	129
1. Religion and Philanthropy	133
2. Leisure, the Secular World and Self-Help	149
3. Crime and the Temperance Movement	153
4. The Gospel of Education	175
Chapter Four. Politics, Power and Self-determination	203
1. Internal Relations	203
2. External Relations	218
Appendices	244
Epilogue	247
Biographical notes	249
Notes on place names	269
Bibliography	270
Sources	278
Names Index	282
Subject Index	289

LIST OF ILLUSTRATIONS

(between pages 62 and 63)

Plate
1. Wellington Street, from Todd's Pictorial Map, 1862.
2. Aerial photograph of Wellington Street and New Town.
3. Ordnance Survey map of Wellington Street area.
4a. Chase Street.
4b. Liverpool Road.
5. Interior of 38, New Town Street, taken in the 1950s.
6a. Windsor Street.
6b. King Street.
7a. Lea Road (Blackwater Lane).
7b. Tower Hill.
8a. Jones' Yard.
8b. Market House c.1867.
9a. Market Hill c.1866.
9b. Market Hill and the Corn Exchange, c.1869.
10. George Street.
11. Cheapside.
12. Ceylon Baptist Church, Wellington Street.

(between pages 182 and 183)

13. Park Street, from Todd's Pictorial Map, 1862.
14. Chase Street, from Todd's Pictorial Map, 1862.
15a. The minister and deacons of King Street Congregational Church, c.1868.
15b. James Adams.
16a. William Bigg.
16b. Frederick Brown.
17a. Henry Brown.
17b. Rev Henry Burgess.
18a. John Cumberland.
18b. Hugh Gunn.
19a. Rev James O'Neill.
19b. William Phillips.
20a. John Webdale.
20b. Levi Welch.

Back cover. Stages of hat making from the *London Illustrated News*, 1878.

ACKNOWLEDGEMENTS

The feeling of isolation experienced during the production of a local studies volume needs to be revised when one looks back and considers the assistance which various individuals have provided. The staff at Bedfordshire's excellent Record Office provided great help in guiding my general requests for information towards specific items in their holdings and the staff at other offices around Bedfordshire and Hertfordshire were always most accommodating and informative. All at the Hertfordshire Record Office, the Hertfordshire Local Studies Library, the Luton Reference Library, the Bedfordshire County Library and St. Albans Reference Library were outstanding in this respect. The service provided in these institutions put that of some others further afield to shame.

My former colleague at Luton Museum, Marian Nichols, provided helpful observations to the original text; neither have I forgotten the suggestions made by Alan Taylor and Mark McCall. It is also appropriate to recall an enormous debt of gratitude to my original thesis supervisor, Professor Martin Daunton, for the advice which he gave, constantly guiding me towards placing the results of my research in a wider perspective. Particular gratitude is extended to the BHRS General Editor, Gordon Vowles, doubtless even more relieved than the author to see the publication of volume 78. Sylvia Woods heroically volunteered to produce an index and Pauline Newbery has also assisted with its preparation for the printer. Mere acknowledgement seems inadequate for such a service. Alison Wood and James Collett-White kindly proof read the original drafts, Christine Rees and Chris Stow helped in the production of the maps and the assistance of Chris Grabham and Elizabeth Adey in providing photographs has been greatly appreciated.

An equal debt lies with my parents, to whom this volume is dedicated, and to my wife, Melanie. In their different ways they provided crucial support during the period of research. Although sharing a study has now become intolerable, Melanie knows how much I owe to her.

ABBREVIATIONS

BRO	Bedfordshire County Record Office.
Beds Times	*Bedfordshire Times*
BHRS	Bedfordshire Historical Record Society
BL	British Library
Herts CRO	Hertfordshire County Record Office
LM	Luton Museum collection
LM/BI	Luton Museum copy negative held by Bob Irons
PP	Parliamentary Papers
PRO	Public Record Office

Introduction

Luton is one of a number of towns and cities, mostly located in the south-eastern quarter of England and including Oxford, Slough and Coventry, which experienced rapid economic expansion during the first half of the twentieth century. In fact, it is little exaggeration to claim that in the last two centuries Luton has twice undergone a profound economic and social transformation. The second industrial revolution, accelerating from the Edwardian era onwards, was sustained through the inter-war period when the town became a magnet for migrating workers, many of whom came from the depressed regions of Britain. Dominated by the large Vauxhall car manufacturing plant, Luton became the home of 'the affluent worker', a specimen worthy of sociological study.[1] In parliamentary terms it became a barometer seat: since 1918 by and large the party which gained the constituency containing the bulk of the Luton urban area also won the country.

This volume, however, is concerned with the first transformation of industrial Luton during the middle of the nineteenth century. Apart from its staple industry, the hat trade, this has been a relatively neglected period, a possible reason being that in many respects this is a difficult subject for assessment. For a start there still remains insufficient published work on the smaller cities and towns of mid-nineteenth century England which would allow appropriate comparative study. Most effort carried out has been digging along the richer seams presented by London, Manchester, Liverpool, Leeds and Birmingham, with more occasional studies of places such as Newcastle, Bradford, Nottingham or Bristol. For example, during an era distinguished by volunteerism, there would be few spheres of activity more conducive to parochial enterprise and originality than philanthropy. F.K. Prochaska's study of this in *The Cambridge Social History*, for example, cites 44 post-war titles in its bibliography. Setting aside the ten devoted to London and two on Scotland, there are just three drawn from studies of a defined locality.[2] W.D. Rubinstein's recently published general history of nineteenth century Britain also reflects this imbalance. The second part of the volume is devoted to social and cultural history, citing 97 texts in its bibliography. Seven of these are based upon analyses of specific localities, five of them concentrated within the capital.[3] Professor Rubinstein makes clear that he excluded articles from this bibliography, the vehicle through which most local studies see the light of day, but it is reasonable to claim that local history has yet to make a full impact upon wider historical understanding. Much remains to be done, particularly on the smaller urban centres, although perhaps the new journal *Family and Community History* will help to redress the imbalance.[4] Until then it remains difficult to draw broad conclusions in a number of areas, such as the evolution

1

of workshop industries, the involvement of the different sectors of society in local politics or patterns of small scale property ownership.

Notwithstanding the scholarly excellence of much recent research, therefore, it frequently becomes difficult to compare Luton, the chosen town of this study, with other similar urban areas. This is partly because each is a distinctive entity with its own peculiar social and economic make-up, possessing also a unique relationship with other populations in the vicinity. As stated, studies on the smaller towns between 1840 and 1875, the formative years of modern Luton, still tend to be few and far between, frequently concentrating upon individual features – a Board of Health in Heaton, carpet making in Kidderminster and so on – rendering parallel comparisons over a 35 year period nigh on impossible. Yet the work which has been published so far illustrates the great vitality and local variation which existed across a multitude of themes in English history. These demonstrate also how important it is to deepen our awareness of the subtleties of the past by stepping out of the shadow cast by the large metropolitan centres. The present research and publishing culture in British universities does not encourage the awkward long-term task of digging through the far more fragmentary data connected with smaller urban centres. This is to our considerable loss in terms of historical understanding, and the need remains to examine more closely towns such as Luton – or Leighton Buzzard, Dunstable, Biggleswade and Bedford.

Luton does not offer itself up for comparison at another level: its rate of growth was such that long term juxtaposition with other towns is simply not possible. In 1821, for example, Luton bore much in common with nearby Leighton Buzzard, both being market towns in the straw plaiting region of the south-east Midlands with roughly equal populations (2986 and 2749 respectively). Forty years later Luton was four times the size of its near neighbour. Other towns which were larger than Luton in 1821, such as Hemel Hempstead or Hitchin, were barely half its size in 1871 (for a broad representation of comparative growth see graph on page 3). The 1851 census returns revealed that Luton was already bigger than more than half the municipal boroughs in England and Wales.

Further afield, towns such as Canterbury offer only fleeting opportunities for comparison as Luton's population swiftly rises from behind to first match and then surpass them. Centres such as Oxford, Leicester or Coventry present interesting common perspectives on economic progress over the nineteenth and twentieth centuries as a whole, but when examined in detail Luton's experience was too dissimilar on too many levels for a useful comparison to be made. To grab at random a clutch of towns (Chester, Honiton or Burnley, for example) just because one perhaps possessed a cottage industry and another a strong local Liberal party, even if there existed accessible source material, would be of very limited use.

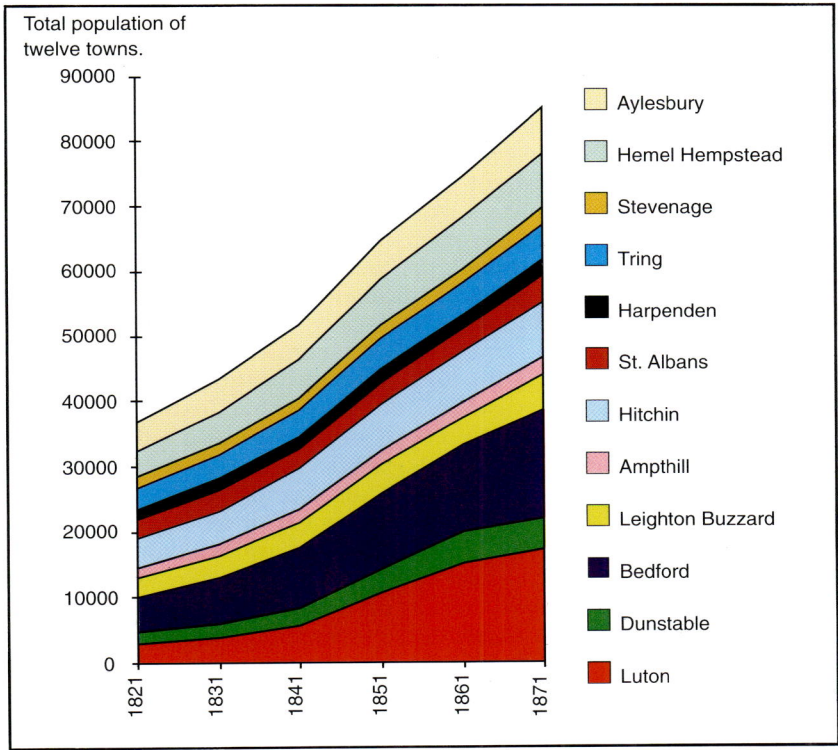

Total population of twelve towns.

The story of modern Luton is very much the story of the middling sectors of society and, in particular, the ranks of shopkeepers, small masters and traders who, more than any other class, collectively formulated the town's economic and social composition. A German visitor to Luton in 1835 felt moved to write:

> I have now had the opportunities to be convinced how incorrect the assertion so constantly repeated on the continent, is, that in England there are only rich people and beggars. In no other country perhaps is a very prosperous middle class so numerous as in England; and this class, in which industry, integrity, simplicity and purity of morals, and a truly religious spirit prevail, forms the real healthy heart of the nation, and gives it such extraordinary vigour.[5]

This, the visitor attributed to the fact that for 'nearly 800 years, England has not seen (at least for any length of time) any foreign enemy'. His abiding impression of 'extraordinary vigour' and a 'very prosperous middle class' (albeit, in Luton's case, in a very middling sort of way) is certainly one which shines through this community during the nineteenth century, although had he taken a closer look at the town he may well have wished to qualify his assessment with regards to the 'purity of morals'. Richard Cobden did not know Luton well and so, when he described it as 'the Manchester of Bedfordshire', he was not drawing any precise comparisons with the great pioneering industrial city but rather was referring in general terms to the busy spirit of the town: an enterprising centre of industry which operated free from the influence of the aristocracy.[6] Working class activity remained unorganised, disregarded and unrecorded, the aristocracy represented only by a steadily diminishing land holding around the town, and the gentry largely remote from most aspects of local life. Even within the local middle class there were no examples of major industrialists, men who measured their employees in the high hundreds or thousands and whose personal wealth could be measured in the tens or hundreds of thousands of pounds. There were no examples of men who exercised great sway over local politics and perhaps who aspired towards the aristocracy either through personal advancement or through marriage. Luton became a town characterised by a small number of medium-sized manufacturers and a vast number of independent, small-scale units producing goods and services.

It is here that a profound problem lies in researching Luton, a difficulty accounting for its economic development and assessing this subsequent effect upon its evolving institutions, character and values. Simply put, there has been, as Crossick put it, an 'unease' about accounting for the petty bourgeoisie in Britain. This has partly been caused by a problem of generic definition, the blurring of the lines between the artisan and the independent outworker at one end of the spectrum, and between the scale of production which marks divisions between subdivisions of middle class at the other. This stands in stark contrast with the continent and is made more difficult, in the British context, by the absence of data and primary sources of information. The humorist George Mikes added a further uneasy element here when he succinctly observed that the 'one class you do not belong to and are not proud of is the lower middle class. No one ever describes himself as belonging to the lower middle class'.[7] Consequently, after the culmination of Chartism, the petty bourgeoisie in Britain as a whole often appear as a negative dead weight, balking at reform promoted by liberal reformers, a group with whom many modern historians would probably share a natural affinity. This does many thousands of people scant justice, failing to allow for their own personal struggles, tenuous economic stability and feelings of social isolation brought about by the solitary nature of many of their occupations and long hours of work.

With fewer mechanisms than other classes for social and political organisation, the petty bourgeoisie remain a grey area in British history, one which does not present an inviting area of study. In Luton, a town principally built upon the activities of the middling orders, this presents awkward obstacles. Of the other significant group, the class of larger builders, manufacturers and professionals, there at least survives some small amount of data upon which to build an assessment of their contribution to their time: a history of freemasonry in Luton, chapel histories, handbills and campaign posters, fragments of company records. Above all there are newspapers, dominated by the terminology, attitudes and correspondence of the upper strata of the local middle class. For the less affluent sectors, leaving no tangible evidence of their lives and work (save for a dwindling number of dwellings in the centre of the town), the task is far more difficult, leading one perilously towards the misrepresentation of class stereotyping. This would be inadequate, as to do so would be markedly at odds with the sense of individualism which was so potent in Luton, certainly far more so than any notion of collective identity, be it social, religious, parochial or political.

It is almost impossible to enter the minds of individuals who left so few clues as to their personal aspirations and principles: no diaries, no memoirs, no private correspondence, no business and property records, not even a short letter to the local paper. Literacy levels were poor and business deals were frequently made verbally, especially in the straw hat trade. Even the leading manufacturers, such as Edmund Waller or John Everitt, preferred to travel personally to local markets in order to purchase straw plait. Waller would rise early each Wednesday, walk the several miles to Dunstable market in order to buy plait and would carry a quantity of it on his back on the return journey, arriving back in Luton by 8 am in order to open his draper's business. Everitt, who evidently worked for the Wallers in some capacity, would also attend Dunstable market and return with the plait in a 'capital strong cob and trap'.[8] Much of what occurred is hidden in a network of personal relationships, family connections and social, business, political and religious links which crossed and re-crossed one another within the small town. John Dony, recalling late Victorian and Edwardian Luton, claimed that the town did not need a borough council: during the day if one walked down George Street past the hat warehouse of Asher Hucklesby – Liberal, Congregationalist, self-made man and five times Mayor of Luton – there one might see Hucklesby and a handful of Luton's other great and good discussing various affairs of the town on the steps of his premises.[9] Aside from illustrating the power which a handful of manufacturers were able to exert over the town at the turn of the century, this observation also indicates that discussion, debate and decision were frequently made beyond the forum of public office. This applied especially in the mid-nineteenth century when Luton was a much smaller town, bereft of an all-encompassing local authority. The biographical notes at the end of the volume will go some way to illuminating part of the tangled web of personal connections in the town.

Luton is a difficult town to fathom and, for all its economic buoyancy, assessments of the place have always been, at best, mixed. Deprived of easily appreciated distinguishing features – a harbour, coastline, slums, cathedral, medieval streets, peculiar social customs – it presents a bland perspective to visitor and resident alike. Unable to understand the imperative which drives the town many outsiders resort to cheap sneers:

> Luton is an easy place to have nothing to do with. Drive past on the M1 and you wont [sic] register much more than an urban smudge amid the green of Bedfordshire. Arrive by train on your way to the airport, and the diesel-belching Luton Flyer bus offers little in the way of views beyond multi-storey car parks and ring roads.[10]

Other descriptions have been even less kind: 'Luton has an airport. It is situated on the highest point of the gigantic rubbish heap that the town has become... Its airport lounges should be fitted with signs announcing, "Welcome to Luton, the trash capital of the British Isles".'[11] A London woman, evacuated with her children to Luton in 1939 complained: 'Heaven preserve me from ever becoming like Lutonians. I never met such a snobbish, selfish, unfriendly, rude lot in all my life. All they think about is their houses. House-proud, that's their trouble'.[12] For the indigenous population, resentful though they may be at perpetual lampooning by outsiders, their own complaints have long born a marked degree of consistency, frequently focusing upon the town centre, an area only recently reinvigorated partly due to the establishment of the university in 1993.[13]

A sense of disenchantment with the town persists in spite of its many good features, or at least absence of negative ones. There are no slums in Luton, indeed there never were on a scale found in towns such as Nottingham. The town's industries have traditionally thrived, and until the 1980s, even during periods of national recession, Luton was markedly less affected than other manufacturing centres. It sits advantageously at the hub of an air and land communications network. Since the early nineteenth century Luton has been a place to which thousands have migrated in search of work and housing, a testimony to the fact that, for all its shortcomings, it was regarded as at least preferable to those places from whence they came. Luton is a congenital product of its own economic and social heritage and has not suddenly acquired its allegedly negative features through recent aberration. Throughout its modern history, whilst tens of thousands were being drawn to the town, people simultaneously complained about Luton's perceived defects – its brash pursuit of wealth, the lack of architectural beauty, its paucity of recreational facilities, the absence of careful planning and a preparedness to sacrifice evidence of its past for the sake of the present. All of these have been noted and commented upon.

Even in the century before industrialisation descriptions of this south Bedfordshire town were so varied that it is difficult to believe that they were talking about the same place. Thus we discover that 'North East of Dunstable is Luton, a pretty little Market-Town, pleasantly seated amongst Hills. It has a large Market House and a very great Market on Monday' (1715). We also find in contemporary descriptions that it is 'pleasantly situated between two hills' (1764) but that Arthur Young felt 'If the Earl of Bute's park at Luton Hoo was not an inducement, there certainly could be none to visit that town: Notwithstanding the wretched roads I was forced to crawl through' (1769). Luton is both a 'handsome town' (1772) and a 'long dirty market town of one street, meanly built' (1776). Luton is a 'small dirty town' (1782), a 'considerable market town' (1806), 'irregularly built' (1819), 'tolerably, but very irregularly built' (1827) and a 'poor town' which 'evinced marks of decadency' (1828).[14]

Most detailed descriptions of the market town in the early nineteenth century are drawn from the recollections of Lutonians recorded at a later date. Little is known of the medieval town but the extent of the urban area (known as the township) which lay within the large parish of Luton had grown little since at least the late seventeenth century. Luton was essentially two main streets from which five others, plus a number of lanes and courtyards, also ran. From the Luton Hoo northward ran Park Road and Park Street which, at its northern extremity, contained the Long Pond, stagnant and smelly. From here Church Street ran away at an angle of 90 degrees to the right. Veering to the left from the Long Pond, Park Street was connected at the junction of Market Hill with George Street, and further to the left, Castle Street – the beginning of the road to St. Albans and London. At its northern end (at Cross Hill) George Street divided into a 'Y' shape with Dunstable Lane to the left and Tower Hill to the right. Until 1832 the road to Bedford left Tower Hill opposite a tavern known as the *Red Cow*, crossing the River Lea. Castle Street and Hog Lane, which ran parallel with it approximately 75 yards away, were only developed to a limited extent. On its south-western side Luton was overlooked by the Dallow Hills, to the immediate south lay the parks of Stockwood and Luton Hoo, and across the northern and eastern edge of the urban area lay the Great Moor. Through this ran the River Lea which, although at this point was not very substantial, occasionally burst its banks during heavy rain – sometimes with loss of life.[15]

Frederick Davis in the first edition of his *History of Luton* (published in 1855) wrote of his home town at the beginning of the nineteenth century:

> Luton a little more than half a century ago was a dirty town, with streets narrow and low, so that there were few places in which two carts could pass each other; there were banks on each side, covered with grass, in almost every part of the town; the houses were generally very low and overhanging in front about two feet, many of them thatched.[16]

Since Davis was not born until 1815 many of the details which he gave were beyond his recollection. His sources probably included elderly Lutonians and perhaps a survey of the town dating from 1804.[17] This, plus Davis' account, shed light upon the very rural nature of the town at this time: George Street contained four farms and a row of trees. A large chestnut tree stood near to the site of the present Town Hall. Davis' recollection was reinforced by a contemporary: successive letters to the *Beds Times* in 1848 lamented the passing of 'old Luton'. The picture painted was of a town containing 'houses with overhanging stories, mossy tiles, open gutters . . .' and also apparently, a set of stocks, still functioning in the first quarter of the nineteenth century but derelict by this time.[18]

An account of the development of Luton, from market town to manufacturing centre, is essentially an account of a town building itself upon the fortunes of the straw hat industry. John Dony's seminal work traced the growth and structure of the trade, as well as the reasons for its concentration in the south-east Midlands and since then a number of other studies have been made of the industry.[19] These render further detailed accounts largely superfluous but, nonetheless, a brief outline of its structure would probably be helpful at this stage.

During the middle of the nineteenth century there were two strands to the local hat trade. The plaiting of straw was undertaken principally in the rural areas whilst the production of hats was concentrated in the town. Plaiting of straw was found across the fertile corn producing region of the south Midlands, into Essex, and scattered elsewhere in places such as Devon, the Lake District and Orkney. As a domestic industry it declined into eventual extinction in the face of reduced import duties from 1842 onwards (they were finally repealed in 1860) which brought increased competition from Leghorn, Switzerland and Saxony. The south Midlands was initially able to withstand this competition (50% of imported plait was re-exported) but was finally killed off in the last quarter of the century with the addition of imports from the Far East. Within the Luton Poor Law Union, 60% of the women over the age of twenty were engaged in plaiting in 1861, a work which also absorbed some young boys and men as a secondary occupation.

Plaiters were independent producers with straw dealers (selling to the plaiters), and plait dealers (buying the finished product), as separate entities. The cost of the straw represented approximately 20% of the finished selling price and a plaiter, therefore, had to work continuously in order to make a living. Between 4s. and 6s. was the average weekly income in mid century, but the proximity of the plaiter to a particular market, or the person to whom the plait was sold, could make a difference in earnings of between 2s. and 10s. a week. Most plaiters lived a hand to mouth existence, and as soon as sufficient plait was produced they sold it to the village grocer either for money or in exchange for goods. This latter deal could help keep the income of the plaiter secret from the Relieving Officer or indeed from husbands whose income, if working as a general labourer, was unlikely to be much greater.

Like plaiting, bonnet sewing had become concentrated in the southeast Midlands. The quality of the finished product steadily improved in the face of competition from Leghorn, improvements which were spearheaded by the Wallers, amongst others. The Wallers were a remarkable clan, descended from London merchants who had long been connected with the manufacture of straw hats. They were related to another London hat manufacturing family, the Whites, as well as (through marriage with the Whites) to the Huguenot family of Goujon. An early nineteenth century member of this latter group, Samuel, became involved in the hat trade in High Town, arriving c. 1818 and leasing land there from Edmund Waller.[20] James Waller settled in Luton during the late eighteenth century, having at least five sons, Edmund, Thomas, James, John and Robert. All were businessmen of considerable ability, making an enormous impact upon the small town, with Edmund and Thomas being the most formidable. Edmund, as a draper and hat manufacturer, did much to develop the system of 'making up' by dealing with sewers who worked within their own cottages, as well as those directly under his employ at his factory. He sold his product through his national (and international) agencies. Whilst Edmund developed the manufacturing side of the trade, brother Thomas concentrated upon improving the quality of locally produced straw plait. With supplies of the fine quality Leghorn plait from Tuscany cut off during the Napoleonic Wars, Waller resorted to buying straw plait produced by French prisoners of war at Yaxley Barracks near Peterborough (virtually all of these camps produced straw plait) and experimenting with ways of improving the quality of English plait. Although the production of straw plait by the prisoners was suppressed by the authorities, much work was smuggled out for the Luton merchants by local travellers and tradesmen, often with the connivance of the guards. With the Napoleonic Wars over and the duty upon plait steadily decreasing, Waller twice visited Tuscany (once in 1825) and began importing straw from that region for production of a variety of plaits which he patented.[21]

It would be most interesting to know precisely why the Wallers chose to come to Luton and to stay there. The town was centrally placed within the straw plaiting district of the south Midlands, but for Thomas

Waller, at least, not the ideal point from which to operate a semi-illicit trade with the prisoner of war camp near Peterborough. Hitchin, lying near to the Great North Road, or even Shefford, would have been a better location. St. Albans lay closer to London. Whatever the reason, the presence of the Wallers, with their commercial contacts with London hat producers and their manufacturing resources, made an immense impression upon the development of the Luton trade in the first quarter of the nineteenth century, which the land market was able to sustain. In 1826, Vyse became the first of the big London firms to open a factory in Luton, a year later also opening a branch in Tuscany. The straw hat trade was flourishing in the Hertfordshire market towns at the same time that Luton's begun to develop. Most places of significant size contained hat production units, many run by women, although how many there were it is not possible to account for accurately. Within small towns such as Hoddesdon, Baldock, Hatfield and Bishop Stortford could be found at least a handful of manufacturers, and in larger towns such as Hertford there were appreciably more. St. Albans possessed eighteen listed hat manufacturers in 1832, against Luton's thirteen (four of these the Wallers) in 1830. At least one London hat manufacture, Thomas Henley of Goodge Street, had also opened a branch factory in St. Albans. Vyse and Sons were also there – by 1854 at least.[22]

Exports steadily increased during the middle of the nineteenth century: 235,000 hats were exported between 1871–5, compared with 31,000 in the corresponding period in the 1830s. Sewing paid more than plaiting, a powerful inducement for the plaiters to move into towns, but these earnings also varied greatly. The biggest hat factories, many of which were branches of London firms, employed as many as 300 sewers, with further home workers and sewing rooms located in the town or in neighbouring villages. In a large factory a skilled bonnet sewer could earn approximately 18*s.* a week, being paid by the piece. Most towns in the region – St. Albans, Hertford, Dunstable, for example – possessed large and medium sized factories but the distinctive feature of Luton, for reasons which will be suggested in the first chapter, was the array of 'makers up'. These produced the whole or part of hats in small domestic units which were then sold on to a factory or warehouse which operated a counter trade. T.G. Austin estimated that in 1871 this accounted for 75% of the Luton trade. For little or no capital outlay it was possible for an individual to set up business: men perhaps blocking downstairs whilst women, family and lodgers alike, carried on sewing elsewhere in the house. In addition to the makers up, there were many individual rooms where just sewing was undertaken and which could be then sold through numerous outlets in the town. In addition to the big factories and the counter trade, there were also a number of medium sized hat factories.

The definition of what constituted a 'large' or 'medium' sized hat factory remains arbitrary. It is hard to give a precise definition because of the absence of data and also the fluctuating numbers involved in both direct employment and the counter trade. Charles Robinson, whose conduct and belief could offer him up as a typical member of Luton's middle class citizenry, employed just 23 people in 1869 (although in better times this probably would have been greater). Anything between 20 and 100 employees could be classified as 'medium', and above that figure, 'large'. With perhaps not much more than a couple of exceptions, around 200 was the maximum number employed at a large factory, and there were only a handful of these.

Little production was mechanised during the mid-nineteenth century. Hat sewing machines were being introduced in the middle of the 1860s, but these were not refined enough for use in factories for another ten years. This part of the production process, therefore, depended upon the dexterity of the sewer working on the plait from the crown outwards. After stiffening, the hat was blocked, a process which had once required wooden mallets and mushroom shaped glass slicken stones, but from mid-century onwards becoming mechanised with the development of large blocking machines. Bleaching, done to give attractive variations in colour to the plait, was also developing as an ancillary branch of the hat trade.

The small production units paid less than the big factories, between 5s. and 13s. a week. These were attractive earnings for young girls in villages with no other prospects other than farm work, domestic service, plaiting or, in the north of the south Midlands region, lace making. Thousands of girls would temporarily migrate to Luton from the surrounding villages to work in the hat trade during its busy season. This was at its most intense between December and May. Because of the discrepancy in earnings the small production units became the focal point for younger girls who, as soon as they were more proficient, moved to the larger factories where the pay was better. The hat trade was a mobile industry, and for the luckless and 'disregarded' Factory Inspector, a largely hidden one. It absorbed many more women than men – a ratio of ten to one in the bigger factories. Men could carry on tasks such as blocking (a skilled activity), and also dyeing and packing. A blocker in mid-century could earn between 20s. and 30s. a week, but a bleacher or dyer earned no more than the sewers – between 12s. and 18s.

Despite the difference in pay, there were parallels between the lives and work of the plaiters and sewers. Both were paid by the piece and both worked long hours in order to maximise income, the urgency being greater for the poorly paid, hand-to-mouth plaiter. It was supposed that hat sewers were not wanted back in their lodgings too early in the evening, a further inducement for them to stay late, making as much as possible of the busy season before the leaner times over summer.

Factory discipline was loose as a consequence of piecework: sewers arrived late and stayed late. From such a working life came the allegations from various employers, clergymen and assorted moralists that outwork led to a sinful life (even though straw plaiting had been deemed to be beneficial to the needy by the Poor Law Commissioners in 1833). Relatively high earnings gave women economic power which it was feared compromised their station in marriage, so the theory ran. Furthermore, the obsession with producing goods led to untidy homes and neglected children. There is slight supporting evidence for this last point, not only in the appalling plait 'schools' to which children were farmed out, but also in the succession of tragic deaths of infants from administration of 'Godfrey's Cordial', a lethal opium based sedative. One can sympathise with a distracted, if misguided mother, attempting to quieten small children in order that she could carry on working during the respite that the opiate gave. Recent research, however, has indicated that fears of immorality represented by a supposition of a high number of illegitimate births, in the villages at least, have been greatly exaggerated.[23]

A consequence of this type of economic activity was that it produced two varieties of Lutonian: those who were resident and those who migrated to work for the 'busy' season, usually commencing around October and increasing in intensity from February through to the end of May. This cycle of production was determined by the summer fashion market, both in Britain and abroad, and to a lesser extent by the availability of labour after harvest time. For the latter group, predominantly young and female, Luton's straw hat trade offered wages which were unapproachable in other spheres of employment, plus plenty of lodgings. For the permanent residents, a number of whom were also originally migrants, Luton offered myriad economic opportunities – hat manufacture and related activities such as dyeing, block making, property speculation and ownership, shopkeeping, retailing and wholesaling.

Stemming from this, however, a number of questions remain to be answered. Starkest of all, and the starting point for this study, is simply why it should be Luton that became the principal centre of the trade. The town was only one of a number of similar sized market towns – St. Albans, Dunstable and Hitchin being the most notable – which at face value also possessed the potential to become the heart of the industry. Yet, despite possessing decidedly inferior communications until the late 1850s, Luton swiftly outgrew its immediate neighbours (see again graph 1.1).[24] The underlying reasons for this are examined in chapter one, together with an account of the physical growth of the town. In the first chapter, it will be argued that the fluid land market within Luton was the catalyst for the establishment of the town as the centre of the straw hat trade. Its nature was favourable to the spawning of the small units of production which gave the town a distinctive and decisive edge. This, however, is in no way to deprecate the contribution made by the Wallers, Vyse, Munt and Brown, plus others, who, in the late eighteenth and early nineteenth centuries, did so much to establish the base for later expansion. The spawning of houses and factories in Luton was a process devoid of planning and which, in the early stages at least, was little short of anarchic. The facilitator for this development, and of decisive difference in accounting for the growth of the town in relation to its neighbours, was the nature of the local land market. Bereft of local authority control, and with major landowners (in particular the Marquess of Bute) departing the town, speculators were encouraged to rush in, creating a momentum of expansion.

From this burst of frenetic activity flows two other areas which are worthy of study. First, a new society was created, the existing social and economic elite disappeared (with the notable exception of the Quaker family of Brown). Second, a new set of institutions and values were created in its wake. Gertrude Himmelfarb has argued most persuasively that Victorians thought in terms of 'virtues', not 'values'. The former noun possessed a universal, timeless quality at odds with what Professor Himmelfarb regarded as its subjective, relativist corruption in the twentieth century.[25] In fact, closer inspection of one small Victorian society qualifies this sweeping assessment. With the concomitant and varied effects of the Evangelical Revival, licensing legislation and sanitary reform also making an impact, modes of behaviour and standards of acceptable conduct shifted. Clearly apparent was a divergence of opinion over the respective roles of the individual and collective public authority in determining the town's development. A subtext to this was the sense of a growing obligation upon the new Lutonians to come to terms with the town which they had helped to create. It fell to the local Board of Health to wrestle with the consequences of economic growth. This was both in respect of the excesses of unrestricted urban development, and with the attitudes of a large class of independent producers and sellers who remained suspicious of the intrusion of local authorities upon their lives.

From what source decisive power and influence was wielded is difficult to establish precisely. In terms of exercising authority Luton was superficially a town of the middle class, but it becomes very clear that there was a sharp difference in attitude which carried overtones of more complex relationships. The small bourgeoisie of professionals and larger manufacturers tended to be more interventionist, advocating the creation of public bodies (supported from a locally levied rate if needs be) in order to acquire the facilities and trappings commensurate with a modern town. From the much larger ranks of small traders, artisans and builders, jealously defending their independence and economic gains, there was demonstrated a clear preference to remain unencumbered by local authorities. More pertinently, it was often expressed as a desire to pay as little in the way of rates as possible. It was, therefore, the upper reaches of the middle class who initiated and piloted within Luton the more positive aspects of the Board of Health, the formation of a railway company, the creation of public utility companies, the provision of public education and the achievement of incorporation: changes which they genuinely regarded as being for the benefit of the town as a whole. Unable, for a number of reasons, to organise and initiate their own programmes, sections of the petty bourgeoisie were driven into a reactive role. Sometimes they were passive, sometimes sullen, and just occasionally (when organised by dissenting members of the upper strata) turning upon the promoters of reform with a negative but ultimately inconclusive venom. It is possible to see that an evolving awareness of collective identity was, therefore, perceived quite differently by various sectors within Luton's population. It would be convenient if one could address the issue of the exercise of political power and social control in clear, class based terms: the waters, however, are murkier than this.

At a fundamental level, there remains an encumbrance in the meagre extent of Luton's records. The nature of the town during both the nineteenth and twentieth centuries, deriving its population from recent migration, has ultimately mitigated against a sense of collective identity and, consequently, an appreciation of Luton's heritage. This has applied not only to Luton's wholesale demolition of older buildings, oblivious to any value save monetary gain, but also in the total destruction of whatever personal records were compiled, as well as the official records for the town. On more than one occasion records have literally been retrieved from disposal skips by staff from Luton Museum. It is precisely these generations of migrants, however, who have played a key role in the evolution of the culture which pertains to the town. Parish records are poor and the societies and organisations which were spawned during the middle of the nineteenth century have, for the most part, left no evidence of their existence other than reports in local newspapers. A significant proportion of those records which were preserved during the nineteenth century were presumably kept, uncatalogued, within the Town Hall, but were mostly destroyed when the building was burnt down during the Peace Day Riot on the night of 19 July 1919.[26] Requests for records are still proffered the lame excuse that the papers were destroyed during the Town Hall fire, even for material which post-dates the event!

The chapters which follow are as much an account of what happened as to why events unfurled as they did. The narrative approach is as essential as wider analysis in tracing the development of a town whose history in this important period has not yet been accounted for in any detailed sense. In its long and distinguished history, the Bedfordshire Historical Record Society has pursued its commitment to make widely available the records of the county through its annual volumes in a wide variety of ways. Some records are of sufficiently narrow definition to allow publication with a minimum of commentary. Others have required a greater degree of explanation. Some volumes have encompassed a collection of essays but it is more rare, although not unprecedented, for the Society to publish a monograph. In the context of the observations made at the beginning of the introduction, a very deep appreciation is due to the Society, therefore, for enabling the fragmentary records connected with the county's largest town to be gathered, considered and laid before a wider audience.

Modern Luton, its economy, its society and its institutions, was forged (or, more aptly plaited) during the first half of Victoria's reign. The absence of much in the way of comparable research and, crucially, the absence of even basic data (such as comprehensive land prices) inevitably leaves some questions unanswered. What follows, nonetheless, is an attempt to elucidate the cottage economy antecedents of a modern engineering town. This involves a consideration not merely of its industrial base, but also the society, ethics and institutions which were subsequently created during the mid-nineteenth century.

NOTES

1. Goldthorpe, J.H., Lockwood, D., Bechofer, F. and Platt, J. *The Affluent Worker in the Class Structure* (Cambridge, 1969).
2. F.K. Prochaska 'Philanthropy' in Thompson, F.M.L. *The Cambridge Social History of Britain 1750–1950, vol. III, Social Agencies and Institutions* (Cambridge, 1990).
3. Rubinstein, W.D. *Britain's Century. A Political and Social History 1815–1905* (1998).
4. *Community and Family History*, issued by Maney Publishing from November 1988. The Journal of Regional and Local Studies now publishes lists of MA and undergraduate theses covering local history.
5. Waagen, G.F. 'Works of Art and Artists in England', vol. 3, (1838), pp. 357–9. Quoted in Houfe, Simon (ed.) *Through Visitors Eyes. A Bedfordshire Anthology.* (Dunstable, 1990).
6. *Luton Times* 12.4.1851
7. Crossick, Geoffrey. 'Urban Society and the Petty Bourgeoisie in Nineteenth Century Britain' in Fraser, Derek and Sutcliffe, Anthony *The Pursuit of Urban History* (1983), chapt. 15, pp. 307–26. Mikes, George. *How to be Inimitable* (1960).
8. Hawkes, Joseph. 'Memory Sketches of Luton'. Published in the *Luton Reporter* between 1895 and 1897.
9. Recorded interview between J.G. Dony and Stephen Bunker, 1988. Copies in University of Luton Sound Archive and Luton Museum.
10. *Sunday Times* 15.10.1989. The article was entitled 'Who Loves Luton?' (evidently not the snide hack who produced this unoriginal, ill-informed piece). This article provides some context for the same paper's squalid assault upon the town's university nine years later.
11. *New Scientist* 14.4.1988.
12. Luton News (compiler). *Luton at War.* (Home Counties Newspapers Ltd., Luton 1947).
13. Luton Borough Council. *Gulbenkian 'Out of Hours' Study for Luton Town Centre. Draft Report* (1990). History and Heritage Consortium report on feasibility of the

'Luton Adventure' (1990). In 1981 Luton's total population of 163,209 included 6,591 who originated from Eire (4.04% of total population), 4,589 (2.81%) from Scotland, 2,384 (1.46%) from Wales, 3,302 (2.02%) from the Caribbean, 2,784 (1.70%) from India, 1,487 (0.91%) from Bangladesh and 3,455 (2.11%) from Pakistan. It is certain that a greater number of Lutonians would associate themselves with one of the above groups, particularly the long established Irish, Scots and Poles, even if they themselves were not born in those countries.

The Borough of Luton calculated that in 1988 66% of Lutonians were classified as owner occupiers (above the national average), and that 23% were council tenants (below the national average). Unemployment was 5% (below the national average) but within four years this had climbed to 11%, 2% above the national average. There was a high level of car ownership, unsurprising in a vehicle manufacturing town with a poor public transport network, 62% having access to at least one car.

14. Cox, Rev Thomas *Magna Britannia et Hibernia. Bedfordshire* (1715). *England Illustrated, or a Compendium of Natural History, Topography and Antiquities, Ecclesiastical and Civil of England and Wales.* Bedfordshire section, printed for R. & J. Dodsley (1764). Young, Arthur, *A Six Months Tour through the North of England* (1769). Spencer, N. *Complete English Traveller. Bedfordshire* (1772). Gough, Robert 'Notes taken at Luton' (1776). Pennant, Thomas H. Esq. *The Journey from Chester to London* (1782). Lysons, Rev Daniel and Lysons, Samuel *Magna Britannia. Being a concise topographical account of the several counties of Great Britain.* (1806). *The New British Traveller. Bedfordshire, General Description of the County* (1819). Parry, Rev I. D. *Select Illustrations, Historical and Topical of Bedfordshire...* (1827). Phillips, Sir Richard *A Personal Tour through the United Kingdom describing living objects and contemporaneous interests* (1828).

15. Flooding occurred in 1795, drowning one member of the Brown family, and again in July, 1828, when several houses were damaged so severely they required rebuilding. Fortunately no-one was killed on this occasion.

16. Davis, Frederick. *The History of Luton with its Hamlets, etc.* (Luton, 1855).

17. 'The Town of Luton in 1804.' (LM collection).

18. Letters from 'Edward', *Beds Times* 9.9.1848, 16.9.1848 and 23.9.1848.

19. Dony, J.G. *A History of the Straw Hat Industry* (Luton, 1942). Publication of Ph.D. thesis, *University of London*, 1941. Pinder, D.A. 'The Luton Hat Industry' Ph.D. thesis, *University of Southampton*, (1970). Dony, J.G. 'The Straw Hat Industry' in Silverman, H.A. (ed.), *Studies in Industrial Organisation* (Methuen). Dony, J.G. and Law, C.M. 'Luton and the Hat Industry' *The East Midlands Geographer*, vol. 4, part 6, no. 30. Horn, Pamela L.R. 'The Buckinghamshire Straw Plait Trade in Victorian England', *Records of Buckinghamshire* vol. XIX, part 1, (1971) pp. 42–55. Grof, Lazlo L. *Children of Straw. The Story of a Vanished Craft and Industry in Bucks, Herts, Beds and Essex* (Buckingham, 1988). Publication based upon a thesis submitted for the Certificate in Local History, Dept. of External Studies, Oxford University, May 1987. For contemporary analysis see Austin, T.G. *The Straw Plaiting and Straw Hat and Bonnet Trade...* (Luton, 1871) and for a mix of statistical and anecdotal information see also *The Hatters Gazette*, published from 1877 onward.

20. Dony, J.G. et al. *The Story of High Town.* (Bedfordshire 1984) pp. 6–9. Luton Museum correspondence file, September 1989: papers related to Waller and Goujon families. Land tax records at the BRO show the Wallers well established in Luton in the second decade of the nineteenth century as property owners as well as tenants. Hat manufacturer James Munt was renting property from Edmund Waller in 1822. Richard Vyse first appears as a resident in 1832 (he is not listed in 1830). My thanks to James Collett-White for obtaining these details. See also Higgins, D.M. *Old Luton* (Luton, 1885). According to this recollection, the premises of the Wallers' alone shone brightly at night in the 'dull and dreary' town.

21. Walker, Thomas James. *The Depot for Prisoners of War at Norman Cross*

Huntingdonshire. 1796 to 1816. (1913), pp. 133–45. Walker contradicts Davis and others who claimed that Luton merchants ever directly dealt with the prisoners of war at Norman Cross. Dony, J.G. *A History of the Straw Hat Industry*, pp. 38–41; Phillips, Sir Richard *op. cit.* pp. 6–7.

22. *Pigot & Co.'s Commercial Directory* (1832). *Pigot and Co.'s Commercial Directory* (1839). *Kelly's Directory of Hertfordshire* (1850). *Craven & Co.'s Commercial Directory* (1854), Hertfordshire Local Studies Library. *Pigot & Co.'s Commercial Directory* Bedfordshire section, (1830).
23. Grof, Lazlo *op. cit.* The original focus of Lazlo Grof's study was the village of Edlesborough. His research emphasised that, contrary to censorial allegations made at the time, illegitimacy rates in straw plaiting districts were in fact below the national average. See also chapt. 3 of Rose, Lionel. *Massacre of the Innocents. Infanticide in Great Britain 1800–1939* (1986).
24. I am indebted to Nicola Clarke, the Local History Reference Librarian at Luton Central Library, and Rosie Dugeon and Beryl Housley at St. Albans District Library, for obtaining these statistics.
25. Himmelfarb, Gertrude. *The De-moralization of Society. From Victorian Virtues to Modern Values* (1995).
26. It is difficult to establish what precisely was held within the Town Hall. Although Luton already possessed a public library, founded in 1883 and given a new building opposite the Town Hall thanks to financial assistance from Andrew Carnegie in 1911, few records were kept there. Luton Museum was not established until 1927 – in the Carnegie Library. Medieval Papel Bulls adorned the walls of the Mayor's parlour (and were destroyed in the fire) and Board of Health records also resided in the Town Hall, the minute books fortunately surviving the conflagration.

Chapter One. Hats, Land and Houses

We must in the end make plain how the land was built upon in the way that it was. (H.J. Dyos, in the foreword to *The Provincial Towns of Georgian England* by C.W. Chalklin).

The building of houses for the working classes has, I am sorry to say, not been attended to at all in this borough. (Evidence submitted by Charles Harrison to Parliamentary Select Committee on Town Holdings, 1887).

In the middle of the nineteenth century Luton experienced a transformation from a slightly shabby market town, where hats were made, to principally a manufacturing centre. Land was the key to this physical growth, a development which was accompanied by profound social change. This small Bedfordshire town possessed few advantages which predestined its status as the centre of the straw hat trade, and it certainly achieved its dominance without the benefit of a good communications network. A unique blend of factors removed its rather typical market town social elite whilst Luton was simultaneously expanding. These two factors assisted and hastened a metamorphosis already under way in the first third of the nineteenth century.[1]

Compartmentalising a process spanning forty years, one which dictated the pattern, quality and fortunes of thousands of lives, has its drawbacks. Luton's physical, economic and demographic revolution comprised numerous strands which intertwined in a nature which was as complex as a length of straw plait. Nonetheless, for the sake of clarity it is necessary to draw distinct threads from the myriad personal ambitions, activities and experiences which collectively built Luton. The logical starting point for this lies with Luton's position, established by the end of the second quarter of the nineteenth century, as the principal centre for the manufacture of straw hats. The supply and demand relationship between the hat trade and land development is of central importance in plotting the progress of a town which developed its own variation of the cottage economy. In Luton's case there was a mixture of small, independent masters and artisans, an extensive putting out system and a significant proportion of property owners in all but the poorest sector of the population.[2] The answer to why this should be so lies with the approach which principal local landowners had towards their holdings: it was here that the stage was set for change. This was to have consequences both for the form of land tenure and the type of economic structure which came to be built upon it. With estate control minimal, the running was made by an army of small speculators who relentlessly pursued a policy of rapid return from their piecemeal investments. This is how Luton grew and why it became the town that it did.

It is also important to look at what this process produced in terms of a living environment. Luton's growth produced more than the mere grafting of a new town upon an old social structure or degrees of mutual assimilation. With the departure of the old property owners, a new breed arrived. This chapter will seek to identify the speculators and builders who built Luton. Later chapters will examine institutional, political and ideological change.

Part One. A Distinctive Local Economy

The influence of land upon the hat trade

The evolving structure of Luton's hat trade was both complemented by the method of land disposal and property development. The pattern of estate disposal remained consistent throughout the period in question. There were frequent, sometimes large scale, and occasionally ill-judged disposals of freehold land, subsequently carved up into smaller plots to meet demand. From the 1820s Luton developed a distinctive model of the cottage economy: partial or complete hat production was integrated with factories and warehouses located within the town. As such, the town contained a number of integral features which were typical of an early industrial society: a substantial number of workers were self-employed and local industry was distinguished by a significant labour input from women and children. This latter element was especially prevalent in the textile trades. Little capital was required to start up a production process which generally encouraged marriage at a young age and the early begetting of children.[3] The Luton process of urbanisation, notable for affordable, plentiful, unconditional freehold, allowed market forces to be freely expressed.

Writers on the Luton hat industry have identified a number of features which they are agreed were the fundamental reasons for Luton's emergence as the centre of the straw hat trade.[4] These factors all pre-date the arrival of the railway, which is acknowledged as reinforcing an existing dominance already held by Luton. The period in which this pre-eminence was established was the period of depression following the end of the Napoleonic War, through to the resurgence of the hat industry in the 1840s. Important was the establishment of large branch factories by several London firms, plus the development of good quality but cheaper hats – an initiative attributed to Edmund and Thomas Waller. This enabled much work to be carried out by the small domestic production units undertaking the 'making up' of the hats. The small units were also flexible enough to meet any changes in demand and the developing industry substantial enough to support a number of specialised ancillary trades – bleaching, dyeing and blockmaking amongst them.

Although important, these factors alone could not have given Luton the decisive edge over neighbouring towns. The firms which came from London were only part of the expansion of the industry relying upon the hundreds of small 'makers-up'. These small units were crucial in giving Luton a broad and flexible base, but without suitable land the growth of the town could never have reached the levels that it did. Land was the key, the abundance of which in the 1830s and 1840s sucked in workers from the surrounding agricultural areas, providing an irresistible momentum of growth.

The larger factories, therefore, possessed not only a large and growing pool of labour to recruit into their firms, but also another to whom outwork could be sent. William Hunt, the manager of London based Munt and Brown, estimated that in the early 1860s the company employed 215 persons at their Luton factory and also engaged between 300–500 outworkers elsewhere in the town.[5] William Willis reckoned that there were 'eight or ten' factories in Luton on the scale of his own or Munt and Brown. They all operated on a similar system by augmenting a factory workforce with outworkers in the hundreds of small workshops and dwellings around the town. This process, apparently unique to Luton in its extent, encouraged the abandonment of plaiting for the more lucrative sewing of hats. Plaiting rapidly became the activity of the very young and very old within the town.

Before the end of the nineteenth century Luton had become dubbed 'Strawopolis'. There were no felt hats made, neither were there any other complementary crafts such as silk manufacture or umbrella production. The London firms which opened up branches in Luton (and neighbouring towns) did so, in all probability, to get closer to the supply of plait and to the pool of labour. They arrived in Luton long before the onset of mechanisation, their factories initially being no more than large sewing houses. The details of their economies of scale are, regrettably, not known. Swiftly, an escalating momentum of activity developed in Luton, receiving only the occasional check. The prospect of higher wages encouraged migration and the part played by word of mouth should not be underestimated in understanding migratory patterns. The straw plait and hat trade, with its network of markets, was ideally suited to accommodate a relay of news. Information concerning the auction of some building ground in High Town, the need for more sewers at a factory, empty cottages awaiting tenants in Dumfries Street, all of these matters could be discussed at Luton market on a Monday and, by the end of the week, would have reached ears in places as far afield as Tring, Hemel Hempstead, Hertford and into Essex.

The industry required much more female labour than male, William Hunt reckoning that 250 women 'keep about twenty men employed in blocking'. A high number of these women would be single, seasonal migrants, reducing significantly the need to provide complementary employment for spouses. The traditional spheres of employment, such as brewing or milling, did not require large numbers of employees, so for men opportunities lay not only in the various functions of the hat trade, but also in the construction industry and various fields of general labouring. Comparative figures are difficult to utilise since the census enumerator's employment classification for Luton (as with Hitchin but unlike Bedford) covers a substantial agricultural district as well as the urban core. It is interesting to note, however, that when agricultural labourers are accounted for, those engaged in more general labouring were more than twice as numerous in Luton (7%) as the county town (3.2%). Many would be drawn into the various branches of the vibrant construction industry.[6] Out of sheer necessity a number of men had more than one string to their working bow and the occupations given at the time of a census may not accurately represent an individual's means of accruing income over an entire year. The hat trade would have attracted some seasonal labour, as would have the building trade, and there still remained the (diminishing) rural tradition of hiring of labour at the September 'Stattie' Fair.[7]

The 6724 males listed on Luton's census return for 1861 shared a town with 9332 females. Returns for New Town in 1841 demonstrate that it was in two key age groups that the difference was most pronounced. Amongst those aged between eleven and twenty there were more than three times (93 : 30) as many females as males. In the next age bracket (21–30) the ratio was nearly as substantial (81 : 34). Luton's hat trade, operating to the extent that it did from domestic premises, permitted a preponderance of women and children, rare for the textile industry. The carpet trade in Kidderminster, for example, employed fewer women than men in its larger production units.[8]

The economy and the family

In Luton, it was thus possible for a woman to stay at home, fulfilling the functions of mother and wife whilst simultaneously exceeding her husband's earnings. As well as the mother, the importance of children to the family based economy must be stressed. This is reflected in the absence of evidence for any significant numbers of the notorious plait schools within Luton, an institution which was exceedingly common in the surrounding villages and even in smaller towns such as Leighton Buzzard. The family oriented mode of production is at its most noticeable here, with children from the earliest possible age concentrating upon the more lucrative sewing of the plaited straw. There was little discernible benefit to a Luton family in packing their children off to a plait school at the cost of threepence, payable to a 'mistress' (some of whom could not even read or write), whilst the mother and older siblings remained at home, deprived of the extra help which the young child could provide. Mothers and older children could teach young children plaiting and sewing at least as well, probably better. They were most unlikely to be worse at imparting the general rudiments of education.

The surplus male labour in the south-east Midlands, plus the generally low wages, gave an impetus for women and children to seek a living in domestic industry. Earnings varied enormously, fluctuating according to individual proficiency and the fortunes of the market. To repeat, within an industry where it was possible to begin work at four years of age, there lay the opportunity for a plaiter to earn anything between 3s. and 18s. a week. A good sewer could earn between 18s. and £1 a week, although for those who were less swift or working in smaller workshops, the figure might be nearer 10s. to 12s.[9] These rates can be compared with the wages of a male agricultural labourer which spanned approximately 9s. to 14s. during the mid nineteenth-century period.[10]

The comparison in fortunes can be made by the following example taken from the 1841 census for New Town Street, one of the earliest areas to be developed. The census was taken in June, at the end of the busy season. In one of the cottages lived Joseph Barber, a 35 year old labourer, together with his wife Martha, ten year old daughter Mary and a lodger named Mary Fisher, aged around twenty.[11] All the females were bonnet sewers with the only non-earner recorded on the census being the nine year old son, also named Joseph. Although occupations were not listed for children under the age of ten it is possible that Joseph junior also contributed his labour, if not as a sewer then perhaps as a plaiter instead. In any case, as Levine pointed out, it would be wrong to assume that children were a 'drag' on the family economy. Before the advent of compulsory education they were able to assist in a number of domestic chores whilst mother and (in the Barber's case) elder siblings were busy at work. Presumably Mary Fisher also paid a proportion of her earnings as lodgings.

The Barber weekly income could, therefore, be estimated to be in the region of £2 to £2. 6s. This can be compared with the lot of a labourer from rural Bedfordshire, Phillip Peddor, from Cranfield, south-west of Bedford. Peddor emigrated to Derbyshire around 1836 where he was able to almost double his income whilst retaining his occupation. The members of his family also greatly increased the family income by taking employment at a local mill. At Cranfield their weekly earnings were as follows: Phillip (age 39) 7s.; his wife (not named), lace maker, 1s.; handicapped daughter Mary (19), lace maker, 1s. 6d.; daughter Sarah (16), lace maker, 2s. 6d.; son Thomas (14), ploughboy, 2s. 6d.; daughter Betsey (nine), lace maker, 10d.; son Phillip (four), nothing. Total family income for the support of seven persons, with six contributing, was 15s. 6d. Phillip claimed that he was on the verge of starvation in Bedfordshire.[12]

The depression in agriculture which persisted from the end of the Napoleonic War until the end of the 1830s was a powerful imperative for families to migrate to a location offering conspicuously higher wages. Within Bedfordshire, a period of aching poverty and social unrest culminated in a spate of rioting across the county in 1830, with further riots centred upon Ampthill five years later.[13] Luton was not immune from these troubles since a depression in the straw plait trade in the late 1820s led to riots in 1828 and 1829. On the first occasion, a 200 strong mob focused their efforts upon an attempt to burn down the home of John and Richard Jones, straw hat manufacturers, but were repelled by gunfire from the latter. Both riots took place on 5 November, an event in Luton's social calendar which occasionally resulted in spontaneous disorder. At the depth of the depression earnings plummeted, as elsewhere, but serious though it was the depressed state of the straw hat trade was not as sustained as it was in the agricultural areas. For those not able or willing to migrate to northern mills or to endure the risks of emigration, Luton presented an attractive haven from desperate circumstances.

Of those residing in Prospect Place and New Town Street in 1841, 282 (63.4%) were born within Bedfordshire, although the precise number from Luton is not known. The role of Luton as a centre for local migration is demonstrated further by study of the places of birth within the Luton sub-district at the time of the 1851 census. Of the 25,087 people listed, 16,338 (65.12%) were born in Bedfordshire and 4979 (19.8%) in Hertfordshire. The percentages for the remainder were as follows: Buckinghamshire (5.2%), Middlesex (2.4%), Northamptonshire (1.4%), Essex (0.4%), Cambridgeshire (0.3%) and Scotland (0.3%). Within the 25,087, the population of the township amounted to little more than 45%. The 86 from Scotland were comprised overwhelmingly of women (78) and it would be interesting to know whether they came from a single region, perhaps a depressed plaiting district such as the Orkneys.

Luton's economy offered an enticing range of opportunities to those from the rural hinterland who beheld few options other than agriculture, domestic service or unemployment. The occupations of the senior males in New Town Street and Prospect Place in 1841 give witness to that diversity. Thirteen worked within the hat industry: one warehouseman, one plait bleacher, seven bonnet pressers, three plait dealers and one 'straw manufacturer'. A further 32 were associated with the construction industry (eleven labourers, ten bricklayers, two sawyers, seven carpenters, one plumber and a timber merchant). There were also those whose occupations were typical of any urban centre; four grocers, a shoe maker, a shoe dealer, a baker, a sieve maker, a potato salesman, a schoolmaster, a general dealer, a butcher, a coal brazier, a miller, a thatcher and a coach maker. In addition there were eight resident tailors, one commercial traveller, one of independent means and three whose occupations are unreadable.

No beer shops were identified in this part of the census, but a number of the men listed above must have had this as a second source of income as there were by this time several (nameless) beer shops being opened up in New Town Street. Some of those working in public houses and retail would have acted as plait dealers and some were also cottage landlords. The link between the handful of large factories and the myriad domestic workshops was the ubiquitous plait dealer, an individual coming in a number of guises.[14] A handful would be specialist merchants such as Josiah Wright, with warehouses in George Street and Hemel Hempstead, but a greater number would combine this with other trades. Examples of this type included William Smith, a Market Hill plait dealer and furrier, and George Tearle of Hastings Street, principally a block maker. Still more would deal in plait as a sideline – shopkeepers as well as publicans being especially well placed to trade in this way. Lutonians were building homes, owning homes, working in homes, selling from homes, selling to homes and drinking in (usually) licensed homes: the town was built upon a cottage economy.

Although comprehensive data is lacking, Luton's cottage economy throws up a number of interesting areas for further investigation. Did those who lived and worked in Luton – especially in the hat trade – marry (or at least cohabit) at a younger age than elsewhere? Did they have their children at an earlier age? What proportion of migrants were single? Certainly it is known that the town was attractive to girls from their mid-teens upwards and there were a number of men who also would have been drawn to the town. These would have been fewer in number than the women. The New Town Street returns show that whereas the percentage ratio between women born within and beyond Bedfordshire was more or less even (49 : 51), for men there was a small divergence in favour of Bedfordshire birth (55 : 45). A higher proportion of men would have been seeking permanent, rather than seasonal, opportunity and they would in all probability have been slightly older.

These same returns for New Town can give some indication of the ages at which couples began producing children. Disregarding those over 50 years of age (whose children may well have left home) the figures for those working in textile-domestic related trades (sewers, tailors, dressmakers, all men in the hat industry) reveal a slightly lower age at which they produced their first child to those in other occupations. These figures stand at 22.22 years and 24.87 years for men, and 22.61 years and 23.18 years for women. These calculations are based upon the rounded up ages of adults on the census and tentatively point to a feature of the domestic economy – a predilection for marriage and the consequent bearing of children between the ages of twenty and 25. There was little incentive for girls to marry much before the age of twenty. They were mobile, only living in one place for around six months, earning good pay (as good or better than most of their male contemporaries) and able to spend this cash on attractive dresses and other consumer goods. Hat sewing was clean work, undertaken at the heart of the fashion industry and Luton girls were noted for their vivacious looks. After all, as Lazlo Grof observed, the example of early marriage, from which many girls were escaping to work in Luton, was hardly an attractive one.

To also judge by the census returns, couples did not provide enormous broods, 2.95 being the average number of children per household in New Town Street and Prospect Place in 1841. Naturally there were great variations with cases of families of up to nine children living close to young couples who had as yet little opportunity to produce families within this relatively new district. It is noticeable, however, that many couples in their late twenties had not borne offspring at short intervals. Carpenter Robert Taylor and his hat sewer wife Frances, for example, (recorded as being aged '30' and '25' in 1841) had three children: Ephraim (five), Robert (two) and Richard (five months). Next door, labourer Samuel ('30') and hat sewer Elizabeth Barlow had two daughters aged five and three. Two doors along, George Bull, a carpenter ('35'), and Caroline, a sewer ('30'), had children aged ten, eight and four. In Luton's economic context this was a prudent approach. Family income could be seasonal and uncertain. Whilst children could be an assistance during times of intense domestic production, the reverse was the case during the 'slow' season or the worse circumstance of a full depression. Instead of vast numbers of children, it appears that Luton families sought to augment family income by taking in migrant lodgers during the busy season who could then leave when the work eased off. Unlike children, lodgers were not a burden when times were bad. The Taylor's thus had one lodger, an eighteen year old bonnet sewer. The Barlow's also had one, Jane Axtell, a fifteen year old 'apprentice'. The Bull's had three of these 'apprentices', two aged fifteen and one aged ten. More than half of the houses in New Town Street (53%) had lodgers at the time of the 1841 census.

Part Two. Vendors and Builders

The other hat towns

During the second quarter of the nineteenth century other leading centres of the hat trade included St. Albans, Dunstable, Hitchin, Tring, Hemel Hempstead and Leighton Buzzard. In addition, there were also minor plait markets at Hertford, Baldock and Shefford. Luton's communications were no better than any of these places, and certainly inferior to those of Dunstable. Through its roads and railway this latter town could certainly boast of a superior network until 1858, and an equally good one until 1868.[15] In fact, it had not been until 1784 that

Luton acquired anything like a satisfactory road link with Dunstable, a town which was popularly supposed to produce a better quality hat in its larger factories.

The comparison of land ownership is relevant to the discussion as to why Luton should have become predominant from such an unpromising initial position. Records are fragmentary but a comparative source on one of the neighbouring towns is provided by a tithe award list for Dunstable from 1840.[16] The intersection of the town's main roads effectively cut the built up area in the middle of the century into quarters, urbanised Dunstable being virtually restricted to those buildings abutting onto the roads. The south-eastern quarter lay mainly in the ownership of the church. The remaining three quarters were mostly within the control of five owners: William Frederick Brown, the executors of James Hopkins Oliver (his son succeeded), George Hooper, Edward Burr and Richard Gutteridge. The latter two were related to the Luton landowning families of the same name. Of these, Gutteridge and Brown, neither of whom were listed as tradesmen and industrialists, owned the most.

The marked difference between Luton and Dunstable was in the degree of availability of land in the crucial period during the second quarter of the nineteenth century in which the hat trade expanded. Only one of the main property owners in Dunstable released land during this period. This was Edward Burr, who had succeeded to the ownership of the Dunstable Brewery in 1835, but retired just eight years later. In quitting the business Burr sold the entire brewery and its holdings, the neighbouring Brewers Hill Farm and 50 acres of land. The brewery was turned into a hat factory by Messrs. Cooper of Manchester and the land was built upon. The isolated sale, however, was insufficient to provide the necessary stimulus for developments which could have provided a similar, rival mode of production to that which existed in Luton.[17]

The next major sale of land did not occur until after the death of Richard Gutteridge. Although having a son, Matthew, most of his lands were purchased by the British Land Company in 1861. They laid out several streets upon them before disposing of the acquisition in small plots (with some difficulty) through several sales in 1862, 1869, 1871 and 1877.[18] Well before this time Luton had stolen a march and established its pre-eminence as the centre of the industry. Again, there is an inclination to peer into the veiled activities of the preceding century: the Dunstable charities held land in Luton, more than they did in their own town, suggesting that there existed disparity in the level of activity of land markets in the respective localities which predated the expansion of the hat trade.

Similarly, there was little change in land ownership in either Hitchin or St. Albans. At the former, land upon the southern and eastern sides of the town was held by two, long established families – the Radcliffes and the Wilsheres.[19] Frederick Delme Radcliffe, then owner of Hitchin

Priory, was the latest in the line which stretched back to the sixteenth century. He owned other country homes, and a 'town' house in Grosvenor Square, and was the model of a country squire. He spent a good deal of time in Hitchin where he sat on the local magistrates' bench and, at every opportunity, indulged in his favourite pastime – hunting. It was a sport in which Delme Radcliffe, a friend and fellow horseman of the Prince of Wales, particularly excelled.[20] He had neither reason nor inclination to sell the estate upon which he hunted, his home protruding into the heart of the town with the park fanning out behind it. Upon his death in 1875, the lands of Frederick Delme Radcliffe remained largely inviolate.

Neither were the Wilshere family, whose home lay at Welwyn, inclined to sell at this time. They were the biggest landowners in the Hitchin area with William (an MP) owning 818 acres, Charles 145 acres, and another William 227 acres. They were not to dispose of their holdings until the twentieth century. The remainder of the land was owned by a number of families, many of whom were Quakers. These included the Lucases, brewers, bankers, artists and writers; the Ransoms, principally millers and farmers; Joshua Sharples, a banker, and John Whiting. Hitchin serves as a vivid example of a town where the close interest of the landowning families in their local estates acted as a bulwark against industrial expansion.

At St. Albans there was an even greater fragmentation of land with a number of local men (and some women) owning substantial field holdings in the centre of the city, alongside those of the Earl of Verulam.[21] Such an arrangement might have been more conducive to market driven land dispersal than at Hitchin or Dunstable. Again, however, relatively limited building had taken place by the 1880s, most of which was in the vicinity of the railway station. Dunstable, Hitchin and St. Albans did not share with Luton the same impetus for growth where speculators were encouraged by a continuous supply of freehold building ground, (from a much earlier point in the century). Both Tring and St. Albans contained silk mills which provided alternative employment for female labour, and in the latter city, as with Berkhamsted, Hemel Hempstead and Leighton Buzzard, between 24–29% were working in some capacity within the straw hat trade in 1851. By contrast some 60% of Luton women were working in that trade (plus 10% of men). It may be the case that alternative forms of factory based employment diminished the demand for domestic units, which were so striking a feature in Luton.

Dunstable's hat industry was not shackled by a desire to service only the more affluent sectors of the fashion world. Its factories, like Luton's, were operated by businessmen some of whom were from Manchester and London. Two of the biggest, Munt, Brown and Company, and Gregory, Cubbitt and Company, had branches in both Bedfordshire towns. There was no intrinsic element within Dunstable's hat industry which prevented it from adopting similar methods of production to Luton. Rather it was the case that there was literally no room for it to expand, to locate new units. By the time that space became available the initiative had long since passed to Luton where the large factories engaged in a reciprocal arrangement with the small production units springing up all around. In Dunstable, this two way relationship was stifled by the absence of land. The consequence of this was that most production was carried out in large factories, leading to a stunting of potential development.

Luton's land

Details of land ownership in the eighteenth century are very scanty but no Act of Parliament was ever passed dealing with a comprehensive enclosure of commonable lands in Luton. The Luton Enclosure Act of 1808 dealt with specific portions of commonable land totalling just under twenty acres. William Austin, who took a great interest in matters concerning land ownership, concluded that the absence of a general enclosure act was because inter-commoning had virtually ceased within thirty years of the commencement of the eighteenth century. Thereafter, Austin supposed, enclosure took place in the following years through mutual agreement between respective landowners largely at the behest of Lancelot 'Capability' Brown, acting as agent for the Earl of Bute.[22] Whatever the truth of the matter, it is evident that there had been considerable movement in the local land market in the mid-eighteenth century, allowing newcomers such as the Wallers, Burrs and Goujon to build up holdings. This is tantalisingly obscure as here lies a root influence over the events which subsequently occurred in the second quarter of the nineteenth century but is rendered impenetrable by the inaccessibility of the Bute archive. A tentative comparison can be made with the machine lace city of Nottingham. There, the presence of vested interests (essentially the freeholders) upon the moribund Corporation prevented the enclosure of the extensive land which the Corporation owned around the edge of the city. This inhibited Nottingham's development well into the nineteenth century. Such matters were largely settled in Luton before the passing of its 1808 Enclosure Act, but how and when are not precisely known.[23]

In the early nineteenth century, John Crichton Stuart, second Marquess of Bute and owner of Luton Hoo, was pre-eminent amongst local landowners. The second Marquess was the great-grandson of John, third Earl of Bute, who had purchased the 4468 acre estate in 1763. The third Earl combined an ultimately disappointing political career with a love of books, works of art and botany – fields in which he built outstanding private collections as well as a considerable level of knowledge. Through his activities as collector and patron of the arts, the Earl of Bute established Luton Hoo as one of the finest houses in England. At its peak it was observed that 'the rooms are hardly to be equalled for grandeur of dimensions and luxury of decoration; the library is inferior only to that at Blenheim; and there is a large collection of paintings by the finest masters'.[24]

A common feature of the Butes was their accumulation of wealth and property through marriage. By the time of his marriage to Lady Maria North in 1818, the second Marquess owned property in London, the Isle of Bute, Galloway, Glamorgan, Bedfordshire, Ayrshire and Durham. The last two of these contained coal mines. By marrying Lady Maria, Bute added estates in Essex and Cambridgeshire.[25] Propitious marriage and personal vanity apart, the second Marquess was a significantly different character to his immediate forebears. He was meticulous, hard working, enterprising – but not a collector. His serious commitment towards his scattered estates was reflected in the carefully planned tours which he regularly undertook. No amount of travel, however, could allow even the most conscientious estate manager to spend sufficient time in holdings so widely spread. Although the administrative headquarters of the Bute estate in England and Wales, Luton Hoo was becoming of diminishing importance to the Marquess. Thomas Collingdon, who became secretary to the Bute estate in 1817, officially resided at the Hoo, but like his master frequently was obliged by affairs to be absent from Luton.[26]

The logistical difficulties presented by scattered estates, as well as the burden of family debts, prompted the Marquess to attempt to rationalise his holdings. Between 1821 and 1824 he endeavoured to sell the Hoo but received no suitable offer. At the same time the Marquess dabbled in a little property speculation of his own in Luton, attempting to build 'superior houses' in order to attract 'superior people' to the town.[27] The location of these homes is not certain but in all probability it was Wellington Street, laid out around this time by Bute. The purpose of 'superior people' coming to Luton during a slump in the plait industry is also unclear and Bute's first (failed) attempt at house building in Luton was also his last. Following the failure to sell the Hoo, the Marquess commissioned Robert Smirke to undertake expensive alterations in 1829.

Although extended absences determined that he was not usually active in Luton's affairs, the Marquess was not uninterested. He was closely involved with the early development of the Board of Guardians, John Davies quoting this boast made by the Marquess at the time of the first elections to the Board in 1835:

> I put the wealthiest Baptist in the Town, the most moderate of the Quakers and a friendly Methodist on my list. The radicals had a meeting for the express purpose of getting up a contest but the list was admitted to be so respectable that they were obliged to give up their intended agitation.[28]

This statement speaks more of the Marquess' vanity than his real power in Luton. Bute and Rev Macdouall were ex-officio members of a Board which included Edmund Waller, Frederick Burr, Richard Marks Brown and Thomas Partridge as Luton Guardians. Far from being creatures of the Bute influence, these men were from prominent local families and possessed opinion, ability and influence in their own right. As such it was certain that they would have at least considered election to the Board; it was highly unlikely that they would need or require the blessing of a remote Lord of the Manor (nor agitating radicals) in order to secure a place.

At the first meeting of the Board of Guardians, held at Luton's George Inn, in April 1835, the Marquess was shown due deference and elected chairman. Henry Bebb Morris, the Caddington Guardian, was elected vice-chairman.[29] Although Bute attended most weekly meetings in the first two months of office, from the end of June until the elections the following April he attended just three of the 42 meetings. He was absent between September 1835 and March 1836. Bute was re-elected chairman of the Board for the second year of operation (at a meeting which he did not attend) as well as for subsequent years, but remained an irregular attendee, being rarely present from April 1839 onward. Bute did, however, chair every Board meeting between 4 November 1836 and 6 January 1837, and again between 9 November 1838 and 22 February 1839. These patterns reinforce the image of the Marquess as someone conscientious but frequently absent. It was the Marquess who provided the land upon which the workhouse was built, a contributory factor no doubt to his election as chairman, but it serves also as an example of his sense of responsibility towards Luton.

The position of the Marquess of Bute was, therefore, that of someone who maintained an interest in the affairs of the town but could only do so as far as commitment to his other estates would allow. Inevitably, this led to neglect. By 1834 the market place in Luton, the responsibility and benefits of which lay with the Marquess as Lord of the Manor, was in a poor state of repair. An approach was made to Collingdon by surgeon, Thomas Waller, in an effort to cajole the Marquess into making good the dilapidated facilities. The letter finished 'the cry is, Luton is improving and we want more accommodation in the very place now offered'.[30] Little, if anything, was done and it was more than 30 years before the town's markets received substantial improvements at the hands of the Board of Health. It is hardly surprising, therefore, that the Marquess was regarded by Lutonians as a distant figure who did not command a great level of affection or loyalty. An attempt by Frederick Chase to raise subscriptions towards a portrait of the Marquess had to be abandoned through lack of support. Hat manufacturer, Thomas Waller, and remarkably the St. Mary's curate, Thomas Sikes, were amongst those who refused to subscribe.[31]

In the light of his remote relationship with Luton and his increasing financial commitments, especially in Glamorgan, it was logical that the Marquess would come to regard the Bedfordshire estates as a saleable asset. Consolidation of land around Cardiff was taking place through purchase and sale in the 1840s, but indebtedness was obliging the Marquess to abandon purchases. Additional capital was required since income from his estates was insufficient to meet debt burden and his other financial responsibilities.

The decision to put the Luton estates on the market was finalised by the disastrous fire at Luton Hoo on 10 November 1843. This destroyed the 'Great Hall', the library and the chapel and left the Marquess with repair costs which he had neither the will nor the resources to meet. Twelve months later, on 29 November 1844, virtually all the Marquess' holdings to the south of Luton were put up for sale at a public auction.[32] Lot 1 comprised the mansion (requiring repair at 'the cost of a few thousand pounds'), the park and its farm, lodges and surrounding land, all this totalling nearly 1300 acres. Also in lot 1 were Someries Farm and the remains of the 15th century manor house which stood alongside. In the same lot were a further six farms, three mills, two public houses, 'a capital freehold brick built residence', forty cottages, brick making land and the title and privileges of the Lord of the Manor.[33] Most of this land lay in East and West Hyde but there were also gardens of twenty cottages at Leagrave which were let at one shilling.

Lot 2 comprised the advowson to the vicarage of Luton (as an incentive potential buyers were reminded that 'the present incumbent is in his 70th year') which, with its accompanying property, was purchased on behalf of the curate, Thomas Sikes. Lot 1 was sold to C.T. Warde of Warwickshire for £160,000. This was considerably less than the upwards of £200,000 which Luton Hoo had been valued at when placed on the market more than twenty years earlier, although property prices had generally fallen since then.

Thus the link between Luton and the Hoo were severed, as Warde (and the Leighs who followed) had no interest in the town. The links between the Marquess and Luton, however, remained. The Manor of Dallow (later purchased by J.S. Crawley), Maiden Common Farm and the Bury Farm were not included in the sale. The most significant omission was that of the Bute lands around the centre of the township. These lands are shown in appendix one, based upon the earliest detailed map available, surveyed by E. Brown of Silsoe in 1839.[34] The Marquess remained the dominant landowner in Luton; his land encircled the urban centre in an almost unbroken band. The decision not to offer this land for sale was a shrewd one. If not quite a stranglehold (there were other landowners within this band), the Bute estate remained a powerful influence over the rate and direction of Luton's expansion. Perhaps the decision not to sell Luton land at that juncture was influenced by one of the periodic slumps in the hat trade which would have undermined the price. It is wholly characteristic that Bute should decide to wait in order to obtain a greater return at a later date.

The Bedfordshire estates were used to finance the development on Bute land elsewhere. It can only be conjecture to try to assess what would have happened had the Marquess' priorities been different from what they were. Perhaps Luton's growth would have followed a different pattern altogether, one in which the rate of expansion as a centre for the straw hat trade would have been considerably retarded. If this had been the case, towns such as Dunstable and Hitchin, with their superior communications, may well have assumed a degree of commercial parity. They might also then have even seized a trading initiative, leaving this 'long dirty market town' trailing along in their wake.

Although the Marquess of Bute was overwhelmingly the largest owner of land in the township there were other families whose fortunes, and the extent and location of their lands, made them significant figures in determining the direction in which Luton spread. One of these was the Burr family of whom two brothers, Charles and Frederick, were the third generation of a prominent local brewing concern. Following the retirement of Charles in 1850, and the death of Frederick in 1856, the family ceased to play an active role in local affairs, selling the brewery to Thomas Sworder the following year. Although the Burrs had only been in Luton since the 1770s they had established a substantial catalogue of property by 1839. Apart from the brewery's 90 or so tied houses, the Burrs held land chiefly on the south-eastern side of Luton in the vicinity of Park Street and High Town, although there were other parcels adjacent to Old Bedford and Dunstable Roads. It is not known from whom the Burrs acquired their land – the Dunstable charities were amongst what appears to have been a number of local vendors.

The family of the Marquess of Bute's solicitor, Frederick Chase, also held a substantial amount of land within the township: a further 200 acres were owned by Frederick's father, John, in the Stopsley district. John, Frederick and his elder brother Edward, owned smaller but still significant portions in the vicinity of Park Street and Castle Street. The Chase family bear much in common with the Burrs, possibly being established in Luton for a little longer but abruptly ceasing to play an active part in the town when Frederick left in 1851.

By contrast the Gutteridge family had been living in the Luton area since the sixteenth century. Like the Butes they had accumulated considerable wealth through fortuitous marriages, albeit at a more parochial level. The last prominent member of the family was James Gutteridge, a Baptist of considerable pride and volcanic temper.[35] Upon James' death in 1831, the complexities of his will obliged his executors to go to the High Court which then ordered the estate to be sold by auction. The *Hertfordshire County Chronicle* carried the notice of the sale providing the fullest account of the late James Gutteridge's holdings in 1833:[36]

> To be peremptorily Sold, pursuant to a Decree of the High Court of Chancery, made in the cause of "Thomson-v-Waller", with the approbation of the Rt. Hon. Robert Lord Henley, one of the Members of the said Court, at the Red Lion Inn, at Luton, in the County of Bedford, on Monday the 30th September, and each Tuesday, the 1st day of October, 1833 at One O'Clock in the Afternoon of each Day in Lots the Freehold and Leasehold of the late James Gutteridge, of Luton, in the County of Bedford, Esquire, Deceased, situate and being of several Dwelling Houses and Cottages, including the late residence of the said James Gutteridge, in the Town of Luton, with the coach-house, stabling, and suitable out-buildings, garden pleasure grounds, and plantations thereto belonging. Also two Farms, known by the respective names of Limbury Farm, and Crawley Green Farms, and several pieces of arable meadow, and pasture land, containing altogether upwards of Five hundred and fifty acres, some part of which are contiguous to the Town of Luton, and are very desirable for building.

The sale could not have been a total success. Brown's terrier shows that in 1839 the 550 acres referred to in the sale advertisement (just over 555 according to the terrier), were still in the hands of the executors, at least at the time that the terrier was being compiled. 'Executors of James Gutteridge' has been crossed out and replaced with the name of Edmund Waller beside the entry for Limbury Farm (348 acres). 'Thos. Waller' has been inserted in the margin alongside some parcels of land which include the gardens of Gutteridge's former home: Austin claimed that it was John Waller who bought the house and gardens and the 1844 tithe award list supports this. 'John Waller' and 'Jones' have been added to other lands. The 136 acre Crawley Green Farm, however, (eventually purchased by Samuel Crawley) remained in the hands of the executors. Within five years this, and the remainder of Gutteridge's land in the township, had been disposed of.

It would be interesting to know why the sale was unsuccessful. Perhaps the same slump in the hat trade, which may have influenced Bute's decision not to sell the township land, inhibited speculation. The Marquess was an interested party and appears to have joined in a dispute with the Wallers over the sale of land, as this letter from Collingdon to Stanton indicates:

> I must say that I am surprised considering what took place previous to Mr Gutteridge's sale and the present proposed accommodation to Mr Waller's family, that Mr John Waller should make the least objections to his arrangements you have submitted to him – he distinctly pledged himself to Mr Roy (the Lord Bute's solicitor) on the understanding that Mr Roy was not to

oppose him Mr John Waller in lot 26 that he would let the Marquis have whatever land he required to complete his arrangements in that quarter after the sale was settled, and with that understanding Mr Roy actually purchased Lot 26 for him . . .

You will be so good as to not proceed any further with the valuation of Mr Thomas Waller's premises until the arrangements of the land beholden to the Marquess of Mr John Waller is finally settled to his Lordship's satisfaction.

It would be better for Mr Austin not to be placed at Mr T. Waller's mercy but that he should make the purchase of garden from the end of the Barn from his Lordship to which I dare say there would be no objection upon his Lordship being paid what you think a proper sum for such accommodation.

I cannot understand what Mr Austin means by the pledge he mentions from the Marquess. I am quite aware that he wished to have part of the Barn but he can hardly expect the sale of his property to be injured for this accommodation when it be open to him afterwards to meet with Mr. Waller.[37]

In the absence of full evidence this letter has a certain cryptic tone. Bute already owned land in the area on the eastern side of George Street running down towards the River Lea (known as Seven Acres). He may, through purchase of Gutteridges' ground, have been attempting to further consolidate in this district and improve his points of access to George Street. There does appear to have been eventually a clarification of boundaries between Bute and the Wallers. Since the latter got the best of it, however, it is also apparent the Wallers were muscling in where they saw business opportunity. It has to be also said that they were using their position as executors of the Gutteridge estate to get the better of the deal, demonstrating a marked lack of deference toward the Marquess in the process.

The other lands purchased by John Waller from the Gutteridge estate were situated adjacent to the London Road (Cutenhoe Closes) and in High Town. Besides the Limbury Farm, Edmund also purchased a small amount of land in the Dallow area and he also rented land (on the opposite side of George Street to John) from Charles Cox. At some time between 1839 and 1845 this passed to his brother Thomas whose widow, Jane, allowed a linking road (George Street West) to be made between George Street and Stuart Street over this land in 1847.

Bute, Gutteridge, Burr, Waller and Chase were thus the leading landowning families within Luton township during the first half of the nineteenth century. A substantial amount of land lay beyond family control and in the hands of the Luton and Dunstable charities. These were, in fact, second in extent to the Bute interest within the urban area. The Luton charities numbered seventeen in all, classified under five headings: Bread Fund, Apprentice Fund, School Fund, Distribution Fund and Repairing Fund (for St Mary's). All but three of these charities were the responsibility of the churchwardens. An investigating committee, appointed by a vestry meeting in March 1853, concluded that these charities were not being discharged in accordance with the donors' original intentions.[38]

In addition to the main landowners, there were others worthy of mention. William Townrow, a yeoman farmer and Baptist, owned small fields in the vicinity of Stuart Street (three acres), Bailey Hill (two acres) and several other pieces on the northern side of town. Townrow's plots near Stuart Street were the first in the area to be utilised as building ground: Austin claims that the original conveyance was made in 1845.[39] It is very possible, therefore, that Townrow purchased this land specifically for building and the pattern of ownership in this area suggests that the vendor may well have been the Marquess of Bute.

Charles Cox was one of the few Luton landowners not to reside in the town and little is known of him. His address was given as Finchley, Middlesex and all but one of his scattered fields were rented as arable land – the Burr's numbering amongst his tenants.[40] As mentioned, Cox also owned premises in George Street, these eventually passing into the hands of his erstwhile tenants, the Wallers. Henry Brown, the Quaker timber merchant, also owned a number of scattered pieces of land mostly concentrated in the area of Chapel Street and London Road. Like Townrow his acquisitions could have been recent, but it is not known from whom.

The notable omission from this list is the Crawley family of Stockwood. Following the failure of Samuel's political career, the preoccupation of both himself and his son, John Sambrook Crawley, was the consolidation of the family estate through a succession of purchases of land and farms around Luton. On their estates the Crawley's concentrated upon improving agricultural techniques.[41] The family holdings were on the periphery of the town centre and, with very minor exceptions, this remained the case. The rest lay in a band, from the south-west of the town, around to its north, via Stockwood Park, Dallow, Biscot and Stopsley.[42] These lands, second in extent only to those of the Marquess of Bute within the parish of Luton, were added to during the course of the nineteenth century and reached their greatest extent by its last decade. They were to be the base upon which twentieth century Luton was built.

Early urbanisation

A little over a quarter of a century, following the death of James Gutteridge in 1831, saw the eclipse of the major landowning families in Luton. John Chase died in 1843 (aged 87) to be followed two years later by Thomas and Edmund Waller, the latter with no surviving heir. A year later the Marquess of Bute cut his close links with Luton. Frederick Chase left Luton in 1851, Frederick Burr died in 1856 (brother Charles quit the town) and John Waller died in 1859. Although Thomas and John Waller had heirs, the power of the family declined appreciably from this point. Remnants of the Burrs and the Gutteridges were still to be found in the district, but their prominence was lost. The Chase family disappeared altogether.[43]

Potential property speculators were thus offered a double enticement: an expanding local industry allied to a steady abundance of freehold building ground. Details of land and property prices are scarce, usually no more than a scribbled note in the margin of a surviving sale catalogue, making a clear picture of overall prices difficult to assess. What is important, however, is the fact that in Luton there was sufficient affordable land for the small, first time investor. From 1839 onwards, speculative activity gathered momentum as individual fields were purchased and carved up in anticipation of building being able to take place.[44] The physical removal of the existing landowner weakened the potential for estate control, a factor enhanced by the quantity of building ground which was available. It was the consumer, the property speculator, who had the decisive influence over the sort of town which Luton became. Rarely were any conditions placed upon the sale of land.

The steady supply of land was lubricated by major auctions interspersed with smaller sales. By 1845 urban development had already taken place on the lands of four owners (see appendix 2): the Burrs in High Town, Townrow and Chase in New Town and Bute upon Seven Acres in the heart of Luton. Upon the latter, the first tentative stages of building were taking place, the development serving as an example of the difficulties caused by the lack of close control.[45] In Collingdon's absence many local details were handled by two solicitors, Frederick Chase and Alexander Parkes, the latter possibly a recent arrival in town. John Waller, in partnership with the builder John Williams, had approached Collingdon in order to secure the purchase of some of this land but had been rebuffed because his offer was 'not consistent with the value of the property'.[46]

Delays and confusion caused by Collingdon's repeated absence reached comic proportions in 1842 when he and Parkes sold the same piece of Seven Acres to two different developers, John Gray and Charles Tomson. Both Gray and Tomson were tenants of the Marquess elsewhere in Luton, Tomson having recently purchased the 'piece in common' which was named Prospect Place. Parkes accepted Tomson's offer of £5 per pole (receiving a £60 deposit) and Collingdon accepted Gray's tender of £6 per pole. Gray began building. Collingdon blamed Parkes whilst Tomson dug in his heels, threatening legal action. Eventually, agreement was reached between Gray and Tomson, whereby it seems that the former offered to sell some compensatory ground to the latter. Still, however, Collingdon meddled from afar, claiming to be protecting the Marquess' interests.[47] Frederick Chase clearly thought otherwise and placed the blame clearly upon the Marquess' absentee steward.[48] He wrote to Collingdon, on behalf of Gray, who appeared to be getting the worst of the deal:

> I have taken an opinion on Tomson and Gray's case, and the result is that Gray cannot be allowed to execute the Deeds of covenants as now sought to be altered by you, it would be an act of injustice towards Gray and would involve him serious consequences and which if the case was properly explained to his Lordship would not I am sure for a moment be entertained; by allowing Gray to take possession and build, with the terms of the Covenants settled, you cannot afterwards turn round and introduce fresh clauses to bind subsequent purchases, I do not hesitate to say whatever trouble damages or expenses Gray may be put to, or sustain, you will have to bear it, the works are all suspended in consequence and Gray cannot fulfil his contract entered into with Tomson which of course will render him liable to an Action for damages.[49]

The bitter fiasco involved another solicitor, William Hunt, with whom Gray had a 'violent quarrel'. Collingdon went so far as to order the removal of a roof from one of Gray's constructions which the steward claimed was overhanging the road, thereby serving as an 'injury to the rest of his (Bute's) property'. In the light of Collingdon's unsatisfactory oversight it is hardly surprising that two other prospective purchasers of land in Seven Acres, Frederick Davis and Frederick Gee, showed a marked reluctance to complete their transactions. There were always alternative sites for speculation and Davis eventually opted to pull out altogether.[50] The Marquess of Bute was distant and passive, and the speculators made all the running. It was inevitable that mistakes would be made.

The first stage of Luton's building boom is a clear, if not exactly shining, example of pure *laissez-faire* economic activity. Maximum financial return was not only the primary consideration, it was virtually the only concern which drove on speculation. The meadows and gardens of John Waller's estate, which was auctioned upon his death, were headed on the sale catalogue simply as 'eighty acres freehold building ground', unequivocally illustrating how open space in Luton was regarded by this time.[51] Referring to the areas fronting onto Chapel Street, lying between George Street and Stuart Street, the sale catalogue ended with this optimistic footnote: 'Lots 16 to 24 inclusive would be a very desirable Investment to any Capitalist disposed to erect a Straw plait Market, which is very much needed in the Town of Luton, and there is no doubt it would pay a liberal interest for the Capital employed'. In a town devoid of any promoting public body, private enterprise was to view the priorities very differently. Housing offered a swifter return for smaller outlay, although some of Luton's more elegant buildings (in George Street West) were to be included in the development. The town would have to wait until the advent of public institutions for the provision of a purpose built plait market.

In the late 1840s building activity became concentrated in the New Town area close to Chapel Street. The momentum at Prospect Place diminished temporarily and the debacle at Seven Acres seemed understandably to have inhibited speculators.[52] E.C. Williamson, however, who lived at the junction of Tower Hill and George Street (and owned cottages and land nearby), was pressing to buy further parts of Seven Acres situated immediately to the rear of his garden. Williamson was not planning to plant an orchard – he was acquiring land for a little property speculation of his own. By no means were all Williamson's peers so motivated: a public auction in 1847 resulted in Richard Vyse securing Kidmans Close, three acres of meadow between Chapel Street and Castle Street, for £4000. In taking this land out of commission Vyse apparently left a number of disappointed speculators. He also snuffed out the possibility of low grade New Town housing coming too close to his home.[53]

The new streets under construction were almost entirely for dwellings. Virtually all public buildings were restricted to nonconformist chapels (four substantial examples between 1835 and 1850), public houses and schools (just two of these). The one outstanding example of a public building was erected in 1847, the Town Hall built at the northern end of George Street. In addition, there existed a 'reading room' in Castle Street, and 'public baths' owned by John Gray in New Bedford Road and situated next to his brewery.[54]

The five years after 1845 saw approximately 500 houses built in Luton. The census returns for 1841 and 1851 record that there were 1139 and 2081 houses in the township in these respective years. A tally drawn from the 1845 rate book numbers 1481. This figure includes public houses and shops as 'habitable buildings' and may even be a slight underestimate because individual retail premises are sometimes referred to in the plural (i.e. 'houses and shops').

Urbanisation, 1850–76

On Monday 7 April 1851 the Burr family placed more of the estate on to the market. 'To Capitalists, Builders and Others Seeking Desirable Investments . . . Eligible Building Ground'.[55] There is no evidence to suggest that the leading brewer in Luton was in need of money and there was no expansion of the business that required additional capital. During the 1850s, however, further land was released with a new thoroughfare (Albert Road) being laid out upon a meadow which linked Langley Street with Prospect Place. Still unsold, by 1855, were the Burr's brewery and its tied houses, fields along Langley Street and a few unsold assets left over from the 1851 sale. A series of fields in the south-east of the township, which the Burr family had acquired between 1803 and 1853, were bought by John Shaw Leigh in July 1856.[56] It appears that the Burrs were deciding to cash in on the investment made by their family over the preceding half century, but if Frederick Burr was planning any sort of further investment his death, in 1853, halted it. The business was sold off soon after. Leigh did not build upon these lands but left them as a buffer between his park and the town seeping towards it from the north.

By the mid-1850s the Chase family had relinquished nearly all their Luton holdings and quit the town. At the same time the Bute trustees released more fields along Stuart Street as far as the lane to Buxton Wood. Much of the New Town lands, however, remained undeveloped and, with the disappearance of the Burrs and Chases, the Bute monopoly of land had, if anything, strengthened. The policy of the Bute Trustees towards their lands in Luton is unknown.

The buoyant property market of this period encouraged other, more minor, landowners to sell. The freehold which in 1839 was owned by a non-local clergymen, Rev Lewis, was situated on a prime site between Manchester Street and Stuart Street, dissected by Upper George Street. All of this was disposed of in one auction in June 1855, realising £9961.[57] Elsewhere, there was further building taking place along Guildford Street, but for a while this was not at a rapid rate.[58] The commercial potential of this area was to change when Luton's first railway belatedly arrived in 1858. Running from Hertford the route of the track crossed land still held by the Burrs near to the Brache, and across that owned by Ashton's Charity at the foot of Hart Hill. From there it gouged through Seven Acres, thereby cutting off High Town from the rest of Luton, before crossing Lucas' fields and away from the urban area via the fields behind the Bury Farm along Dunstable Road. Its entire route traversed open country and, although necessitating the re-routing of roads between Luton and High Town, caused relatively little disruption. Inevitably, the ground adjacent to the station and goods area at the top of Bute Street became extremely desirable and almost immediately bids were made for this land near to the station.[59] This area between the station and George Street was to feature the concentration of the larger hat factories.

Following the death of William Townrow in 1861 his widow placed the entire estate on to the market.[60] Some parts of his land, at sites scattered around Luton (Bailey Hill, Dallow, Leagrave and High Town), had already been disposed of in the spring of 1860. The sale was a considerable success, realising prices between £100 and £165 per acre in the face of great demand.[61]

It was during the 1860s that the Bute estate substantially diminished its land holdings in the township. The first major sale was held at the George Hotel on 26 June 1862, at which a smattering of lands was auctioned.[62] Much of this lay in the vicinity of Park Street and a local newspaper reported that there was 'good competition' for the garden ground which made 'very good prices'. Part of this site was purchased by James Hopkins, a Park Street builder, but remained undeveloped until the latter part of the nineteenth century (a section becoming the East Ward Recreation Ground). A further five acres were acquired by the Board of Health, at that time developing a sewage treatment plant.[63] The Bute trustees had made an astute calculation in the timing of the sale which coincided with the emergence of the hat trade from a brief depression: 'there was a large attendance of gentlemen and the bidding was spirited'.[64]

In 1867 Bute's trustees miscalculated, overplaying their hand whilst seeking to take advantage of Bute land near to Coney Hall.[65] The sale resulted in the creation of new streets but took place at the beginning of a deep recession in the straw hat industry. There was an added disadvantage in the decision by the trustees to shackle the various lots with conditions of sale, stipulating the type and value of what might be erected on them. Each lot was sold but although 'there was a good company present . . . the biddings were not spirited . . .'.[66]

Similarly, the sale of the late Richard Vyse's Luton estate two months later was also a failure, necessitating a second sale in 1872, once the straw hat trade had improved.[67] The rate of urbanisation was noticeably dwindling during the late 1860s and the early 1870s. King Street, the last road to connect George Street with Stuart Street, was built up only along its eastern side. This street, 'one of the most imposing thoroughfares in Luton', contained a number of elegant three storey houses for the middle classes, together with a small number of shops.[68] The effect of the recession was pronounced, making clear the correlation between building activity and the hat trade. Although the hat industry recovered in the early 1870s, up to incorporation and beyond there were no major sales of land. Instead there was a period of consolidation upon land already released.

Part Three. Property and the Hat Trade

Housing and building before 1850

Much of Luton's housing stock in the mid-nineteenth century was built to contain the early stages of the urbanised hat industry. Later in the century, a greater proportion of the workforce was to undertake its labour within the confines of primitively mechanised hat factories. During the early stages of growth, however, the 'putting out' system of the 'counter trade' represented the urban evolution of a cottage economy. Luton's homes doubled as workshops as thousands were drawn into the town on a seasonal or permanent basis. The construction industry needed to be flexible in order to meet this peculiar demand. The ease with which farmers, brewers and retailers were able to diversify economic activity, or to slip into entirely new areas altogether, illustrated the dynamic stage of economic activity which existed before full industrialisation and the greater specialisation that went with it.

Many of Luton's earliest (and consequently worst) examples of housing were removed in various private and commercial developments during the late nineteenth and early twentieth centuries. Those that did survive were virtually all swept away by a series of slum clearance programmes which were undertaken by Luton Borough Council between 1930 and 1938.[69] A few lingered on in isolated pockets, reprieved by World War II, but disappeared (along with much else of the Victorian town centre) during the redevelopment plans of the post-war era.[70] By contrast, the period between 1830 and 1850 was one unfettered by building regulations. Consequently, houses were erected in little short of a free-for-all, the limitations upon developers being restricted to location, size of plot and availability of capital. It is not easy to provide typical examples of Luton's housing in this period but there are some common features.

Virtually all houses were built of locally produced bricks, these usually being of a distinctive plum colour.[71] During the course of the nineteenth century brick-fields opened up at Stopsley, Round Green, Caddington, Bailey Hill and close to the Dunstable Road. It is difficult to establish precise dates for the opening of all the brick-fields, and it is possible that there were others, records of which do not survive. Within Luton's township there were three kilns which were known to be operating before 1845. All of these were on land owned by the Marquess of Bute, thereby illustrating another dimension by which he, and later his trustees, contributed to Luton's urban growth.

The oldest kiln was situated on the eastern side of Dunstable Road, close to the *Fox* public house. Operated by William, and subsequently Elizabeth, Gregory, it was already functioning by the 1830s but appeared to have ceased by 1855. In 1834 John Williams successfully negotiated access to the brick earth in White Hill Close, between the present London and Tennyson Roads. This necessitated the abrupt removal of the sitting tenant, farmer Charles Tomson, who naturally objected to what he saw as the shabby treatment which he received at the hands of Collingdon – not for the last time, as the Seven Acres experience was to prove. Collingdon wrote to Tomson in September, 1834:

> I am sorry to find that it is unavoidably necessary to take the whole of White Hill Close for the purpose of Brickmaking ... although you do not like to give up this land, that as it will be a considerable benefit to his lordship; you will not object to do so.[72]

Tomson did indeed object but, realising that there was little he could do, hung out for alternative land and compensation (he had been intending to sow barley). His correspondence with Collingdon demonstrated his annoyance:

> ... I understand that White Hill Close is intended for Williams if it must be so I hope you have secured the Bush Piece he bought at Gutteridge's sale, if you cannot Buy it must be rented of him, <u>We must have it</u> ... you will please observe that I will have nothing to do with Mr Williams, therefore Whatever sum of Money I am to Receive for giving the field up, I shall Expect to Receive from you ... NB Pray write to me very <u>soon</u> and where to address you.[73]

Although he was unable to prevent himself being turfed off the land, Tomson was able to secure compensation mutually acceptable to himself, to the Hoo estate and to Williams. Clearly, the Hoo appreciated that mollifying a disgruntled farmer was worthwhile when set against the return to be derived via Williams' operation, one which far outweighed the agricultural value of the land. The fourteen year lease arranged between Bute and Williams required the latter to pay a yearly rental of £12 for the land plus a further £35.5s. for its use for brickmaking. Williams was obliged to pay 2s. 6d. for every thousand bricks produced and further amounts for every thousand tiles, according to size: 2s. 6d. if six inches square, up to 7s. 6d. if twelve inches square.[74]

The monitoring of brick and tile production presented something of a problem as Collingdon felt that the estate's income was not something which should depend upon a gentleman's agreement with Williams. The matter was drawn to the attention of Frederick Chase when the latter was in the process of drawing up the legal agreement between Bute and Williams:

> There is one difficulty to which I will draw your attention that is how it is to be ascertained the number of each awhile to be made, we can check the Bricks only by the duty paid to the Excise, but if the Duty should be taken off what is to be done then? This must be defined in the lease; it must not be left to the lessee.[75]

There was no duty upon tiles and, therefore, Chase recommended that Williams be obliged to swear an affidavit. The agreement required Williams to keep clear records of bricks and tiles produced for the purposes of payment to the Hoo estate and also to agree not to sublet the site. In 1846 the site was sold, although it is not known whether Williams was the purchaser.[76] Two years earlier a similar agreement was drawn up between Bute and another Luton builder, Robert Smith. At £10 per annum, Smith secured the tenancy of land near Kidney Wood (further along the London Road from Williams' site) on a fourteen year lease.

Although there were to be other brick-fields opened up elsewhere, these agreements gave Smith and Williams a temporary monopoly of brick production close to a main area of building activity. They were in advantageous positions and both men were amongst purchasers of land, especially Smith who owned a substantial number of cottages in the New Town/Park Town area. The identity of mid-nineteenth century house builders is unknown but it is reasonable to suppose that Williams and Smith contributed a good proportion.

There are few descriptions of working class housing erected during the late eighteenth or early nineteenth century. One of the most vivid accounts of the type of conditions which the poorest had to endure comes from the public inquest into the cholera outbreak of the autumn of 1853, an outbreak concentrated in Adelaide Terrace. There, the 33 back-to-back, one-up, one-down cottages seemed to be held together by plaster and lathe. Amenities by 1853 comprised a communal (but defective) well, an open cesspit and four communal privies. Inherent difficulties, due to the poor standard of building, were further exacerbated by the proximity of Jennings and Gates' candle factory, divided from Adelaide Terrace by a high wall which ran along its length. The smell of fat from the factory frequently caused the inhabitants of the Terrace to vomit their meals.[77]

The period between the late 1830s and the early 1850s witnessed many examples of the desire to cram as many dwellings as possible into an allotted area for building. The prevalent building style was noted in a wry letter to the *Beds Times*:

> Having bought a bit of land, and intending to build a house for himself, the Lutonian sees no reason why the house should not be his in every sense as well as in one, and he therefore stamps upon it at once the marks of and the peculiarities of his own mind. If he was to build precisely like his neighbour who could tell that the buildings did not belong to one man? One therefore puts his house a little askew; another sets the roof at a different angle from that of his neighbour; a third aspires nearer to heaven; a fourth will be more humble and let another tower over him. One may admire the popular sense of the proverb that an Englishman's home is his castle, but it is to be regretted that it has not been greatly curbed by a deference to public convenience and order, and that private whims have not been counteracted by the salutary provisions of a local building act.[78]

The unregulated period of building which lasted until the mid-1850s provided the greatest diversity in housing which Luton was to see in the century. That is probably the best that can be said for it.[79] Ill-ventilated, shoddily constructed, no facilities for lighting or sanitation: districts such as Spring Place, Bryden's Passage, Gaitskell Terrace and Chase Street soon became bywords for squalor and its associated problems.

These dwellings, quite appalling though they were, should not detract from the fact that there were also many other examples of housing being erected. Many cottages were small, but they were also adequately ventilated, equipped with the necessary facilities and, overall, provided at least tolerable living conditions. There were also examples of housing – in George Street West and London Road, for example – that were considerably better than that. Bad though many parts of Luton certainly were, the extremes of tightly packed squalor to be found in medium sized and large urban centres were not to be found in what remained a small town. There were no cellar dwellings, such as had proliferated in the early industrial cities, notably in Manchester. Because the land market allowed construction to take place on scattered sites there was not, therefore, the dense alleys and rookeries, impervious to sunlight and fresh air (not to mention officers of the law), that could be found elsewhere in Britain. Nonetheless, with utterly unregulated building, by 1850 it was clear in which direction Luton was travelling.

Housing and building after 1850

Despite the thinness of contemporary evidence, it is clear that the housing free-for-all, if not stopped short by the Board of Health, had at least been curtailed by 1860. Many houses built after this time were still deemed habitable when later standards were applied, escaping the clearance programmes of the mid-twentieth century. In many respects this represents quite a remarkable achievement given the inherent weakness of central legislation, especially the 1848 Health of Towns Act and the 1858 Local Government Act. The permissive nature of this legislation, relying upon local discretion for the enforcement of minimum standards in housing, made it vulnerable to assault from vested interests. As shall be seen in the following chapters there lurked in Luton, as elsewhere, examples of this selfish sort of person.

Detailed analysis of the local construction industry during the mid-nineteenth century is severely hampered by the absence of records but it is apparent that an improvement in standards coincided with a greater uniformity of building materials. With tighter controls being enforced by the Board of Health from the mid-1850s, it was no longer permissible to construct external, internal or party walls out of wood or 'composite' materials as had once been the case. The dimensions of houses increased, thoroughfares became wider and streets of compacted mud became paved, curbed and metalled. With few exceptions, Luton's housing stock became typified by brick built two storey terraced houses fronting onto (or close to) the street and topped by pitched and gabled slate roofs. There were some houses with rear extensions, dedicated to the manufacture of hats, but more typically domestic dwellings were built with a large scullery or back room in which this cottage industry was continued. No back-to-back houses were built after 1850, with all properties possessing at least a communal back yard in which was located a privy. Water-closets became prevalent from the mid-1860s with the Board of Health anxious to promote them. Their adoption, however, was by no means universal.[80]

Although uniform in basic materials and design, a diversity of ornamentation and design was to be found in all but the poorest of streets. Doorways were either square headed or carried a semicircular arch, often with accompanying minor ornamental features. These included protruding wooden lintels, decorated architraves or elaborate keystones topping an arch. Windows were universally rectangular or occasionally arched, and a sliding sash was most common.

With no power over constructions already standing, the main impact of the Board of Health lay in the regulation of new buildings. In essence this meant ensuring that none was built which could impede upon the light, sanitation or stability of another, or which would be injurious to those inhabiting it. To this end the Board was empowered to inspect plans for new buildings and to ensure that no dwellings were occupied before completion. Attempts at improvement over existing properties, however, were disdainfully ignored by landlords. The degree of vigilance which the Board's officers could bring to bear upon homes and lodging houses can also be doubted, and the competence of some of its officers left a great deal to be desired. In the light of all this, some of the optimistic reports which were made to the Board of Health should not be relied upon absolutely. Working within a town whose staple trade encouraged periodic overcrowding, it is hardly surprising that a Board with limited powers, inattentive appointees, many low calibre members and embattled by occasional bouts of litigation, could not be a heavily interventionist body.[81]

In this context, therefore, of greater importance in a town such as Luton was the application of central government enforcement, chiefly through the provision of bye-laws. In Luton's case this was reinforced by the more progressive Board members, coming to power from the mid-1850s and buttressed by the 1858 Act. Section 34 of the Act was concerned with the space around buildings, construction materials and sanitary facilities.[82] Dead end, dog-leg developments, typified by Spring Place, cease from this time onward. They were replaced by typical bye-law housing: rows of solid, if plain, terraced cottages, an increasing number with their own piece of private space at the rear and differentiated from their neighbours in the street only by minor architectural adornments. By curtailing abuses on the part of the unscrupulous, the bye-law provided legal parameters in which the developers could operate. What went on within this framework depended upon the discretion and conscientiousness of the local Board of Health.

Luton's housing was shockingly bad in parts, but its squalor never reached the depth or scale of larger urban centres, such as Nottingham. Bald declarations such as this, although true enough at one level, can trivialise the experiences of people who had to live in them. It would be of little consolation to the hapless tenant of Adelaide Terrace or Jones' Yard to know that although their own children were ravaged by disease caused by their living conditions, even greater numbers were suffering elsewhere. The context of any discussion of Luton's slums, nonetheless, entails analysis of individual courtyards and small streets, instead of whole districts. Although public attempts to remove the slums were ineffective, the improvement in building standards from the middle of the 1850s ensured that they formed a diminishing proportion of the total housing stock as the town expanded. The local Board of Health established minimum standards, encouraged good practice and took action against certain infringements. It was crucially abetted by the limited building which had taken place prior to its formation and by the plentiful supply of land which relaxed the demand for intense development. A less abundant availability of building ground might have severely tested the Board's ability to hold the line.

With the exception of lodging houses, overcrowding within dwellings was not a prominent feature of Edward Cresy's report of 1850, which served as the catalyst for the establishment of a local Board. Overcrowding was regarded as a low priority by the Board, doubtless aware that the problem would go away come May as the busy season ended and migrant workers quit the town. A comparison of the number of persons per house shows virtually no improvement in the half century between 1831 and 1881, density falling from 5.22 to 5.21. The peak density was in 1861, at 5.63 persons per house during a revival in the hat trade. The apparent lack of movement must be mitigated by the undoubted improvement in the overall quality of the housing stock which increased from 758 to 4597 in this period. Five residents of a Chobham Street terraced home in 1881 enjoyed a far better quality of life than five who had the misfortune to share an Ainsworth Passage hovel thirty years earlier. Amongst similar sized towns in 1881, the density figure of 5.21 for that year compares with 4.90 for Peterborough, 5.18 for Colchester, 5.48 for Tunbridge Wells and 5.72 in Chatham. Locally, Luton had greater densities than Dunstable (4.36), Hitchin (4.75) and Bedford (5.02). Interestingly, the density in Luton was also greater than the larger textile cities of Nottingham (4.84) and Leicester (4.90). So many local circumstances determined the density of housing: the census was invariably collected during the peak of the busy season, when Luton's population was swollen with migrants. It would be interesting to be able to analyse Luton's figures on a month by month basis.

Influences upon housing demand

There were many influences upon building patterns. Amongst those cited by writers on housing are central government legislation, existing local social structures, price and availability of land, the power to exert social segregation, location of employment, landlord control and the nature of the local economy. The overwhelming demand in Luton between 1840 and 1876 was for dwellings which could also serve as production units. As a consequence two styles evolved locally. The first was by far the more common: the two storey home in which whole families, seasonally augmented by lodgers, lived and worked. The latter part of the nineteenth century saw an evolution in this type away from the straightforward two-up, two-down pattern and towards houses with a third room downstairs in the form of a short extension, later having a storey placed above it. The second variation were premises which required a retail outlet on the ground floor. Examples of this type were to be found mostly in the commercial heart of the town: Bute Street, Waller Street, Cheapside, George Street and Park Street. The three storey domestic dwelling was to be found in only a handful of middle class homes. Rothesay Road, Castle Street and Wellington Street (soon converted into the retail units for which its buildings were ideally suited) were amongst a handful of examples of this latter type.

The fact that land for development was spread between a number of estates was of great importance in holding down prices, the power of the landowning interest being further diminished by death and removal. Luton's land was usually abundant for even the smallest investor, almost entirely freehold and governed only by local bye-laws. Even the Bute estate was not in a position to force up the price by withholding land – as the father of John Shaw Leigh had done in the dockland area of Liverpool earlier in the century. The availability of plentiful ground in the hands of several other smaller, but still significant, owners ensured that there was little foreseeable advantage to the Bute estate in not relinquishing its town holdings. Only once did it attempt to influence the type of buildings erected upon it – at the disappointing sale of 1867. Although able to shape growth, the role of even the biggest local landowner swiftly became restricted to that of purely a vendor.[83]

In common with other towns, Luton's builders were locally based, small scale operators. With little capital outlay, it was relatively easy to enter the building trade, and not much harder to drop out of it. Little direct experience was necessary: numerous self-help guides, such as *The Builder's Practical Director*, were available to the small timer who, according to Dyos, constituted some 80% of the trade.[84] This group was defined as those employing less than 50 men and it is probable that all of Luton's builders would have fitted into this category. Many of these had probably seen few towns other than their own and, once building regulations made it impossible for speculators to throw together the likes of Bryden's Passage, they were left with the town's traditional pattern as their benchmark. This, to repeat Frederick Davis, was 'in general very low'. With no pressure upon them to do otherwise, it is not surprising that Luton's builders stuck with patterns with which they were familiar.

The decisive influence lay with the hat trade itself. In what was an inherently unstable cottage industry, carrying fluctuating labour demands, the two storey dwelling made sense for the landlord and owner-occupier, providing maximum flexibility for minimum outlay. Although a modest speculation and a compact home, during the busy season it could be crammed to the rafters with migrating workers. The relationship between the hat trade and the construction industry was, as a consequence, a precarious one: to be dependent entirely upon the fortunes of straw hat production must have left the finances of many builders in a perilous state. In attempting to respond to demand it was impossible to tell whether a downturn in trade would last a few months or would be measured in years.

Data is limited but some pointers to the relationship between the two sectors can be identified. After a number of years of expansion, the hat industry slid into a gradual downturn from the mid-1840s. The building trade continued to be active until 1846:

> For the first time in many years there appears to be a halt in the passion for building in this highly prosperous town. There are several houses to let, and the fact is looked upon as a curious phenomenon by those who have acted as if no bounds could be assigned to the increase of the place. The business is as prosperous as ever, but the trading in bricks and mortar has been overdone ... the little check this building propensity has received will probably be salutary. Like a nipping frost in March, it will make further operations more safe and sure.[85]

The property market remained active with 'considerable estates to small tenements' as well as a good supply of building ground continually being available. This factor was to hold true for the rest of the nineteenth century and for most of the twentieth.[86] If, as was likely, the overbuilding of the early 1840s led to a downward pressure upon rents, then this may have served to alleviate the financial distress of individual families and assisted in the recovery of the trade. In 1844 it was reported that every house in Luton was full, sometimes with 'exorbitant' rents being charged. Three years later the landlords were struggling to fill their homes with apparently two or three empty in every street, shops abandoned and people 'forced into sales under distress'.[87]

Rents would not rise until the building trade had also recovered. In Luton, this appears to have occurred very swiftly, assisted by the healthy property market and the incentive to catch up with the rejuvenated hat trade. Both these factors would lead to a demand for housing. Together with the anticipated construction of the Watford to Luton railway line (never built), this was leading to the production of 'millions of bricks'. 'Some months ago' estimated the *Beds Times*, there had been an estimated 200–300 empty houses in the poorest streets in the town – Burr Street, Duke Street, Gaitskell Terrace, Adelaide Terrace, High Town Road, New Town Street and the like – all were now full with returning workers. By August 1851 it was reported that the estimated 100 houses built in the preceding twelve months were all full. The output of the construction industry was encouraged to increase accordingly: two hundred houses were erected in the year to July 1853.[88]

With land plentiful, even during a serious slump in the hat trade during 1853–4, the building trade was to continue to boom throughout the decade: half a million bricks were reported for sale in March 1857.[89] It was not halted in its tracks until the following decade when a small slump in the plait trade in 1860–1 was followed, after a brief recovery, by a catastrophic depression in the hat industry as a whole which lasted from 1867 until the early 1870s. The revival was attributed to the reopening of the Paris fashion market after the ending of the Franco-Prussian War.[90] The building boom of the 1840s and 1850s fizzled out as the market became saturated with houses and land. In 1861 the census revealed that there were 54 uninhabited buildings out of a town total of 2778 or 1.93% of the total stock. By 1871 the proportion had risen to 7.23%, a total of 261 houses. The rate of population increase in the decade slowed down to 13% between 1861 and 1871 (compared with 83% and 44% in the previous two decades). It is even possible that the total population fell during the recession of the latter part of the decade.

Local evidence is scanty but the slow down of construction, sooner or later inevitable in the wake of such a prolonged recession in the staple trade, would inevitably have placed an enormous pressure upon many businesses. Those builders who were also landlords would have felt the squeeze on another front as rents eased down. W.H. Attwood went bankrupt at the beginning of the depression (but bounced back) and the Luton Savings Bank closed in October 1871. In the light of this depression, the decision by the Bute trustees to attempt a large scale sale of land in 1867, (just five years after the previous one), can be seen for the ill-judged adventure that it proved to be. It would be interesting to know to whom they turned for local advice. Richard Vyse (junior) had that intimate knowledge and declined to sell his plots of land in Castle Street. The attempt by his executors to do so in 1867 was a failure.

Clearly the distinctive structure of Luton's hat trade, the large number of 'makers up' in small domestic units, determined that there would be a concomitant relationship between the hat and building trades. The strength of the hat trade stimulated the building cycle and Lutonians fed the ranks of both. John Waller certainly had no hesitation in pleading the poor state of the hat business when negotiating with Collingdon over the price of land. The latter had refused his offer of £1000 for a leasehold plot and, in declining to make a better one, Waller suggested instead that Bute should consider the 'gloomy prospects' for the hat trade before naming a price.[91]

Whilst Bute's trustees and Vyse's executors had certainly overestimated the demand for housing in 1867, the reason for the large number of vacant homes by 1871 was probably due to people quitting the town, just as they had moved in when work was plentiful. The building trade seemed to operate a cycle of activity which echoed that in the hat industry, and it is inconceivable that Luton builders would continue to erect whole streets on the off chance that something might turn up. The 1869 Board of Health rate book, compiled as the recession deepened, recorded 160 empty or partly empty buildings, the occupants having 'absconded'.[92] Two years later there were to be 101 unoccupied buildings. A sizeable proportion of these empty places must have been completed before 1868 which, if correct, illustrates how dormant the building industry had become.

The property owners

In many respects property is synonymous with power, historically a source of political influence and a symbol of wealth and attainment. At the apex of pre-industrial social hierarchies it was usual for the leading landowners to exercise power in their localities through the dispensation of justice. Historic examples also exist whereby property has been used to either stifle or promote economic activity. Broadly speaking, the pattern of property ownership is indicative of the social and economic forces at work within a society.[93]

In the first instance it is clear that, from the late 1830s, Luton's balance of power began to shift. It ebbed away from its old market town elite, with a Marquess at its peak, and the process became formalised with the granting of a charter of incorporation in 1876. By the time of incorporation it did not even occur to anyone to invite the aristocracy to take on a figurehead's role within the new order. It would be an over simplification to claim glibly that a vacuum of power caused by the decomposition of one social order was filled by the richest of the ranks created by concomitant economic transformation. Relationships in small urban centres are far more subtle and fluid than that. It is fair to say, however, that Luton's economy and society fundamentally changed in the middle of the nineteenth century. Property ownership and the balance of power also altered as a consequence. Within its tiny core, Luton's pre-industrial society was broadly what would be found in any south Midlands market town. In 1785, for example, the town's listed trades and occupations contained the usual mixture of shopkeepers, maltsters, millers, provincial attorneys and just one hat manufacturer (Williamson and Son).[94] The Chase, Brown and Burr families all feature.

The 45 families listed in the 1811 rate book included the following: the Crawley's at Stockwood, two clerics, eight farmers, three lawyers, a surgeon, two millers, an innkeeper, five brewers and maltsters, two shopkeepers, a cooper, a painter and the steward of Luton Hoo.[95] Within this rate paying elite, only a small number owned more than one property. Those who did so in 1827 were the Marquess of Bute, the Wallers, Joseph Everitt, William Burr, William Adams and Thomas Kidman (maltsters), Benjamin Harrison, William Burge, Thomas Butlin and Henry Brown.[96] By 1860, this composition, the Browns apart, had disintegrated.

In considering the nature of the change that was undergone, it is worth recalling the method of land disposal and tenure which existed in Luton, a feature possessing striking uniformity well into the twentieth century.[97] In virtually all cases the freehold only was conveyed. A plot of land would be purchased (sometimes directly by a builder), an auction being the usual mechanism of transfer. Buildings erected by the speculator, usually a small scale operator, would then either be retained for rental or sold on to a third party. Evidence on this last occurrence is scanty, suggesting that a substantial proportion of the properties were retained by the developer. Leases were few and long-term leases unknown. Rarely were any conditions attached to a purchase and, after 1854, the Board of Health were able to apply minimum standards to the building construction.

Certain groups were the beneficiaries of this burst of activity in the property market. An indication of those who were able to take advantage in the early stages is provided by the 1841 census augmented by a contemporary local guide compiled by John Waller.[98] In New Town in 1842 there were 104 separate owners of property, including ten women. A large number of these (39 or 41%) do not appear in the nearest available poll book, suggesting that they had not previously held sufficient property to qualify for the franchise (the women of course not counting in any case).[99] Only seven of the owners (6.7%) were listed as non-Luton residents. Occupations can be attributed with reasonable certainty to half of the property owners in New Town. Of these 16 (30.76%) were connected with the construction industry; eleven (21.15%) in retail; seven (13.46%) were connected with the hat trade.[100] A comparison can be made with the proportions which these occupations held within the town's overall economy by looking at the nearest available trade directory, that from 1839.[101] Amongst the 492 individual tradesmen, 31.9% were retailers, 10.9% were connected with the straw hat trade and just 4.2% were involved with building and allied trades.[102] Those involved in building were advantageously placed, an advantage which they pressed home by forming a new phalanx of landlords out of all proportion to their numbers within the town. More than half of the 134 houses in New Town (55.97%) were owned by those associated with building, compared with 10.44% from those involved in retail, 9.7% in the hat trade and 6.71% being the nine properties owned by those associated with brewing. The remaining 23 properties (17.16%) were owned by individuals from a range of occupations and backgrounds.[103]

Luton, therefore, although distinctively a town built upon the straw hat trade, was one which offered ample opportunities to other groups through its dynamic property market. Within New Town Street and Prospect Place in 1842 there lived 451 people, 7.7% of Luton's population, in 97 households. Thirteen of these households owned their own as well as other properties. Chief amongst these was William Lewington, an unmarried timber merchant in his twenties, living alone and not a registered voter. Lewington owned seventeen cottages in the immediate area. It is apparent that even those of humble origin were able to find the necessary capital and to meet repayments. Although women do not constitute a large number of property owners in their own right, their contribution to household incomes was, as witnessed already, of vital significance. An example of this is provided by the family of James Clark. In 1841, Clark, a 40 year old plait dealer (born in Bedfordshire), owned two cottages in New Town. In one of these he lived with his wife Mary, eight children and a lodger, Emma Edwards, aged between ten and fifteen years of age. Mary was a straw plaiter whilst four of the children and Emma Edwards were hat sewers. It is possible that the younger children also plaited straw and having a family member who was a plait dealer was a cost saving bonus. Virtually all members of the household could, therefore, augment James' income.

John Parkins, a middle aged carpenter, owned six properties in New Town. His own household was much smaller than Clark's comprising just himself, his wife Frances and a teenage lodger, Ann Birden. Like many tenants, Ann Birden would probably leave her lodgings at the end of the busy season. Owner occupier Abraham Fountain was a carpenter in his early thirties living with his wife Mary, a sewer, and three year old daughter Kitty. Fountain was far from being the model of a prudent, sober artisan. He was frequently in trouble, on one occasion assaulting an inspector of the Hertfordshire Constabulary.[104] Ann Peach, listed as 'thirty' in the census, owned her own house and two others. Beside the rent derived from these, Ann's household income was considerably supplemented by the work of herself, her mother and her daughter as hat sewers.

Although these are striking examples, the bulk of the people in New Street rented their homes. Of the thirteen households who did own property, however, ten had more than one source of income. In all but two of these the hat trade constituted a significant source of earnings. An abundance of affordable land, a vigorous construction industry and the structure of the local hat trade were mutually supportive.

Bricklaying, blocking, carpentry, plumbing, plaiting, paper hanging, renting, retailing and sewing, all provided employment opportunities in Luton. For families such as Clark, Parkins, Fountain and Peach, diversity of income provided greater security in an environment where the seasonal, fluctuating nature of local trades encouraged less reliance upon one source of income in order to provide greater security.

An astonished *Beds Times* commented upon this frenetic activity. 'For some years past everyman who could scrape a few pounds together has built himself a house; success has encouraged him to further speculations, and cases have occurred of labourers and journeymen mechanics erecting whole streets'.[105] Whilst this was a slight exaggeration since no speculator was responsible for an entire street, it does indicate that a fundamental change was taking place within the fabric of Luton's society, as well as in its physical environment. In a letter to the General Board of Health in 1854, Luton's Board reminded it of the pattern of ownership in High Town. 'The majority of the owners of property in this particular area are comparatively poor . . .' it observed, referring to the difficulty in raising a rate to pave the district.[106]

Initial conclusions drawn from the early 1840s are reinforced by a later survey made when High Town and New Town were more fully developed. Fragmentary though Luton's records may be, a surviving rate book from 1869 provides further data for analysis of the town's burgeoning property owning sector.[107] The list of people owning individual properties to whom an occupation could be attributed with reasonable accuracy numbered 526 (out of 754). This roll is headed by Thomas Sworder with his array of tied houses, brewery yards and cottages.[108] The brewing interest distorts the picture since the bulk of its property was licensed premises: Sworder had 88 properties and the trustees of Frederick Burr still had 22. Aligned behind Sworder were a series of (mainly) men with a diversity of occupations, from which the same broad occupational groupings stand out, as they did in 1842. Again, these are the hat trade (149 individuals, 28% of the total number), retail (136 – 26%) and building (62 – 12%).[109]

The strong position of those from the construction industry who wished to become landlords has already been alluded to. The 62 builders owned 436 properties, 386 of these owned by individuals with four holdings or more. This is an indication of the extent to which builders were also establishing multiples of homes for rent. The names of Smith and Williams stand prominent in the list but they are by no means the only example of builder/rentier dynasties. The Attwoods were one family who endured bankruptcy, one member, (Arthur Bennett Attwood), being able to set up in business at twenty and retire at 48. He did so to pursue a public career, eventually becoming Mayor of Luton on two occasions.[110] The Smiths, Williamses and Attwoods were all Conservatives, which seems to have been a feature of Luton's bigger builders. Although the principal property owners from this occupational group are the larger scale builders, there are also carpenters, decorators and even bricklayers owning more than four properties in the town.

When the housing stock itself is considered, a fourth group emerges – farmers. Out of the 2502 individual properties in the town, thirteen farmers owned 220. The farmers, therefore, continued to hold a vested property interest in Luton and they were not merely a residue from Luton's semi-rural past. Like the builders, they too were in an ideal position to engage in property speculation and, with better access to capital than many, some clearly took advantage of this opportunity.[111] The Sibley family from East Hyde, of whom Henry was the most prominent in Luton's affairs, was the most active. From having virtually no presence in the town in 1839 (certainly no land), they had acquired 77 properties by 1869, usually cottages of the most miserable kind. Their property was mainly concentrated in the lower end of High Town and largely in housing erected before the application of minimum building standards by the local Board of Health. Perhaps deterred from further investment by the limited obligations set by the Board, the Sibleys' callous indifference to the suffering (sometimes fatally so) of their tenants mark them out as one of the most contemptible examples of landlord. Of similar ilk was Joseph Dancer, whose property was largely in the New Town district.

There were a number of notable omissions from the list of major property owners. Their role as vendors of land apart, the Wallers owned few buildings other than those in which they lived and worked. It has already been seen that Richard Vyse bought land but allowed it to remain undeveloped. The London firms had no real interest in the town other than the manufacture of hats, being neither qualified nor structured to diversify into anything else. The list of 1869 property owners with connections with the hat trade was headed by Thomas Lye, the bleacher and dyer, with just sixteen. The hat manufacturer who owned most was John Day with eleven. A.T. Webster, for example, owned nothing apart from his modest mansion along New Bedford Road. The 149 individuals from the hat trade, owning 436 individual properties, comprised mainly the small operators, including sewers.

No more than five individuals drawn from the professional classes operated as landlords. The tiny band of doctors, clergy and gentry were not prominent amongst controllers of property. Perhaps more surprisingly, neither too were the solicitors, estate agents and auctioneers. The latter group were, however, in a position to benefit substantially from the housing boom by the very nature of their work. Conveyancing (the bread and butter of provincial solicitors), land auctions, house sales, the occasional litigation or bankruptcy – all provided a steady income. This was not a guarantee of riches and at least one of the town's small complement of lawyers, William Hunt, became so financially embarrassed that he was obliged to quit his home and, temporarily at least, his practice.[112] Frederick Chase and Edwin Brickwood left their Luton practices at the height of the building boom.

A key role for the solicitor was oiling the machinery of property development through the arrangement and management of mortgages, a substantial proportion of which were provided by private individuals. Here was the solicitor's advantageous position: he could act as both arranger and provider of a mortgage. A surviving account book sheds some light upon the identity of those who provided the necessary finance for housing and purchase. It belongs to the Luton firm of Cooke and Son, whose founder Richard Cooke took over the business from Thomas Sworder when family obligations obliged the latter to take on the running of the family's brewing business.[113] This account book reveals that in addition to the Luton Equitable Building Society and the South Bedfordshire and North Hertfordshire Permanent Building Society (based in Hitchin), ten individuals appear as acting as mortgagees in the period between 1853 and 1857. Henry Gates (presumably the George Street grocer and ironmonger) made several loans of between £30 and £350. In 1854 Gates called in a mortgage of £200 made to John Steel (or Steed) for property in Langley Field. The reasons for Gates to do so are unknown and the available evidence does not make clear how frequently this occurred.[114]

Like Gates, Richard Cooke also made a number of loans. One of these was for £1000 to Samuel Lane, who wished to build four cottages near to his own home in Chobham Street. Other mortgagees included William Brown (whose death in 1856 necessitated the transfer of loans), Thomas Beeson, William Clarke (the builder), Charles Lawford (building society director), and Henry Coles Brown. Sworder was also able to secure loans from contacts in his home town of Hertford and acted on behalf of Robert Smith, who does not appear to have required loans for any of his activities.

The aristocracy, gentry, professions, large hat manufacturers and Quaker Browns remained immune to the lure of property speculation and ownership. One possible reason was that the risky returns were not worth the investment of time and money. A handful of cottages were hardly worth the bother, a substantial number simply too much trouble. It seems that few Luton proprietors employed agents or collectors to gather the rent. Most were too small scale (or too mean) to pay someone else for what they could well do themselves. A busy, more physically removed landlord drawn from the professional classes would have neither the time nor the inclination to trail around grimy streets listening to the well-rehearsed excuses for not having the rent or complaints about defective downpipes. They would have to pay someone else to do it – and the return really was not worth the trouble. It is even possible that Luton's social elite regarded the burst of energetic acquisition with a measure of faint disdain. Land auctions and the humble, sometimes squalid, houses which clustered around the town may have been viewed as an activity for grasping aspirants with limited income. Not only is it the attributed occupations for property owners which lends credence to this. The identity of those who were to form the nucleus of the 'clean' party, campaigning for building controls and effective sanitary reform, were drawn from the large hat manufacturers and members of the professions. These were men conspicuous for their absence of property owned for rent. As far as the more affluent sectors of Lutonian society were concerned, the closest which they were prepared to go into the local property market was through loans and mortgages. This offered profit with none of the risks, what H.J. Dyos described as the 'passive, safe as houses, five per cent way of taking part . . .'.[115] Some individuals would advertise loans (anonymously) through the local press. One, to give an example, offered separate mortgages of £800 and £300 respectively, it being stipulated that neither sum was to be divided.[116]

The building boom led to a rash of building societies being formed in the 1840s and 1850s. There was already one in existence when the Luton Benefit Society was formed in 1847.[117] By all accounts this achieved immediate popularity with great competition among local solicitors for the Society's posts of secretary and solicitor, as well as a considerable demand for shares.[118] Despite initial success the Luton Benefit Society hit unspecified trouble in the mid-1850s necessitating a reorganisation and new trustees. At this time it had 60 members.[119] The Luton Equitable Building Society was perhaps the oldest in the town. It was certainly in existence by 1849 when it let out £2040 on mortgages and received an income of £2239.13s.10d. Frederick Chase was its solicitor.[120]

The longest surviving building society in the town was the Luton Permanent Benefit Building Society, formed in 1851.[121] Samuel Toyer was the first president and William Hunt the first secretary. Also possessing a strong Luton component was the South Bedfordshire and North Hertfordshire Permanent Building Society. It included a number of the town's small tradesmen: Edmund Baisley, J.R. Brown, Alfred Barrett, John Keeling, Charles Lawford, Joseph Clarke, John Godwin and Charles Jones being amongst its directors.[122] There was also the Luton Improved Building Society (the secretary of which, J.W. Pressey, was accused of embezzlement in 1859), and the Luton Equitable Loan Association, which existed to make small loans (£190 in 1859–60).[123] In 1847, the London and County Bank opened a branch in Luton, transferring William Bigg from Witney, and swiftly promoting him to be manager.[124] Whilst it is widely acknowledged that banks were not usually prepared to advance mortgages, there is some indication that William Bigg was more willing to promote growth in the town in ways which went beyond merely helping to finance public undertakings.[125]

There was one further way in which philanthropic elements could become involved in land development. The Luton Freehold Land Society, formed in June 1849, was influenced by the example of the Birmingham Freehold Society. The driving force behind the local imitation was A.J. Tansley, a man who does not appear to have been involved in direct speculation himself. Also prominent within the Society was Tansley's fellow hat manufacturer and radical, William Willis, as well as James Waller. Promoters of the Birmingham Society, William Scholefield MP and James Taylor, were invited to Luton. Scholefield and Taylor addressed an audience of nearly 800 people at a meeting of the Bedfordshire and Huntingdonshire Freehold Land Society in December 1849. The finances of the Luton Freehold Land Society were based upon a weekly (unspecified) contribution 'within reach of everyman' in order to raise shares of £20 each. Within two months the Society had upwards of 50 members, and by the beginning of 1850 it was in a position to purchase some pasture land in the township for development. In accordance with the Society's rules, upon completion of purchase the field was then divided between the shareholders, apparently by ballot.[126] The extent to which conscientious control was exerted was seen in the subsequent building which took place. The sewering of the streets was ensured at a time when there was no guarantee of enforcement by a limp Board of Health.

Although detailed evidence is not abundant on this point, Tansley's vision behind the formation of the Freehold Land Society was essentially to provide ordinary working men with an opportunity to own their small piece of Luton, something which might otherwise be beyond them. In promoting this property owning democracy, equal emphasis was placed upon the enfranchisement which would come as a consequence of the value of each allotted parcel of freehold. Upon reflection it would, therefore, have been no small disappointment to Tansley that, in his earnest desire to promote this cause, he neglected to apply certain conditions upon membership. Consequently, many of the 50 successful allottees turned out to be men who were using the Society as a vehicle for speculative activity. These included at least one man from outside Luton, a 'Mr Bontems' of Hemel Hempstead. Upon acquisition these men, who included George Bailey and tradesmen such as Raban, Charles Hanwell and Joseph Gardner, promptly sold their holdings at a considerable profit.[127] Perhaps it was due to disillusionment on Tansley's part that little further was heard of the Luton Freehold Land Society.

In contrast with the arms length approach of the upper middle class, the shopkeepers cashed in to a great extent during Luton's burst of growth. Even with merely fragmentary intelligence concerning the price of land during this period, it is clear that it was within the means of retailers to secure property amounting to almost a quarter of Luton's built up area. Like the builders they were well placed, living and working within the heart of development areas and able to keep tabs on their investments and tenants, using knowledge to fill vacancies.

An element of disbelief remains with the evidence that a Park Street ironmonger (William Barrett) could possess a property empire second only to that of the leading brewer. It may be the case that he was related to the builder Thomas Barrett. William Barrett's holdings included a third of the buildings in Regent Street, laid out in 1861, a rare example of concentrated investment. Another such example is George Sole, whose houses included the 28 former almshouses on Tower Hill, as well as a scattering of cottages in High Town. Barrett and Sole were atypical, however. More common were men such as Frederick Davis. Davis' investment was periodic and piecemeal, with four properties in George Street West, one in Wellington Street, one on Market Hill (his own shop), three in Stuart Street and one in High Town Road.

More modest, and more typical of the new breed of landlord, were Samuel Oliver and Thomas Puddephat. Oliver, in addition to his drapery business in Park Street, owned two houses in Park Street West and two pairs of cottages in New Town Street. Puddephat owned four buildings in Alma Street, one of which was his own residence and bakery, with the other three homes rented out. He also had a single property in Stuart Street and a further two in Buxton Road. Many of their peers owned fewer than this. The pattern of ownership amongst shopkeepers indicates that they were mainly small-scale opportunist speculators, investing when something affordable came on to the market. Of other identifiable occupations there are some interesting comparisons to be made. Thomas Mabbot, listed as a labourer in 1869 and as unemployed in 1871, owned a row of four cottages in Chobham Street, one of which was his own. It is unlikely that he was not working through choice and someone of independent means would have been entered as such on the census return. The unemployed Mabbot owned one building less than surgeon Kit Tomson. There are examples of people whose occupations would not immediately mark them out as owner occupiers, let alone landlords. Ann Cawdell, a widowed nurse of 70 (in 1871) owned two dwellings in John Street (one her own) and another in Dumfries Street. Engine-driver William Hudson owned his own home in Lea Road as did three other railway workers. John Young, a stone sawyer, owned his cottage on Pepper Hill.

Just as the majority of Luton's citizens did not own property, there are plenty of examples of those men of apparent wealth who did not invest in property. One example is William Allen, a builder employing two men. Another is Charles Robinson, hat manufacturer, with a direct workforce of 23. Farmers such as Kidman at Biscot and Partridge of Leagrave, did not imitate Sibley. Colonel Lionel Ames did not extend his close involvement in many aspects of Luton's public life into the property market. The Bute estate deliberately diminished its town centre holdings until it retained just a handful of cottages in St. Anne's Lane. As demonstrated already, John Shaw Leigh's involvement in the property market was a defensive one. In 1865 he added to his buffer between the Hoo and the town by purchasing White Hill Piece from Samuel Lane.[128] J.S. Crawley was not active in any aspect of the Luton land market. Henry Coles Brown and Lydia Brown owned a handful of cottages between them but, on the whole, this notable business family refrained from direct property speculation. The churches and chapels restricted ownership to their sanctuaries, vicarages, manses and schoolrooms. The Tower Hill almshouses, acquired by George Sole, had been sold to him in 1862.[129]

Property ownership in Luton was not of the type which was able to support a rentier class. With fewer than 1% owning twenty or more buildings, it was rarely a source of substantial wealth. Just four people on the 1871 census are described as living on 'income from houses', three of these (all women) owning two or less in the town.[130] The fourth, Samuel Toyer, was a retired builder. Other property owners of independent means included Charles Burr, by then retired, two female Browns (probably both of the Quaker family) and Ann Higgins. This 71 year old widow was listed as an annuitant in the census but also owned pairs of houses in Victoria Street and Davis Field. Approximately 95% of Lutonian property owners had at least one other way of making a living; even for the Smith family property ownership was just one source of income. This demonstrates that property ownership served as a supplementary part of income.[131] Those whom it attracted were almost entirely the first generation of Luton's burgeoning entrepreneurial class, the self-employed of limited assets such as carpenters, small plait merchants, grocers and shoemakers. Alive to constant opportunity, all of these people worked and lived in a district where there was a plentiful supply of small plots of affordable freehold. In very general terms, a typical Luton landlord was likely to be a self-employed craftsman or trader, living in a modest terraced house (or shop), from which he practised his occupation. He would perhaps own the cottages adjacent to his own, plus a couple of others a short distance away.

In a population of 15,584 in 1871, Luton's males amounted to 7956.[132] The town's 750 property owners represented, therefore, 9.4% of the total. If those too young to own property are deducted from the calculation (there being no break down of age groups within the enumerator's summary), the figure could well stand at between 12–15%. At another level this figure looks at only half the picture, the male half. It is utterly inadequate when considering the character of nineteenth century Luton. George Bailey's evidence to the incorporation enquiry in 1875 (see chapter four) estimated that there were some 650 female ratepayers in the town, although how many of these were owners of property is not known. At a time when married women were not entitled to own property in their own right, a Luton property owner was invariably male, nominally the head of the household. As such, this does a disservice to the thousands of married women who made a decisive contribution to household incomes and whose earnings could match, even exceed, that of their husband's. In this respect it is possible to surmise that adults with a property owning interest in the town amounted to anything between 18–25%. Estimates on national property ownership are sparse but Luton's figures can be compared with the 'unsupported' 10% quoted by Avner Offer as being the case by 1914.[133]

The uniformity of housing throughout Luton, caused in part by the application of building controls during the 1850s, ensured an even spread of occupationally based landlords throughout the town. Only at the poles of housing quality represented by, for example, Spring Place and Cemetery Road, would there likely to be a greater proportion of carpenters and tailors at the former and their exclusion from the latter.[134] The demands of Luton's economic make up ensured that the demand for the more substantial properties, in places such as Cemetery Road or Cardiff Road, would be limited. Alma Street and Adelaide Street were more typical examples of Luton building. The town was not an administrative or commercial centre, so there was no need to accommodate an army of Pooters. Exporting hats rather than people to the capital, the streets close to the railway stations (situated closer to the town centre than at Hitchin, Harpenden, St. Albans or Hemel Hempstead) contained not the modest villas of metropolitan commuters, but workshops and factories. Luton has never presented its most favourable aspect from a railway carriage window. With no military, ecclesiastical or academic tradition there was not a demand for the substantial homes inhabited by an active or retired collection of officers, clerics, scholars or ex-colonials (such as at Bedford). Most important of all, because Luton did not possess more than twenty or so medium to large factories of any type, there was only a small managerial class.

At the time of incorporation, there was a striking residential mix between the various sectors of Luton's population. The influence of the Bute trustees had ensured the exclusion of the working classes from the eastern side of New Bedford Road, upon which a short line of moderately sized villas were built, but this was an exception. A number of similar houses were built on rising land between Farley Hill and London Road, but more humble cottages were close by. Crescent Road was laid out at the end of the 1850s from which the affluent occupants could gaze out of their elegant residences at the railway sidings which ran along the length of the avenue. Crescent Road spanned the bottom of Hart Hill, destined to become a middle class enclave by 1914, but which had seen only partial development by 1876.[135]

Many of Luton's senior figures involved in manufacturing and the professions still preferred to live within the heart of the town during the middle of the nineteenth century. William Bigg continued to reside in Castle Street until his death, not far from the homes of Thomas Sworder and Edmund Vyse. William Willis lived in King Street and C.A. Austin in Upper George Street. Still clinging (just) to the status of a small town, living within central Luton was tolerable whilst open countryside on the surrounding hills remained visible and accessible. The development of Luton's suburbia, with its irresistible pressure upon the Crawley estate, did not take place until the end of the nineteenth century. This all means that there was no desire for landlords or the more affluent to create exclusive suburbs of their own, as Pooley demonstrates occurred in Liverpool. Many of Luton's landlords shared the same requirements as their tenants: an abode that would serve as a production or business unit or a home that was within walking distance of work. The method of land disposal ensured that landlords with limited resources would continue to live close to their tenants. Differences in standards of living between individuals were more likely to be expressed in minor variations in architectural adornment (perhaps a token front garden), rather than exclusive social enclaves.[136]

The approach of individual speculators towards their property varied considerably. Some behaved as Thomas Puddephat did in the 1850s, repeatedly buying and selling land and buildings. Some would sell their houses in order to finance the purchase of more land for building elsewhere. A substantial number who purchased property, however, regarded it as a long-term investment rather than a short-term speculation: 28 out of the 53 surnames which feature on a list of property owners in New Town Street in 1842 were still there in 1869. Some people in New Town Street had steadily increased their stock, Joseph Dancer added twelve further houses to the two which he owned 27 years earlier. Others continued with exactly the same, Ann Peach remained in her cottage with two others rented out further down the street. Peach and Dancer typify the type of small cautious investor who comprised the bulk of Luton property owners.

The period 1830–50 saw the development of an economic base which was consolidated in the decades which followed. The growth of the hat industry was central to this but it was crucially underpinned by the availability of land. It is clear from the analysis of property ownership that hats were not the only way to earn money. On an individual basis, the hat and building trades provided many opportunities, but not for enormous fortunes, a fact partly reflected in Luton's modest housing. Frederick Davis, a successful example of a small businessman, left less than £2000 at the time of his death in 1874, and George Sole half that four years later. Of the class of larger businessmen, Charles Robinson and A. J. Tansley (who died in early middle age) possessed personal estates of under £5000 at death. The estate of E.O. Williams, the second generation of a successful business family, amounted to £4284 when he died in 1886. The examples of William Bigg (leaving £16,000) and Henry

Brown (just under £30,000) were rare exceptions. Far more typical were Frederick Brown, a Wesleyan and a hat manufacturer in Inkerman Street, who left £249.8s. when he died in 1890. William Dancer was a grocer who cut his throat in 1863, his suicide coming as a shock partly because he was regarded locally as a prudent and successful businessman. His estate amounted to under £300.[137] Many other small builders, hat merchants and manufacturers would have operated on the borders of insolvency. What Luton did unquestionably offer was the chance of a level of affluence which can best be described as 'comfortable'. It presented the opportunity of a standard of living which for so many migrants was beyond anything which they could have dreamed of elsewhere. All this frenetic enterprise, graft, ambition, profiteering, failure and success generated a network of streets, the ageing remnant of which serve as virtually the only evidence of the forces which transformed a town. No planning process played any part in the early growth of Luton – and it showed.

NOTES

1. Dony, J.G. *A History of the Straw Hat Industry* (Luton, 1942). Publication of Ph.D. thesis, *University of London*, 1941.
2. Cannadine, David. 'Urban Development in England and America in the Nineteenth Century: Some Comparisons and Contrasts', *Economic History Review*, 2nd series, vol. 33, no. 3, (1980). Hudson, Pat. 'From Manor to Mill: the West Riding in Transition', in Berg, M., Hudson, P. and Sonenscher, M., *Manufacture in Town and Country Before the Factory* (Cambridge, 1983).
3. Levine, David. *Reproducing Families. The Political Economy of English Population History* (Cambridge, 1987).
4. Dony, J.G. and Law, C.M. 'Luton and the Hat Industry'. *The East Midlands Geographer*, vol. 4, part 6, no. 30. Pinder, D.A. 'The Luton Hat Industry', Ph.D. thesis, *University of Southampton*, (1970).
5. *Children's Employment Commission (1862) 2nd Report of the Commissioners.* Evidence submitted by William Hunt, p. 207.
6. *Census of England and Wales for the Year 1861. Population Tables. Volume II, Ages, Civil Condition, Occupations and Birth-Places of the People.* (HMSO, 1863). P. P. Brit. Lib. The Luton and Hitchin returns are for the sub-district, Bedford's are for the Borough.
   For the purposes of this discussion those bracketed within 'building' or 'construction' include carpenters and joiners, as well as thirteen masons and one paper hanger.
7. The early work of oral historians recorded patterns of migration which might otherwise be difficult to trace. For example, after harvest many East Anglian farm workers went to work in the Bass brewery in Burton, see Ewart Evans, G. *Where Beards Wag All. The Relevance of the Oral Tradition* (1970). Many examples of seasonal or short term migration would have existed in Bedfordshire families. Millbrook farm workers, for example, migrated to Derbyshire in mid-century to work in the mines for a short period, most returning to their home county.

Plate 1

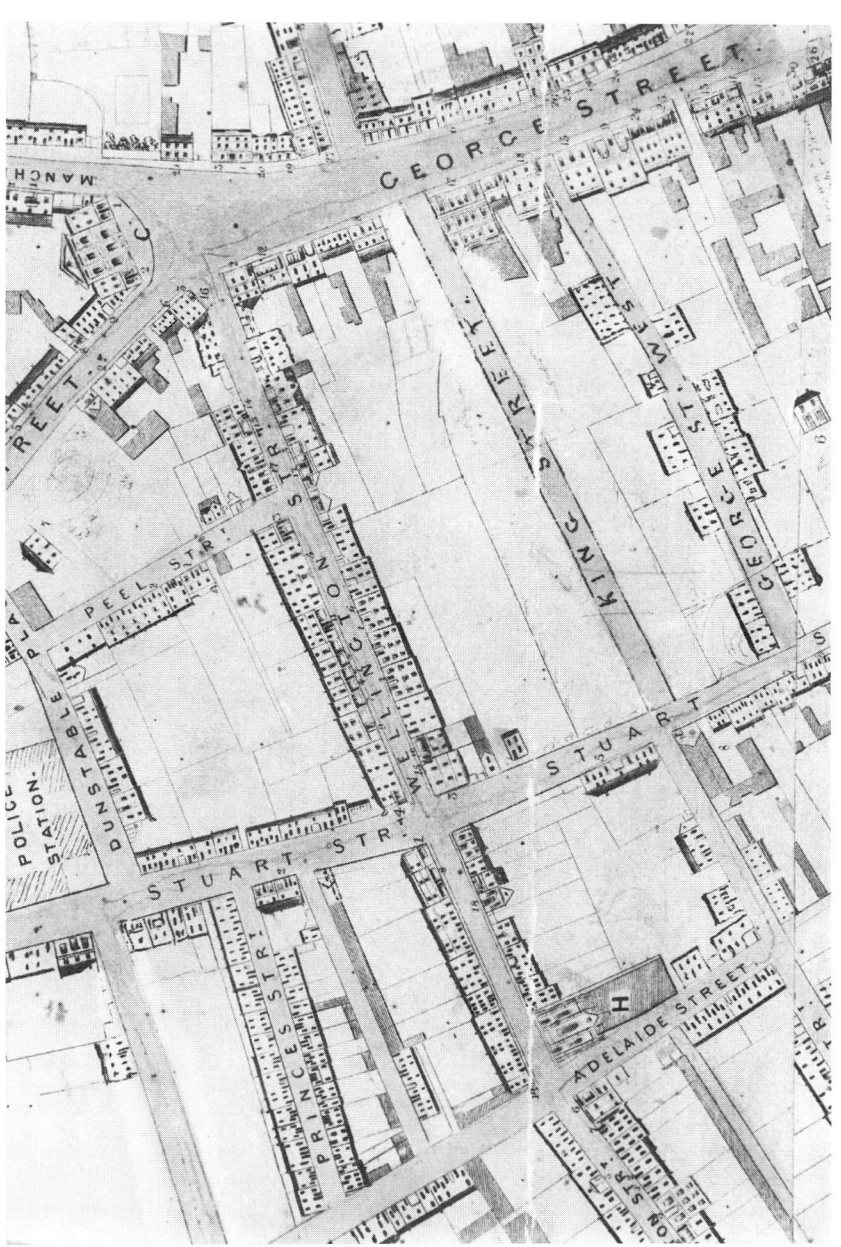

A section of Richard Todd's pictorial map of Luton, 1862 (BRO).

Plate 2

Victorian Luton, photographed from the air around the time of the Second World War, looking across New Town towards Stuart Street, and on the facing page a section of an earlier Ordnance Survey map covering the same area. The photograph centres upon the Ebenezer Baptist Church in Hastings Street. This photograph shows the scar in the urban landscape caused by the demolition of Spring Place and New Street, the large number of small workshops and a significant number of cottages with attic skylights (LM).

Plate 3

Plate 4

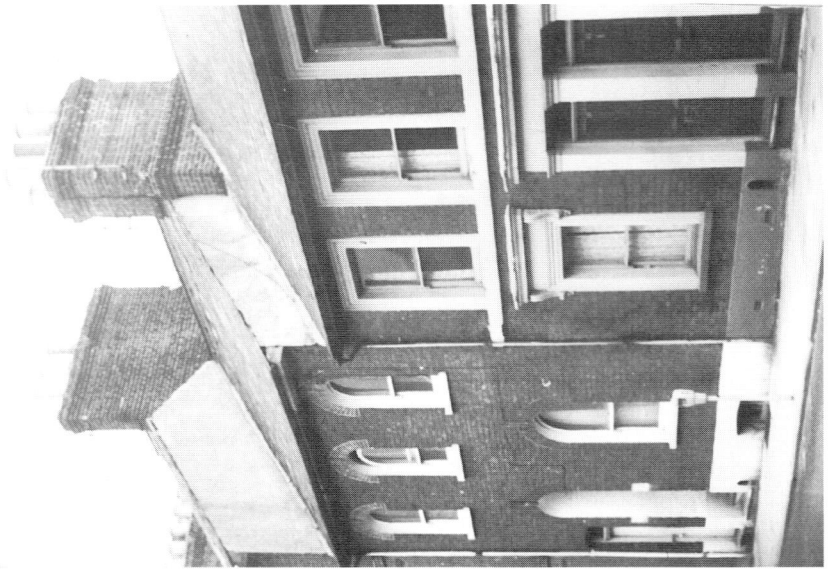

(b) Liverpool Road, photographed in the late 1960s (LM).

(a) Chase Street, built in the 1860s and photographed shortly before its demolition 100 years later (LM).

Plate 5

The amenities of 38, New Town Street are tried for size shortly before its demolition in 1956 (LM).

Plate 6

(a) Windsor Street, photographed in the late 1960s (LM).

(b) King Street c. 1870, before the development of its northern side (LM).

Plate 7

(a) Lea Road (Blackwater Lane), c. 1890 (LM).

(b) Tower Hill, c. 1870 (LM).

Plate 8

(a) Jones' Yard, photographed by Frederick Thurston, 1899 (LM).

(b) Market Hill and the old Market House photographed from Castle Street, probably by Samuel Debenham c. 1867 (LM).

Plate 9

(a) Market Hill c. 1866. Photographed probably by Samuel Debenham (LM).

(b) Market Hill and the newly completed Corn Exchange, c. 1869 (LM).

Plate 10

A view of George Street taken by J. Taylor of Bute Street, probably in the mid-1860s. This photograph was lent to Luton Museum by the daughter of William Sandoe (print in LM).

Plate 11

Cheapside, the location for many of the larger hat factories, photographed c. 1920, looking towards George Street. At their junction once stood iron gates marking the entrance to John Waller's gardens (LM).

Plate 12

Ceylon Baptist Church, Wellington Street, photographed by Henry Gregson, 1870s (LM).

8. Smith, L.D. 'Industrial Organisation in the Kidderminster Carpet Trade, 1780–1950'. *Textile History* 15 (1), pp. 75–100, (1984). Article based on Ph.D. thesis, University of Birmingham, 1982.
9. Dony, J.G. *op. cit.* p. 108. *Children's Employment Commission op. cit.* pp. 196–200. It was admitted that young children could earn '3s. a week or so . . . and many of course, earn from that down to nothing'.
10. *Children's Employment Commission op. cit.* Agar, N.E. *The Bedfordshire Farm Worker in the Nineteenth Century* (BHRS, vol. 60, 1981). Publication of Ph.D. thesis, University of East Anglia, 1979. Agar, N.E. *Hitchin's Straw Plait Industry*, (Hitchin, 1982).
11. The census enumerator rounded up the ages to the nearest five for all persons over the age of ten.
12. Agar, N.E. *The Bedfordshire Farm Worker . . . op. cit.* pp. 129–30.
13. Cirket, A.F. 'The 1830 Riots in Bedfordshire. Background and Events' in *Worthington George Smith and Other Studies* (BHRS, vol. 57, 1978) pp. 75–112.
14. A deputation to the Luton Board of Health in May 1868, comprising Kershaw, Welch and Willis, reckoned that the small workshops constituted 'probably one half of the town' (see chapter two). *Luton Times* 7.5.1868.
15. One Dunstable historian attributed the decline in the Dunstable trade to the loss of the stagecoach service with London in the 1820s. Derbyshire, W.H. *The History of Dunstable*, 2nd edition, (1882).
16. 'Apportionment of the Rent Charge in lieu of Tithes in the Parish of Dunstable, in the County of Bedford'. BRO, MAT 12/1. 'Map of the Parish of Dunstable in the County of Bedford'. Surveyed by John Darnham in 1822 and revised by Joseph Mead for the Commutation of Tithes in 1840, BRO, MAT 12/1.
17. Sale catalogue, BRO, DDBH 409. Derbyshire, W.H. *op. cit.* p. 100.
18. BRO uncat. 355/4–8.
19. 'Apportionment of the Rent Charge in lieu of Tithes in the Parish of Hitchin in the County of Hertford . . .' (1844). Terrier and map at Herts CRO.
20. Hine, Reginald L. *Hitchin Worthies* (1932). Hine, Reginald L. *The History of Hitchin* vol. II (1929).
21. 'Apportionment of the Rent Charge in lieu of Tithes in the Parish of St. Albans . . . in the County of Hertford', (1847). Maps and terriers of the Abbey and St. Peters (as well as St. Michael's) in Herts CRO.
22. Austin, William. *The History of Luton and its Hamlets* (Isle of Wight, 1928) vol. II, chapter 11, 'The Enclosure of the Open Fields'.
23. Church, Roy A. *Economic and Social Change in a Midland Town. Victorian Nottingham* 1815–1900 (1966).
24. *Leigh's New Picture of England and Wales* (c. 1820).
25. Davies, John. *Cardiff and the Marquess of Bute* (University of Wales, 1981).
26. Ibid. p. 17. See Luton Hoo papers at BRO (G/DDA) which contain much correspondence concerning Bute, and Collingdon in particular.
27. Ibid. p. 47 and p. 191.
28. Letter from Bute to Edward Priest Richards concerning the tactics to be used at the forthcoming Cardiff municipal elections in 1835. Quoted in Davies, p. 128.
29. Guardians of Luton Union Minute Book No. 1., BRO PULM 1.
30. BRO G/DDA 150/92, 7.8.1834.
31. BRO G/DDA 151/16.
32. Sale catalogue. 'Particulars at Luton Hoo . . . which will be sold by Messrs. Hoggart and Norton at the Auction Market . . .'. LM 238/81.
33. This 'capital freehold brick built residence' was occupied by the solicitor Edwin L. Brickwood. The benefits of being Lord of the Manor did not amount to much. At the time these accrued less than £30 per annum through rents and tolls of the market stalls.

34. 'Plan of the Township of Luton in the County of Bedford. 1839. Reduced from the Plan of Luton Parish by E. Brown, Silsoe, Beds'. Scale – 8 chains to one inch. BRO C 2264.
    The identity of E. Brown is not known. Thomas Brown was the land agent for Earl de Grey at Wrest Park, Silsoe at this time. The Brown map for Luton township (one for Limbury and Biscot also survives) provides a comprehensive list to the ownership of land in Luton parish, being accompanied by a terrier giving (alphabetically, in order to occupier), the occupier, owner, field name or type and size. Questions can be raised as to how up to date was the map: neither the gas works (built upon land owned by the Burrs) nor the workhouse are shown, although both were standing by this time. This, however, should not detract from the map's usefulness as the earliest detailed survey of the town.
35. *Luton Times* 21.10.1881: 'Sundon and its Memories – By a Lover of the Past'. The author said of Gutteridge '. . . he had many good qualities but he was a man of war . . .'.
36. *Hertfordshire County Chronicle* 28.9.1833.
37. Copy of letter from Collingdon to Stanton, 12.5.1834. BRO G/DDA 150/54.
38. *Report of the Luton Charities in the County of Bedford and the Proceedings of the Vestry in connection therewith*. 1853. LM 476/33. The investigating committee comprised William Willis, J.K. Blundell, Robert How, A.T. Webster, Alfred Tansley, John Brett, Frederick Clarke and James Muir. It investigated the conduct of the charities' management over a sixteen year period and its report was damning of the 'inefficient manner' in which the distribution fund had been managed (there had been no annual statement of accounts). Because of this, the committee concluded, 'Several Hundreds of Pounds have been lost to the Poor of this Parish'.
39. Austin, W. *op. cit.* p. 134.
40. 1841 Poll Book. BRO RV 903.
41. Information concerning the Crawley family can be found in Austin, W. *The History of a Bedfordshire Family* (1911).
42. Tithe Award List, 1844 and map of the Crawley estate (with register) made around the same time. Both in LM collection. The Crawley family owned approximately 3200 acres in Luton parish, an amount exceeded only by the Bute estate with its 4000 acres.
43. The builder John Williams purchased Blackwater Field on the eastern side of town in 1844 from the Gutteridge estate, although this was never built upon. BRO LHE 7 & 8.
44. *Who's Who in the Town of Luton in 1842? The Question Answered by John Waller.* LM 117/43. According to this source, of the land developed to date, three cottages and yards belonged to Samuel, John and David Lane, two belonged to Charles Squire and one garden (soon to be built upon) belonged to Richard Brown, owner of the Sun Public House in High Town.
    Elsewhere in the town, around 1841, Frederick Burr had laid out (or allowed to be laid out) a street in High Town which was to bear his surname. Judging from the field boundaries, it appears that Burr Street chopped off a portion of the adjacent field which belonged to Ashton's Charity. Townrow's development on the western side of Chapel Street instigated the building of what was to become New Town: New Street and Spring Place were the first streets erected. Although owning property in the Park Street area, as well as Stuart Street, Townrow owned none of the New Street and Spring Place cottages by the time of his death in 1861. A little further up Chapel Street, another new road – Windsor Street – was commenced between 1843 and 1845, upon land once owned by the Marquess of Bute. This land had been tenanted in 1839 by Thomas Waller, and it is possible that he was an interested party in the development.
    In the area bordered by Park Street and Castle Street the Chase family were active in releasing pasture land for house building. What were to become Langley Street

and New Town Street were being developed between 1841 and 1844. The Chase family and Bute were also allowing building to take place upon an isolated arc of land not connected with any existing street. This was dubbed 'Prospect Place' (on Brown's map the fields are referred to as 'Piece in Common'). The complexities of land ownership in this area suggests that a degree of collusion between the Bute and Chase estates allowed this development to take place.

45. The Marquess of Bute owned another field also by the name of Seven Acres. This lay between Dunstable Road and Leagrave Road. Collingdon's letters, although presumably the first draft of that which was subsequently sent, contain a great many alterations, suggesting a hurried man with much on his mind.
46. BRO G/DDA 151/11, 151/19, 151/20.
47. BRO G/DDA 151/53. 1842 was the date later given for the laying out of Bute Street. See PRO MH 13/120, letter book of General Board of Health re Luton, 1.5.1855.
48. BRO G/DDA 15/37. Chase to Collingdon, 14.7.1842: 'You are to blame for not letting Parkes know you had sold your land to Gray'. He described Tomson as an 'obstinate stupid fellow'.
49. BRO G/DDA 151/55.
50. BRO G/DDA 151/61, 151/68, 151/87.
51. Sale catalogue 22.10. 1845, LM collection. Frederick Chase acted upon behalf of the widowed Jane Waller. The sale catalogue provides details of Waller's estate situated in the heart of town. This included land formerly owned by Edmund Waller and by Cox.
52. BRO G/DDA 244 & 265. Letter from Thomas Hyde, surveyor, of Park Street. He reported that he had twenty men working in Seven Acres at that time.
   The laying out of Windsor Street was virtually completed by the late 1840s, and Elizabeth Street, Dumfries Street and Hastings Street were by now commenced. Peel Street, running off Wellington Street (by now a public thoroughfare stretching as far as Stuart Street) was also begun in this period. In the main, urbanisation was taking place on pieces of land released by the Burrs in two areas: in Park Street, around Queen Square, and in High Town where a further part of a field was sold off allowing a second road (Duke Street) to run parallel with Burr Street. The Chase family land close to Market Hill was covered with a link road between Park Square and Market Street, rather unimaginatively named Park Street West.
53. *Beds Times* 6.3.1847, 17.4.1847.
54. 'Valuation of Messuages, Lands and other Hereditaments Liable to Poor Rates . . . 1845'. Borough Treasurers' Dept., Luton Town Hall. Unfortunately no illustration of these buildings exist.
55. Sale catalogue, BRO LHE 33. Lots 1–5 were freehold building ground situated on part of the remainder of the Burr's Field between Hitchin Road and High Town Road. Lot 4 was not sold but those in Duke Street went under the hammer for £54 apiece, the section fronting onto High Town Road (just under thirteen poles) for £50, and a smaller piece (nine poles) fronting onto a new street (York Street) was sold to Henry Sibley for £28. Land at Park Road (in Hyde parish), and at Hart Hill was also sold, but a small strip of meadow adjoining the Old Bedford Road, a small garden opposite the workhouse, and Hagdell Common, close to the Farley Road, did not find buyers. The reserve price for the large piece abutting the Old Bedford Road ('Coney Hall Field', fourteen acres) and the remaining leasehold (379 years) upon two cottages in Castle Street, are also noted in the sale catalogue but it is not clear whether they found purchasers. Judging from development in the immediate future, it seems not.
56. BRO LHE 85. The land had been purchased from a number of different owners: Daniel Chase, the Gutteridges, Joseph Brown, Francis Coupees and the Marquess of Bute.
57. Copy of sale catalogue lent to Luton Museum by a member of the public. Lot 1 comprised three large fields on the road from Luton to Dunstable. Lot 3 was situated along the Luton to St. Albans road. The remainder were within the township,

lots 2 and 4 sandwiching land belonging to Bute. Here, Alma Street was already marked out as an 'intended road'. Lots 5–11 included a farm, outbuildings and fields, being bordered by Stuart Street, Upper George Street and Dunstable Place. All was in the occupation of George Gregory, who had farmed the land for a number of years. The newspaper report of this sale is none too helpful: there appears to be a discrepancy between the lot allocation between it and the sale catalogue. The identity of the purchasers are not given.

58. James Hopkins, a Park Street builder, felt that the asking price for building ground was far too high. BRO G/DDA 340.
Following the death of John Waller in 1859, his executors sold portions of his estate (the pleasure grounds behind his house) laying out John Street, Waller Street and Melson Street. The latter was named after one of his executors. The Bute Street end of John Street was later renamed Silver Street. This network of streets crossed Cheapside, once terminating at the gates of John Waller's garden, but now connected to Guildford Street.
59. BRO G/DDA 488. 15.11.1859.
60. Sale catalogue, LM 10/93/28. Lot 3 comprised:
'... a very valuable freehold building ground having a frontage to Chapel Street of 84 feet by a depth of 366 feet or thereabouts, and an entrance from Hastings Street and Spring Place, and contains 1a 1r 4p (more or less). The valuable plot of Building Ground is well adapted for a New Street, and being so near the Centre of Town, offers an opportunity for Builders, Speculators and others that cannot occur again on account of the absorption of Building sites in the centre of Town.'
It is not clear why Townrow had allowed this area (to become Regent Street) to remain undeveloped. Perhaps he was holding out in order to achieve a better return at a later date. Other pockets of land which were not yet built upon still remained in Windsor Street and Hastings Street. Besides the undeveloped land, at the time of his death Townrow's New Town estate contained two large houses and a bakery in Stuart Street, and three moderately sized houses in Stuart Street (one occupied by Mrs Townrow). There were also fourteen grim dwellings in Lea Road and one large house in Church Street.
61. BRO G/DDA 340. *Luton Times* 17.3.1860 and 24.3.1860.
62. Sale catalogue, LM M/354.
63. The lots purchased on the western side of Park Road were just within Hyde parish and were bordered in part by the estate of John Shaw Leigh. Parts of this land had already been built upon and the streets that were to rise here were mainly for working class housing. The roads laid out were Bailey Street (the boundary lane), Wood Street, Kings Road, and Park Street West.
Lot 18 comprised a row of small cottages in Old Bedford Road, and lot 29 was a small garden in Hitchin Road. Lots 20–28, and lot 43 were fields and gardens situated at the junction of Church Street and Hitchin Road on the western side of the railway. This separated them from lot 44, the Upper Pondwicks Gardens. Lots 29–42 were a series of gardens bordered by the River Lea, Henry Coles Brown's field to the rear of the vicarage, Ashton's Charity land and the Pondwicks Road: this was built to provide a right of way alongside and then over the railway to the tenants' gardens on the other side.
The land in the region of Hitchin Road, Church Street, St. Anne's Hill and the Pondwicks Gardens were sold. Apart from a few cottages on the corner of Church Street and Hitchin Road, however, these lands were to see no building development whatever in the short term, and only one (Henry Street) in the distant future.
Lots 20 and 21, plus lot 43, were described as being within part of the hamlet of Limbury-cum-Biscot. The tenants of the properties in this area had been given notice until Michaelmas 1862 to quit. A number of the tenants attempted to buy their plots – the surviving catalogue showing that John Keeling, a tenant of lot 39 (a garden),

purchased his twenty poles for £37. How many were able to do so in the face of lively bidding is another matter.
64. *Luton Times* 28.3.1862.
65. Sale catalogue, LM M356. Wenlock Street, Mill Street, Boyle Street (not named by 1870), North Street and Dudley Street were created. A house had already been built at the corner of North Street and was up for auction. Given the proximity of this street and Dudley Street to the railway line, it was not surprising that they were to see a mixture of small industrial units and domestic premises.
66. *Luton Times* 22.6.1867. The land at the corner of Old Bedford Road and Mill Street was described in the sale catalogue as 'unquestionably the most suitable spot for the Erection of a Railway Hotel or Tavern'. The purchaser (Gray) took the hint and the Royal Hotel was built upon the spot. Lot 32, on the opposite corner, however, carried the condition that the 'Purchaser of this Lot will have to bind himself, and his heirs and assigns for a period of 21 years, not to erect any Inn, Ale House, or Public house on the same, or to carry on the Trade of Beerseller, Innholder or Victualler'. This applied to a number of lots. Lot 32's nine poles were purchased by the builder, Smart, for £70.
A private carriage road (now Villa Road) linked Old and New Bedford Road. Between this and the River Lea, purchasers were obliged not to erect any house of an annual rateable value of less than £35. This stipulation also applied to a plot on the corner of Cardiff Road, part of a meadow formerly used as a 'Working Men's Recreation Ground'. The division and development on this field may have prompted the compensatory acquisition of People's Park. On the other side of the future Villa Road the three plots of land were not permitted to support houses of an annual rateable value of less than £25. Two of these plots had already been purchased by J. C. Conder and the Smart brothers, although it is not clear if further purchasers were found for the Villa Road area at the 1867 sale. Two of the four plots in the Dunstable Road/Cardiff road junction were sold to Cooke, the solicitor, for a total of £780.
The impact of the arrival of the railway upon High Town has been covered elsewhere (see J. G. Dony et al, *The Story of High Town*, Bedfordshire, 1984 pp. 13–15). Its route followed a similar one to that of the Great Northern, but slightly to the east. Apart from High Town, the lands that were affected were mostly those owned by the Bute estate and the charities. A helpful side effect for builders, caused by the extensive demolition of property in High Town, was the availability of a considerable amount of second-hand building materials and fittings.
67. Sale catalogue, M/340. The accompanying sale catalogue provides an insight into the Vyse's activity in the property market. Since 1840 they had purchased land from Frederick Chase and Henry Brown – acquisitions from the latter including Vyse's home, Holly Lodge. The land purchased from Chase lay between Union Street and New Town Street, through this Holly Street was now laid (but not built on, except at the corners). The land was divided into a series of plots with frontages to Holly Street of approximately 18 feet.
68. *Luton News* 7.6.1862 and 27.4.1861. John Everitt had purchased the building ground and was offering terms to potential speculators. Purchases could be spread over five years and loans were available. Building continued over John Waller's former gardens although patches with trees still lingered on. Behind the Town Hall Inkerman Street, Liverpool Road and Collingdon Street were virtually completed. Liverpool Road was advertised as 'admirably situated for the erection of private Residences, being high and dry, and commanding a pleasant view of the surrounding country', (*Luton News* 16.8.1862). This commanding vista, becoming rapidly hemmed in by the developing Inkerman and Collingdon streets either side of it, included the workhouse, a gas works and two railway lines. This area was swiftly developed, leaving just one street (to become Gordon Street), still to be built upon

by the time of incorporation. It contained a mixture of housing for artisans and the lower middle classes, plus some small hat factories.

At Prospect Place, after some years of stagnation, there was a burst of building activity with New Town Street and Albert Road being connected across a field sold by Ashton's Charity. The Bute family appear to have sold off no more of their dwindling stock at this moment. The laying out of Wenlock Street and Havelock Road were completed and initial preparation had taken place for further streets in the High Town district by 1876.

69. BRO BOR L/EH 19/1–9.

The 1930s clearance programmes contain the best details of housing in Luton erected before the establishment of a local Board of Health. These records contain details of inspections of individual properties, notes on defects, recommendations for action to be taken, relevant correspondence, overall plans of the area and descriptions of room size (often area rather than dimension) with some notes on building materials. They do not, however, contain plans of individual properties nor, sadly, were photographs taken (at least that have survived). Aerial photography was undertaken just a little too late to provide details in most instances, their former location being represented on photographs by blank scars across New Town and High Town.

70. The slum clearance programmes, together with a population increase of 18,000 between 1931 and 1945, necessitated an urgent house building programme. This, and other aspects of the town's housing programme, was identified in two reports: Grundy, F. (Medical Officer of Health) and Titmus, R. (Statistical Adviser to the Council) *Report on Luton* (Luton, 1945).

Tomlinson, Charles G. (Senior Administrative Officer, Public Health Dept., Borough of Luton *Families in Trouble. An Enquiry into Problem Families in Luton* (Luton, c. 1950).

71. Cox, Alan. *Survey of Bedfordshire. Brickmaking. A History and Gazetteer* (Bedfordshire County Council and Royal Commission on Historic Monuments, 1979) pp. 87–9.

The 1839 trade directory lists a number of 'Brick and Tile Makers and Lime Burners'. These were Henry Brown 'near Market Place', William Clarke at 'Cold Arbour', John Gray in New Bedford Road, James Gutteridge at Darley Hall and Frederick Pigott in Caddington. The exact nature of these businesses is not clear, nor is it certain that the addresses given are the location of the site or the address of the owner/operator for business communication.

72. BRO G/DDA 150/104, 10.9.1834.
73. BRO G/DDA 150/106. Tomson to Collingdon, 12.9. 1834.
74. BRO X448/2. Lease dated 31.1.1835.
75. BRO G/DDA 150/103. 10.9.1834.
76. *Beds Times* 10.10.1846.
77. *Luton Times* 5.11.1853, 12.11.1853 and 19.11.1853.
78. *Beds Times* 23.9.1848. Letter from 'Edward', writing to 'Tom . . . across the sea'.
79. Borough of Luton Clearance Areas numbers 2,3,4,9,13 and 14, BRO BOR L/EH 19/1–9. These provide some evidence as to the standard of speculative building in the 1830s through to the 1850s:

6, Spring Place

The houses in Spring Place and New Street offer examples of what came closest to a typical style of construction before 1850. 6, Spring Place was built at some point between 1842 and 1853, being constructed of brick and topped with a slate roof (see appendix 3a). It contained two rooms on the ground floor, the front measuring 10' × 11'10". The height of the front room was 7'5" with the rear room 3" higher. The house was inspected in June 1936 prior to a wholesale demolition of the area in which the report noted that there was a housing density of 42.1 per acre. The inspection report does not make clear the precise location of the staircase but in all

probability this was between the two ground floors since the front room would have been entered directly from the street. The staircase (which contained a coal place underneath) rose 8' in a going of 7'6". This was considered 'dangerous' by the inspector.
The stairs led to two rooms upstairs, both 7'3" in height and both with equal dimensions to the corresponding rooms downstairs. Fronting onto the street, the house had a yard at the rear which was twenty yards wide and was shared with 8–10, Spring Place. Within the yard was a wash house and water-closet, although these were almost certainly provided at a date after construction. There was no damp course and facilities were restricted to a fireplace in three of the rooms.
Natural lighting in the ground floor back room was obstructed by the gable of 4, Spring Place. The report concluded that 'the unsatisfactory condition of these premises is due generally to the manner in which they were constructed originally'. At the time the owner was County Alderman S. H. Godfrey, of Marlborough Road, Luton.

93, New Town Street
Inspected in 1935 (see appendix 3b), this house was also a two up, two down. Linking the floors were stairs rising 7'9" in a going of 4'7".

8, Back Street
This was a surviving remnant of a High Town street which was largely demolished to make way for the Midland Railway line (see appendix 3c). Unlike many other properties, at the time of inspection Back Street's rear ground floor rooms was referred to as 'sculleries' and may have been built as such. 8, Back Street contained a larger ground floor than the New Town properties (145 square feet), but this was at the expense of the scullery which was just over 67 square feet. Both rooms were just 6'10" high, with the bedrooms above being 7' in height. Three feet beyond the back of the house was a hopper WC which was shared with no. 6. Although an early form of water closet, the hopper was not early enough to have been installed when the cottage was originally constructed.

Bryden's Passage
Built probably between 1845 and 1850, Bryden's passage provided a striking example of concentrated development upon a limited space, in this case a narrow strip of land. Access to the six cottages was gained via a passage running between 105 and 107, New Town Street (see appendix 3d). The land had been conveyed to Peter Bryden (or Briden) some time before 1842. He then built the two New Town Street houses, choosing to live in one himself. The properties in Bryden's Passage were built of brick and were boarded at the rear and side (presumably a cladding). There was no damp course on any of the properties, three of which comprised two rooms (one up, one down): the others had two bedrooms. At the time of inspection the passage had one stand pipe between the cottages. In 1850 there was just the one shared privy, although this would have been one more than in some courtyards. When inspected in May 1934, Bryden's Passage still had no gas, electricity or sink waste drainage. See also Cresy, Edward Report to the General Board of Health on a Preliminary Enquiry into the Sewerage, Drainage and Supply of Water, and the Sanitary Condition of the Inhabitants of the Town of Luton (HMSO, 1850) p. 11.

Taylor's Yard
Built at around the same time as Bryden's Passage, this contained five cottages (three of them with one bedroom) lying between New Town Street and a parallel alley, Manor Path (see appendix 3e). Some were built back-to-back with the neighbouring sculleries in New Town Street and, whilst two hopper closets were located in the yard, these again were not contemporary with original construction. The common yard was used as a thoroughfare between New Town Street and Manor Path and, as elsewhere, there was no damp course in any of the buildings. 1–2, Taylor's Yard

were single storey cottages and no. 3 had a corrugated roof by the time of inspection. No. 4 was built of brick and part cement rendered but no. 5 had been constructed out of 'wood and composite material'. Its external walls were wooden.

Bailey Hill Cottages
There were few houses in Luton poorer than these. Built in the 1840s, they comprised twelve cottages built back-to-back, reached via a narrow passage from Chase Street (see appendix 3f). These cottages contained no amenities whatsoever (some do not appear to even have fire places) and even by the time of inspection they had just one external tap fitted to the wall of no. 7. The owner at the time was the publican of the nearby *Mother Redcap*.

Other properties in New Town were built with rooms in the attic, and in Back Street there were rare examples of properties with both attics and cellars. 8, Gaitskell Terrace contained a wooden internal wall between the living room and scullery. The Sibley family still held property in High Town in the 1930s.

80. The local Board of Health conducted an exhibition of the working of the water closet at their offices in Stuart Street.
81. Over the years the Board passed a number of individual resolutions in order to strengthen its bye-laws. In 1860, for example, it voted (by a margin of six votes to three) that the party walls of all future buildings should be 9" thick (Board of Health minute book, vol. III, 17.4.1860). In 1868 it resolved to approve no plans which showed dumb wells (Board of Health minute book, vol. IV, 4.8.1868).
82. Daunton, M.J. *House and Home in the Victorian City. Working Class Housing 1850–1914* (1983)
83. Examples of the Influence which landowners could exert can be found in the following: Cannadine, David. *Lords and Landlords: The Aristocracy and the Towns 1774–1967* (Leicester, 1980); Johnson, J.H. and Pooley, C.G. *The Structure of Nineteenth Century Cities*, chapter two, 'Rent and Ground Rent. Housing and the Land Market in Nineteenth Century Britain', (1982); A good introductory guide is provided in Gaskell, Martin *National Statutes and the Local Community. Building Control, National Legislation and the Introduction of Local Bye-laws in Victorian England* (1983).
84. Cannadine, David and Reeder, David (eds.) *Exploring the Urban Past. Essays in Urban History by H.J. Dyos* (Cambridge, 1982).
85. *Beds Times* 4.4.1846.
86. An example of the intense activity which took place in this period occurred when there was a 'great competition' for just 'a small piece of building ground' that was put up for sale by the Chase family on the corner of Park Street West. It went to Samuel Oliver for £290. *Beds Times* 17.10.1846.
87. Daunton, M.J. *op. cit.* p. 157. *Beds Times* 20.11.1847.
88. *Beds Times* 12.6.1847, 29.9.1849, 16.8.1851, 30.7.1853.
89. Ibid. 1.4.1957.
90. *Luton Advertiser* 25.3.1871. Dony, J.G. *The History of the Straw Hat Industry op. cit.*
91. BRO, LHE 151/19 and 151/20.
92. Rate book now in possession of Luton Museum.
    One estimate was that up to 1000 young women and girls would leave Luton within a week at the end of the busy season. Evidence given by William Hunt to *Children's Employment Commission (1862) 2nd Report of the Commissioners* p. 207.
93. Offer, Avner. *Property and Politics 1870–1914* (Cambridge, 1981). Clark, Peter and Slack, Paul *English Towns in Transition 1500–1700* (Oxford, 1976). For a study of those at the top of the tree see Rubinstein, W.D. *Men of Property* (1981).
94. Herrington, John Franklin. *The Merchants Miscellany and Travellers Complete Compendium ...* (1785). Facsimile reprint, (1885).
95. The location of this original source is not known. Summarised in Austin, W. *The History of Luton and its Hamlets op. cit.* p. 110.

96. Luton Overseers First Rate, BRO DDP 85/11/4.
97. Evidence submitted by Charles Harrison (based upon information supplied by George Bailey, Town Clerk) to the *Select Committee on Town Holdings (1887) XIII*. University of London, Senate Library.
98. Census enumerator's return for New Town, 1841 (copy on microfilm in Luton Central Library, Reference Library). *Who's Who in the Town of Luton in 1842? The Question Answered by John Waller.* LM 117/43. This is a reasonably detailed list giving property owners and the names of some of the occupants.
99. 1841 poll book for Bedfordshire, Luton section. BRO RV 903.
100. These calculations were made grouping known occupations into broad categories. These comprise the following: *Building* Builder, timber merchant, carpenter, joiner, painter, decorator, bricklayer, plumber, plasterer, tiler; Retail Grocer, baker, confectioner, general dealer, bookseller, butcher, ironmonger, chemist, fishmonger, draper, corn merchant, tea dealer, milliner, shoe maker and tailor. The last three occupations would have included a sizeable number who worked from purely domestic premises, but it is not possible to differentiate between these and those who also operated with a retail outlet; *Brewing* Brewer, publican, cooper, beer house keeper, victualler, wine merchant, F. Burr's trustees; *Hat trade* Hat manufacturer, straw manufacturer, blocker, plait dealer, plait buyer, sewer, block maker, bleacher, hat presser; *Farmer* Farmer, retired farmers, farm bailiffs; farm stewards; Clarke's devisees; *Independent* Independent, landowner, gentleman, annuitant, pensioner, Charles Burr. *Public Institutions* Postmaster, police superintendent, Board of Guardians, assistant overseer, Town Hall Company. *Church* Mostly church buildings and clergymen's homes. *Craftsmen* Coach builder, rope maker, blacksmith, harness maker, saddler, stonemason, wheelwright. *Professional* Solicitor, estate agent, auctioneer, surveyor. These were the professionals who had a close involvement in the land market during the early stages of the property boom. *Other* This category includes labourer (many of whom would have worked within the building trade), miller, poulterer, surgeon (who overall showed a marked disinclination to become involved in the property market), engine stoker, hotelier, market gardener, coal merchant, railway car man, gardener, warehouseman. The tallies do not include the following: Thomas Hawkes, bricklayer and baker; William Hawkes, publican and wheelwright; Richard How, publican and baker.
101. *Slater's Directory of Bedfordshire, 1839* (Luton section). The figure of 492 is by no means a comprehensive list of the town's businesses, being less likely to include the small workshops at the expense of 'high street' operators. The occupational summaries in the enumerator's summaries are too general ('Buyers and Sellers', 'Textiles', 'Mechanic Products', etc.) to provide precise comparisons. *Slater's Directory* must be also qualified by the listing of businesses in more than one category.
102. This figure does not include milliners or tailors, both occupations which could be undertaken from domestic premises. It does include small manufacturers such as clock makers, who would in all probability have an additional retail unit.
103. The properties of Thomas Hawkes, William Hawkes, Richard How (for reasons stated above), plus those to whom a trade could not be attributed, have been omitted from the total.
104. *Beds Times* 7.2.1846.
105. Ibid. 4.4.1846.
106. PRO MH 13/120. 1.12.1854.
107. 'General District Rate Book of the Local Board of Health for the District of Luton ... prepared by George Bailey, Law Clerk to the Local Board of Health for the Luton District. Made 16th February 1869' (LM collection).
108. 'Property' is defined here as a dwelling, public house, commercial building, vacant premises, public building, building ground, garden and any vacant land in the urban area of less than one acre.

Frequently the nature of property is not specified and one unit of property can be classified as two or more individual items (i.e. house, workshop and stables). This thereby exaggerates the amount which some owned. J.S. Crawley, with just a few lodges and a cottage on the western perimeter of the township, has not been included.
109. A fair margin of error when attributing occupations to individuals must be allowed for here. Occupations are not given in the rate book and these have been established by drawing upon entries from the lists in the Luton section of *Kelly's Directory for Bedfordshire, 1869*, and the township returns in the 1871 census. The two year gap may compound further errors made by the compilers of the rate book, the directory (itself not a comprehensive guide), the directory's printers, the census enumerator, and not least of all, the present author. Vagaries of handwriting and spelling, of which there are all too many examples, have not helped.

The duplication of names also reduces the likelihood of establishing precisely who owned what. There are four, or five, men called 'Samuel Lane': these include one who is a butcher or builder, two carpenters and two lived just a few doors from one another in Cumberland Street! Occupations may have changed between 1869 or 1871, or simply be described differently. George Hodge, for example, who owned eleven houses in Liverpool Road, is listed as a builder in 1869 and a brick layer in 1871. In these two years a number would have died or moved away (especially during the period of recession) and it is very possible to confuse a property owner living outside Luton with someone else with the same name who lives within it. It is not possible to precisely assess the number of speculators and landlords who came from beyond Luton parish.

Where there is a multiplicity of occupational categories which can be placed against a single name, these have been placed in the occupational groups cited in n.100. Unless there is a virtual certainty, labourers and hawkers have been discounted as owners of property. The presence of some labouring men in this category shows this to be something of a presumption but, overall, probably does not grossly underestimate their numbers.
110. *Tuesday Pictorial* 28.1.1936.
111. In allocating the total number of properties held by those from within the farming interest, there remains the problem of William Clarke. There were at least two, and possibly more. Those connected with agriculture were in an advantageous position to gain access to capital and credit. See Daunton, M.J. *Progress and Poverty. An Economic and Social History of Britain 1700–1850* (Oxford, 1995).
112. BRO G/DDA 214, 234, 235, 238, 241, 248, 253 and 254. Judging from the directories Hunt appears to have resumed practice by 1862.
113. Account book of Cooke and Sons, solicitors, George Street West, Luton. The first entry dates form 1854 when the business was operated by Sworder. The format of the entry is altered in 1857, when the practice was taken over by Richard Cooke, and it becomes more difficult to glean worthwhile information.
114. In this particular it was for a Mr Waring 'to complete the business'. This was a reference to Richard Waring, solicitor, who was possibly part of Sworder's practice in Park Street West. F.C. Scargill apparently foreclosed on a number of occasions.
115. Cannadine, David and Reeder, David *op. cit.* chapter 10, 'The Speculative Builders and Developers of Victorian London'.
116. *Luton Times* 25.5.1855.
117. *Beds Times* 30.1.1847.
118. Ibid. 20.2.1847 and 5.6.1847.
119. *Luton Times* 20.9.1856.
120. *Beds Times* 3.3.1849.
121. Ibid. 16.8.1851. The Luton Permanent Building Society was eventually absorbed by the Town and Country Building Society. Generous help was offered by T.H. Pashley,

formerly of the Luton Permanent, but efforts to trace the whereabouts of the minute books through the Town and Country Building Society proved fruitless.
122. *Luton Times* 28.2.1857.
123. Ibid. 30.10.1859 and 1.9.1860.
124. *Beds Times* 27.2.1847.
125. *Luton Times* 8.3.1878. Obituary of William Bigg.
126. Sadly no records of this Society have survived. All evidence, therefore, comes from local newspapers. *Beds Times* 9.6.1849, 18.8.1849, 15.12.1849 and 21.1.1850.
127. Ibid. 9.11.1850, 13.11.1850.
128. BRO LHE 185, November 1865.
129. Sole purchased this 'very eligible property' for £365. *Luton News* 29.3.1862.
130. Martha Mortimore owned two, and Elizabeth Butt and Ann Bellshaw one apiece. These alone would not have provided them with a living but their other sources of income are unknown.
131. This percentage may be reduced slightly by the fact that there could be a number of persons, unidentified, who would be outside investors and, therefore, have had no attributed occupation.
132. Figures taken from *Census of England and Wales, 1871, Population Abstracts. Ages, Civil Condition, Occupation and Birth Places of the People*. (HMSO, 1873). Thanks to Valerie Walsh of Bedfordshire Central Library for obtaining these statistics.
133. Offer, Avner *op. cit.* pp. 119–25. In 1945 Luton Borough Council estimated that 20% of Luton's householders owned their own home.
134. Attributed property owners in Spring Place (32 houses, average rateable value of £6) in 1869 included two builders, a beer retailer, a coal merchant, ironmonger, housewife, medical practitioner, publican and baker, plait warehouseman and bricklayer. In nearby Adelaide Street, built during the 1850s and 1860s (37 properties, average rateable value £11) the houses were owned by, amongst others, two hat manufacturers, two plait dyers, two bakers, a builder, a carriage builder, a grocer and a retired medical practitioner. Alma Street (63 properties, average rateable value of nearly £12) contained a similar mix of landlords: ironmongers, a grocer, a tailor, two hat manufacturers, a blocker, a plumber, estate agent, widow, decorator, rope maker and warehouseman.
135. *Luton Times* 26.11.1859.
136. Johnson, J.H. and Pooley, C.G. *op. cit.* Daunton, M.J. 'Public Place and Private Space. The Victorian City and the Working Class Household' in Fraser, D. and Sutcliffe, A. (eds.) *The Pursuit of Urban History* (1983).
137. Probate returns from Somerset House.

Appendix 1. Land ownership in Luton, 1839.

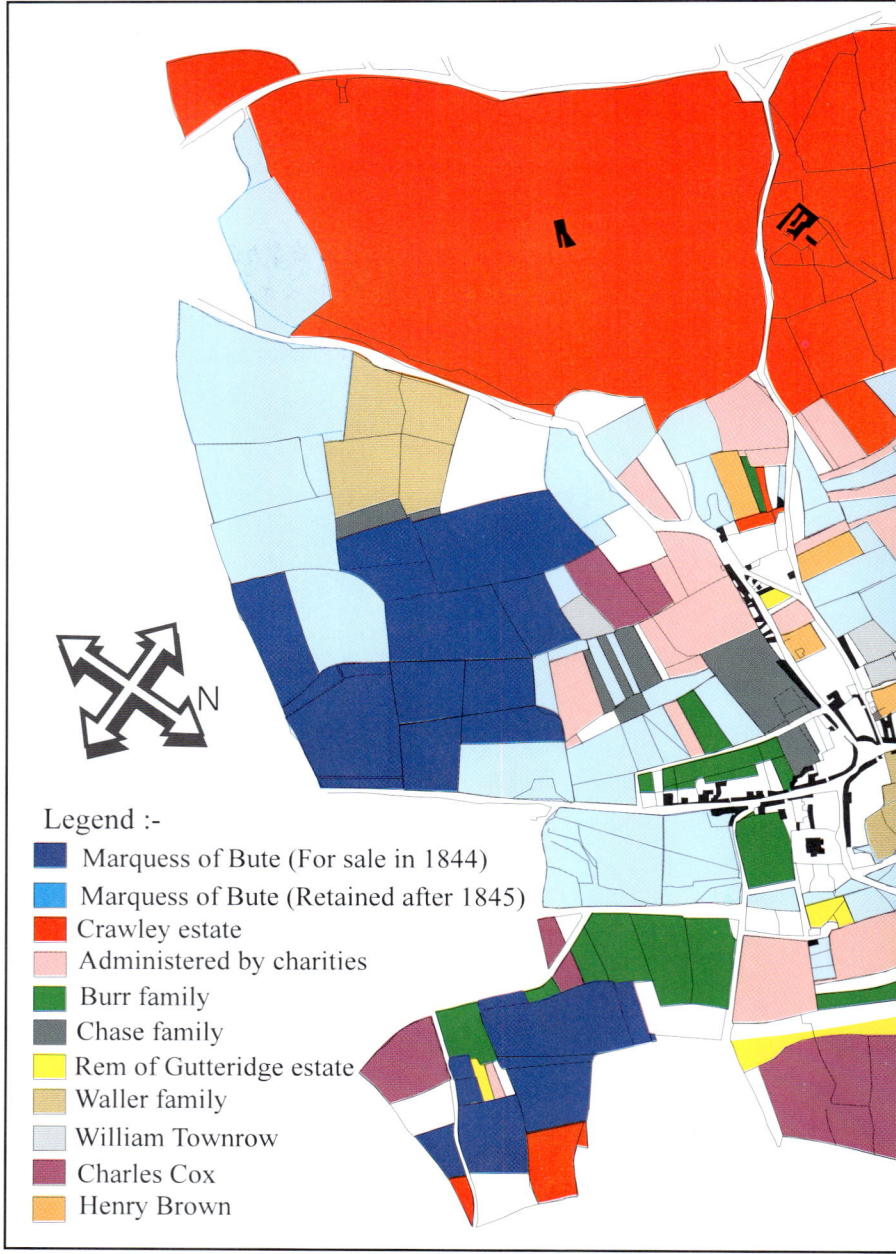

Appendix 1. *continued*

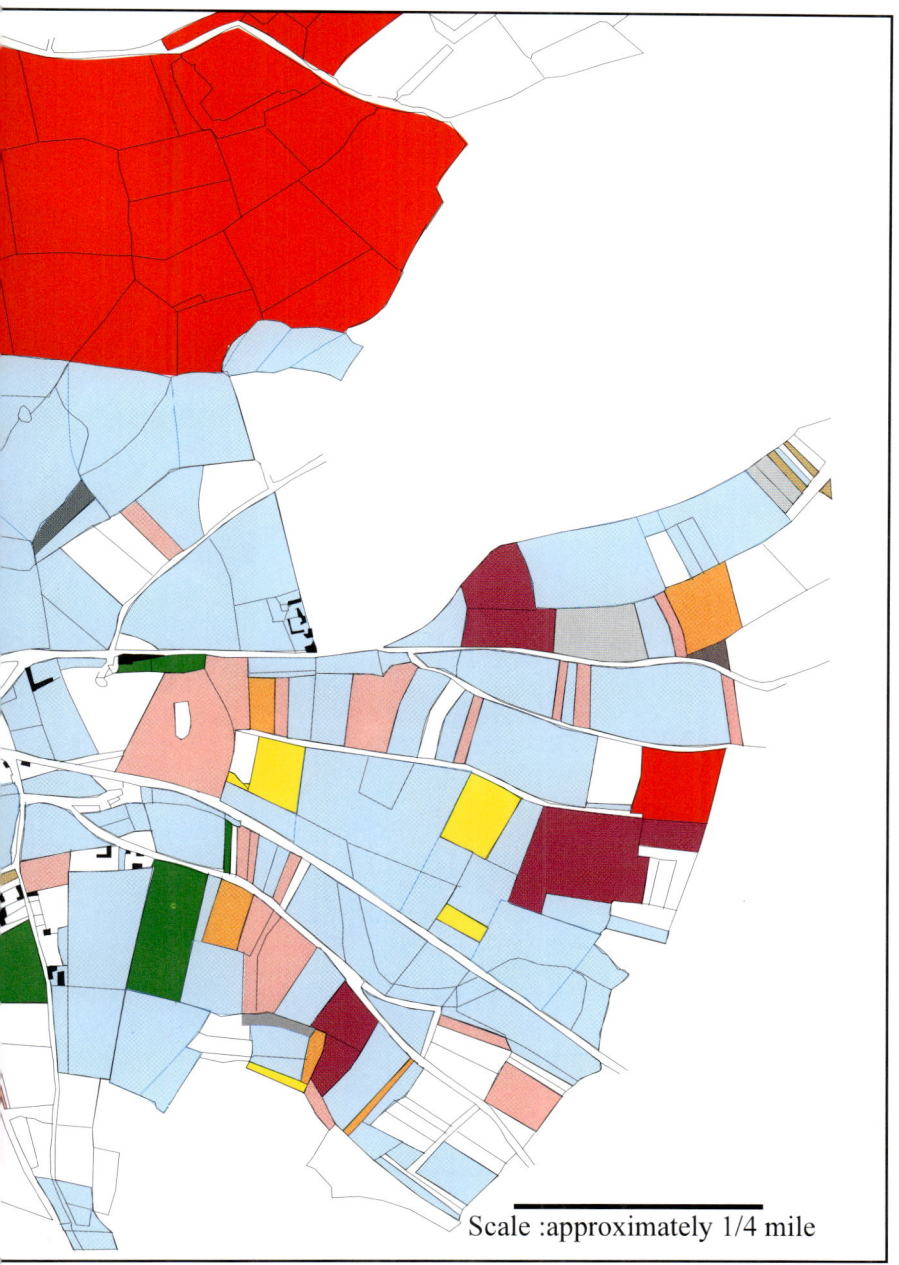

Scale :approximately 1/4 mile

76 STRAWOPOLIS

Appendix 2. The growth of Luton, 1840–76.

Scale: approximately 1/4 mile

78 STRAWOPOLIS

Appendix 3. A selection of examples of housing erected before the application of bye-laws.

(a) New Street and Spring Place. Surveyed in June 1936, prior to demolition (BRO).

(b) New Town Street and Albert Terrace. Surveyed in January 1936, prior to demolition (BRO).

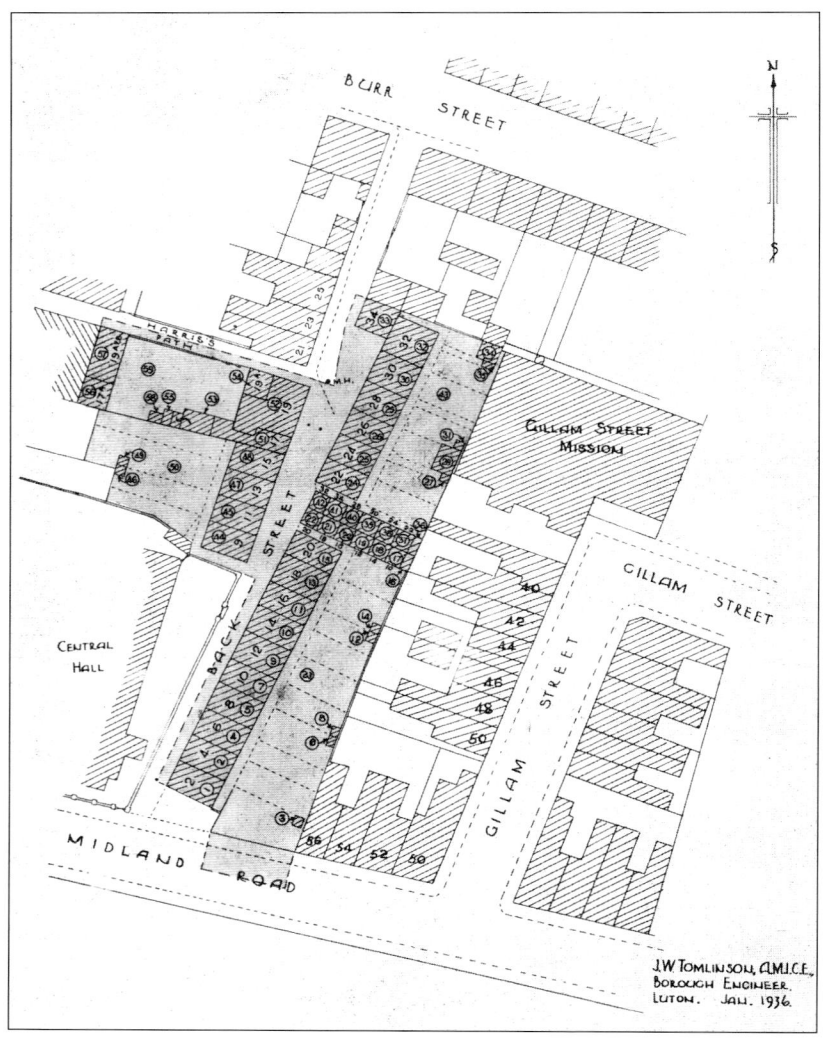

(c) Back Street, High Town, from a survey made in January 1936 prior to demolition (BRO).

HATS, LAND AND HOUSES 81

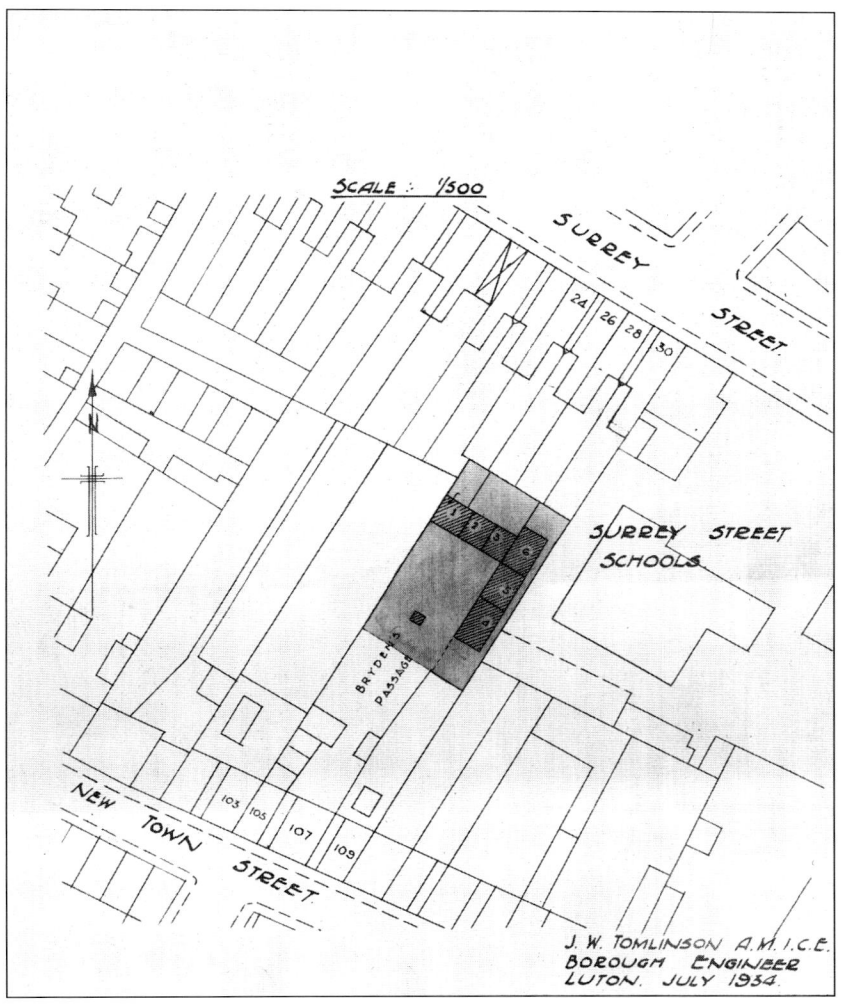

(d) Bryden's Passage. Surveyed in July 1934, prior to demolition (BRO).

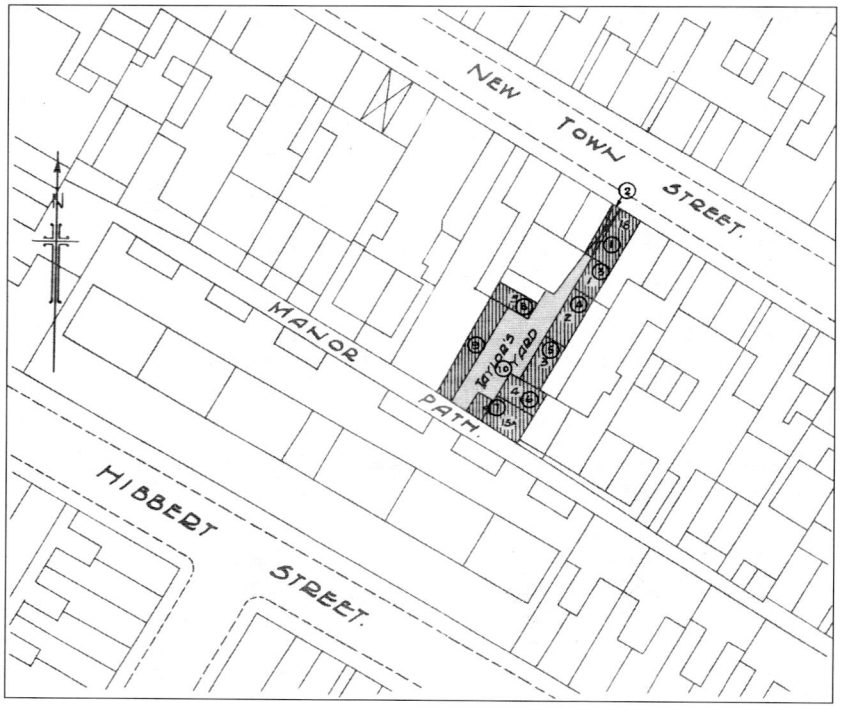

(e) Taylor's Yard, New Town. Surveyed in July 1934, prior to demolition (BRO).

HATS, LAND AND HOUSES 83

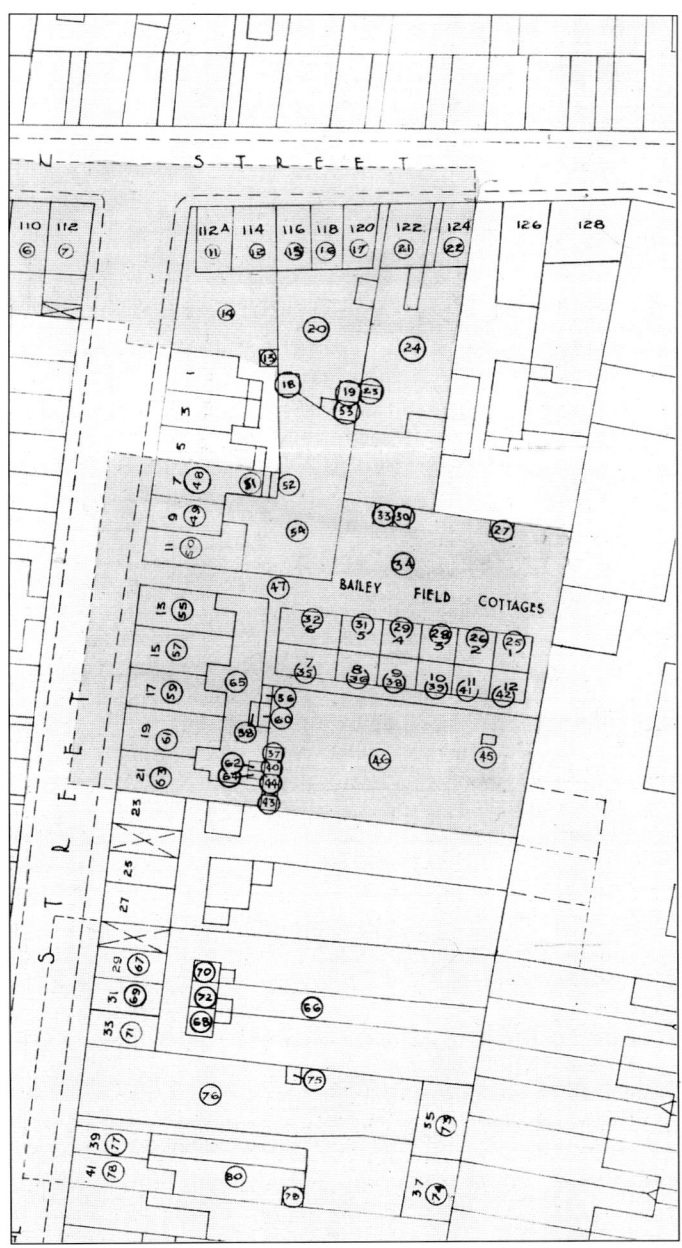

(f) Bailey Hill (Field), Chase Street. Surveyed in March 1935, prior to demolition (BRO).

Chapter Two. The Board of Health

> *Know ye the stream where the cess-pool and sewer*
> *Are emptied of all their foul slushes and mire,*
> *Where the feculent stream of rich liquid manure*
> *Now sickens the people, now maddens the squire?*

(*Luton Times* 18 March 1856. Poem entitled
The Luton River).

Before incorporation in 1876 the most powerful of Luton's public institutions was the local Board of Health. General questions of power are dealt with separately, in chapter four, but the local Board's history forms an undercurrent to the development of the town in this period. In this respect it warrants a chronological account as the Board served as a bridge between the medieval and modern systems of local government for the town, beginning as a health authority but developing into Luton's 'little parliament in Stuart Street'. It came to be regarded as a shadow town council, a role for which it was ill-equipped and for which it received more brickbats than bouquets.[1] The more that the Board became involved in various areas of the town, the more was expected of it. The local Board of Health came, therefore, to exemplify Luton's inadequate administrative structure and political impotence: it became the focus for frustrated criticism for perceived failings in areas which were far beyond its remit. The Board also became a focal point of public debate, just one of the former functions of the Vestry, which it steadily superseded in relevance. The only other public body of similar significance was the Board of Guardians (see also chapter four).

A second distinctive feature punctuated the period in which the local Board was operational. This was the way in which it served as a vehicle for the promotion of the interests of certain sections of Luton's social structure – interests not always in harmony with those of their fellow citizens. As such, it became a forum for occasional power struggles between the new urban elite of professionals and bigger employers on the one hand and the old market town circles, such as the farmers (supported by smaller tradesmen) on the other. The occasional nature of these struggles must be stressed and the limitations of power and influence of each of the above groups were made apparent by the battles which were fought around and beyond the Boardroom. The farming influence dwindled, the less affluent elements of local society were a largely negative force and the upper echelons of the middle class found that the local Board of Health could only serve to fulfil aims which were close to their hearts if usurped for a specific issue. Relatively early in the life of the Board, a number of Luton's leading citizens were to discover that it was not a suitable substitute for borough status.

Pre-Board Luton

The imperative which caused a Board of Health to be established in Luton can best be understood by the manner in which the perceived problem of sanitation and public health was addressed. The break with the world of market town Luton in the second quarter of the nineteenth century was a traumatic one, far more profound than the later transformation from hat town to car town at the beginning of the twentieth. The failure was not one of investment in the 'social overhead' during the early stage of industrial driven urbanisation, as some historians have suggested. It was a failure of institutions in the face of profound change. Some Lutonians (such as John Williams) switched occupations, some diversified economic activity, others quit the town and a great many more individuals arrived. Just as the ways of making money changed, so also would the bodies which administered the town have to alter. The scarcity of land (and consequent high rents), which Jeffrey Williamson cited as being a major contributory element towards rising mortality in the towns and cities, was not, as we have seen from chapter one, a significant factor in Luton.[2]

No amount of investment would have helped the Vestry which was simply outgrown by the town which it administered: between 1801 and 1851 Luton's population trebled to over 10,500, by which time the standard of public health and sanitation in parts of the town had become appalling. The problem lay in two particular areas – old cottages and recent property developments. The town had long lived with the pockets of squalor which existed in courtyards in the centre of town, such as Adelaide Terrace and Spencer's Yard in George Street and Bull Court and Old Yard in Park Street. In such places 'the alleys are in some case about four feet wide so that the houses stare at one another in most dark and ominous proximity'.[3] What really concentrated the minds of those considering the viability of municipal reform were the even greater problems caused by the housing boom of the previous twenty years. The waste from houses constructed without adequate means of disposal spilled over onto the street beyond. At the foot of Wellington Street (built on a slight incline) lay an accumulation of water and 'filth' beside the new Town Hall.[4]

The main centres of concern were in the expanding districts of New Town and High Town. Part of this problem was caused by building activity itself: 'Middle-aged people now give up hope of seeing Luton a clean town, on account of the constant trade in bricks and mortar, which is not likely to cease in their time', lamented the *Bedford Times* in 1847. It went on to report that 'the late high wind has carried much brick rubbish into the eyes of Lutonians, and caused much inconvenience'.[5] Specifically though, the problem lay in what the builders produced. Unlit High Town presented a number of hazards: one unfortunate gentleman recorded how, after attending a meeting at the

Methodist Church, he lost his way 'and was detained above a quarter of an hour in the midst of slippery turf, heaps of stones and muddy pools'. Suggesting that Lutonians concentrate upon fundamental issues, the correspondent referred to a recent series of letters in the newspaper concerning literary societies, adding that 'before Luton enters into any controversy respecting literature and the graces it would be well if the town were to study municipal reform'.[6] The hazards lay beyond falling into unlit trenches: in February 1847 two deaths in Back Street were attributed to the 'mud and filth, emitting the vilest odours, (which) occupy the centre of the street through all its length'.[7] However unscientific was this kind of diagnosis, the link was established in many minds between dirt and disease. With the only check upon building activity being the law of supply and demand, there lay only the prospect of an increase in the depths of destitution.

It was from this perspective that the state of Luton's sanitation was addressed: according to the Board of Health report on the township, made in 1850, the death rate for Luton in that year was twenty-seven in every thousand, with the average life expectancy being twenty-five years and one month. Statistics, however, were not then, and are not now, easy to come by as the Registrar General's reports (published from 1837) provide insufficient detail. The township was grouped into the large Luton Registration District together with Dunstable, Houghton Regis, Caddington, Barton, Sundon and Hyde. This leaves only generalisations possible. In many respects though, debate over mortality is irrelevant as a factor which influenced the promotion of a local Board of Health. There was no local discussion over diminishing life expectancy, rising mortality and certainly no evidence of awareness of the link between poor sanitation, bad housing, poverty and the nature of a local economy which provided seasonal wages. Stagnant pools of waste water, news of epidemics, squalid houses, dangerous building sites, overcrowded lodging houses – the visible signs of change – these were what provided the motivation.

Clearly, the Vestry was no longer capable of dealing with the problems of an expanding manufacturing centre and, in the absence of any other modern machinery of local government, the Board of Guardians attempted to fill the breach. From the mid-1840s it had two Acts of Parliament at its disposal. The first of these, the Nuisances Removal and Diseases Prevention Act of 1846, gave local authorities (including Boards of Guardians) the power to apply to the Court of Petty Sessions for the removal of those things deemed hazardous to the public health. This Act was consolidated a year later by the Town Improvement Clauses Act. The Luton Board of Guardians had not waited for the arrival of legislation: in November 1845, the clerk (E.C. Williamson), was ordered to write to James Newman regarding the defective drains adjacent to his properties in Old Yard, although

Newman attempted to dodge responsibility by claiming that Old Yard was a public thoroughfare.[8]

The composition of the Board included Henry Tomson as the Sundon representative, plus Richard Marks Brown, Richard Vyse, John Brett, J.J. Johnson from Luton and Richard Gutteridge of Dunstable. Henry Tomson, as Vice-Chairman, frequently chaired meetings, as did Richard Marks Brown, in the absence of the Marquess of Bute. It was the conscientious son of Henry Tomson, Dr Kit Tomson, in his capacity as medical officer for the Luton District, who inspected the condition of selected hovels in Luton and reported to the Board of Guardians for action. Twenty copies of the Nuisances Removal and Diseases Prevention Act were ordered and sent to each medical officer and parish clerk in the Union, accompanied by a letter requesting enforcement.[9] In November 1847, Williamson issued notices of intention to obtain an Improvement Bill – although there is no evidence that this was carried through.[10]

Armed with this Act, Kit Tomson began listing various properties which, as he saw it presented nuisances, and submitted these to the Guardians. Old Yard, Tower Hill, Adelaide Terrace, Gray's Yard, Lawford's Yard (in Church Street), cottages on Hitchin Road, together with numerous properties in High Town (including Wren's Yard, Gaitskell Terrace and at least one public house), all were identified as problem areas. Initially, the Guardians attempted direct communication: George Gregory, like Newman, was written to by Williamson on two occasions and ordered to remove nuisances (unspecified in the minutes) at cottages which he owned in Old Bedford Road. Dr Tomson followed up the second letter within three weeks and reported back that the 'nuisances were not removed to his satisfaction'.[11]

After the failure of the personal approach towards first Newman, Gregory, and then a number of other property owners, the Board of Guardians, chivvied by a frustrated Tomson, resolved to take the next stage. Legal action was prepared against the owners of the Tower Hill almshouses, the Hitchin Road cottages (William Clarke), a public house in High Town (unidentified) and the laughably named 'Mount Pleasant' in High Town (John Wren). Magistrates made an order against the latter to remove his 'foul cesspool' but the continued presence of 'Wren's Yard' (presumably the same place) on subsequent nuisance reports suggest that, at best, this could only have brought temporary alleviation.[12]

Edward Cresy's Report

The Health of Towns Act, passed in September 1848 by Lord John Russell's Whig administration, created a General Board of Health with defined but limited powers. Because there was no other authority in Luton to approach, the General Board of Health wrote to the Board of Guardians in November 1848 enclosing copies of the Nuisances

Removal Act (not realising that the Guardians already had copies) 'trusting that this Board give immediate and careful attention to them'. The Guardians responded by unanimously resolving 'to report to the Board (of Health) all Nuisances in their respective Districts'.[13] Over a period of three years George Street was paved, this being paid for by a levy on the poor rates.[14]

Despite Tomson's efforts, the failure of the Board of Guardians to make headway against problem areas showed that the existing legislation which applied to Luton was inadequate to cope with the growing problem which unrestricted building development represented. The adoption of an Improvement Commission under the auspices of the 1847 Act did not spare Bedford from an outbreak of cholera in 1849. A fever ward was prepared at Luton but the dreaded epidemic never struck. Luton's escape can only be attributed to good fortune although, perversely, Bedford's suffering could have been taken by some as proof that central government legislation was an ineffective additional expense.

More fundamentally, the supervision of public health was simply not a duty of the Board of Guardians. The Poor Law Board were already requesting that the Luton Guardians keep separate accounts for work done for the General Board of Health and, anticipating that initial contact with the General Board was probably the thin end of a very long wedge, the Guardians attempted to disengage themselves. In January 1849 they wrote to the churchwardens and overseers of Luton to see whether there was any prospect of a visit from an inspector from the General Board of Health. This request was evidently passed on as the General Board replied (via the Vicar of St. Mary's, Rev Thomas Sikes) that they were giving their attention to Luton.[15]

As the local Board of Health were eventually to find out, fulfilling duties which were not strictly theirs only served to make the Guardians vulnerable to criticism from the ill-informed. 'A Friend of the Poor' wrote to the *Bedford Times* complaining that the Guardians were neglecting to inspect adequately the 'filthy' areas of Luton 'which defy the power of language to define them'.[16] In any case, there was clearly not universal confidence that the Guardians were fully capable of controlling their own affairs. The same correspondent described the Union workhouse as a 'miserable pauper prison': fever had swept through it in the summer of 1847 carrying away Gardner, the workhouse master.

The Health of Towns Act allowed for the creation of a local Board of Health if 10% of ratepayers in a district petitioned for one. Locally, this was swiftly raised, largely at the instigation of one of the Guardians, Richard Vyse. The total number of ratepayers was 1863 – nearly a fifth of the town's population – and 187 signed the petition.[17] In March 1849 Edward Cresy was sent by the General Board to make a report on the sanitary conditions in Luton.[18] Cresy, whose report was published in

February of the following year, spent several days in Luton where he heard evidence at the Town Hall before being conducted around the route of his inspection by a phalanx of Luton's bourgeoisie – Richard Vyse, James Muir, C.A. Austin, William Phillips, William Willis, Robert How and Doctors Tomson, Heale and Beale.[19]

After noting that in 1847 21 people had died of 'endemic, epidemic and contagious diseases', Cresy made some general observations on Luton. There was no general system either for the drainage or a supply of water.[20] Worse still it was evident that the drainage from the bleaching houses of straw hat factories was seeping into some of the wells used for drinking water. Also reporting 'a total absence of ventilation', Cresy then made specific observations upon individual areas.[21] In Tower Hill he discovered that there was '... one privy for 28 houses. The utensils made use of are all emptied into open brick channels within 5 feet of the doors and windows and the earth is saturated'.[22] The appropriately named Blackwater Lane had 'not a house with a healthy inhabitant'. These cottages were more than 200 years old, whilst at High Town the buildings were barely twenty: yet, at the latter, the sanitation was no better and Cresy found that 'in some instances the stench is scarcely to be endured'. In a lodging house in one room '12 feet × 9, was a dead child 4 years of age ... it was stated that the previous night three persons slept in the other beds in the room where the corpse lay'.[23]

Cresy made six recommendations: a supply of clean water; the removal of cesspools and dungheaps; the construction of sewers; the establishment of a public slaughter house to replace the unsanitary ones in existence; 'better arrangement and superintendent of the public lodging house' and improved construction of small tenements. Cresy coupled these recommendations with another: 'I therefore humbly recommend the application of the Public Health Act and appointment of 9 persons, to be elected as pointed out by the Act ...'[24]

Establishment of the Local Board

The debate over whether Luton should adopt the Health of Towns Act was fought principally within the middle classes, naturally enough between those who were significant landlords and those who were not. Because of this there also existed an undercurrent to the division: the landlords comprising a substantial proportion of established families, notably farmers, were pitted against the non-landlords, drawn from relative newcomers to the town, who were promoting the Board. The subsequent debate, therefore, also carried overtones of economic division, perhaps even personal antipathy. The opposition to the proposed formation of a local Board of Health was slow to move but finally manifested itself at an acrimonious meeting of the Vestry on 30 May 1850. The identity of all those present is, regrettably, not known. Richard Vyse, in advocating the proposed Board was confronted by Edwin L.

Brickwood, 'a keen-witted "waspish" lawyer who gained an unenviable notoriety in his day as being always in opposition on public matters'.[25] There was an angry exchange between the two at which the meeting sided with Brickwood and 'overstepping the bounds of propriety hissed Mr Vyse out of the room'.[26] The Vestry meeting then passed the resolution 'that this Vestry protests against the Health of Towns Bill being applied and extended to Luton' and further resolved to find out who had raised and signed the original petition. It is remarkable that there still remained uncertainty as to this last matter: Cresy had spent several days prodding around in virtually every street, courtyard and midden of a small town in the company of some of its leading citizens, during which he held a public meeting on 20 March. That the visit could not have escaped local attention is indisputable and it can only be attributed to the detachment and indolence of the Board's opponents that they waited until the horse had bolted before they attempted to slam the stable door. In the introduction to Cresy's report the Secretary of the General Board, Henry Austin, had requested comments on or before 1 April 1850, and yet it was 1 May before the special Vestry meeting was called.

It is no surprise to see that the fiercest critics of the Board were to be found amongst the ranks of the principal property owners: even the most insensitive and hard-nosed landlord would have been stung to see their property condemned in such a trenchant manner within an official report. Under the provision of the Health of Towns Act tenants paying less than £10 per annum would not be liable for the local rate to support the work of the Board, this being borne instead by the landlord. For landlords in Luton, the immediate consequences of the application of the Act was the cost of providing a system of drainage to their property. Certainly, there appeared to be a widespread fear amongst ratepayers (stemming partly from ignorance) of the prospective cost to the town of fulfilling all of Cresy's recommendations – particularly regarding water supply and sewage – as well as employing full-time officials to the Board. The constitutional argument which was used by those who opposed the passing of the Act in 1847–8 (that it represented a dangerous move towards continental despotism) was also echoed locally, but in Luton, if not at Westminster, this argument was a thinly veiled disguise for the fundamental motives behind the opposition.

The main preoccupation of those resisting the Board was clear enough: economic self-protection. That this was recognised locally is apparent from a handbill produced by an unnamed supporter of the Board immediately after the Vestry meeting in May 1850.[27] The handbill, referring in particular to the speech made by Brickwood, concluded that the Board's opponents 'know they are now exacting the highest possible rent for their human pigsties, and they fear they shall be compelled to expend a portion of their 101 per cent profits in adding to your comforts'.

If a local Board of Health was established, few men would face a greater outlay than Henry Sibley. An affluent farmer, who had proposed the motion at the Vestry meeting protesting against the need for a local Board, Sibley owned at least fifty cottages in High Town as well as the squalid dwellings in Adelaide Terrace.[28] The latter, a courtyard running off George Street, contained 33 cottages which provided Sibley with an estimated income of over £165 per annum from a mixed rental of between £4 and £8. Sibley also owned many of the cottages in the notorious Back Street. Another farmer who was a substantial property owner was William Clarke: like Sibley, Clarke owned new cottages in the area of High Town (those along Hitchin Road, already mentioned) as well as an older courtyard, 'Clack's Yard', at Amen Corner (opposite the Parish Church), in which Cresy had noted that the twelve cottages shared one pump and one privy.[29] In addition to these, Clarke owned a scattering of cottages in Park Street. Other opponents of the Board included solicitor, Frederick Chase (who had chaired the Vestry meeting) and farmer William Townrow. Both these men owned property in the recently developed New Town, which had been singled out by Cresy for particular attention because of poor sanitation.

The most senior of the proposed Board's opponents was John Waller. He owned a large house fronting onto George Street and the extensive grounds to its rear comprised the largest parcel of land within the small urban area. Unlike the other leading opponents of the Board, he did not own a substantial number of dwellings. In this Waller had more in common with the pro-Board faction, amongst whom there were few substantial landlords and comprising at its head principally those in the hat trade and professions. The Wallers had, however, been active within the property market – chiefly in land speculation – and John may have calculated that the proposed Board would inhibit activity in this sphere.

It was not immediately revealed that 187 persons had signed the petition calling for the establishment of a local Board of Health, the details of which were to give the anti-Board lobby some powerful ammunition.[30] In response to this, the opponents had, by mid-June, raised a rival petition of 1423 names. It soon became apparent that some of these people (34 according to Richard Vyse) were also signatories to the original petition. When details of the original petition became known these 34 included some embarrassing signatures. Most notable was Frederick Chase, plus three others who were subsequently to be anti-Board candidates – J.J. Johnson, William Clarke and James Waller. By no means were these stupid men, yet the fact that they should find themselves straddling both camps within the space of eighteen months is a stark demonstration of the slowness with which realisation of the consequences of central legislation seeped into this provincial town. Armed with this knowledge the anti-Board lobby reinforced their petition with a series of objections sent to the General Board of Health.[31] They claimed, somewhat unconvincingly in the light of Cresy's observations, that Luton was not an unhealthy place and added that the heavy rates would put an extra burden upon households made more vulnerable during the 'dull time' in the hat trade. More reasonably, they pointed out that the original petition did not contain 187 ratepayers, thus falling short of the 10% minimum requirement. The contents of this letter became known to Vyse (perhaps the General Board showed it to him) because he provided a riposte to the anti-Board's points. Conveniently ignoring the fact that some prominent ratepayers had clearly changed sides, he wrote pointing out that the 187 in favour of the Board paid rates to the value of £6572 5s., whilst the 715 (why he selected this figure is not known) against the Board paid rates to the value of £5026 18s. Furthermore, Vyse added that 135 signatories against the Board were not ratepayers and that landlords had 'induced' their tenants to sign.[32]

The General Board refused to receive the anti-Board petition. A delegation comprising Waller, Brickwood, Clarke and Henry Brown, on behalf of the Vestry were unable to gain access to the Board. A second petition of 600 names, hurriedly raised and presented to the House of Lords, also failed.[33] The Board were not listening to those who opposed their work, no matter how loud they shouted. Far more persuasive was their own inspector. In June 1850, he responded to the anti-Board's petition:

> No Town, has come under my inspection, that so much needs, the application of the Public Health Act, as the Township of Luton . . .
>
> The Builders of small Tenements, ought to be obliged, to construct healthy habitations – at present. They are under no control, and mortgaging their homes to the full value, when called upon to repair or cleanse, are utterly unable to do so . . .
>
> I shall exceedingly regret, if the opposition which has been got up . . . should defeat the wishes of the most respectable Rate Payers and Inhabitants who desire to see their Town properly drained and supplied with water.[34]

The whole episode, from the raising of the original petition, had uncovered depths of bitterness and acrimony not seen in Luton within living memory. The *Bedford Times* dryly noted that 'the threatened operation of the Health of Towns Act at Luton seems to excite some parties to be as offensive as they can in proportion as their time is limited'.[35] Those resisting the Board continued to hold meetings resolving to 'offer an obstruction . . . to those who incline to centralisation principles,' but their delay in organising a defence of the *status quo*, plus

Luton's high death rate (which at 27 per 1000 was above the legal minimum required to establish a local Board – 23 per 1000 – by the Act), meant that there was no prospect of the ratepayers being able to prevent its application to Luton.[36]

Paradoxically, the opposition forces found their refuge in the Health of Towns Act itself. In unincorporated districts the Act laid down that a local Board would comprise nine men elected by the ratepayers with property owners possessing plural votes, one for each £50 of the rateable value of their property and up to six in total.[37] Against such a limited and inequitable voting system it became apparent that the Board's supporters stood little chance in any election. A supportive lecture at the Mechanics Institute from R. Fish (a contributor to the *Cottage Gardener*) attracted a 'respectable but not . . . a numerous audience', indicating that the Board did not have a large number of supporters to call upon. Fish shrewdly declared that whilst Luton would adopt the Act, it would probably need central government authorisation for effective measures.[38] When news was received on 24 July 1850 that the General Board was to appoint Richard Vyse as Chairman of a local Board, Brickwood and Chase seized the opportunity to petition successfully the Board for an election to be held immediately. Luton's small electorate then split into two factions, the 'Blue' (pro-Act) and the 'Yellow' (anti-Act) for the first election of its type ever seen in the town. In reporting this development the Luton correspondent of the *Bedford Times* was able to speculate as to the likely outcome: '. . . if the Bill must be carried out, it will be at the least expense possible to the town.'[39]

Faced with an increasingly confident opposition the 'Blue' faction could do little more than assume the moral high-ground. They could reiterate their reasons for advocating the creation of a Board and claim, in Williamson's words, that an effective Board was the desire of 'all the respectable inhabitants whether owners or occupiers'.[40] A letter to the *Bedford Times* from 'A Reviewer' contained what was essentially the 'Blue' manifesto: '. . . wherever the eye is turned it rests upon batches of newly-built, ill ventilated, badly drained cottages. The sole design being a large percentage for the outlay.'[41] Like Cresy before him, the writer then singled out individual properties: Bull Court in Park Street (partly owned by Brickwood) and the Tower Hill almshouses (where it was claimed that there were ten persons in one room) were cited as particularly bad examples. Henry Sibley may have been riled to find that Adelaide Terrace 'baffles all description' where the 'stench is intolerable' but it was the 'putrid' Blackwater Lane, whose cottages were owned by a number of small landlords, for which was reserved the most cutting invective: dead dogs, cats, and carrion were listed amongst the 'thousand ills' contained within the ditch which ran along its length. Against all of this, the writer concluded, the existing machinery for the improvement of sanitation had been found to be 'defective', hence the urgent necessity for the establishment of the Board of Health whose expenditure would be controlled by the ratepayers. The letter is also evidence that none of the landlords of the said properties had felt so moved or threatened by Cresy's report or its consequences to attempt any improvements.

The same article also carried details of a well-attended meeting at the Town Hall organised by the 'Yellow' party. This was addressed (for two hours) by the barrister Toulmin Smith of the Anti-Centralisation Society and a local man, Mr. Bambray, who had recently switched camps. The chairman of the meeting, Frederick Chase, opened the proceedings with an attack upon the Act: 'The spirit was bad; it was opposed to the British Constitution and the best interests of a free people'. Edwin Brickwood also spoke, concurring with Chase's view that the Act would 'annihilate freedom', but candidly also admitting that 'personal considerations' influenced his position on this issue. Even at this stage Brickwood still appeared to be entertaining ideas of preventing the Act from being applied to Luton.

Reporting 'great excitement', the *Bedford Times* listed the candidates standing for the nine places on the Board, eleven from the 'Blue' faction and nine from the 'Yellow' faction.[42] There were no independent candidates. The result of the election, never in any real doubt, was published in the newspaper the following week. The votes cast were as follows:

Elected		*Not Elected*	
John Waller (Yellow)	760	James Muir (Blue)	458
William Clarke (Yellow)	739	Henry Brown (Blue)	296
James Kidman (Yellow)	717	Richard Vyse (Blue)	277
John James Johnson (Yellow)	713	William Phillips (Blue)	247
Daniel Davies (Yellow)	704	Samuel Daniels (Blue)	239
Thomas Smith (Yellow)	698	Frederick Brown (Blue)	232
John Clark (Yellow)	690	E.C. Williamson (Blue)	231
Henry Sibley (Yellow)	680	J.K. Blundell (Blue)	224
William Townrow (Yellow)	672	Thomas Sworder (Blue)	212
		Robert How (Blue)	115
		A.T. Webster (Blue)	60

It was a bitter irony for the 'Blue' party that the legislation which offered the hope of transforming the town had been ambushed by those who had already shackled or ignored the existing institutions for sanitary improvement. The weakness of the General Board (which tended to leave efforts to local initiative), the limited extent of the Act and the nature of the voting system, all served to produce a frustrating result, especially for Richard Vyse. Set against the numbers on the rival petitions, the result indicates that the 'Blue' party had maximised their vote. It was, nonetheless, an overwhelming victory for the 'Yellows'.

The immediate future for the reformers must have appeared bleak: the 'Yellow' party, comprising men whose greed and negligence had harnessed them to an institution which they would rather have avoided altogether, had at least been able to gain control of the beast. They would now be able to 'carry out every necessary measure, at a very trifling cost, as compared with what would have been the case had their opponents been successful'.[43] Vyse informed the General Board of the disastrous outcome, with undisguised bitterness:

> ... each of the members elected is known to be opposed to the introduction of the Act ... I have reason to believe that they are indebted to their election to assurances held forth to the lower class of electors that the operation of the Act would add very considerably to their Rates and that if they elected the present Board, they the Board, would <u>do nothing</u> and thereby defeat the object of the Act.[44]

The establishment of the Luton Board of Health conformed to the processes as laid down in the Health of Towns Act. Edward Cresy's visit and report followed the normal procedure, and his observations and recommendations could have been applied to any number of English towns containing old and new slums bedevilled by thoroughly inadequate sanitation. As with other towns, the mere fact of a death-rate exceeding the legal minimum ensured that once the petition was raised nothing could prevent the creation of a local Board and Finer's conclusion was that 'assisted by the full weight of the Board, the "clean party" (dubbed the "intelligent minority") triumphed everywhere ...'.[45] In Luton, the 'triumph' possessed a hollow ring as the conservative forces gained the initial advantage. If by 'intelligent minority' Finer meant the upper reaches of the middle classes then their clear division decisively altered the outcome. That the anti-Board forces gained the upper hand can be attributed to the tenacity and energy of Edwin Brickwood and Frederick Chase. It is probably not a coincidence that their departure from the town was to coincide with a revival of the 'clean' party interest.

Trial and Disrepute, 1850–58

The victorious nine members of the 'Yellow' Board held their first meeting at the *Cock Inn* on 12 August 1850: John Waller was elected chairman and Frederick Chase, able to overcome his misgivings about the Board's threat to Englishmen's freedom, accepted the post of Clerk. Richard Vyse, in his capacity as Returning Officer, was admitted to the meeting just long enough to deliver the ballot returns.[46]

The immediate priorities for the Board were to consider the state of the town's streets and drainage. John Cumberland was appointed Surveyor and requested to make an assessment of the drains.[47] Contracts were obtained for the supply of stone flags. A general rate of 9*d.* in the pound was levied and it was 'ordered that when the annual value of any cottages or tenements liable to assessment... does not exceed the sum of ten pounds a composition shall be made by this Board with the Owner of such premises for the payment of the said rate ... and levied upon such a reduction of the net annual value of the premises as shall leave two-thirds to pay the assessment.'[48] Little detail of the Board's early financial arrangements are recorded, the auditor later reporting '... I have only once been called on to audit the Accounts which I then found in a very unsatisfactory State as to form ...'.[49] There is little reason to dispute the opinion of the Luton correspondent of the *Bedford Times* that the Board was weighting composition in favour of the landlords in the town.[50]

The initial attention of the Board was focused in particular upon Blackwater Lane, an area which not only urgently required improvement but which also was not owned by any member or official of the Board. Rev Thomas Sikes was ordered to widen the path near to the lane, and sewers were connected to the property. Work that was scheduled to take two weeks engaged 22 men, this achievement being marked by the changing of the name to Lea Road in October 1850. An Inspector of Nuisances was appointed and, following his report that the nearby Old Yard in Park Street (part of the Bute estate) was in a 'filthy condition', the Board ordered the Trustees of the estate to make the necessary repairs otherwise this would be undertaken by the Board and a bill presented to them.[51]

Plans for new buildings were scrutinised and if they did not meet the requirements of the Health of Town's Act were refused: moreover, proceedings were undertaken against those who built contrary to the Act or without the Board's approval.[52] Nonetheless, for the first two years the Board undertook the absolute minimum to satisfy its legal obligation which was, of course, its members' precise intention. Nowhere is this more apparent than in the Board's highly selective approach towards Luton's sanitation: notwithstanding the fact that they owned some of the poorest dwellings in the town, no measures were commenced to improve the conditions of the tenants of Board members. On only one occasion was action taken against a member of the Board when William Townrow, after refusing an informal request, was ordered to make a drain to run from one of his properties in New Town into the recently laid main duct in Stuart Street. Townrow must have regretted not being present at this particular meeting.[53]

Before the Luton Board had served a full year it was clear that the 'Yellow' interest was on the wane. Frederick Chase announced his intention to leave Luton and resigned as Clerk in March 1851. Although Chase was replaced by Edwin Brickwood the following month this appointment only lasted until July when the latter also left Luton, to live in Putney. Brickwood's successor as Clerk was George Bailey who had served his articles in Chase's practice.[54] Details of elections until

1853 are not available, but a contested one may have occurred in March 1851 when Sibley, Townrow and John Clark were replaced by James Warr, Joseph Mead, a Park Street grocer, and James Waller. These appointments did not alter the balance of the Board but the following year came the significant election of Henry Brown, the first of the 'Blue' party to obtain a seat.

Meanwhile, the Board plodded on. Sewers were begun in Gaitskell Terrace and Tower Hill. The lighting of the town was undertaken: the tender of the Luton Gas Company, the only local company, being accepted. A register of lodging and slaughter houses was prepared and people were ordered not to push wheelbarrows along Barbers Lane.[55] The rate was increased to one shilling in the pound.[56] This progress did not impress the former members of the 'clean' party. Under the heading 'Industry and Filth', a critic of the Board of Health opened a letter to the *Bedford Times* thus: 'Sir, As a general rule the above terms are and always have been diametrically opposed, but an exception is afforded by the busy town of Luton.'[57] Although many of his specific allegations were not strictly true, and were subsequently refuted by John Cumberland, it was clear that the defeated 'Blues' were regrouping. Prior to the annual elections in March 1853 a public meeting was called at the Town Hall at which the performance of the Board to date was criticised as achieving no fundamental improvement for Luton – despite expenditure of £2000.[58] Proclaiming 'efficiency with economy', the meeting put forward five candidates for the approaching election. Four – William Willis, Frederick Brown, A T Webster and Thomas Sworder – had stood for the 'Blue' party in 1850. They were joined by a fifth, the energetic John Everitt.

From a total of ten candidates, three 'Blues' – Brown, Sworder and Everitt – were successful. Re-elected was William Clarke and also joining the Board was John S. Crawley, making a rare excursion into Luton's affairs. This election altered the balance of the Board with the Browns, abetted by Sworder and Everitt, the dominant members. Henry Brown usually chaired the meeting although he deferred to Crawley on the infrequent occasions that the latter attended until his resignation the following February.

The changing composition of the Luton Board of Health was not due to an expression of electoral dissatisfaction in its early performance. It appears rather that the bitterness and fears that were so swiftly formed in 1850 faded in the light of experience of a cautious and only partially effective Board. So, whilst the justifiable criticisms of Luton's sanitary conditions continued to motivate the 'clean party', in the absence of Brickwood and Chase there were none on the other side with the energy and organisation to prevent its electoral success. This success was achieved through the disintegration of the 'Yellow' interest and the votes cast at subsequent elections reflect this: in 1856 William Bigg and

Thomas Sworder topped the poll gaining 328 and 295 votes respectively.[59] Six years earlier these votes would not have secured them a place on the Board.

If the 'Yellow' members of the Board had to choose an epitaph for their early work it would be that, in the words of one supportive correspondent in the *Bedford Times*, they undertook improvements to the town 'gradually but surely'.[60] Their abiding and more fitting legacy was to be harsher and, indeed, tragic – cholera. Whilst the consequence of the cholera epidemic was to reinforce the necessity of electing 'clean' members, it was a political irony that it was the 'Yellows' erstwhile opponents who were to reap the results of the previous three years' negligence.

It is hardly surprising to record that it was in a property belonging to a 'Yellow' member that Asiatic cholera first struck. After suffering for nine hours, a child died in Adelaide Terrace in October 1853. Kit Tomson had attended him and, after receiving his report, the Board of Guardians wrote to Sibley requesting that he take some action, as well as asking the Board of Health to offer assistance and co-operation.[61] The Board of Health responded by forming a Cholera Committee: John Everitt, J.S. Crawley and the Browns were members of both the Board of Guardians and the local Board of Health.

Within four days, as the respective Boards desperately attempted to apply such primitive measures as were at their disposal, it was reported that another child was fatally ill. The Union Relieving Officer was ordered to ensure that someone in Adelaide Terrace maintained a supply of at least three pails of boiling water and the Medical Officer ordered a quantity of brandy. The Board of Guardians engaged three nurses and the Board of Health a full-time assistant who distributed peat charcoal and chloride of lime to a number of properties. Cottages owned by Brickwood (Bull Court), Elizabeth Gregory (in Old Bedford Road), Richard Haselgrove, Joseph Dancer and J.S. Crawley, amongst others, were ordered to be whitewashed and have their refuse removed. Five hundred notices advising people on remedial actions against cholera were printed and sent to local clergymen for distribution amongst their congregations.[62]

Although the cholera did not spread, these belated efforts were not sufficient to prevent a deterioration in Adelaide Terrace. The approaches to Sibley on the part of the local authorities suggesting joint action were ignored: it was obvious that Sibley was indifferent to his tenants suffering and it was also clear that there were other landlords in the town who would follow his example. The authorities, therefore, intensified their efforts. On 1 November 1853 a joint emergency meeting of the Cholera Committee was held which also included William Willis, Rev Sikes, Dr Benson, Dr Tomson and R.D. Grainger, the Medical Superintendent Inspector of the General Board of Health.

Grainger had already made his own inspections of the town. As a consequence of the meeting, two medical assistants were appointed to assist Tomson, specifically working in door-to-door visitation. Preparation was made for two further medical assistants to be engaged for the following two weeks at £4 4s. per week, including medicines.[63] The joint Cholera Committee met twice on the 2 November and daily thereafter.

Adelaide Terrace presented a particular problem which required a direct remedy. At the end of October, as the cholera in the courtyard intensified, Kit Tomson reported that it was 'so overcrowded, so filthy and unfit for human habitation that nothing short of an entire removal of the inhabitants to some distant place and the property put under quarantine until declared fit for habitation would meet the urgency of the case'.[64] Faced with Sibley's non-co-operation the local authorities took matters into their own hands. Some outbuildings belonging to Everitt in High Town were converted by a local builder at a cost of £60 to act as 'places of refuge' for people who needed to be removed from their homes. Once the Adelaide Terrace refugees were safely on the other side of the town, their sties were cleansed with lime.[65] By the middle of November Tomson was able to report that the cholera was easing and by early December there were no further cases. The Board of Guardians paid £20 remuneration to Kit Tomson on behalf of a grateful town.[66]

Meanwhile, the inquests on the death of one of the Adelaide Terrace victims, an eleven year old boy named Frederick Green, focused the attention of Luton not only upon the squalor in its midst, but also upon the inadequacy of its relevant local authority.[67] At least ten of the fifteen people who died as a result of the cholera came from the two hundred or so who constituted the population of Adelaide Terrace. The inquest jury found that there were but four privies in the Terrace and that their doors had been removed for firewood. There was one well (broken) and an open cesspit. On behalf of the Board of Guardians, T.E. Austin reported that there had been previous complaints about Adelaide Terrace but that the Guardians felt that it was a Board of Health responsibility. The 'clean' party members of the Board made no attempt to defend their 'dirty' colleagues and predecessors. Everitt gave evidence stating that not a single bye-law had been passed by the Board in three years up until the March 1853 elections. He reinforced this in a subsequent letter to the *Bedford Times* specifically highlighting its failure to fulfil Cresy's original recommendation of regulating lodging houses and slaughter houses. Against this, Everitt claimed that an Inspector of Nuisances had been appointed to relieve a busy John Cumberland of this extra responsibility. Between one hundred and two hundred conveniences had been built on existing properties in the previous twelve weeks. Bye-laws had recently been prepared.

Evidence from George Bailey and Joseph Anstee showed that Sibley had made little effort to improve his property but it was an Inspector from the General Board of Health (possibly Grainger) who put this into its proper context. His evidence concluded that the cholera outbreak would have been avoidable but for the activities of the 'dirty' party upon the Board who used their electoral power to protect their own interests and to subvert the health legislation, even at the expense of their tenants' lives. Sibley (with his one hundred cottages) and his confederates had the power to be able to swamp all opposition in any election: Henry Brown pithily remarking that 'Mr Sibley's property in Adelaide Terrace, is a terrific proof of the power of filth'. The inspector concluded that '... there cannot be any doubt that the sanitary state of the town is worse than before the Act was applied'. The *Beds Times*, viewing these events from the county town, applied comments to the inquests. It lost no time in administering a ticking off (laced with a degree of patronising smugness) to the brash, upstart community growing in southern Bedfordshire:

> In this great emporium of commerce, political freedom and social happiness, there is the most terrible want of all features which would stamp it as a clean and wholesome town ... open sludgy gutters ... accumulations of muck ... decomposing animal and vegetable matter in snug places, dumbwells ... cess pools and open soil pits daily and hourly invite Typhus and cholera to come and hold a great field day.[68]

The Luton Board of Health, it concluded, was just an 'ornament'. If they were honest, the 'Yellows' would have admitted that they never intended that it should be otherwise.

Tragic though it was, the cholera epidemic had one salutary effect: never again was the Board run in such a negligent fashion. Cholera threatened again in October 1857 and a Board of Health sub-committee was formed to meet it, but the Board's improvements were not put to this particular test. From the mid-1850s onwards the 'clean' party ensured that the Luton Board adopted a more vigorous position, although this was no more than commensurate with the pace of Luton's expansion and its stark problems.

A series of inspections were made and a report was compiled by the newly appointed Officer of Health (surgeon F.J. Clarke) in the autumn of 1854.[69] This gave considerable detail but also demonstrated how little had hitherto been achieved. The worst of the landlords, notably Henry Sibley, Joseph Dancer, Richard Haselgrove and Edwin Brickwood, were pestered to comply with the law: on the occasions when they failed to do so the work was carried out by the Board.[70] Byelaws were published in 1854 outlining the duties of officers and detailing the responsibilities of the Board in maintaining standards of cleanliness in the town.[71] Immediately, the Board showed a willingness to bring actions against those who contravened them.[72]

Amongst the Luton Board of Health's acts in its first 'clean' phase of existence was the appointment of an Inspector of Nuisances, Common Lodging Houses and Slaughter Houses. Edward Godfrey, Superintendent of Police, was appointed to this post in June 1853, but dissatisfied with his performance the Board dismissed him a year later.[73] The Board had not yet learnt their lesson, still persisting with the appointment of part-timers. They fared even worse with Thomas Lloyd Evans, from Torquay, who was appointed Surveyor in May 1854. Evans resigned four years later before a vote of no confidence in him could be passed: the Board had discovered that he had kept no proper financial accounts for his work but, although there appeared to be some discrepancies, they were difficult to verify because he had kept few records.[74] The Board found itself in the embarrassing position of having to request contractors to supply details of charges for work which Evans had asked them to carry out. It seems that Evans made a complete hash of the drainage work. In 1855 the General Board's inspector (Henry Austin) dismissed Luton's facilities as 'imperfectly laid out, and . . . apparently devoid of systematic arrangement'. Little if any of this was Evans' fault but his own proposal was no better, Austin describing it as '. . . a very imperfect one. It is merely a skeleton plan . . .'. The Luton Board's application for a loan to finance the work was, in this instance, refused.[75] The Board, however, continued to use the Police Superintendent as Inspector of Nuisances, Lodging Houses and Slaughter Houses, rather than appoint an officer dedicated to that work alone. By 1858, Superintendent Samuel Pope was confident that the condition of the lodging houses (at least the regulated ones) had improved to the extent that he was able to report that they were in a 'clean and healthy condition . . . I have no cause to prefer any complaint.'[76] Pope's optimistic report, if correct, showed that there had been a remarkable improvement in the condition of Luton's lodging houses in a very short space of time. In the early spring of 1856, the *Luton Times* highlighted the plight of one visitor to Luton. Arriving late at night with his family, he made his way to a lodging house in New Town. There the family was shown to a small room (swarming with vermin) which contained two beds and a bedstead. Already in the room were seventeen other occupants. One suspects that Pope was not looking too hard. A successor, William Sandoe, confessed in 1864 '. . . one great difficulty which we cannot reach is the crowding in lodgings, owing to the number of girls who come in from the country for work.'[77]

Most of the township was paved and, as a result of the cholera epidemic, Luton also acquired two cemeteries. In addition to criticising the Board, Grainger's report also passed some observations upon the poor state of some of Luton's graveyards. The result of these inspections was an order from the Home Office, made under the terms of the General Interments Act, to close all burial grounds by the 1 June 1854. A Vestry meeting was called to debate how best to comply with this order. The proposal, by E.C. Williamson and John Waller, that a new cemetery for the town should be opened immediately revealed a serious split between Anglicans and nonconformists. William Willis (in a characteristically lengthy speech) and Joseph Everitt both objected to paying for a Church of England controlled cemetery and an amendment, opposing the Act as detrimental to Dissenters, was carried by a large majority.[78] Subsequent attempts to find common ground between the two sides, through the formation of a Joint Stock Company, foundered in squabbles over voting rights. Of this shambles the *Beds Times* wearily remarked that 'there appears to be something mysterious in the atmosphere of Luton, for even so peaceful a subject of the grave and its decent requirements cannot be discussed unless accompanied with an unseemly exhibition of oratorical stream.'[79] Consequently, Luton acquired two cemeteries in 1854. The General Cemetery stood on a hill overlooking the town (secured from the Bute Trustees), and the Church Cemetery lay on a hill on the opposite side of the valley upon land secured with financial support from J.S. Leigh and J.S. Crawley, who provided £100 each.

Loans were sanctioned by the beleaguered General Board of Health for sewage, paving and other works. By October 1856, the local Board held three separate mortgages with the General Annuity Endowment Association amounting to £1900, £1408 and £570, all payable over thirty years.[80] The local Board's spending plans, however, were always threatened by an electoral backlash from the ratepayers and, wherever possible, it tried to ensure that the cost of sanitary improvement was borne by those in the locality for whom the work was being carried out. This itself caused problems with some property owners and, occasionally, sympathetic Board members. The Board's finances were delicate: William Bigg and Alfred Tansley, who comprised the Finance Committee, reported in February 1858 that because of the 'accumulating obligations of the Board it is obvious that without a vigorous collection of the outstanding rate, and the speedy preparation of another of at least equal amount, the position of the Board will shortly become embarrassing and discreditable.'[81]

As the Board tried to establish itself, the inescapable image is of a legally hamstrung institution, not fully in control of the affairs over which it was required to have jurisdiction. It was repeatedly turning to the General Board in London to request elementary advice. The weakness of its position was most clearly illustrated in the manner in which Luton's first sewage treatment plant was built. Less tragic than the 1853 cholera outbreak, this was the most damaging legacy of the 'dirty' Board. Although there was not yet a piped water supply, some homes certainly had water closets by the middle of the 1850s. From 1850 drains and sewers were laid out in parts of the town augmenting a rudimentary system of drainage which had been installed by the parish surveyors around 1815, designed to take off surface water. It seems that some of Luton's enterprising populace unilaterally connected drains from their premises to take away their miscellaneous waste via this system.[82] The contents of all this surface water, plus a growing volume of miscellaneous commercial and domestic waste, passed into the River Lea. Flowing out to the south of Luton, the Lea widened near to the Brache Mill worked by Richard Marks Brown and thence on into John Shaw Leigh's Luton Hoo estate, where it widened still further into a small lake before continuing its journey south towards the Thames. Leigh understandably took umbrage at receiving the untreated effluent of ten thousand Lutonians and by 1854 was threatening legal proceedings against the Board.[83] Forced into action, the Board investigated sewage treatment systems at other towns such as Hertford and Tottenham whilst fighting a legal rearguard action against Leigh. A loan was eventually sanctioned by the General Board and tenders were invited for the various tasks.

Erection of a deodorising works was commenced in 1856 on land purchased by the Board near to Windmill Road. Throughout 1857, as contractors struggled to overcome various practical problems (a fall of earth in Guildford Street after heavy rain hindered progress), Leigh kept up the pressure upon the Board by continuing with his legal suit, successfully obtaining an injunction preventing the Board from discharging any new sewage into the Lea. Not until January 1858 was this abandoned, by which time the Board was involved in another lengthy legal battle, this time with Richard Marks Brown of the Brache. Brown claimed damages caused during the erection of the plant and for loss of water caused by the intercepting works. All of this occurred at a time when the Board were discovering that their Surveyor, appointed to oversee construction of the sewage works, had simply not been fulfilling his duties. The work by contractors around the town predictably caused considerable inconvenience: gaping holes and noisy navvies were the oft-repeated complaints. More serious was the ominous threat that loomed in the form of the Ratepayers' Protection Society. This was formed as a direct result of Leigh's legal action and the fear of its effect upon the rates.[84] Builder Thomas Barrett chaired the first meeting at the Town Hall at which the 'reckless spending' of the Board was criticised. Wild accusations concerning the Board's motives appeared in the local press.

Fortunately for Luton, the organisation of the Board's opponents did not match their opprobrious language. With the farmers a diminishing presence, the Wallers a lesser force and both Chase and Brickwood gone, the Ratepayers' Protection Society wore a far more distinctively lower middle class profile – with weaknesses in sustained organisation as a consequence. Although agreeing at its first public meeting to levy a subscription of 1*d.* a week, it did not formulate any rules and for the 1856 elections it was rumoured that there were to be seventeen candidates. In the end only eleven stood. The Society failed to whip up the 'dirty' backlash of 1850 and achieved only partial success in a moderate turnout (the average number of votes for an elected candidate was 280). Thomas Barrett was elected and Tansley and Anstee, both 'clean' members, were unseated – Tansley, with 94 votes, spectacularly so. Bigg, Sworder and Everitt, however, remained in place. Although more or less obliged to publish the ill-informed (and usually anonymous) criticisms of the Board in its correspondence columns, the *Luton Times* steadfastly sided with the Board on the question of sewage: if the Board members were so scurrilous, it reasoned, then it was a poor reflection upon the town which elected them. In a later leader article it came out strongly in support of the Board's areas of expenditure and against those who argued for 'economy'.[85] A year later Tansley and Anstee were re-elected unopposed.

Relations with the Luton Gas Company were often strained, with a fair degree of mistrust on the Board's part. They often quibbled over the price of gas that the Company supplied and even called in independent assessors to measure the power of illumination. In the absence of any other source of gas, however, they were obliged to accept the Company's tender each year to light the town. In 1858 the Board were successful in altering some clauses in a bill placed before Parliament to incorporate the Gas Company, which it felt were detrimental to the interests of itself and other consumers in the town.[86] Essentially, the Board was resisting the company's monopolistic powers and it is clear that many in the town were expecting the Board to make representations on their behalf. This issue split the Board, some of whose members were also directors and shareholders in the company, and who subsequently resigned.[87]

Involvement in disputes such as this were not the affair of an authority formed to undertake the requirements of the Health of Towns Act. The gas issue was one example which demonstrated, however, that the Board was filling a breach left by the absence of any other local authority. Increasingly it was assuming the mantle of the defenders of Luton's 'interests' on a number of issues, and in doing so was only reflecting the desire of many who saw that this should be the case. An example was provided by one misguided correspondent to the *Luton Times* who complained of the lack of lighting in Victoria Street, requesting that the Board undertake to supply it.[88] Another correspondent, complaining about the condition of Bute Street, referred to the Board members as 'councillors'.[89] There were numerous requests for Board of Health work from residents all around the town – possibly even from those who were simultaneously members of the Ratepayers' Protection Society.

THE BOARD OF HEALTH   105

Shadow Council, 1858–68

Before the end of its first decade, the leading figures of the local Board – the Browns, Bigg, Sworder and Everitt – had resigned or retired their positions and were not to stand for election again. From March 1858 onwards the Board acquired a slightly more conservative composition. John Brett became Chairman of a Board which comprised William Willis, Charles Robinson, A.J. Tansley, Joseph Anstee, Joseph Bailey (who attended infrequently and who showed a very cautious approach to matters involving expenditure), plus shopkeepers Joseph Mead (returning to the Board) and George Sole (an owner of various properties). Attendance was often poor, as few as three at a meeting on 10 February 1859.

From this time the Luton Board also acquired something of a second rate character with shopkeepers replacing those drawn from the professions and larger businesses. Crawley and Williamson were amongst others who never stood again; Rev James O'Neill and Kit Tomson on no occasion offered themselves for election; Cumberland, Scargill and Willis are examples of those who chose to serve for no more than short periods, usually seeking election to pursue a specific issue. Luton's leaders, the men who subsequently were to fight for control of the School Board and lead the Town Council, had deserted the local Board of Health. Presumably each had his own motives, but in all probability it was frustration with the Board's impotence in the face of the many demands made upon it. Certainly, from the 1860s, former members such as Willis, Bigg and Anstee were becoming involved in the movement for Borough status or *ad hoc* issues such as the railway or control of the markets – issues which occasionally involved working through or with the Board of Health. What must also be counted was personal incompatibility: Frederick Brown's decision to stay away from the Board may have been influenced by animosity toward the type of people with whom he would have to deal. In a letter to John Shaw Leigh, concerning the dispute with the Board over compensation for damage to the Brache Mill incurred by the sewage works, Brown was typically forthright:

> I am quite sure judging from their (the Board's) past conduct (which I consider to have been exceedingly disgraceful) that if any power is placed within their hands, that it will be abused – some are proverbially well versed in the art of flattery and invective, and indulge in the one, or the other, as it best meets their purpose, but no confidence can be placed in the professions of such men . . . [90]

This small-minded conservatism became even more pronounced the following year when Brett, Anstee and Sole retired and were replaced by three shopkeepers, Frederick Davis, Gustavus Jordan and Samuel Lane. All three men were elected on a ticket of opposition to the levying of a special district rate and they gained reinforcement the following year with the election of Joseph Hawkes, who supported them. This was coupled with the second defeat of A.J. Tansley, an advocate of the rate, who according to the *Luton News* 'lost some of his previous supporters by having publicly denounced existing nuisances and other malpractices'.[91] The position of the anti-rate group, however, still remained that of a minority and this was undermined still further by Lane's failure to attend meetings regularly. It was no surprise that he lost his place after a year when the durable Tansley was re-elected and assumed the Chair.

The issue of the special district rate was one of the few issues around which a party gathered to fight elections, and even this appears a tame affair when compared with the antagonisms of the early 1850s. The 1861 election, which was fought over this question and which resulted in the election of three supporters of the rate (John Cotchin, A.J. Tansley and Samuel Toyer), was conducted 'in a most orderly and respectable manner'.[92]

There was no issue confronted by the Board which resulted in a polarisation of economic interest or political allegiance. Although the upper middle class were abandoning the Board of Health, the petty bourgeoisie did not possess the necessary means by which to assert control over it. The shopkeepers, representative of small ratepayers, never acted as a cohesive force dividing amongst themselves upon particular issues, a feature which applied also to the hat manufacturers. No occupational group dominated: for the most part the local Board comprised individuals, not parties. Luton at this stage possessed little in the way of party political organisation and it was in this vacuum that the Board limped on, in fits and starts.

The major effort on the part of the local Board of Health from the late 1850s to the early 1860s was devoted towards the complete paving and curbing of Luton's streets. A loan had been secured for £2300 but the Finance Committee's report in February 1858 concerning the Board's slender finances prompted it to levy a special district rate of 10*d.* in the pound. The result of this was the election in March 1859 of three men (Jordan, Davis and Lane) who campaigned against the rate and the bringing of a case by Davis at the Quarter Sessions, disputing the rate's legality. Undeterred, the Board resolved to collect the rate, taking legal counsel from Frederick Day, a Hemel Hempstead solicitor.[93] Day's advice was to proceed with the rate and take legal action against those who refused to pay, hoping that this would deter the rest.[94]

The Board's Minute books do not provide details of the difficulties the collector experienced in pursuing those who refused to pay the rate, nor their identities. That he had considerable difficulties is apparent but, although divided, the majority on the Board persisted in resolving to redeem the rate.[95] They, therefore, had little choice but to resist also a further appeal to the Quarter Sessions by Davis.[96] The issue was finally settled by the victory of three advocates of the rate (Cotchin, Toyer and Tansley) in March 1861 over three opponents of it (Allen, Lane and Pledge) in the highest poll for at least eight years. At the first meeting after the election, on 2 April, the Board passed a compromise resolution allowing those ratepayers who undertook to pave the areas adjacent to their property to have the cost deducted from the amount of the rate for which they were liable. Whilst this still left the problem of dealing with ratepayers who would neither pave nor pay, it was sufficient for Davis immediately to withdraw his appeal.

In 1859 the local Board applied to the General Board of Health for confirmation of its bye-laws. Comprehensive in range, these covered the following areas: the level, width, construction and sewering of new streets; the structure and safety of walls within buildings; the ventilation in and around buildings; the closing of buildings unfit for habitation; drainage; the halting of construction or even pulling down of any buildings erected in contravention of the bye-laws; the prevention of nuisances; the regulation of slaughter houses; the cleansing of streets; the removal of refuse; and the cleansing of privies.[97]

As Luton continued to develop, an increasing amount of the Board's attention was devoted to the inspection of building plans in which it appears to have been diligent. The bye-law concerning the width of party walls on new buildings required that they should be a minimum of nine inches.[98] The builder W.H. Attwood was warned that legal proceedings were being considered against him for allowing occupation of cottages in John Street before the Surveyor had certified that they were ready for habitation.[99]

Much of the credit for the Board's conscientiousness through all its tribulations rests with its surveyors. Joseph Keyte was active in the period 1860–61, making a number of inspections and reporting nuisances to the Board. Heading the list of problem areas was, naturally enough, Adelaide Terrace, which was condemned as 'unfit for human habitation' and requiring a number of remedial measures.[100] The Medical Officer was also making inspections and his findings were reported in the local press. The *Luton Times* summarised his conclusions thus: 'One of the most important social reforms that could be effected, is the entire destruction of the hovels ... they endanger the PUBLIC HEALTH'.[101] As should have been expected such descriptions did not worry the breed of landlord typified by Henry Sibley, who made little effort to comply with the Surveyor's requests. At the same time Keyte inspected another slum, Spencer's Yard, on the opposite side of George Street to Adelaide Terrace, owned by a man named Pigg. What his tenants chose to call him can only be imagined but Pigg, like Sibley, chose to ignore Keyte's recommendations until the Board in despair voted in January 1864 to take proceedings to close Spencer's Yard. Either this failed or was not followed through, and Spencer's Yard outlived the Board.

In 1863 complaints were received by the Board alleging Keyte's 'inattention and inefficiency' in discharging his duties and he was promptly given his notice, a somewhat harsh decision.[102] Keyte's replacement was William Sandoe who, during his six years in office, was the most energetic of the Board's surveyors. Sandoe supervised an extensive programme of paving, curbing, metalling and sewering of Luton's streets, in addition to inspecting individual properties and pursuing recommendations for improvement – the installation and repair of privies and the trapping of drains, for example. In connection with his diligence the names of How, Haselgrove and Brickwood recur in an unfavourable light. Bleaching and dyeing factories were also regulated and not permitted to be built in the centre of town, an enforceable decision whilst there remained sufficient building ground on the outskirts of Luton – as there always was.[103]

Improvements to the efficiency of the sewage works were necessitated by a further injunction from John Shaw Leigh, who found that sewage had been seeping into the Lea. Dissatisfied with the Board's measures Leigh gave notice of another lawsuit in 1861, which the Board staved off by purchasing land owned by Leigh next to the deodorising works for the laying down of two large filtering beds.[104] After a visit by the clerk to the Chelmsford Board, pumps were purchased similar to the models used there.

During the 1860s there were many issues with which the local Board increasingly became identified, and identified itself, as defending the 'public' interest (or at least the ratepaying section of it). In November 1860 notice was received of a proposal to form a company to supply piped water with a reservoir on Hart Hill. Backers of this move included William Phillips, Thomas Sworder, T.E. Austin, Alfred P. Welch, and Col. Lionel Ames. The Board's response, influenced by the strained relations with the Gas Company and wary of a private company over which it would have no control, was that such works were unnecessary since 'at the present time the water supply is abundant in quantity and good in quality'.[105]

This scheme was abandoned in February 1861 but four years later a bill was again introduced to establish a Luton Water Company with (according to William Austin) the crucial support of a local bank, Sharples.[106] The branch manager, Edward Lucas, was one of the first directors of the Company – as were William Bigg, Frederick Brown, Charles Robinson and Welch. Faced with a more formidable proposal the Board first considered placing a number of public pumps around the town, thereby immediately conceding that the supply was not 'abundant in quantity'.[107] It also resolved to raise a petition against the bill and then took issue on the failure of the Water Company promoters to give a guarantee concerning the supply of water to the Town Hall.[108] Finally, the Board shot itself in the foot: in December 1864 it adopted A.T.

Webster's proposal that it should offer a premium to establish its own Water Company (Waller, Cotchin, Pledge and Pearman voted against) and then resolved to hold a referendum on the 19 December. Faced with the choice between establishing a Water Company on the rates or through a joint stock company, Luton's ratepayers chose the latter proposal by a margin of 453 votes to 67. Although the local Board remained unanimously opposed to the establishment of a Water Company, and succeeded in winning some concessions from its promoters, the referendum effectively put an end to its opposition. In 1865 the Luton Water Company was duly incorporated with its headquarters in what was to become Crescent Road.[109]

Whereas the responsibility for the supply of water was now definitely not the responsibility of the Board, the disposal of waste water most certainly was. In this field the Board of Health had more success. In 1868, the Lea Conservancy Bill threatened the Board with being obliged to change its method of sewage disposal (Higgs Patent) at the deodorising works to one which used a costly irrigation process. Having expended so much money and effort to achieve the sewage system it possessed, the Board of Health correctly concluded that the additional cost of changing the system (feared to be between £50,000 and £70,000) would be too much for the ratepayers to bear. As the bill passed through the committee stage, E.O. Williams (as chairman) and John Higgins attended Parliament daily to give evidence.[110] For once, Luton was united in its gratitude to the Board when the bill failed.

In contrast with its approach towards the Water Company, the Board of Health supported the establishment of a railway line for Luton. In this they were reflecting Luton's universal desire for a line and some Board members were active in promoting the two railway companies concerned. The railway lines did not intrude directly upon any of the Board's functions but, in particular with the work on the Midland line, it again undertook the role of the guardian of public interest. The planned route of the line carved through High Town entailing the demolition of some 90 buildings and the diversion of two roads. The Board found this 'highly objectionable' but eventually acceded to the plan in August 1865, which, whilst separating High Town Road from the rest of Luton, also removed some of its slums.[111] The Board requested that the Railway Company place a bridge across the line to maintain a link between Luton and High Town Road and repeatedly asked the Company to ensure that the bridge was maintained: when it was reported to be unsafe the Board ensured that the Company replaced it.[112] Complaints of damage caused by excavations for the Midland line were addressed to the Board who, in turn, applied pressure upon the Company.

In proceeding to assume control of Luton's markets the local Board of Health went far beyond the role envisaged for it by Edward Cresy and the original promoters, and closer to the role of a town council. The town and its main industry had outgrown the existing facilities for market trading. Each market day (Monday) virtually the entire length of George Street from Market Hill to Wellington Street was occupied by 'rickety old trestles and stalls exposing their goods and the people to all weathers in the open street'. The market was mainly, but not exclusively, devoted to straw plait. An evocative description was made of this in 1861:

> It had been described to me as something combining many features of the picturesque ... when the crowds from the country would hilariously display the golden Plait on stalls ... and cheerful matrons and smart lasses would stand quietly on the pavement, each with scores of plait hooped on their arms. It was my misfortune to see this assemblage on a morning when the rain came down with a settled determination, that destroyed all the gaiety of the scene ... every gateway that could give shelter, was filled with the poor women who brought their week's work to a certain market.[113]

With the town's main street, and all its traffic, blocked for a whole day every week it was evident that improvements were needed. In addition to this the Market House was in a very poor condition. As early as September 1859 the Board agreed to approach John Shaw Leigh in order to lease the tolls of the town which Leigh held as Lord of the Manor. This move was temporarily spoilt by bad relations caused by disputes connected with the sewage works but this did not remove the demand nor the necessity for improvements to Luton's market facilities. A public meeting was called in April 1864, under the chairmanship of Henry Brown junior, to investigate the possibility of erecting a Corn Exchange and a Market Hall. From this a committee was formed which looked at three sites (two in Cheapside and one on Market Hill on land at the rear of the *Crown Inn*), but was unable to decide upon any one.[114]

In June 1865 the Board was informed that the ageing Leigh would consider an application to lease tolls. John Cumberland appears to have been the driving force behind this move and, after representations to the Steward of the Manor acting upon Leigh's behalf, it was agreed that the Board could lease the tolls for 75 years at an annual rent of £150 on condition that the dilapidated Market House was demolished and replaced with another costing not more than £2000.

The Board opted for a controversial site for the Corn Exchange in Middle Row, the island of shops and a public house which stood on Market Hill. On a split vote (W.H. Higgins, Cumberland, Joseph Green, Shepheard and Frederick Davis for, and Pledge, Toyer and James Higgins against), the Board opted to purchase the site.[115] Those who opposed the Market Hill scheme meanwhile placed their hopes in the 1867 and 1868 elections to the 'little Parliament in Stuart Street'. Their arguments dipped below that of unnecessary expenditure to the level of accusations of 'trickery' toward the pro-Market Hill members who they claimed were seeking to make personal profit from the development.[116] Davis, whose shop on Market Hill would have to be purchased and who was nearing the end of his active business life, and Cumberland, the leading estate agent and auctioneer in Luton, were obviously vulnerable to this line of criticism – and a little of the mud stuck. Although Green and W.H. Higgins were returned at the 1867 elections, Henry Blundell, a leading advocate of the Market Hill and Plait Hall development, failed badly in his bid to win election. The following year Cumberland (419 votes) lost his place on the Board in which Toyer (722 votes) and James Higgins (1007 votes – topping the poll) were re-elected. Whilst the anti-Market Hill faction had mounted a reasonably successful campaign amongst the voting ratepayers, the electoral formula ran against them in trying to turn a six–three deficit into a majority on the Board. It was also apparent that the pro-Market Hill faction had a broader level of support within Luton, regardless of whether any member of the Board stood to make personal gain, as was amplified at a number of public meetings.[117]

The majority on the Board then voted to proceed to purchase the freehold of the tolls for markets and fairs from Leigh. At the same time the Board began to purchase land in Cheapside and Waller Street for the erection of a Market Hall to remove the plait market from George Street. The old Market House was pulled down and a temporary wooden building was erected whilst designs were submitted in the form of competition for the Corn Exchange. The temporary Market House was nearly more temporary than originally intended – it only narrowly escaped destruction by vandals on Guy Fawkes' night in 1867.[118] Surviving this, it was replaced the following year by the new Corn Exchange, designed by the London architects, Grundy and Messenger. The Luton building firm, Smart Brothers, successfully tendered for both the Corn Exchange and the Market Hall. In order to complete this programme a loan of £15,000 was requested from Whitehall and approved.[119]

Although less prominently placed than the Corn Exchange, it was the Plait Halls which drew most attention in the town. The *Luton Times* now had the opportunity to sing the praises of the Board:

> Travellers tell us no town in England is better paved than Luton; and the local Board of Health have done a great and useful work in the miles of streets new and old under their authority, but beyond all doubt their crowning achievement is the erection of the plait halls in Cheapside.[120]

An impressive procession of dignitaries, headed by the American Ambassador, Reverdy Johnson ('representing the most powerful nation in the world' according to the *Luton Times*), gathered for the opening ceremony at the Plait Halls and (in a shorter, smaller affair) for the Corn Exchange. In a day of lavish celebration it was a proud moment for the Board of Health and the supporters of the markets development scheme.

In other spheres the Board was also beginning to assume the role of the pre-eminent local authority. It subdivided itself into various committees – Finance, Gas, Deodorising and, upon the conclusion of the Market Hill transactions, a Tolls Committee. A Fire Brigade Committee was added after the Board assumed control of the local brigade in February 1864.[121] Whilst there is little doubt that many in Luton saw the Board of Health as a shadow town council, the fact remained that the Board was neither empowered or resourced to satisfy all the demands made upon it. In addition to the repeated dilemma of incurring the wrath of one ratepaying section for 'needless expenditure', i.e. meeting the demands of another district of the town, the local Board often appeared to act in an amateur, even petty way. Many Lutonians would have regarded its attempts to negotiate a low price with the Luton Gas and Coke Co. as laudable, but to others the expenditure of what one disgruntled letter writer estimated to be 'four to five hundred pounds' in a futile dispute with a local monopoly was simply throwing good money after bad. This was especially the case when the resulting *impasse* was likely to leave the town in the dark.[122] Ten pounds per annum were saved in 1859 by leaving the new Town Hall clock unlit.[123] Most embarrassingly of all, allegations in 1861 by the Board against Mr Clarke, their rate collector, regarding discrepancies in the books, were suddenly found to be false because a mistake had been made by the bookkeeper. It was not, of course, unprecedented for a local authority to be defrauded by one of its employees (John Congreve, the assistant overseer embezzled £27 in 1872 and had to be retrieved from Newcastle), but the hasty manner in which the Board jumped to the worst conclusion with Clarke reflected badly upon them and showed the lack of confidence which they had in their officers.

In the absence of anything better, therefore, and despite its inherent limitations, the middle period of its existence saw the local Board become increasingly involved with the details of everyday life: in June 1860 it resolved that anyone found writing obscene graffiti 'or otherwise' on fences and walls would be liable to a 40 shilling fine or fourteen days in prison. The Board also concerned itself with traffic problems in George Street: it ordered the forcible removal of Inskip's photographic van if he persisted in parking it in front of the Town Hall.[124] The one example of the Board raising its eyes beyond mud and rates was a message of sympathy to Mrs Lincoln and the American nation following the assassination of President Lincoln.[125]

Whilst relations with Luton Hoo improved, those with the other large landowners remained distant as the Crawley family played a remote role in the life of the town. The Board was able to enlist J.S. Crawley's support to 'use his influence' to help thwart the proposed water company in 1861 but, in the main, contact between the Board and Stockwood was restricted to clarification of land ownership around Stockwood Park.[126] There was a skirmish with Crawley concerning a public right of way over Winsdon Hill which he had stopped up, and, more amicably, an exchange of land following the completion of the Midland line which provided Luton with a park in High Town and Crawley with land between Dunstable Road and the railway upon which he built houses. The Board was a peripheral mover in this latter development in 1867. The principal institution involved was the separately constituted Moor Committee.[127]

Whilst attention was paid to multifarious aspects of Luton's affairs, it drew back from fulfilling one of Cresy's original recommendations – the construction of a public slaughter-house. This was deferred even though the Board had resolved that many of the existing facilities were 'prejudicial to the health of the inhabitants of the town.'[128]

Dying Days, 1868–76

Dogged by the same failings and controversies which had marked its first twenty years, the Board of Health imperceptibly slipped out of prominence in the minds of Lutonians. It ceased to be seen as a shadow town council when the prospect of the real thing seemed within the town's grasp. Two major undertakings featured during the latter part of the local Board's existence, one of these causing the last instance of a controversy settled by election. In August 1870, a Committee of the Board was formed to consider the desirability of erecting public swimming baths on land owned by the Board in Waller Street, next to the Market Halls, the land having cost £650. This proposal was supported by a public meeting, still officially a Vestry meeting, which resolved that the Board should 'proceed to their speedy economic and efficient construction'.[129] Following this, on 4 July 1871, the local Board of Health formally resolved to commence work, with two of the shopkeepers on the Board (Barrett and Oliver), voting against.

The decision to build public baths had split the Board and, in October 1871, Frederick Davis presented a twelve feet long petition of 367 ratepayers requesting that they not be built. Unimpressed, the members of the Board who supported the baths proposal disparaged the petition. Scanning the list, John Higgins claimed never to have heard of some of the signatories and Drewett went further, stating that he had reliably been informed that some had signed simply in order to be rid of persistent attention from the petitioners.[130] The Board's vote to continue revealed that, besides Davis, two other Board members – William Barrett and Dr H. A. Squires – were also opposed to the construction of public baths (Oliver apparently changing his position). Beyond the

Boardroom, the 'ratepayers' backlash was beginning to wind itself up. Samuel Toyer was again the guiding light for the opposition to expenditure, drawing together kindred spirits at 'one of the most absurd and ludicrous public meetings ever held . . .'.[131] Toyer's proposal for the formation of a 'Board of Health Ratepayers' Protection Society' was altered to 'The Owners' and Ratepayers' Protection Association' but the original nomenclature was essentially correct – it was the Board of Health's plans which Toyer and his supporters had their stern eyes upon. Toyer was one of the Association candidates, along with Joseph Bailey and J.W. Haselgrove: it was clear that the forthcoming elections in the spring of 1872 would decide the issue.

In contrast to the 1871 elections, passions ran high. 'No more interest was taken in the Board of Health elections last year than in the selection of an errand boy or washerwoman' commented the *Luton Times*. It was very different now. For the last time in a Board of Health election, the labels 'Blue' and 'Yellow' were used: the former campaigning for the erection of the baths, the latter, the Ratepayers' Protection Association, against. The debate cut across party political allegiance with the three 'Blue' candidates comprising John Webdale and Frank Chapman Scargill, both Liberals, and John Cumberland, a Conservative. This was also reflected in the nominations of the 'Blues' which included both Conservatives and Liberals, whilst T.C. Johnson, a former member of the Board, nominated both 'Blue' and 'Yellow' candidates. The 'Blue' candidates were formidable, with Scargill in particular being a fluent public speaker. It was clear that Luton's manufacturing and professional elite were combining to thwart Toyer and his band of small tradesmen, although their combined votes alone would not have been enough – they had to win the argument. Meanwhile, the local Board had accepted the Smart Brothers' tender of £4895 for the erection of the baths and had successfully requested permission to borrow £1250 from the central Board to complete all the necessary work.

The result of the election, in the highest turnout of any in the local Board's history, determined that the baths would be built: [132]

Elected		*Not Elected*	
John Webdale (Blue)	1214	J.W. Haselgrove (Yellow)	618
John Cumberland (Blue)	1133	Joseph Bailey (Yellow)	644
Frank C Scargill (Blue)	1039	Samuel Toyer (Yellow)	560

The other major effort of the Board was to purchase the Town Hall from the company which had built it in 1847. According to William Austin and J.G. Dony, the unsatisfactory way in which this purchase was concluded was a major contributory factor in the decision of the town to press for incorporation as a borough.[133] This is certainly true but, even had the transaction proceeded smoothly, it is unlikely that it would have made a significant difference to the development of the campaign for incorporation which was already under way. The ownership of Luton Town Hall by a public body subject to the justices at Bedford could only have acted as a spur to those campaigning for borough status, one of the main campaigning points being the establishment of a locally controlled Magistrates' Bench.

As it was, the Board initially refused the Town Hall Company's low offer of £2250 in October 1873 before finally settling at £2125 in August the following year.[134] Again, according to Austin, it seemed likely that the Town Hall would have been sold to another buyer had not two Board members, G.C.H. Lockhart and John Higgins (who was also a Director of the Company), secured a provisional contract privately and then persuaded their colleagues to take this over.

As its period of operation drew to a close the local Board remained actively preoccupied with the enforcement of building and street regulations. The Water Company was warned to repair a road (unnamed) which had been opened up for the laying of water mains; otherwise, the Board threatened to carry out the necessary work, charging this to the Company.[135] When after heavy rainfall it was discovered that the new roads in High Town had inadequate drains the Board completed the work, succeeding in obtaining £50 from the Midland Railway Company (who was responsible) in compensation.[136] In more general terms, the Board continued to clash with the public utility companies of whose monopolistic powers it remained suspicious and who, therefore, undermined the Board's own authority within Luton. It persisted in querying the price of gas, (enlisting the support of one Professor James Copcutt) and even considered building its own gas works – an idea which, had it been so foolhardy to try, would have surely brought down upon it the wrath of more than just Samuel Toyer and his confederates.[137] At the same time as this, the Board of Health was in dispute with the Water Company over the supply of water, the cost of sinking wells and gauging the level of water.[138] The sewage plant continued to give cause for concern: in October 1869 its foreman was dismissed for not ensuring that the water was sufficiently 'clarified'. Whatever the problems with the sewage works – and there were many – Luton at least found some reward in a lack of ambition. The idea of selling liquid manure, in order to recoup some of the expenditure on the sewage works, was mooted but never adopted.[139] This was in imitation of an initiative promoted by one of the more enterprising Boards, at Leicester: that city's scheme, however, eventually proved to be an economic failure.[140]

To the end, the names of Sibley and Brickwood feature in the Board's minutes, a testimony to the Board's persistence as well as to its weakness. Brickwood – by then living in Brighton – ignored demands to build privies to his Park Street properties and was presented with a bill by the Board for £20 10s. 10d. There is no record that he paid.[141] The Market Hill controversy lingered on: not all the adjacent properties had been purchased for demolition by 1871, even though this had been agreed with the owners in 1868. An 'uproarious' meeting of the ratepayers failed to decide whether the shops of Frederick Davis, W. Taylor and the late Thomas Wingrave should be purchased, but eventually the Board undertook the last part of the scheme.[142]

The fire brigade continued to be a source of occasional embarrassment despite the purchase of a new engine in 1869. Inherent weaknesses stemmed from its amateur status and were made worse by the highly inflammable (and ill-designed) nature of buildings devoted to the manufacture of straw hats. Like the Board of Health, frequently it was castigated for failings which were none of its business. 'What use is the Luton Fire Brigade?' asked the *Luton Times* after the brigade had failed to reach Stopsley, a village over which it had no jurisdiction, in time to put out a fire.[143] The *Luton Times'* suggestion of copying the London Fire Brigade's system of fining members who failed to turn out in time might have ensured a better performance than the brigade mustered in August 1873. A serious fire in a Cheapside draper's shop, half a mile from the station, had been put out by the shopkeeper and members of the public before the brigade arrived.[144]

The 1872 election for places on the Board marked the last in which a single issue (and personal abuse) created any excitement in Luton. The elections of 1874 were, according to the *Luton Advertiser* 'characterised by an amount of apathy that was almost unprecedented'.[145] By this time the attention of the town had moved to battles being fought elsewhere, chiefly to the fight for control of the School Board and to the incorporation as a borough, a series of events in which the Board of Health played no part.

The decision to apply for incorporation marked the beginning of the end for the Board although it continued to operate for another two years and three months (becoming the Urban Sanitary Authority on 25 April 1875) as the formalities for incorporation were proceeded with. The last meeting was held on the 9 March 1877 at which it resolved to be merged into the Rural District Sanitary Authority of Luton Union and its debts and property transferred to the Urban Sanitary Authority of the Borough of Luton.[146]

The Luton Board of Health in Retrospect

Assessment of the performance of the Luton Board of Health, or indeed any other Board, has to be qualified by an appreciation of the limited extent of the powers vested in it by the Health of Towns Act. Sir Edwin Chadwick, the driving force behind the Public Health Bill, watched with frustrated anger as the legislation was repeatedly compromised in order to secure its safe passage through Parliament. Thus, the emaciated powers with which the General Board of Health attempted to operate placed the onus for improvement upon local initiative and the result was that the performance of the Act differed in each area in which it was applied.

As Chadwick correctly forecast, powerful vested interests could thwart and nullify the effectiveness of the Act in many localities.[147] The Merthyr Tydfil Board of Health (formed in the same year as Luton's) was dominated by the local iron masters with the support of the smaller ratepayers: consequently 'implementation of the Public Health Act of 1848 was a half-hearted business'.[148] At Hanley, an area of the Potteries with a larger population and with greater squalor than Luton (the death rate for the district of Shelton in the period 1846–8 was thirty six per 1000), there already existed by 1850 Watching and Lighting Commissioners, Market Trustees and Highways Boards. There was, therefore, determined resistance by older authorities which regarded the creation of a new one as an encroachment upon their traditional rights and powers. The latter bodies successfully led the opposition to the proposals for a local Board and the Market Trustees continued to oppose (unsuccessfully) the move towards incorporation.[149] Similarly, at Stratford-on-Avon the old Corporation, responsible for choosing nine out of the twelve members of the Board, also operated as a focal point for opposition to the Board from vested interests.[150]

Of the limited number of localities available for comparison, it is Burton-upon-Trent and Chelmsford which bear strongest similarity with Luton.[151] With a population of 7934 in 1851 Burton, like Luton, comprised the old township plus two more recently developed areas, Burton Extra and Horninglow. The two towns also shared a similar standard of sanitation and neither possessed borough status. Edward Cresy was also the inspector for Burton (in 1853) but there the parallels end and the contrasts begin: Cresy only inspected Burton Extra and Horninglow but did not recommend the application of the Act to these areas without Burton itself. Consequently, Burton was left with the Town Improvement Clauses Act (adopted in 1853) but which proved to be a poor substitute for a local Board of Health. Both the Improvement Commissioners and the Highways Committee were 'hopelessly incapable' of dealing with the town's sewage which was polluting the Trent, and it was not until after a local Board was established (in 1863) under the Local Government Act of 1858 that various improvements to Burton's sanitation were commenced.[152] A.J. Archer's conclusion was that 'what was lacking in Burton was not the will to improve, but the power to do so effectively and permanently.'[153] For all the failings of the Luton Board, Burton's miserable experience puts a favourable perspective on Luton's performance.

Chelmsford also bore similarities with Luton. It too was inspected by

Cresy (in 1848). Here pockets of deprivation in old courtyards were contrasted with the miserable conditions in the new part of the town. Five hundred houses had been erected after 1839 (although only 300 were occupied) when land to the south of Chelmsford was sold by the Mildmay family. No building controls were exercised and contemporary descriptions echo those of Luton: houses were ill-ventilated and ill-lit, with open cess-pools and stagnant ditches.[154] Also established in 1850, the Chelmsford Board of Health, however, appears to have met with greater success than either Luton or Burton, reducing the death rate per 1000 to nineteen by 1871 (see table on page 120), and its sewage works acted as a model for Luton's Board.

A striking feature of Luton in 1850 was the power vacuum which existed in the town. There were no powerful local institutions with vested interests which could suffocate the Board; no Corporation nor Improvement Commission, no Highways Committee nor Tolls Trustees. There was, of course, the Board of Guardians but it appears to have had little contact with the Board of Health and no involvement in its affairs. The two most extensive landowners for the most part sought not to exert any influence over the life of the town. Both John Shaw Leigh and J.S. Crawley concentrated their interests upon their immediate estates. Whilst Leigh can take indirect credit for the sewage and market improvements, both he and Crawley remained inactive in Luton's affairs. Neither were there large scale industries whose owners could exercise a baleful influence over the town, forcing a local Board to bend to their will. The experience of Merthyr Tydfil could not be repeated in Luton where the town's elite were individually not powerful enough to alter the affairs of the town in order to satisfy selfish ends. Collectively, they were far more inclined to promote 'clean' issues, with, at times, a striking degree of unity. That is not to argue, however, that Luton provided typical examples of a national type. Nottingham Corporation was dominated by an oligarchy of middle-class, nonconformist Whig traders. By all accounts the majority of the Nottingham Corporation were inert, ineffective and corrupt, unwilling to court unpopularity and the possible loss of their seats by revealing and tackling the intense squalor of which they were all aware.[155] This would be a far too uncharitable assessment of most of Luton's members but it probably explains why most of the leading Luton 'Blues' stayed away from the Board, apart from specific forays in the early 1850s, in 1861 and again in 1872. They recognised that lengthy tenure of office was not compatible with effective performance: John Cumberland and A.J. Tansley were two who did not follow that approach and both suffered electoral defeat at the hands of lesser men as a result.

There is no indication that party politics played in any way an important part in the Board's affairs. In a Liberal town, that leading Conservatives such as Sworder, Williams and Cumberland could be elected, and serve as chairmen, is proof of that. Divisions and disputes in Luton on Board of Health matters took place on cross party lines. The fiercest critics of expenditure – Samuel Toyer, Frederick Davis and Abraham Hobbs – were all Liberals. What did matter was the issue of expenditure or, more accurately, effective expenditure. Comparative data is limited, but a selection of the general district rates levied shows it rising from 1s. 4d. in 1851, to 2s. 6d. three years later. By 1861 it stood at 3s., by 1865 it had been reduced to 2s. 6d., after which it levelled off at 2s. 9d. by 1872.

The early figures clearly reflect the Board's intention to spend, and do, as little as possible: the rise in the general district rate after 1854 demonstrates circumstances forcing the Board to change its approach as its membership alters also. Tansley and Bigg's grim financial report of February 1858 can be taken as much an indictment of earlier mismanagement as of the Board's current predicament. Loans secured for sewage and for paving put pressure on the Board's delicate resources necessitating a rate in December 1857 of 1s. 3d. dedicated specifically for highways, and a further one of 1s. in July 1858. The decision to levy a special district rate of 10d. in June 1859 (to offset the loan and interest for paving the town) led to two years of bitter fighting at Board meetings, the polls and the Courts. Although the more progressive elements on the Board eventually got the better of the final compromise (the Board voted to allow all ratepayers who undertook the paving of adjacent premises to have this deducted from the special district rate), the first decade of its operation, in particular, demonstrated the vulnerability of a local Board to the brand of myopic, corner-shop economics which had stifled the advancement of public health elsewhere in England.[156] Never capable of organised, sustained influence, these people had little in common except property and selfishness. The threat of their ability to organise an occasional electoral or legal backlash forever haunted the operations of the Board. Also constant was the continued sniping of those who wished the Board to undertake expenditure in their particular locality or upon their pet scheme.[157]

A more informative comparison of the Board's effectiveness can be made by observing the death rates of a selection of similar towns.[158] A qualification that must be repeated is that Luton's return covers a Registration District and, therefore, includes the Borough of Dunstable plus neighbouring villages. In Luton's case the statistics are not those of an urban area. This factor might well apply to the returns of some of the other towns and cities in the table below. The figures are as follows:

	Population, 1871	Deaths per 1000 1861–70
Chelmsford	9,318	19
Peterborough	16,310	20
Stafford	12,212	20
Aylesbury	6,962	21
Burton-upon-Trent	24,565	21
Coventry	37,670	21
Luton (and Dunstable)	21,875	21
Cambridge	30,078	22
Colchester	26,343	22
Oxford	33,292	22
Derby	64,180	23
Northampton	41,168	24
Stockport	29,931	25
Leicester	95,220	26
Stoke-on-Trent (including Hanley)	124,523	26

Luton's figures had improved since 1850, but not outstandingly so. These statistics echo conclusions already drawn, namely the larger the town, the higher the death rate, and suggest two important factors when considering the effectiveness of local Boards of Health. First, there were a number of influences upon the standard of public health within nineteenth century industrial towns: a Board of Health (or similar authority) was just one of these and rarely a decisive one. Second, with regard to Luton, in carrying out its functions the Board was fortunate that the town in 1850 was still a relatively small one. Unable, for a number of reasons, to remove existing slums and other nuisances (no public slaughter house was built as recommended by Cresy in 1850), it was able to make sure that minimum standards of good building were applied for the future. The consequence of this was that as Luton expanded the proportion of its inadequate dwellings diminished within the town as a whole. If it is also understood that rural districts generally had lower rates of mortality than urban areas, then it is also possible that a return for the township could well have been higher than the figure of twenty one in a 1000, the figure for the wider district. Regrettably, the Luton Board did not employ a full time Medical Officer of Health and so detailed figures are not available. It must also be remembered that although Luton's worst housing was very poor, it was restricted to individual courtyards and streets and never approached the same scale as towns such as Hanley, Leicester, or Nottingham (where the lack of building land served to intensify the squalor), let alone the big cities.[159] Nonetheless, individual cases of destitution and squalor lingered on, seemingly beyond the help of the Luton Board or of the local authorities.[160]

Ultimately, even the Board's inadequacies made a positive contribution to Luton's development: that it nearly failed to secure the Town Hall, that it had merely nine members, that it was subject to the Justices of the Peace at Bedford, all of these factors focused in Lutonians' minds the need for a more comprehensive representative body. At the root of the matter lay the Board's inability to fulfil the expectations of many in the town. The concept of 'public health' can cover an enormous range of services, including roads, fire prevention, sewage, building control, paving, public baths and graveyards. Yet the terms of reference for the Luton Board of Health were far narrower than this. Its attempts to cover a number of fields (such as the provision of a fire brigade), which were beyond its original remit, simply brought further disapprobation. It was also clear that the Board had a distinct lack of confidence in its officers, with the notable exception of Sandoe. There were many instances, great and small, minor and tragic, where the Board's employees failed to fulfil their duties satisfactorily. In June 1864 a workman was killed by collapsing earth whilst digging sewers in Stuart Street. At the inquest, the Coroner and jury cited the lack of supervision as contributory factors in the accident.[161] Most work for the Board of Health was carried out by private contractors, but each accident, each unattended, unlit and hazardous excavation, each troublesome navvy, was blamed upon the local Board.

Repeated failure to achieve the standards which others set for it did not relieve the Board from further representations. In March 1868, it received a deputation from the owners of the large hat factories, led by Messrs. Welch, Phippen, Kershaw and Willis, concerning the Workshops Regulation Act, 1867. These gentlemen did not oppose the principles of the Act, but feared that the factory inspectors would only visit their premises to see whether employees were working excessive hours. They requested, therefore, that the local Board of Health undertake to apply the Act to all the small workshops which, they acknowledged, constituted 'probably one half of the town'[162] Given that they felt that the Factory Act inspectors would be unable to root out the abuses of long hours of work in Luton's small workshops, it is astonishing that men such as Welch and Willis, who were amongst the better informed in the town, thought that the Board of Health would be equipped to carry out such an arduous task.

Many of the fears initially expressed concerning the detrimental effects of the Health of Towns Act were never realised. The dread of encroachment upon Luton's affairs by central government was most frequently articulated by Frederick Chase but by few others. This contrasts with other towns, notably Nottingham, which possessed more clearly defined administrative structures. Often local authorities attempted to keep central government at arms length, even going through the motions of compliance with the Health of Towns Act in order to satisfy the

General Board of Health. Little fear of London was ever articulated in Luton, a town lying just thirty miles from the heart of the capital and whose economic activity involved frequent contact between the two. Many of the large hat manufacturers, such as Richard Vyse, originated from London and many more frequently travelled there on business, and, after the opening of the railway, for pleasure.

The creation of the local Board of Health did not inhibit building in Luton: the absence of building regulations was advertised by speculators for a land sale at Caddington in 1861 (the development was not subject to 'surveys by the local Board').[163] Caddington, however, remained a small village near to the road from Luton to London, and the issue of building control (applied fairly vigorously by the Luton Board) neither inhibited the property market within its jurisdiction, nor promoted it in areas outside.

Until incorporation in 1876, Brown Brick (the streets on the western side of Park Street – Wood Street, Brache Street, Bailey Street, Kings Road) lay officially within the hamlet of West Hyde, just beyond the limits of the Luton township under the jurisdiction of the Board of Health. T.E. Austin described it as 'a suburb . . . which has sprung up within the past few years', estimating that there were approximately 1000 people in around 200 houses there.[164] Whilst Luton possessed its pockets of pre-1850 established poverty, overall the standard of public health was perceived to be lower in Brown Brick, even though many of its houses were built after 1850. Austin confessed that it was 'a source of trouble and anxiety . . .'. During another of its recurring outbreaks of fever the *Luton Times* asked one of the rhetorical questions with which it occasionally opened its leader column. 'What is to be done with Brown Brick?' was followed by a diagnosis of the fever: the district was without a Board of Health. The filth and squalor of houses erected after 1850 were in marked contrast with their contemporaries in Luton. The large property owners in Brown Brick were reported to be opposed to the Luton Board of Health extending its powers to that district.[165]

It is evident that from early on in its existence the Luton Board of Health began to evolve into a town 'council'. The main reason for this is self evident – the absence of any other local authority coupled with the clear need for one. There is, however, another deeper, and less easily quantifiable reason for this: civic pride. Disparagement of the Luton Board of Health for becoming enmeshed in affairs beyond its remit does not take into account this factor. For a quarter of a century the local Board of Health was the closest which Luton had to a town council, and those who aspired to serve upon it were determined to act like town 'councillors' in the absence of the real thing. In operating in such a way, Luton's Board of Health was no different from many other towns in a similar position. At Heaton, near Bradford, the Board of Health – 'small, impecunious and semi-amateur' though it may have been – performed in a very similar style. It subdivided into various committees (Finance, General Purposes and Waterworks to quote three examples), moved into a cottage which became the Board's 'town hall' and undertook street lighting, which it negotiated with a local gas company.[166] Public improvements in towns such as Heaton or Luton were not merely done for the benefit of the health of the inhabitants. Although lacking the dignity and status of incorporation, the erection of a market hall, the paving of a street, the lighting of a town still became outward manifestations of inward pride. They were tangible evidence of personal, as much as collective, progress.

That Luton made real improvements after 1850 (a statement which could not be applied to all of the towns mentioned above, even those with low death rates in 1871) is undeniable. The contribution of the local Board of Health, willingly or otherwise, was the major factor in this improvement, and no mere coincidence. Inconsistent, tardy, enfeebled both by initial legislation and local vested interests – all of these are criticisms which could be levelled at various times at the Luton Board with justification. There can be no doubt, however, that in the middle of the nineteenth century the Luton Board of Health made a decisive contribution to the making of a modern town.

NOTES

1. Letter in the *Luton Times*, 16.3.1867.
2. For example see Williamson, Jeffrey G. *Coping with City Growth During the British Industrial Revolution* (Cambridge, 1990); Grundy, Fred and Titmuss, Richard M. *Report on Luton* (Luton, 1945).
3. *Beds Times* 31.7.1847.
4. Complaint in *Beds Times* 17.11.1849.
5. Ibid. 1.5.1847.
6. Ibid. 13.3.1847. The pointless literary debate, much of it an exercise in sophistry, had taken up much of the correspondence column in preceding weeks.
7. Ibid. 6.2.1847.
8. Luton Union Board of Guardians Minute Book, vol. 7, BRO., PULM. 7, p. 86, 14.11.1845.
9. Ibid. p. 440, 15.1.1847; p. 444, 22.1.1847.
10. *Beds Times* 20.11.1847.
11. Luton Union *op. cit.* vol. 8, PULM 8, pp. 127–56, 27.8.1847; 3.9.1847; 24.9.1847.
12. Ibid. pp. 240–394, 24.12.1847; 24.3.1848; 14.4.1848.
13. Luton Union *op. cit.* vol. 9, PULM 9, p. 330, 10.11.1848, p. 372, 8.12.1848.
14. *Beds Times* 24.10.1846 and 18.8.1849. The newspaper's Luton correspondent noted that the sight of labourers repairing twenty yards of footpath 'created no small degree of curiosity' and that the ratepayers were 'bracing themselves for an additional levy'.
15. Luton Union *op. cit.* vol. 9, PULM 9, p. 437 19.1.1849; p. 447, 26.1.1849.
16. *Beds Times* 14.9.1847.

17. PRO MH 13/20, letter book of the General Board of Health. The petitioners were headed by Revs MacDouall and Sikes, then Charles Burr, Richard Vyse, E.C. Williamson and A.P. Welch followed. All five surgeons (Benson, Heale, Clarke, Woakes and Tomson) were prominent in the list.
18. Finer, S.E. *The Life and Times of Edwin Chadwick* (1952), pp. 299–300. According to Finer, Edward Cresy, the author of the *Encyclopaedia of Civil Engineering*, was one of a number of engineers who were 'fanatical devotees of pipe-sewers and smallness'.
19. Cresy, Edward. *Report to the General Board of Health on a Preliminary Inquiry into the sewage, drainage . . . of the town of Luton* (1850) p 3. A report of the visit was also carried in the *Beds Times* 24.3.1849.
20. Ibid. p. 8.
21. Ibid. p. 8.
22. Ibid. p. 9.
23. Ibid. p. 13.
24. Ibid. p. 20.
25. Austin, William. *History of Luton and its Hamlets* vol. 2, p. 146, (Newport, Isle of Wight, 1928). William Austin was a young relative of C.A. Austin, who may have been present at the Vestry meeting. Austin also noted that Vyse and Brickwood had already clashed in 1845 over the appointment of an assistant overseer. On that occasion Brickwood lost.
26. *Beds Times* 6.6.1850.
27. 'A conversation between a Master and his workman upon the proceedings at the late Vestry held in Luton.' (LM 5/12/29). Although the publisher of this handbill is not identified it was certainly produced by someone who was at the meeting and who took exception to the manner in which Richard Vyse was removed. It may well, therefore, have been published by Vyse himself. Edwin Brickwood is described as 'the great gun of the Vestry'.
28. The sources for the assessment are *Who's Who in the Town of Luton in 1842* (LM 8721), the accompanying map and a property valuation register of 1845 (LM).
29. Sometimes spelt 'Clark'. There were two men by the name of 'William Clarke' in Luton, both of whom were property owners and electors. Because of inconsistencies of spelling, however, it is not always possible to establish who was who.
30. *Beds Times* 15.6.1850.
31. PRO MH 13/120. The Board's reply was sent to William Clarke.
32. Ibid. 27.5.1850.
33. *Beds Times* 13.7.1850.
34. PRO MH 13/120. Letter dated 29.5.1850.
35. *Beds Times* 9.6.1849. Following Cresy's visit, Rev Sikes and Charles Austin anxiously had written to the General Board on 31.7.1849, chasing up Cresy's report. They clearly wanted to expedite matters, probably before any opposition could get going. PRO MH 13/120.
36. *Beds Times* 6.7.1850. This meeting was held at *The Cock Inn*, of which William Clarke was either the landlord or owner. This spared the expense of hiring a room at the Town Hall.
37. *11 and 12 Vict c 63, (clauses XII, X III, XX and XXX)*. Outlined in Henriques, Ursula R.Q. *Before the Welfare State. Social Administration in Early Industrial Britain.* (1979), chapt. 7, p. 136.
38. *Beds Times* 18.5.1850.
39. Ibid. 13.7.1850. An editorial comment was added to this report from the Luton correspondent – 'few towns require active sanitary measures more than Luton does'.
40. PRO MH 13/120. Letter from E.C. Williamson, 28.3.1850.
41. *Beds Times* 20.7.1850.
42. Ibid. 27.7.1850.
43. Ibid. 3.8.1850.
44. PRO MH 13/120. Letter dated 5.8.1850.

45. Finer, S.E. *op. cit.* p. 436.
46. Luton Board of Health Minute Book, vol. 1, 12.8.1850.
47. PRO MH 13/120. Letter from Chase, 10.9.1850.
48. Luton Board of Health Minute Book, vol. 1, 30.9.1850.
49. PRO MH 13/120. Letter from D.G. Adey of Markyate, 18.3.1855.
50. *Beds Times* 9.11.1850. The Board's offer was described as 'a great boon to cottage proprietors'.
51. Luton Board of Health op, cit. 18.11.1850.
52. For example, proceedings were agreed upon against Benjamin Mills of Burr Street, who erected cottages in High Town (ibid. 3.5.1852) and E.O. Williams for building in Bute Street (ibid. 31.5.1853).
53. Ibid. 16.12.1850.
54. Bailey was to serve as Clerk throughout the remainder of the Board's existence.
55. Luton Board of Health *op. cit.* 6.10.1851. William Clarke voted against and Daniel Davies, a member of the Company, abstained.
56. Ibid. 26.1.1852. Clarke voted against.
57. *Beds Times* 31.1.1852 and 7.2.1852.
58. Ibid. 26.3.1853.
59. Ibid. 29.3.1856.
60. Ibid. 11.9.1852.
61. Luton Union *op. cit.* vol. 13, PULM 13, p. 265, 17.10.1853.
62. Luton Board of Health *op. cit.* 27.9.1853, 18.10.1853–15.11.1853; Luton Union *op. cit.* pp. 275–81, 28.10.1853.
63. Luton Union *op. cit.* p. 287, 1.11.1853.
64. Ibid. p. 285, 29.10.1853.
65. Ibid. pp. 297–8, 1.11.1853–4.11.1853.
66. Ibid. p. 344, 9.12.1853.
67. All evidence was summarised in the *Beds Times* 5.11.1853 to 26.11.1853.
68. Ibid. 5.11.1853.
69. Luton Board of Health *op. cit.*. A series of reports were transcribed in full in September/October 1854. Clarke was appointed as part-time Medical Officer of Health in August 1854. PRO MH 13/120, 25.8.1854.
70. Sibley was ordered to construct privies in Adelaide Terrace (Luton Board of Health *op. cit.* 12.9.1854). At the same meeting Brickwood was ordered to construct privies in Bull Court; repairs to the existing ones plus the removal of 'offensive accumulations' had eventually been undertaken by the Board. A summons was eventually issued to Brickwood for £9 for the repair and for his non-payment of rates (ibid. 13.6.1854). Joseph Dancer appears to have been a particularly truculent citizen: like Sibley and Brickwood he neglected his property, even during the height of the cholera outbreak (ibid. 3.11.1853).
71. PRO HO 45/ OS 6006. The bye-laws ran to 71 pages. They contained the duties of officers and examples of the pages from the rate collection book and the schedule for the register of lodging houses. The scavenger's refuse cart was to pass through every street in the town twice a week from May to September 'and at such intervals as the local Board may direct during the rest of the year'. Notice of the application appeared in the *Beds Times* on 14.1.1854 and these were approved by the General Board on 8.7.1854.
72. Charges were brought against Charles Payne, a saddler, for removing privy soil and vegetable waste during the day (it caused an offensive smell), *Beds Times* 23.10.1854. Samuel Haydon was prosecuted for a similar offence, *Beds Times* 25.11.1854.
73. Luton Board of Health *op. cit.* 13.6.1854.
74. Luton Board of Health *op. cit.*, vol. 2, 7.12.1858.
75. PRO MH 13/120. A note in the margin alongside the correspondence on this matter reads thus: 'This is a case in which Mr Austin thinks the Proceedings of the local

Board should not be sanctioned. He thinks they have not behaved as they should in this matter.'
76. Luton Board of Health *op. cit.*, 1.6.1858.
77. *Luton Times* 22.3.1856. *Children's Employment Commission, 1862, 2nd Report of the Commissioners, 1864.* No. 48 p. 209.
78. *Beds Times* 11.2.1854.
79. Ibid. 23.9.1854.
80. Luton Board of Health *op. cit.* vol. 1, 25.10.1856.
81. Luton Board of Health *op. cit.* vol. 2, 9.2.1858.
82. PRO MH 13/120. Letter from George Bailey dated 3.4.1854.
83. *In Chancery. The Attorney General and J. S. Leigh, Esq., versus Luton Local Board of Health. Judgement* (1856). BRO (LHE 143). Luton Board of Health *op. cit.* vol. 1, 18.4.1854.
84. First meeting reported in *Luton Times* 5.1.1856.
85. Ibid. 8.3.1856 and 27.9.1856.
86. *21 and 22 Vict (session 1857–58).* LM (141 /66). William Phillips' annotated copy.
87. They were replaced by William Willis, Charles Robinson, Joseph Bailey, Samuel Toyer and Joseph Mead. All were opposed to the bill.
88. *Luton Times* 4.10.1856.
89. Ibid. 15.11.1856. Frederick Lawford, in a letter to the paper on 3.4.1858, referred to the town's Board of Health as 'our local parliament'.
90. Letter dated 27.9.1858. BRO (LHE 249). Writing from his home on Farley Hill, Brown was forewarning Leigh who was about to receive a delegation from the Board.
91. *Luton Times* 31.3.1860.
92. Ibid. 30.3.1861.
93. Luton Board of Health *op. cit.* vol. 2, 14.6.1859. Jordan and Allen were not present.
94. Ibid. 19 .7.1859.
95. Luton Board of Health *op. cit.* vol. 3, 4.12.1860.
96. Ibid. 20.121860.
97. Summarised in *Luton Times* 19.2.1859.
98. Luton Board of Health *op. cit.* 17.4.1860. Davis, Bailey and Lane, although Toyer supported Jordan's resolution.
99. Luton Board of Health *op. cit.* vol. 4, 24.5.1864.
100. Luton Board of Health *op. cit.* vol. 3, 14.6.1860.
101. *Luton Times* 2.6.1860.
102. Luton Board of Health *op. cit.* 17.2.1863.
103. *Children's Employment Commission, 1862, 2nd Report of the Commissioners, 1864.* No. 43, p 208. Evidence given by Charles Lutes, blockmaker. Lutes added 'The Board is very expensive, but I suppose it is good'.
104. Luton Board of Health *op. cit.* 22.11.1859 and 27.7.1861.
105. Ibid. 20.11.1860.
106. Austin, William *op. cit.* p. 181.
107. Luton Board of Health *op. cit.* vol. 4, 27.10.1864.
108. Ibid. 11.11.1864.
109. Most of the Water Company's archive is deposited at the BRO (X739). Lea Valley Water Company still retain some material. The buildings in Crescent Road were demolished towards the end of 1987.
110. *Luton Times* 2.4.1870.
111. Luton Board of Health *op. cit.* 3.2.1863. It is not known what happened to the tenants.
112. Luton Board of Health *op. cit.* vol. 5, 28.5.1867.
113. Knight, Charles. *British Almanac and Companion, 1861.* Quoted in Austin, T.G. *The Straw Trade.* (Luton, 1871).
114. *Beds Times* 24.5.1864.
115. Luton Board of Health *op. cit.* vol. 4, 27.11.1866.

116. *Luton Times* 16.3.1867.
117. Luton Board of Health *op. cit.* This meeting of the Vestry empowered the Board to undertake the necessary purchases as long as expenditure did not exceed £15,000. Sums beyond this would require a further meeting.
118. Austin, W. *op. cit.* p 183.
119. Luton Board of Health *op. cit.* vol. 5, 16.7.1867. This was not the design which gained first prize in the competition. Grundy and Messenger had submitted another design and this had come second.
120. *Luton Times* 19.1.1869 and 23.1.1869.
121. Luton Board of Health *op. cit.* vol. 4, 16.2.1864.
122. *Luton Times* 18.9.1858 and 25.9.1858. The correspondent placed responsibility on the Board of Health for failing to come to terms with the Gas Company.
123. Ibid. 6.8.1859.
124. Luton Board of Health *op. cit.* vol. 3, 17.4.1860.
125. Luton Board of Health *op. cit.* vol. 4, 24.4.1865. A message of thanks was received from the American legation on 16.5.1865 and on 4.8.1868 the Board received copies of 'Tributes of the Nations to Abraham Lincoln'.
126. Luton Board of Health *op. cit.* vol. 3, 20.2.1861.
127. Metcalf, Sheila. 'The Provision of Parks in Nineteenth Century Britain.' *University of London* M.A. thesis. pp. 123–7.
128. Luton Board of Health *op. cit.* vol. 4, 19.12.1865.
129. Luton Board of Health *op. cit.* vol. 6, 20.6.1871.
130. *Luton Times* 14.10.1871.
131. Ibid. 8.7.1871. Toyer received a kind press from the *Luton Times* on just one occasion – his obituary.
132. *Luton Advertiser* 30.3.1872. The *Advertiser*, a Conservative newspaper, supported the 'Blue' party. It previewed the election on 23.10.1872 with extremely unflattering pen-portraits of the three 'Yellow' candidates whom they described as being 'a most dangerous party'. Toyer was accused of a public career devoted to self-service and of Bailey it wrote 'We trust that whoever has the welfare of the rising generation of Luton at heart will show their appreciation of Mr. Jos. Bailey by placing him the position he deserves.'
133. Austin, William *op. cit.* p. 187 and Dony, John G. 'How Luton Became a Borough', *Bedfordshire Magazine*. Vol. 15, pp. 135–40.
134. Luton Board of Health *op. cit.* 14.6.1874, 30.6.1874 and 11.8.1874. The minute book does not give full details of the saga.
135. Ibid. 21.12.1869.
136. Ibid. 23.11.1869, 18.11.1870 and 3.8.1870.
137. *Luton Times* 21.5.1870.
138. Ibid. 16.7.1870.
139. *Luton Times* 12.4.1856.
140. Elliot, M.J. 'The Leicester Board of Health, 1849–1872. A Study of Progress in the Development of Local Government.' *University of Nottingham* M.Phil, (1971).
141. Luton Board of Health *op. cit.* 2.12.1873 and 14.6.1874.
142. *Luton Times* 9.9.1871.
143. Ibid. 5.3.1870.
144. Ibid. 30.8.1873.
145. *Luton Advertiser* 28.3.1874.
146. *40–1 Vict. Ch. xxii. Provisional Order for dissolving the Local Government District of Luton.* The Rural Sanitary district of Luton pertained to those remnants not included within the urban Borough of Luton.
147. Sir Edwin Chadwick in a letter to Lord Landsdowne, 13 July 1848. Quoted by Finer, S.E. *op. cit.* p 324.
148. Jones, Tydfil Davies. 'Poor Law and Public Health Administration in the Area of Merthyr Tydfil Union 1834–1894'. M.A. thesis, *University of Wales* (1961), p. 260.

149. Townley, W.E. 'Urban Administration and Health. A Case Study of Hanley in the Mid-Nineteenth Century'. M.A. thesis, *University of Keele* (1969).
150. Penny, R.I. 'The Board of Health in Victorian Stratford-upon-Avon. Aspects in Environmental Control'. *Warwickshire History*. Vol. 1 no. 6, 1971. p. 11.
151. Archer, A.J. 'A Study of a Local Sanitary Administration 1830–1875.' M.A. thesis, *University College of North Wales* (1967).
152. Ibid. p. 108.
153. Ibid. p. 102.
154. Thomas, E.G. 'Chelmsford and the Board of Health Report of 1849' (journal source unknown). This article covers the events leading up to the formation of a Board of Health in that district.
155. Church, Roy A. *Economic Change in a Midland Town. Victorian Nottingham 1815–1900*. Chapt. 8, 'The Reformed Corporation and Urban Society'. (1966).
156. Luton Board of Health *op. cit.* vol. 3, 2.4.1861.
157. It would be nigh on impossible to list all the attacks made upon the Board of Health for its 'inattention' or every ludicrous idea which was promulgated. An example is this complaint in the *Luton Times* on 12.3.1870 concerning Liverpool Road which, apparently, was 'in a state bordering on ridge and furrow, with holes deep enough and wide enough to bury a good size quadruped'. Almost immediately the candidature of Dr Squires of Liverpool Road was announced. Squires was successful in gaining a seat on the Board and the work on Liverpool Road was carried out in February 1871.
158. *Thirty-fifth Annual Report of the Registrar for Births and Deaths* pp. 190–203, Annual Mortality (Deaths to one thousand Living, 1861–1870).
159. Church, Roy A. *op. cit.* pp 162–72. Woods, Robert. 'Mortality patterns in the nineteenth century' in *Urban Disease and Mortality in Nineteenth Century England* edited by Robert Woods and John Woodward (1984).
160. In September 1871, Mr Gardiner, the Relieving Officer for the Luton District of the Union, found one family in Ainsworth Passage, Park Street living in dreadful conditions. The mother, son (aged twenty-seven), daughter (twenty-two), son (seventeen), son (thirteen) and 'idiot' son (eleven) were 'sleeping on the floor of one bedroom having scarcely any clothing and no bedding'. *Luton Times* 9.9.1871
161. *Beds Times* 7.6.1864.
162. Ibid. 7.5.1868.
163. *Luton News* 20 July 1861. The advertisement was entitled 'Bargains for the Working Man'.
164. PRO MH 13/230. Letter dated 30.11.1870.
165. *Luton Times* 15.10.1870. The following week a Brown Brick resident (and landlord?) responded, less convincingly, that the fever in the district was caused entirely by the stench from the Board's nearby sewage works.
166. King, J.F. 'The Heaton Local Board. A Victorian Authority'. *Bradford Antiquary*. Third series, (1985), pp. 31–7.

Chapter Three. Society: Belief and Behaviour

> *It will be readily admitted by all persons conversant with Luton, that there is no place in the county, and I almost said in England, where there is greater independency of thought and action, or a freer or more unrestrained expression of opinion of every kind and shade, whether having reference to civil, political, or religious considerations.*
> (Letter under the heading 'Luton – Its Polemics' *Beds Times* 19 January 1850)

The twenty years following the ending of the Napoleonic Wars had seen a new town created. The economic structure, the community, the topography and the very character of Luton was altered irrevocably by new forces, new demands, new people. Chapter one has shown how the old market town elite of farmers and squirarchy largely disappeared from active involvement in local life. It was replaced in the mid-nineteenth century by a new society reflecting the economic life of Luton – vibrant, open and unstable. If not great fortunes, then certainly comfortable livings could be acquired through activity in the straw hat and building trades – and also swiftly lost.

This chapter will seek to investigate the manner in which physical change was matched by changes in belief. It will endeavour to pursue this by following a thread which begins with religion (which formed an undercurrent to so much of nineteenth century belief and behaviour), through leisure, self-help, perceptions of crime and anti-social conduct, temperance and, finally, education. The establishment of Luton's first School Board occurred two years before the town achieved borough status and the febrile bitterness experienced during the education debate doubtless influenced those promoting incorporation when formulating their tactics. This chapter is, therefore, concerned primarily with the ethics and conduct, less with the structure (political developments are dealt with in chapter four). The focus will be upon the pre-eminent social force created by the town's economic expansion, its middle classes of hat factory owners, workshop masters, shopkeepers, clergymen, publicans and so on. It will seek to analyse the changing morals and conflicting ideologies by highlighting the major concerns of the day.

Luton's aristocracy withdrew behind the walls of their estates. In particular, John Shaw Leigh, by far the richest man in the locality, wished to play little or no part in Luton's affairs. An outsider, he had purchased the Hoo, not the town, and he wished to enjoy the life of a country squire which good fortune had brought him. The peculiar structure of the local hat industry inhibited labour organisation, thereby removing a potential forum for heightened class awareness and possible conflict. It also left those Luton males who sold their labour in a position which was disorganised, transient, marginalised and ignored. In so far as the poor come into the reckoning in nineteenth century Luton, it was as the focal point for programmes which were thought to be good for them, and indirectly, therefore, as a source of conflict between those of moderate wealth.

There are features of Luton's social structure which blur the lines between classes, conspiring to obscure the threads from which broad observations can be made. In historic terms, the most visible and easily defined, Luton's bourgeoisie of large factory owners, the clergy, bank managers and the professions, remained small. In 1850 they probably amounted to little more than 100 individuals plus their families, in a population of some 10,000. Comprising the bulk of the town's population were two broad groups of male occupations, the small retailers and independent producers on the one hand, and those who sold their labour on the other. Women, operating frequently as home builders and plait sewers/dealers, straddled both categories, and it was not unusual for men to alternate between the two according to fortune or season.

There are a number of general observations which are worthwhile making at the outset. First, Luton in the mid nineteenth century was a mobile society – physically, economically and socially. This was a mobility which blunts retrospective suppositions of class and ideology. Asa Briggs' definition of the greatest division in Victorian society was between those who were able to employ domestic servants and those who were not. It is impossible to provide a definitive calculation of how many in Luton employed live-in domestic servants all year round. Partly this is because the functions between 'bonnet sewer', 'lodger' and 'female servant' could easily be blurred – but it is apparent that few in Luton could afford one or were inclined to do so. In terms of housing, as seen in chapter one, the method of land disposal and urban development in Luton led to a high degree of intermixing between people of widely varying lifestyles. The social exclusion which became a feature of cities such as Leeds and Liverpool does not occur here, consequently depriving Luton of distinctive suburbs and ghettos. With many of the wealthiest Lutonians such as Henry Brown and William Bigg living close to their business in the town centre, Luton did not witness the development of a 'carriage society', marking them out as distinct from their pedestrian fellow citizens.[1]

Second, a caveat must be applied when studying Luton's shifting social structure as it is clear that perceptions of identity shift with time. For example, a council election meeting held in March 1876 at the Primitive Methodist Church, High Town, comprised a company of self-professed 'working men', seeking like minded candidates to represent their interests. They saw no discrepancy between that designation and their occupations – shopkeepers, small manufacturers (usually hats), publicans and the like – even though modern historical analysis might regard them as forming the backbone of the local lower middle class. Success in trade could provide a moderate but still noticeable social mobility and it was easy for a man to carry his origins with him, all the way to the detached villa, wearing them as a proud measure of how far he had come. Asher Hucklesby, the richest of Luton's hat merchants in the late nineteenth and early twentieth century, stands as a good example of the sort of social advancement which was possible. Although there were few rags to riches stories, relatively rapid social elevation was possible, however, through a few good years in business. There were many who revelled in their new social standing.

Connected with this aspect of Luton life, care must be taken not to impute motives either to individuals or groups. In a town with such a poor literary tradition as Luton this is compounded by the fact that there is precious little data of any sort to support hypothesis, but the perceived character of the town does provide some pointers. For example, the Hart Hill district on the south-eastern corner of the town developed in the late nineteenth century as a middle class enclave – the closest the town possessed at that time to a distinctive suburb. Yet even within tiny Hart Hill (numbering no more than approximately thirty similar detached houses by 1900) there were subtle nuances of perceived superiority. This was based, in part, on how close one had the misfortune to live to the railway sidings at the foot of the hill but there were other influences at work also. Whilst Luton's small bourgeoisie of larger manufacturers may be reckoned by modern readers to share common interests and objectives, from contemporary perspectives this was not necessarily the case. One second-hand oral recollection from around 1900 recalls how the children of one of the managers of a new engineering firm were forbidden to play with the children of one of the larger hat manufacturers on the grounds that 'they were trade'. Perceptions of being 'different' to one's neighbours ran through every class, every district and every street and this was especially the case in a small town such as Luton with merely fledgling bureaucracies and organisations. Individuals matter more in such places.

An issue which has pre-occupied many historians of the middle class in recent years is the issue of social control. This is a debate revolving around the degree to which institutions, philanthropy, religion and various social causes were manipulated for the imposition of a set of values upon the poorer sectors of society. Following this line of thinking, therefore, education becomes a mechanism for indoctrination; the provision of public facilities through joint stock companies a method of exclusivity; philanthropy a vehicle for self-glorification. In each of the sections where this issue is relevant the validity of this argument will be considered, although in a town such as Luton, where individual activity was more pronounced than collective action, this is not an easy motivation to perceive. The bias away from official organisation, the lack of formal structures and, it must be stressed, the absence of very rich businessmen with close control over large workforces limits the degree to which social control could be applied to Luton. The middle classes in Luton, rarely its upper strata, (and virtually never the petty bourgeoisie), were men and women who gave scant evidence of being bound together by common interest and identity.

The workshop based economy produced its own peculiar set of ideas and values, almost as if freedom of thought and action in the processes of production gave rise to a preference for nonconformist Protestantism and radical politics. Taken as an over-simplification this could distort the fact that there were other forces operating in the town, but at face value this applies to Luton to a very striking degree. For example, the town was ideally suited to the cult of domesticity, a feature of nineteenth century religion and philanthropy. Related to this, Luton possessed some of the characteristics of a frontier town, being devoid of amenities, untidy, unplanned, uncouth and in parts reckoned to be quite hostile. All of these features encouraged a retreat into the sanctuary of the home where it was most likely to find security, comfort and familiarity. Many people in Luton did not possess deep local roots nor the wide family network to be found in long established communities, having little more than the nuclear family around them. These factors were reinforced by the domestic oriented nature of many businesses, whether manufacturing, wholesale or retail, and the absence of formal social institutions abetted this introspection. In a bewilderingly changing world the home was one of the few places over which an individual could retain control. For many it served as the sole manifestation of the work of a lifetime, and as such its sanctity (from punitive local rates) was to be jealously guarded.[2] The commercial and social world of the average Lutonian was a largely hidden one.

As seen in chapter one, Luton's old social elite disintegrated between 1835 and 1860. The Lord of the Manor quit, disposing of his assets in the process, whilst the Established Church barely sputtered out of its slumbers. With the town physically and economically transformed, this did not so much leave a void to be filled as provide a stimulus for the establishment of a new ethos. Leaving aside the politics of the town for now, Luton's Protestant denominations served as the focal point for many people's social activities. They were the mouthpiece of collective opinion and vehicles for reform in the mid-nineteenth century.

SOCIETY: BELIEF AND BEHAVIOUR 133

Part One. Religion and Philanthropy

As Luton industrialised, it also became more conducive to the 'moral entrepreneurship' which took root in Britain's middle class parlours in the late eighteenth and early nineteenth centuries. Locally, the dissenting Protestant denominations were able to expand unfettered by competition from the Church of England. Bereft of active support from the local aristocracy and gentry, and with its traditional rural source of support being eroded by urbanisation, the Established Church lay in a state of utter torpor for the first half of the century. In a town of 10,000 souls, the consequences of this, by the time of the Ecclesiastical Census of 1851, are laid out in Table 3.1.

Table. 3.1. Ecclesiastical Census. Attendance returns for Luton churches [3]

	30 March 1851			Average over previous 12 months		
	AM	PM	EVE	AM	PM	EVE
St Mary's						
General						
Cong.	550	450	1200	600	800	–
Scholars	400	422	130	400	450	–
Old Wesleyan (Church Street)						
General						
Cong.	90	–	48			
Scholars	200	–	–			
Wesleyan (Chapel Street)						
General						
Cong.	600	330	640			
Scholars	58	270	–			
Primitive Methodist (High Town)						
General						
Cong.	500	900	900	200	350	400
Scholars	178	178	178	178	178	178
Total Methodist Cong.	*1190*	*830*	*1588*			
Society of Friends						
General						
Cong.	70	49	–			
Ceylon Baptist (Wellington Street)						
General						
Cong.	430	–	750			
Scholars	200	–	–			
Old Meeting (Park Street)						
General						
Cong.	516	–	621	600	300	700

Union Baptist						
General Cong.	555	555	850	500	250	900
Scholars	450	400	–	450		
Ebenezer Baptist						
General Cong.	150	142	65			
	(130)	(160)	(70)			
Scholars	69	72				
	(62)	(77)				
Total Baptist Cong.	*1651*	*697*	*2286*			

The Church of England

The fortunes of the Established Church remained at a low ebb for much of the nineteenth century, a factor caused in part by a succession of absentee or short-lived incumbents.[4] Charles Henry Hall, Vicar of St. Mary's from 1804 until his death in 1827, never appears to have again preached in the church after his induction. He was succeeded by a relative of the Marquess of Bute, William MacDouall, with Thomas Sikes becoming curate at the same time. MacDouall's most notable act in a twenty year tenure was to remove the old pews within the church and replace them with new ones which, according to Cobbe, separated 'the congregation into classes according to their grade in Society'.[5] Like Hall, MacDouall chose not to live at the vicarage, residing instead at nearby Copt Hall and leaving nearly all the work to Sikes. He refused to allow the church to be lit with gas and consequently in winter evensong took place in the afternoon. By 1850, having had no active vicar within living memory, the spiritual life of the church, as well as its fabric, was in a poor state. Comment was made about the poor standard of singing and music.[6] Upon the death of MacDouall, coinciding with the removal of the Bute interest in the town, the advowson was purchased on behalf of Sikes by some of his friends. For eight years from 1835 Sikes had served as Rector of Puttenham, Herts, leaving unanswered the question as to who had actually carried the Anglican interest in Luton as the town was transformed.

Upon succeeding MacDouall in 1850 Sikes, who had married into the Burr family and was active in local affairs, began to raise the profile of the Church of England. The large numbers apparently attending evensong on the day of the 1851 census suggests how deep was the reservoir of potential support for the Established Church. Immigrants from the rural hinterland would in all probability possess at least a nominal Anglican allegiance. Plans were made to carve out a new parish from the unwieldy St. Mary's to cater for the growing town. Sikes was vicar for just four years, after which he exchanged pulpits with Rev Thomas Bartlett of Chevening in Kent. Bartlett continued Sikes' work. He established Christ Church as a distinct district on the northern side of the township, this eventually becoming (in 1860) a separate parish. The support of the Crawleys appears to have been tapped in order to finance the new venture but the church building itself, opened in 1857, almost immediately presented problems having been built upon the site of recently exhausted clay pits. Bartlett appointed two curates, with one taking responsibility for Christ Church. By dividing the town into districts he was able to instigate a programme of door-to-door visiting. Many clergymen were to be overwhelmed by the effort of ministering to the needs of Luton and Bartlett was such a man: after just three years he found the task 'too onerous' and quit. With Bartlett's resignation the Church of England's revival fizzled out. Bartlett's successor, the scholarly Dr Thomas Williamson Peile made little impact in his three years and his successor, Rev G. Quirk, lasted just fourteen months. A ballot of worshippers (over a choice of times for the morning service) in March 1861 drew 123 votes which, even allowing for a substantial number of abstentions, indicates that a church able to seat 2000 was attracting a pitiful level of support from parishioners. It is reasonable to also question the validity of the high attendance figures of ten years earlier.[7]

Quirk's successor (in 1862) was to very nearly see out the century. For some, Rev James O'Neill was the most remarkable figure to appear in Luton's public life during the whole of the century. For others he was simply the most odious. He was born in Kerry, Ireland, and lost his wife during childbirth whilst they were missionaries in Ceylon. Having served as a curate in Devon, O'Neill came to Luton where he concentrated his energies in a wholesale restoration of St. Mary's (described in 1864 by the *Beds Times* as 'eerie, bleak and desolate') as well as the further subdivision of St. Mary's parish into Limbury and Biscot, St. Matthew's and St. Paul's. All this work, however, was of minor significance compared with the abrasive manner in which he conducted his ministry in other fields.

It is not necessary to record here every battle which O'Neill fought, nor every personal vendetta which he pursued, but for all the extensive restoration of the church building itself it is questionable whether O'Neill's aggressive style restored the spiritual fortunes or the credibility of the Anglican church. This fact has been supposed locally and certainly occurred at a national level in the second half of the century. The cause of Anglicanism in New Town, for example, could not have been helped by an acrimonious and petty dispute instigated by O'Neill in an attempt to force out Rev C.N. Harris of St. John's College, Cambridge. Harris had established a successful, independent, 'Wooden Church' in Albert Road and he also ran a private school in Stuart Street. The dispute was apparently caused by the fact that Harris had married his late wife's sister (an act contrary to the Prayer Book), but no doubt it was also caused by O'Neill's determination to maintain control over religious developments within the Anglican community. By June 1867 O'Neill was appearing before the local bench charged with assaulting his own churchwarden, Samuel Oliver. A verger who gave evidence against O'Neill was promptly dismissed and when Oliver resigned his office O'Neill gave the once prestigious post to Thomas Dunn, the vicarage gardener.[8]

For a man attempting to gather Anglican support around him O'Neill's tactics were, to say the least, bizarre. John Shaw Leigh and J.S. Crawley, men upon whom, above all others, O'Neill relied for financial assistance and personal example in the restoration programme, were so alienated by his behaviour that they refused to serve as churchwardens at St. Mary's.[9] The ageing Leigh proffered the excuse of physical incapacity as reason for refusal to serve, but O'Neill compounded his problems by going to press, a tactic which he rarely could resist. On this occasion he made bitter sideswipes at the two gentlemen and especially towards Leigh, whom, he sarcastically noted, was still able to 'mount his horse at a meet of hounds'.[10] A condemnatory vestry meeting called in support of Oliver did not deter O'Neill (who refused to attend). William Willis, who was his main critic here (and on other occasions), was, according to O'Neill, just talking 'an inordinate amount of bosh'.

Some nonconformists might have sniggered uncharitably as the dispute between O'Neill and Oliver lingered on, fuelled by a sideshow in which O'Neill was simultaneously sued for libel by Shepheard, Oliver's solicitor. By July 1868 O'Neill was facing legal action by Crawley for blocking up the access to the chancel. Legal action was repeated nine months later in a dispute between the two over money for the church restoration.[11] One of the most combative clergymen ever to step into a pulpit, O'Neill is credited with the much needed restoration of St. Mary's, a task which was largely completed by the time of his death in 1896. It is legitimate to wonder, however, how swiftly this work might have been completed had not O'Neill antagonised so many of those who could have featured amongst his natural allies. He had his supporters, who, in the wider sphere of local politics, saw him as a staunch bulwark against the spendthrift inclinations of the nonconformist liberals in Luton, and he improved greatly the quality of the music within St. Mary's. The fact remains, however, that he also alienated many within his own parish.

Of far different disposition was the Rev T. Jones Lee, vicar of Christ Church from 1862 until his death in 1875. Lee was O'Neill's confederate in the formation of the Luton branch of the Church of England Defence Society but kept his distance from his abrasive colleague in other religious and secular matters. This included the School Board issue: although Lee also opposed its formation, he preferred to organise his own tactics. The low profile Lee, together with the other Anglican clergymen in the district, were probably more embarrassed than encouraged by O'Neill's style of ministry. Although O'Neill reformed the content of Sunday services it is difficult to imagine that many could really warm to such a man (Thomas Sworder was an exception). Consequently, it is unlikely that attendance and support for St. Mary's greatly increased, although Christ Church was enlarged under Lee's ministry.

Nonconformity
By the middle of the nineteenth century Luton was the most nonconformist town in England.[12] At the time of incorporation there were four Baptist chapels and one Primitive Baptist chapel (in New Town). The spire of a Congregational chapel, an off-shoot from one of the Baptist churches, towered over King Street. There were Primitive Methodists in High Town with small Methodist outstations on the Hitchin Road and at Brown Brick. Five Wesleyan chapels existed and the Society of Friends had a meeting house at the bottom of Castle Street. Even if the local Anglican church had been in better shape than it was, Luton would still have been a fertile ground for the Dissenters. The correlation between the independent Protestant churches and a 'work ethic' has already been noted by many writers from Weber onwards, a thesis which can be greatly exaggerated in significance.[13] At one level, however, free from the oppressive disciplines of organised production in factories, free from the disapproving glare of clergymen in positions of secular power and free from the coercive peer pressure set by the gentry, people possess greater liberty to think for themselves. This fact was reflected in Luton not only in the strength of the mainstream nonconformist churches but in the number of other sects and independent churches that were scattered around the town. In Luton this factor was undoubtedly accentuated by the weakness of the Established Church and the withdrawal of the old elite from the affairs of the town.

The ethical synthesis between commercial life and evangelicalism – good stewardship, hard work, honesty, self-discipline, sobriety, punctuality, plainness – all suited a town the commercial nature of which precisely required these standards of personal conduct. So much of Luton's trade, the purchase of quantities of straw plait for instance, relied upon the above virtues, particularly honesty. Furthermore, in a town experiencing great social upheaval, where many were rootless and livelihoods often precarious, the teachings of the active Protestant churches provided reassurance, motivation and a sense of wider perspective. No matter what were an individual's circumstance, day-to-day conduct could be seen as possessing a value. Personal redemption, evangelising, setting an example, Christian service – all of these could be lived out through private, public and business life. Activity in both commercial and domestic spheres could embrace thrift, duty and cleanliness. The nonconformist churches, shorn of the rigid class structure which had crumpled into irrelevance in Luton, offered a philosophy which was attractive to so many.

Interlocking with personal conduct was the collective identity which nonconformity provided Luton, a town which often appeared only to be a community in the sense that it was a collection of family homes and production units. The myriad social events and meetings which the churches provided must be appreciated in this context. Barely a week passed in the mid-nineteenth century without Luton's newspapers carrying reports of a tea meeting, invariably in support of a cause associated with one of the Methodist, Baptist or Congregational churches. This may have been a specifically church-oriented act of philanthropy such as a tea provided for the poorer members of the Baptist Meeting House or an attempt to raise support on a wider secular front, such as the Aboriginal Protection Society.[14] In a town lacking recreational facilities the churches served as a social forum, and in the absence of the machinery of local government the churches also did much to fill this gap by acting as a focal point for discussion, agitation and mobilisation on particular issues. It is a great shame that not even a handful of sermons from some of the ministers who filled Luton's pulpits have survived. Did the perceived symmetry between cleanliness and godliness entail support for the provision of public baths in the town referendum? This may be supposed, but without firm evidence it is not easy to state with certainty how firm the churches were in supporting 'clean' issues.

The evangelical and social impact of the nonconformist churches relied, to an even greater degree than the Church of England, upon the energy, ability and integrity of their minister. Despite the transient nature of an incumbency, contrasting with the permanence of the officers and congregation (which set the basic social and theological tone of the church), it was through the pastor that a church succeeded or failed. Progress, therefore, on the vast new Wesleyan church in Chapel Street ebbed and flowed during the 1840s according to the drive of the circuit minister. Building work on the new chapel faltered after Rev John Crofts left Luton in 1846 and, with two weak men following him, did not gather momentum until the advent of the aptly named Rev Wright Shovelton in 1851.[15]

An even more outstanding example was Rev Henry Burgess who flashed, fizzled, and finally flopped across Luton's religious and social scene in the 1830s and 1840s. Burgess became minister at the Baptist House in 1831 at just 23 years of age. He was a fine preacher or, more specifically, a persuasive speaker, and seems to have made an excellent early impression. With no local newspaper, Burgess began a monthly (secular) news sheet and he became involved with various railway schemes that were then being mooted. From his home at the Bury on the outskirts of town he ran his 'Grammar School' and was the driving force behind the early days of the Mechanics Institute and Harmonic Society, both of which met on the church premises. What were Burgess' motives? Working in isolation from his contemporaries he appears to have been driven by a mixture of altruism and a desire to embellish his own *curriculum vitae*. Although his warning of a 'levelling' tone within the Mechanics Institute hints at an innate conservatism, there is no evidence to suggest that his various activities were designed to impress his personal ideology upon others, and in practice he was not sufficiently well organised to formulate any such strategy. Neither did he elicit the support of like-minded men. Sadly, the substance did not match the early promise and Burgess' cavalier approach to spending other people's money undermined his position. William Drewett, a Quaker contemporary, recalled that 'poor people let him (Burgess) have money to invest for them but that trust he betrayed and failed'.[16] The Sunday School anniversary collection was pocketed by Burgess and spent 'as he saw fit': the money which he was spending was placing this once big church in debt.[17] Divisions within the church led to a split to form the Union Baptist Church in 1836 and, more acrimoniously, to the formation of Wellington Street Baptist Church in 1847. Edmund Waller provided the necessary financial prop, personally clearing the debts, but clearly things could not go on as they were. In 1848 the Baptists paid Burgess £250 on condition that he leave. He reluctantly accepted and joined the Church of England in 1850, enjoying a subsequent career successful enough to gain an entry in the Dictionary of National Biography.

Burgess' successor, John Jordan Davies, reinvigorated the church (down to 173 members in 1849). He made changes to its theocratic structure, introducing new posts of assistant deacon and deaconess (a suggestion of John Everitt). By 1852 there were 307 members. A number of these were wooed back from the breakaway church in Wellington Street, an indication of how mobile religious congregations could be and how shallow might be allegiances to churches, the minister often being the principal attraction. Ill-health forced Davies to resign in 1857 (he died a year later) but his rebuilding work was carried on by Rev Thomas Hands, although the office of deaconess was removed. Davies was one of many ministers who found the Luton air too much for their health and that of their families. Hands' successor, Rev Genders, quit after six years to live in the gentler climate of Portsea for precisely this reason.[18] Rev Henry Wonnacott took on the incumbency of the Congregational church in King Street in 1870 at the age of nineteen, but was forced out by ill-health four years later.

The great vitality which, according to Bradley, the evangelicals in England were losing in the mid-nineteenth century (to be replaced by 'a good deal more cant and a great deal less practical piety') was still apparent in Luton. The churches were reflecting a town still experiencing the pangs and momentum of industrial development occurring later than in many other parts of the nation, and which was to continue for most of the 1860s and 1870s. There was no market for revivalists such as Moody and Sankey whose visit to the town in 1875 was not well supported.[19] Luton's chapels were still on an upward curve by 1876, and a number of new causes were spawned by their central bodies in the late nineteenth and early twentieth centuries. Vibrant ministries were needed to fight the good fight against social evils as well as to keep the money coming in. Congregations were certainly prone to mobility, not just within denominations. Richard Vyse attended both the Old Meeting and St Mary's. The ebb and flow of attendance at the latter church suggests that its congregation may have acted similarly to Vyse, but maybe this was from one and then to another, over more definite periods of time, rather than on a weekly basis. Religious roots in Luton were not deep.

Some churches were clearly richer than others, to a certain extent reflecting class divisions between the chapels. The Primitive Methodists in High Town, who with the Ebenezer Baptist Church probably contained the highest proportion of working class support, in their early days required the women members to sell plait to help fund the preacher's stipend.[20] At this time the Luton correspondent to the *Beds Times* speculated that the 'enormous sums lately subscribed to places of worship about to be erected' were having a detrimental effect upon investment in the hat industry.[21] It is not possible to test the accuracy of this statement but it does touch upon a distinctive factor which comes into play in terms of the provision of public facilities of all types in Luton: there was none active in the locality who had access to vast fortunes and the drive for church building placed great demands upon the resources of their supporters. An example of this is King Street Congregational Church formed in 1864 by an amicable split from the Union Chapel. Probably the richest of all the chapels it contrasted sharply with High Town's 'Prims', drawing its leading figures from professionals, manufacturers and builders. These included A.J. Tansley, Charles Robinson, Dr Woakes, William Cotchin, Hugh Gunn, Arthur and George Smart, William Sandoe, A.T. Webster and Charles Tomalin. To these were added John Everitt when he became estranged from Park Street Old Meeting. The 42 founder members who seceded from Union faced an initial cost of £1150 to secure the land and to begin building what was an ambitious architectural project in terms of external features and internal fittings. Although £2500 had been raised by May 1865 costs continued to increase, eventually reaching somewhere between £7000 and £8000 by the time of opening in April 1866. Such a commitment (a loan was required) placed great pressure upon the personal resources of people who, although containing a substantial number of comfortably off middle class, could not turn to any one with vast wealth. Ministers who provided nothing but 'cant', a dilettante (like Burgess) or a bullying oaf (like O'Neill) were luxuries which the nonconformists could ill-afford. The Congregationalists needed a church builder and this they found in the Rev James H. Hitchins, who added over 200 members to the roll by the time he left in 1870.[22] It was the narrow margins upon which Luton's churches operated, as much as their theology and the instability of the town, which gave them their dynamism.

This point is aptly demonstrated by contrasting the burgeoning Baptists and Methodists with the Society of Friends. By the mid-nineteenth century they had become rigid, narrow and insular, relying upon the support of a handful of wealthy people – the Brown, Marsh, Green and Pearman families in particular. Luton, Leighton Buzzard and Hitchin were embattled strongholds in an area in which the Quaker fortunes were swiftly declining. In some respects the Society of Friends represented pre-industrial Luton, its old trades (malting and milling) and the stability, values and practices of a market town. Luton Monthly Meeting (MM) incorporated St. Albans by the time of the Religious Census but undertook no recruiting evangelism whatever. Its active members preferred to direct their energies into promoting the cause of literacy, arguably the most effective form of social action conducted by any religious group.

For much of the mid-nineteenth century, the presiding figure at Luton MM was grocer John Foster. He was recalled as a small, wiry man nicknamed 'Old Pinch Plum' because of the excessive precision which he brought to his business activities – even to the extent of removing individual raisins from the scales when selling to customers. William Drewett recalled that '... he usually waited for one and a half hours before commencing and then spoke for a quarter of an hour the message being usually heralded by a sonorous trumpeting from his nose to which he applied a large silk handkerchief held in both hands and which effectively called attention to what invariably followed.' Such meetings must have been tortuous to the younger Friends and Samuel Drewett recalled walking with his parents to the Luton MM from their home in Park Street against the tide of people going to the Baptist Meeting House and with whom Samuel was forbidden to mix. Until 1859 marriage before a priest would result in disownment, and doubtless local intolerance continued long after this. 'I am sorry to say that as a rule, they were an uncharitable set of persons' wrote Samuel and it is little wonder that in later life so many of the younger Friends kicked over the traces. The case of J.W. Green is one which provides an example laced with an irony which Foster would not have appreciated. As one of John Foster's grandsons, Green benefited from his will when the old man died in March 1864. This he used to build up a highly successful brewing business, eventually renouncing his Quaker and Liberal roots for the Conservative Party and the Church of England. The sons of wine merchant Daniel Pearman (died 1857), Henry and Frederick, squandered his fortune within a generation, indulging in the good life and expanding the brewing side of the business 'regardless of expense'. Pearmans were swallowed up by J.W. Green and Henry also joined the Church of England.[23] The generous, liberal spirit of William Bigg does not appear to have fitted comfortably with the prevailing narrowness at the Luton MM and the town's first Mayor was not an active member amongst them. Whilst the Quakers peacefully declined, other sects established themselves in Luton. Amongst the minor local groups, the Roman Catholics had planted roots by 1846 and the Mormons were meeting in 1851.[24]

There were numerous examples of co-operation between the churches but links were largely informal and joint efforts *ad hoc*. Secular campaigns, such as the promotion of education or incorporation, would involve ministers and their congregations but were not directly sponsored by individual churches or ecumenical organisations. This was entirely natural in a small town where personal relationships were a significant bond. When the Baptist Old Meeting House was destroyed by a gale in February 1866, temporary accommodation was offered to the displaced congregation by the Methodists as well as by fellow Baptists (but not by O'Neill or Lee). The greatest Baptist preacher of the day, Charles Haddon Spurgeon, visited Luton to preach at a service to raise funds for a new Baptist chapel a year later and this service was held at the 1800 seater Wesleyan Church in Chapel Street – described as a 'Cathedral of Methodism' – as no Baptist chapel in Luton was large enough to house the expected congregation.[25] Relief funds for the alleviation of suffering and provision of cheap bread were established during the depression of 1855–6 and this was repeated in 1867 when further recession necessitated another relief fund. The £700 collected by January 1868 included subscriptions from ministers of all denominations (but seemingly nothing from O'Neill) who presumably promoted subscriptions within their churches.[26] Similarly, cross-denominational was the Luton Female Town Missionary Society, an earnest, if short-lived example of middle class evangelism. In November 1855 it was able to report over the previous year nine visits to workrooms, 1006 to individual houses and the greatest achievement of all – 'two couples living unlawfully have been induced to marry'.[27] Attempts at formal ecumenical organisation were usually brief and were not sanctioned by church leaderships.[28]

Relations between the nonconformists were cordial and informal, but those between the Dissenters and the Church of England were another matter altogether. The abrasive nature of O'Neill's ministry did not help matters, but things were bad enough before he arrived. Care must be taken not to exaggerate the depth of the schism between the two wings of Protestantism. Anglicans and nonconformists worked together well enough at a personal level, serving with one another on Luton's various social and political institutions. Debates within the town usually transcended religious lines. The issue of the proposed church rate in the 1830s, which was successfully defied by the nonconformists, did much to define the parameters of Church of England power. If problems arose it was usually where one wing was attempting to resist a perceived encroachment by the other on what it considered were its own rights. Almost any issue was a potential source of dispute: they squabbled over the denomination of the workhouse chaplaincy and the establishment of a town cemetery is probably the best case in point (see chapter two).[29]

The 1851 Religious Census returns indicated that approximately half the population had attended church on the Sunday evening of the day in question, and a third in the morning. This suggests that the observance of the Sabbath in Luton was greater than the national average (47% as against 40%). The striking difference is revealed in comparing the relative strengths of the nonconformists and Anglicans, nationally and locally. Basing the figures upon the evening returns, 11.27% of Luton's total population were at their pews in St. Mary's in the evening. This compares with the Anglican national average of 21%. The nonconformists in Luton on the other hand attracted more than 30% of Luton's population to their evening services, compared with a national average of just over 19%. This imbalance probably does not reflect the Church of England at its lowest ebb: Sikes was already making an impact and had the census been taken six to ten years earlier the gap between the two could well have been greater.

It could be easy to dismiss the nonconformist churches, standing proud and solid within the fabric of the town, as bastions of bourgeois values and virtues. This, however, would be an exaggeration, since there certainly was a substantial, although indefinable, proportion of working class people within the orbit of the church, even if not formally members. That organised religion had a wider social appeal than has popularly been supposed is supported by the limited evidence available, including a list of members of Wellington Street Baptist Church in 1871.[30] Amongst the identifiable occupations were (in no particular order) sewers and finishers, plait dealers, drapers, labourers, builders, hat manufacturers, grocers and carpenters: in short, a reasonable cross section of Luton's population at the time. What is especially striking, however, is the gender imbalance contained within the membership. Of the 313 names listed for Wellington Street in 1871, no fewer than 277 were women, at least 56 of whom were unmarried. A further 54, at the very least, were women who were in membership without their husbands. Some of these women were widows but these figures indicate the attractiveness of church life for unattached females. There they could find companionship and an escape from the isolated confines of home: Miss Rudd, for example, was a 53 year old dressmaker who in 1871 lived at home with an aged mother who seemed to be entirely in her daughter's care. At church also were to be found positions of service, authority and responsibility.

The leaderships of the biggest churches, however, (especially the deacons and elders), were overwhelmingly drawn from the middle classes, with a distinctive leaning toward its upper strata in some churches. With a few exceptions, they were all men. It was not extensive education or exalted social origin, but existing status, which gave individuals standing amongst their peers. It was a sign that socially rather than spiritually a person had achieved something of note. For example, the deacons who supported Rev J. Hitchens at the Congregational Chapel were all men who owned prosperous businesses in the heart of town: G.M. Johnson was a provision dealer with outlets in Wellington Street, Bute Street and Chapel Street; Charles Robinson was a hat manufacturer with premises on Market Hill; W.T. Coates was a Park Street draper; Charles Tomalin was a baker, also in Park Street; and two George Street hat manufacturers, A.T. Webster and Hugh Gunn. Any random sample of Luton's leading citizens would reveal that most played active and prominent roles within the local dissenting churches. The values that these men (usually of business) brought to the chapel, and in turn absorbed from it, permeated throughout Luton's life and affairs. Inevitably such men shaped a chapel to reflect their own values. Architectural design, pew rents and Sunday 'best' reinforced the image that a man had carved himself a niche in a new society. The proud standing of an individual within a church, and the physical position of the temple itself, could be regarded as a rewarding symbol of enterprise, thrift and hard work. It is not possible to know whether it simultaneously alienated some of the poorer people within Luton.

There is ample evidence that many within the middle classes were acutely aware of a barrier between the poorest sections of Luton's population and the rest – even if they remained ignorant of the causes. The sporadic speculative property developments from the 1840s had provided Luton with a high degree of social intermixing within districts, yet there remained a marked degree of ignorance about the manner in which neighbours lived. Luton's poorest streets were regarded as impenetrable, dark, mysterious places where the light of the gospel did not shine. An 1859 editorial from the *Luton Times* succinctly encapsulated this concern.[31] It recommended a visit to the weekly police court (in the awe-struck nature of a trip to the zoo), there to witness the 'haggard, dissipated victims of vice and evil passion'. It continued:

> Probably there are many good people in this town . . . who know very little of the condition of their neighbours. Seeing little of those outside their own circle except in the well-dressed and orderly assemblies of church and chapel . . . they are unaware of the seething mass of moral pollution which in their own immedi-

ate neighbourhood is continually throwing off its deadly poison, and spreading its fearful infection.'

In praising the work of the Gaitskell Terrace School (see part four), Dr Clarke and some nonconformist ministers, the editorial suggested that a few more of the town's leading citizens should visit the poorest streets of New Town and High Town. As a consequence 'many good easy people who are quite satisfied with things as they are, and think they have done their duty to society and to God when they have bestowed their accustomed charities and paid their annual subscriptions, would perceive that there is much yet to be done'.

This editorial touches on another level of wide concern: in the process of urbanisation the close proximity of people exposed them to the 'contagious' nature of poverty and of its associated 'vice and evil passion'. This was not particularly a dread of hordes of dissipated labourers storming the railings of middle class homes (although that was occasionally alluded to), but that the social diseases associated with poverty would contaminate the respectable working class.[32]

Christian middle class disquiet at this state of affairs revealed itself in a number of spheres – education, policing and temperance in particular – but as institutions the churches also sought to evangelise in those districts which they felt were in need. Such attempts, well-meaning though they most certainly were, revealed the gulf that existed between the classes: it showed scant understanding of people's needs on the part of the churches. There were broadly two approaches. First (and the more common) was to establish a separate mission hall or even a church within the district. The second was to send a missionary out into the field, the aforementioned Luton Town Female Missionary Society was one such venture. Another example of the latter was the appointment of a 'Town Missionary' to the affluent King Street Congregational Church.[33]

The unidentified missionary – earnest, sanctimonious and hard working – made a total of 2348 individual visits in less than two years between 1872–4. He followed a clear strategy, visiting an identifiable range of streets spread across Luton, notably Adelaide Terrace, Chase Street, Tower Hill, plus numerous High Town courtyards and side streets. The missionary placed emphasis upon individual visits, in particular praying with (or preying upon) those on their sick-beds to whom the next world seemed more imminent. In between he led cottage meetings and took services at various Baptist and Methodist churches, as well as at King Street. It was a depressingly uphill struggle with few conversions to encourage the naive missionary in his labours. 'The want of suitable clothing' was repeatedly offered as a reason for non-attendance at church. This was not merely a lame excuse but rather an expression of the sharp degree of alienation between the poorest and the rest. This was clearly articulated by the people in Chase Street who openly stated their desire for their own chapel.

The missionary was ill-equipped for the task, able to offer no practical advice in response to stark problems. 'In conversation with a milkman at Tower Hill he told me it was impossible for him to be religious and live; if he did not tell lies in his trade, he should starve'. The missionary's response offered neither help nor hope – there was little point in the milkman feeding himself and his family if in the process he lost his soul. Another man lost to the church. Usually he was confronted by apathy and excuses. In Adelaide Terrace he preached in the open air – 'some of them listened for a while and then went away'. On other occasions he was greeted by outright hostility. A woman living at Amen Corner (in Church Street) was 'much insulted' to be presented with a gift of a dress. When the missionary called and wished her 'good morning', the following altercation took place:

> (Woman) 'I don't want none O' yer blab'
> (Missionary) 'Will you accept a tract?'
> 'No, I don't want none o' yer blab, there's nobody here as does.'
> 'I am sorry for you.'
> 'I don't want you to be sorry for me.'
> 'Well, we will pray for you.'
> 'You want praying for yourself as much as ever I do.'
> 'I know it, I will pray for myself and you too.'

The Missionary's journal continued:

> I then stepped inside the door to put a tract upon the chair hoping she might read it after I left. 'You shan't come inside the house' she said and took the tract, threw it out of the door, picked it up, tore in the middle and slammed the door in my face. She sat within hearing during the whole of the open air service sometimes mocking and sometimes singing in a low tone. The Lord grant that his own word may reach her heart.

Although the heart of the woman in question was apparently 'softened' by illness, this episode encapsulates how the difficult nature of the task was made all the harder by well-meaning but insensitive acts of charity which failed to comprehend the fundamental reasons for poverty or to provide any practical alleviation of it. The resentment of those being patronised in such a way is hardly surprising given the blundering and occasionally offensive way in which some from the middle class approached the intended recipients of the gospel. The *Luton Times*, applauding the establishment of a local branch of the Wesleyan Home Mission Society prepared to work in Luton's alleys and back streets, commented: 'Preachers in pulpits can never do this; sermons are no good for this evil. The dregs of Society will never come to the fashionable chapel'.[34] Charity was frequently accepted, but simultaneously resented as this recollection by Aubrey Darby, a Lutonian born at the beginning of the twentieth century indicates:[35]

> On Good Friday invitations went out to attend the free breakfast. To qualify for the meal one must be the offspring of poor parents. So a multitude of children gathered outside the Congregational Church. Inside, the elders prepared the feast. The Church, a massive structure of grey stone was noted for its high steeple, and gazing aloft we imagined the spire would fall down upon us before we could crowd into the depths of the crypt. Breakfast was a bowl of porridge, an orange, a bun and much salt to flavour the 'skilly', the providers believing this repast would sustain us on the road to salvation. We showed our appreciation by flicking the manna in all directions, like the pauper's lament over his Christmas pudding, if we were to accept charity, something more substantial than a bellyful of porridge would have to be more forthcoming. Before the feast we chanted 'May the Lord make us truly thankful', most evident after the telling of the crucifixion, when we stormed up the stone stairs into the warmth of a cold Good Friday morning.

The other tactic that could be adopted was to plant a mission church within a district. This was especially important in a town whose economic structure deprived the chapel going middle class of sustained contact with the working class through the workplace. Cynically, this sort of development could be regarded as an attempt to fulfil evangelistic duty whilst maintaining the rougher world of the working class as a separate entity, at arms length from the demure sensibilities of the main congregation. It is evident, however, that there was a level of demand from communities such as Chase Street for their own centre for worship, and an awareness of the limited appeal of the vast 1000 seater chapels was recognised on both sides. Mission work, nonetheless, represented hard graft on largely infertile ground and, as in most spheres of life, there were few who were prepared to get their hands dirty. Apathy was by no means the only problem. The Union Baptists had attempted a mission in Chase Street as early as 1847, opening a hall there largely due to the initiative and funding of A. J. Tansley.[36] There was a degree of local support for the mission but the early work was undone by the rift in manners and modes of behaviour between the promoters and the congregation – 'the work was hard and very rough, those who attended having the freest idea as to their liberty of speech and conduct'.[37] The boisterous, and in middle class eyes, uncouth behaviour of the indigenous congregation led to an abandonment of the missionary work although the hall remained in the hands of the Baptists until the work was taken over by the maverick Baptist councillor, Charles Haddon Osborne, at the end of the century. The attempt by Rev Harris to establish a working men's church in Albert Road was also well supported until undone by the sustained animosity of O'Neill.

A substantial proportion of the working class remained, therefore, impervious to the good intentions of middle class patronage. At least two churches, the Ebenezer Baptist in New Town and the Primitive Methodist in High Town, appeared to possess quite significantly different backgrounds from the other nonconformist chapels not only in the make-up of the congregations but also (in the early days at least) of their leaderships. The ministers of these two churches played a notably less prominent part in the public life of the town. The Primitive Methodists had established themselves in High Town through the zealous work and charismatic preaching of two men from the Aylesbury circuit, Rev Henry Higgins and Rev Samuel Turner. The pitch of their appeal, and that of successive ministers, appears to have been specifically to the working people in that district, although it is not known whether they attracted working people from elsewhere in the town. Consequently, for many years they were the only church of any denomination in the area.[38] A presence in High Town from the other nonconformist churches did not come until the end of the nineteenth and the beginning of the twentieth century, again being initiatives of the mission variety instigated by individuals.

So much of middle class evangelical philanthropy was spasmodic, unco-ordinated and largely ineffectual, the Poor Man's Club serving as an example of something which failed to sustain its effort over much more than the short term.[39] The temptation to make sweeping and dismissive assumptions as to its aims and motives, however, must be resisted. It is wrong to impute motives to a great many unknown individuals, long dead, ranging from the leaders of meetings, societies and missions, to the thousands who attended and placed a few coins in the offertory box. Then, as now, people lent support to what they saw as good causes within their own locality, and further abroad, for a variety of reasons: to show off their own wealth; to raise themselves up in the sight of their peers; to score points to be used at Judgement Day; for feelings of guilt; because of pressure from others; for reasons of pure altruism. There were, no doubt, many Mrs Pardiggles who would march into the home (but would be less likely to dare to go to the workplace) and harangue a resentful working class. There were surely also examples of Snagsbys, Chadbands and Jellybys. Undoubtedly, there would also have been Jarndyces (albeit in a smaller way) and most likely of all, people were motivated through a combination of factors. If a form of social control was a primary motivation for evangelism and philanthropy then one is led to wonder why the middle class, with all the power and resources of society at its disposal, did not perform more effectively than it did.

Part Two. Leisure, the Secular World and Self-Help

The field of learning, with its powerful religious and social connotations and significant political overtones, is dealt with separately (see part four). Education apart, it must be acknowledged that, beyond church life, the extent of facilities within Luton was extremely meagre. Beehagg noted that much working class culture remained a largely hidden entity, immune to the attentions of middle class evangelists (and later scholars). Whilst there is probably much in this, the utter dearth of evidence concerning the secular world of the working class points to the conclusion that little existed beyond the public house and whatever the home environment contained.[40] A second point to consider is the suggestion that the provision of the means for recreation and leisure have been regarded as another form of social control. 'The provision of leisure facilities and cultural diffusion had become the concern of rich and powerful citizens' stated Helen Meller, referring specifically to Bristol. Temperance, educational, medical, youth and environmental work in that city were all dominated by a small group, interconnected by social, religious and political ties. From this general observation stems an argument that all forms of social provision were used as a mechanism, in the words of MacLaren, 'by which the whole society was regulated and shaped in an attempt to create an environment in which middle class respectability could flourish at all levels in the social structure'.[41]

This viewpoint has a very limited mileage with regards to Luton, although members of the middle classes were involved in all spheres of local life. The first and rather obvious point to make is that if the provision of leisure served as an example of social control, then in Luton there existed precious few mechanisms for exerting an influence over 'the dregs of Society'. Two distinctive features concerning Luton are also important here. Already it has become clear that Luton's bourgeoisie was of insufficient size and inadequate financial means to be able to exert the influence of, to quote a Bristol example, the Wills family: no Luton entrepreneurs ever received the national recognition of a knighthood. The formal associations, potential vehicles for the exertion of middle class control, necessary in a large town or city for the dispensation of medical care or the provision of libraries, did not exist in tiny Luton, where individual, informal contacts could still be maintained.

The lack of facilities for working class social organisation should come as no surprise in a town where many would be migratory workers in transient, seasonal employment. Neither was the lower middle class, working in isolated retail and manufacturing units, placed in a much better position to establish strong social institutions. A branch of the Royal Industry Lodge of the Independent Order of Oddfellows,

Manchester Unity Friendly Society, was formed in 1842, and a second formed in 1853 by approximately twenty men at a meeting in the *Foresters Arms*. By 1859 the older lodge comprised 202 members and was able to give support to 60 widows and 40 orphans. The younger lodge contained 121 members supporting 63 widows and possessing a half yearly income of £207. 4s. 0d.[42] Three courts of the Ancient Order of Foresters were established in 1843, 1861 (at the *Wheelwrights Arms*) and 1864.[43] By 1875, the first of these (court 'Benevolence') had 517 members. Self-help and respectability were the bedrock of these organisations, reinforced by a strong internal discipline: two Foresters found to have taken part in a prize fight in the 1860s were each fined 20s.

Records of these organisations no longer survive, preventing a thorough assessment of their social and occupational membership. Some of the prominent members of the Oddfellows, however, contained middle class professionals as well as shopkeepers and craftsmen. These included Charles Austin (solicitor), Charles Ellis (saddler), F.J. Clarke (surgeon), William Flower (baker), George Rutland (hat manufacturer) and Thomas Smith (tailor). The founder members of the first Foresters' court comprised eleven shoemakers, two tailors, two bakers, three blockers, a carpenter, a groom and two labourers. At the next meeting these men were joined by, amongst others, George Bailey, Charles Maffey and Henry Sibley. Both Bailey and Maffey served as secretary of the court until Charles Loot took over the position in 1858. This may have been the same individual identified as Charles Lutes, the blocker at Vyses who gave evidence to the Children's Employment Commission in 1862 (see chapter two, n.103). Either way, Loot was a striking example of Victorian autodidactism. Originally a blocker, Loot later established his own hat manufacturing business in Park Street. Much of his self-teaching was concentrated upon book-keeping. This social and economic elevation was more than just a testimony to self-help: Loot apparently paid members' fines and arrears from his own pocket, something which a less affluent leader of a friendly society would not be in a strong position to do. Apparently a kindly and generous individual, Loot served as secretary for 43 years.

Of other contemporary organisations, little is known. A Co-operative Association was formed in 1860, although this appears to have lapsed after a few years. As with the various lodges the limited evidence available suggests that its supporters drew principally from the independent producers and retailers.[44] The Luton Rifle Volunteer Corps drew upon a similar social background. It was formed in 1859 during a scare of possible invasion by the armies of the French Emperor, Napoleon III. Letters had appeared in the national press (criticising milliners in general) and the local press (criticising Lutonians in particular) for not being prepared to raise a force to defend the nation. The (printed) reply to this was straightforward enough: small businesses could ill-afford to lose men to military activity. In any case, war was bad for the local economy, destroying supply sources and export markets.[45] Eventually, sufficient numbers were motivated to form a local corps in April 1860. This did little of note, except, allegedly, disgrace itself at a fete at the home of Lady Frankland Russell by brawling with members of other corps.[46]

Luton's economy was founded upon independent enterprise: a society governed by liberty of thought and action was, in many respects, a logical extension of this. In a town built in such an unplanned manner by small scale developers (operating upon narrow margins), it was almost inevitable that there would be a dearth of communal recreational facilities. This factor was reinforced by the intense seasonal demands on time by the hat industry and the home-oriented values imbued through the churches. In what swiftly became an unattractive town, bearing the character of a large building site, the most comfortable place beyond the chapel or beer house was the home, although for some the beer house would have been preferable to either. Luton swiftly developed a tradition where sustained social organisation, beyond the embrace of the chapel, was very rare. The bucolic institutions of the old market town faded with the onset of industrialisation and the dissenting Protestant ethics which accompanied it. Little evidence survives which sheds light on the nature of the character of pre-industrial Luton. The Agricultural Society had lapsed into inactivity by 1854 and, if the bacchanalian Soaksters Club (only rule – no 'low quarrelling') lasted to the end of the 1850s, it wisely kept its profile low and away from the disapproving glare of the burgeoning temperance movement.[47] The two outstanding institutions of the market town, the fairs and the alehouse, were caught up in specific issues which warrant separate investigation, but other contemporary organisations attracted minimal support and frequently relied upon the enthusiasm of one or two individuals. The Vyse and Burr families propped up the Luton Horticultural Society in the 1840s, particularly after a disastrous year in 1845 when it rained at every show. The Luton Harmonic Society gave performances or soirees at the Town Hall to enthusiastic, but small, audiences until it hit upon the idea of annual Peoples' Concerts. These, providing programmes of popular music, attracted audiences of 300 packed into the Town Hall.[48]

An authority able to promote and plan facilities for recreation and socialising was not the only deficiency from which Luton suffered. The small workshops, less regimented than the large factories, not only diminished the potential for middle class control of leisure but also the opportunity for its paternalistic promotion, a factor which was so important for the development of sport and recreation elsewhere in Britain.[49] The bigger factories sought to act in this way, Welch and

Son taking 100 of their bonnet sewers to the Great Exhibition in 1851, and Munt and Brown organised cricket matches (with a tea) between their Luton and Dunstable branches.[50] Those in the direct employ of large factories, however, represented a minority of the working population and consequently relatively few were able to enjoy these benefits. In any case, many of the large hat factories were branches of London concerns and not fully controlled by local men. Neither did Luton possess a prominent public school presence which elsewhere also did much to initiate the development of mass participation sports such as rugby and soccer. There is a record of one football match being played between the Collegiate School and Villa School but nothing else.[51] Either code of football was rarely played, certainly not on an organised basis. Occasional horse racing events were mounted on the outskirts of town, but the principal sport played was cricket. Again, this was not organised in the form of leagues and cup matches, but *ad hoc* teams representing rival public houses, factories, trades (for example, 'butchers' versus 'bakers'), streets or 'married' versus 'single'. These matches involved middle class and commercial interests rather than those from the labouring class and were played on a ground between Park Street and St. Anne's Hill. The town lost this facility with the arrival of the railway in 1862, which cut right through it, and was not to gain an adequate replacement until the acquisition of People's Park in the late 1860s and the building of 'Bramingham Shott' by F.C. Scargill at the same time. Scargill, a keen cricketer, laid out a fine pitch alongside his house and even had his own team, Scargill's XI.

Virtually no record, written or oral, survives of working class recreation which, given the absence of recreational facilities and opportunity, was restricted to the public house, street or home. Varieties of street gambling, such as 'Crown and Anchor', were apparently popular in Chase Street but being illegal it is hardly surprising that records should be so scarce.[52] Dances were held in barns at the rear of public houses such as the *Roebuck Inn* or the *Antelope*, but details of these only appeared in the local papers when they degenerated into brawls which ended before the magistrates' bench. The General Cemetery was popular as a park where people could promenade at the weekends. Admission, however, was by purchased ticket which served to keep this largely a middle class preserve. In a society which contained, as will be seen, such a high rate of illiteracy amongst its working class there would be little point in written public announcements of events, oral communication being far more effective.

Organised entertainment was, therefore, largely provided by outside bodies. These included visiting theatre groups (often unlicensed), exhibitions at the Town Hall, circuses and other travelling attractions such as Wombwell's Menagerie. Swimming baths existed in New Bedford

Road in the 1840s and baths of a sort in King Street in the 1860s, but these were small and relatively few could afford to use them. Various proposals were mooted by individuals for the establishment of public baths, one of which got as far as the foundations being laid (also in New Bedford Road) before the scheme was abandoned. It was 1872 before public baths were built, credit for which lay mainly with the Board of Health, who remained resolute in the face of stiff opposition.[53] A Gymnastic Society sprang into life in 1873 but had lapsed through lack of support within three years. By 1875 Luton boasted one public bath hall and one public park. There was no theatre until 1880 which, like the baths, saw a number of abortive schemes before one reached fruition. Few would disagree with Henry Wright, when he complained at a public meeting (called to discuss the lack of educational facilities in Luton), that for most people nothing existed between the church on the one side and the public house on the other.[54]

Luton had, therefore, become an outstanding example of the spirit of free enterprise and individual initiative. In the first stage of industrialisation, the termination of which can be marked by incorporation, a crude but nevertheless truthful assessment could be that if an activity bore no profit, then it was regarded as not worth undertaking. The Board of Health, the outstanding public body within the town for the promotion of improvement, was only established by outside intervention, as was the School Board. People were attracted to Luton by the opportunities to make money rather than because it was an appealing place in which to live. It was not until the 1870s that the town acquired the maturity represented by stronger public bodies, public buildings and a diminution in the momentum of growth of the cottage economy. Bedfordshire's largest manufacturing centre remained a place where 'the influx of strangers is really extraordinary. The most unusual and peculiar features are seen in the streets, and shops are opened by people whom nobody knows.'[55] Luton was an urban monument to hard work and self-help but facilities to aid the quality of life came a poor second to making money, as Wright observed. As to the manners of the place, one self-styled 'old Lutonian' lamented in 1850 that visiting buyers 'are almost pulled off their coach by touters and deafened by the din of outstanding claims'.[56] Brash, brisk and unplanned, Luton rapidly became a town in which (to use a modern phrase), people lived to work rather than worked to live.

Part Three. Crime and the Temperance Movement

Whilst experiencing an evolution in its economy, Luton also began to acquire different standards of acceptable behaviour. The extent of the adoption of these is debatable, but it is clear that these clashed sharply with those of the world being left behind. This was most clearly witnessed in the simultaneous assault upon anti-social behaviour which climaxed in the 1860s. This climax was focused upon drinking, which became associated with much that was reckoned to be wrong. 'The history of crime' wrote V.A.C. Gatrell '... is largely the history of how better-off people disciplined their inferiors'. How much did this apply to Luton? Accounts of the value of drink – as Walvin put it, the 'lubricant of the pre-industrial economy' – are well trod ground. Safer than milk or water, alcohol was more than a mere thirst quencher. It was also a medicinal anaesthetic and, more importantly for many, a social anaesthetic too.[57] Drink was a means of temporary escape from squalor and domestic stress and, much more than today, the public house or inn was a centre of a community. Within the pre-industrial economy it was a meeting place which could attract all strata of society, a venue for buying and selling: Dunstable's early pre-eminence in the hat trade has been attributed in part to its coaching inns at which Luton traders sold to travellers. The public house was a place of entertainment and, in pre-railway days, it was a point at which travellers would embark and disembark. The invaluable social function of the public house in Luton was given extra emphasis by the absence of any other competing facility apart from churches. The onset of industrialisation, whilst sharpening the degrees of distinctiveness between different types of drinking establishments, also provided the working man with his own choice of 'club'. For many it was a refuge from the worries of the world and, in the better public houses, an oasis of light and comfort to a degree that could be greater than in their own home.

In mid-nineteenth century Luton, away from the inns and ancient taverns of the main streets, venues for drinking were erected with seemingly little control, appearing as suddenly as the cottages alongside which they stood. Broadly speaking, these can be grouped into two categories – the public house and the beer house. In 1846 the *Beds Times* estimated that there were 90 licensed premises in the town and William Austin reckoned that by 1869 there were a total of 228 – one licensed premise to every 48 people over the age of thirteen.[58] Of these, approximately 100 were public houses, the rest beer houses – the group which in Luton, as elsewhere, had expanded rapidly since the passing of the 1830 Beer Act. The beer shops comprised a wide range of premises ranging from tenanted named houses owned by established local brewers, such as Fordham, Bennett or McMullen, to converted front (or back) rooms carrying neither sign nor name. Given the obscure nature of these places it is indeed possible that there were more beer houses than those accounted for by Austin, some even operating in a shadowy, unlicensed manner. Austin's assessment may have been a calculation made after the cull on beer shops which took place in 1869, and also suggesting a peak figure higher than 228. Control over the beer shops presented a particular problem. Many, for example, gained a licence by being built as more substantial establishments but a stud wall erected on completion would thereby divide the building in two. One half could then be let out as a cottage whilst the other served as a considerably reduced hostelry.

The distribution of public houses around the town appears to be in accordance with the density of population. By no means was the public house exclusively the domain of the lower middle class and labourers, a fact which temperance lecturers were very willing to emphasise.[59] There was, however, great differences between the clientele of individual public houses, and there were a sufficient number of bad licensed premises which offered conspicuous targets for what Bradley aptly described as the 'censorial' elements within Luton society.[60] For such people, the most vocal of whom were drawn mainly from the middle classes, the issue was simple: 'the chief hindrances to all attempts made to improve the habits and condition of the working classes, is to be found in the demoralising influence of the public house'.[61] In their view, the public house or at least the worst of its kind, served as the most constant antithesis to the ideals of sobriety, punctuality, self-control and family life. Those who felt that 'something must be done' about the myriad problems, which seemed to find a common bond in the public bar, did so probably through a combination of motives. There was, of course, fear: fear that lawless hordes might spill forth from the slums and violate the sanctuaries of respectable citizens. For example, an eighteen month depression in the hat trade, coupled with high bread prices in November 1854, culminated in an assembled crowd of between 3000–4000 roaming central Luton in an orgy of window breaking. George Street hat factories, bakers' shops and Wellington Street homes all received systematic treatment. Within a fortnight a Relief Committee had been formed and was distributing cheap soup and bread to the poor of the town.[61] In an age when crime and poverty were both regarded as moral diseases, another motivation was a desire to suppress their contagious effects and to treat their causes. There was also straightforward Christian compassion, often extended into attempts to provide the means by which the poor could escape the crushing embrace of their poverty and ignorance. No doubt there were those who then, as now, became involved in good works simply for appearances sake, maybe from a sense of guilt or, as already witnessed, acted with the best of motives but in a patronising and naive manner. The intertwining of middle class and working class streets ensured that there was no possibility of Luton's social problems associated with poverty being isolated within ghettos, entirely out of sight and, therefore, altogether out of mind.

It was not only the public house which raised the ire of respectable folk. Luton's fairs, in particular the Statute or 'Stattie' fair held in

September of each year, became a target of criticism for attracting all sorts of ne'er-do-wells. One complaint ran thus:

> They form a nucleus for the assembling together ... of the lowest orders; they seduce by their excitement and glitter, hundreds of the lowly born from a regular and honest course of living; they are the means of organising systematic robberies and fraud from the same class; and they bring with them pollution and vice wherever they are suffered to take place.[63]

The Fox fair, which took place annually near to the inn of the same name, disappeared in the early nineteenth century. There was also an April fair, but this was a smaller, somewhat motley, event compared with the orgiastic 'Stattie': 'tall men, fat women, peep shows, ginger bread, and oysters ... conjurers, pugilists and negro melodists. We regret to say ... that the "light fingered gentry" were very busy in their avocations and reaped a rich harvest.'[64]

The fairs, especially the 'Stattie', jarred sensibilities on a number of levels. Its gaudy gaiety offended the puritanical: 'Fair-day. School held, principally as a protest against the fair', David Stalker, the headmaster of Queen Square, sourly noted before adding, '<u>Very</u> thin attendance'.[65] Furthermore, its assemblage of rowdy plebeians aroused fears of riot, and it became the focal point for the perpetration of a number of crimes – fighting, drunkenness (known colloquially as a 'regular stone-blinder'), prostitution and petty theft. The 'Stattie' was also anathema to non-conformist liberal values at another level – the 'slave-dealing custom' of the hiring of servants and labourers, a hangover from a fading era. For human beings to publicly tout their labour was thought by many to be degrading: perhaps this was better done cap-in-hand in a builder's yard or hat factory back door. Luton's evolving economic structure rendered the annual hiring obsolete and the number of labourers dwindled away to just a handful of boys by the late 1850s. Curtailment by the Board of Health, working in close co-operation with the police, reduced it in size and suffocated the potential for crime. The 'Stattie' was eventually suppressed by order of the Home Office (following a local petition) on 21 December 1880. The content and name of the fair, bereft of its labour hiring purpose, switched to the surviving April date where it continued (still with livestock) until 1929 when Luton Borough Council could no longer tolerate a chaotic anachronism which completely blocked the main street of an expanding engineering town. At least until the Edwardian era it appears to have retained the traditional 'Stattie' character, as Aubrey Darby recalled:

> In daylight the Stattie was obscene, with nightfall it seemed like Dante's inferno, flickering lights from kerosene flares haloed in smoke made an unearthly glow, inanimate objects came to life and the faces of the revellers appeared like the gargoyles of Notre

Dame. In this setting the appearance of 'Quasimodo' would have evoked no surprise. Away from the glare, whores entertained any male with fourpence to spare, plagued at times by peeping toms seeking a cheap thrill. Syphilis was common but none cared on Stattie night. The raucous din of machine-made music muffled the whimperings of tiny tots being dragged around by wretched mothers bent on escaping from reality. Tomorrow they would account for the squandering of precious wealth on sideshows, tonight they laughed and squealed with ecstasy, whilst grown men emptied water squirts down their breasts. All inhibitions were gone, young virgins satisfied their curiosity and 'knees up old Ma Brown' was an excuse for matrons to expose a gartered thigh.

Towards the last hour drunks spewed from the pubs, finale to the hectic day and like the titbit left on the plate until last, how we savoured this morsel. Fights broke out everywhere and we scurried here and there alert for overturned stalls. Diving into the wreckage we grabbed all we could lay our hands on before departing into the shadows with the loot. The appearance of the bobbies, the frogmarch of the drunks to the lock-up was of little interest to us. We could see all this on any Saturday night.[66]

Guy Fawkes' Night, 5 November, was not celebrated in any organised sense. The occasion in many parts of England was well-supported by the lower middle class, as well as labourers and artisans, and has been regarded as a regular manifestation of 'Street Toryism'. It was often well-organised and flourished, in particular, in market towns. It was organised to such a degree that local people, who had in some way courted unpopularity with the mob, could find themselves hanged and burnt in effigy.[67] No evidence of this exists in mid-nineteenth century Luton, the worst occasion being the attempt to burn down the wooden structure serving as a temporary Corn Exchange in 1868. That is not to say that 5 November was an event not celebrated: an estimated 2000 people assembled in George Street to watch the fireworks being let off in 1862.[68] The event, however, always appears to have been a spontaneous rather than a co-ordinated celebration, making it a less conspicuous target for the disapproving. 'Street Toryism' was absent in Luton and the crimes associated with Guy Fawkes' Night were petty – pickpocketing, drunkenness and disorderly behaviour – although the fireworks were naturally a hazard. Several minor fires were caused by fireworks in 1858.[69] Luton ceased to be a market town, but perhaps the principal reason that Guy Fawkes' Night was not so vigorously attacked was that, at heart, it was a patriotic, anti-Catholic celebration. Certainly the *Luton Times* and *Luton News*, mouthpieces of liberal nonconformity, did not criticise 5 November events in the way that they grumbled about the September 'Stattie'. Visiting fairs and circuses also caused occasional tremors of concern. The arrival of Wombwell's Menagerie in September

1868 attracted a curious crowd – '. . . the roughest of the backslums of Luton were in full force . . .' commented the *Beds Times*.[70]

Assessing Luton's Crime

The fairs and events such as Guy Fawkes' Night were isolated occasions. The 'demoralising' sale of alcohol, however, remained constant. Remove all the fairs and individual celebrations from Luton's social calendar and drunkenness, poverty, vice and crime would still be there as the public house was still there to spawn them. In the eyes of many, it was the public house that was the root of most that was evil. Luton's unstable economy provided a glut of money for one period and then none at all for another. This factor, however, together with an awareness of poor housing, the dearth of alternative facilities for recreation and any other contributory cause, were given relatively scant consideration by the critics of the public house. Remove the excesses of the drink trade, so they reasoned, and it was possible to remove most of the ills associated with it.

The extent of the association between crime and alcohol is difficult to establish. The unreliability of nineteenth crime figures make clear assessment virtually impossible. Clive Emsley expressed the problem succinctly: 'The gloomy truth might be that the more we understand of nineteenth century crime the less likely any all embracing hypotheses will be to satisfy'.[71] First, the statistics are an accumulation of crimes recorded rather than offences committed. They are, therefore, open to initial distortion through factors such as the efficiency of local policing (not to mention the efficiency of local criminals) and the degree of alienation which some communities feel they have from the administration of justice: in practice, whether an individual sees any point in reporting a crime. The definition of what represents criminal activity alters as a result of national legislation and there can often be local initiatives which suddenly focus upon individual misdemeanours, resulting in a rash of offences brought before magistrates. Luton police, for example, periodically pursued a crackdown on dangerous driving of carts or stray dogs. Petty juvenile crime could be accompanied by a high turnover in offenders – frequent light sentences and subsequent re-appearances before courts when offences are re-committed. The discrepancy in the definition of crime can be seen clearly in the type of offence brought before a bench and the sentence handed down. Luton's magistrates' court was presided over by country gentry and clergy with no representatives from the urban area itself. The deliberations and decisions of the magistrates' court, therefore, represented rural Bedfordshire values, not Luton's. Few Lutonians would lose much sleep over the activities of poachers stealthily going about their business on the estates and farms surrounding the town. They would be more concerned by carts driven by drunkards, suspicious looking vagrants and crimes of petty theft and violence. Yet crimes related to poaching remain prominent in the number of cases brought before the Luton bench in the mid-nineteenth century. Returns from the magistrates' court and the court of Quarter Sessions provide only a sketch as to the degree and extent of criminal activity and are not wholly reliable as a guide for drawing firm conclusions.[72]

At that time, just as now, there was a wide ranging debate about what were the causes of criminal activity and a host of contributory factors were acknowledged as having a part to play. The secretive nature of crime and the unreliability of statistics make firm conclusions hard to come by. Furthermore, technical change can provide new stimulus and variations in criminal activity and its response. The arrival of the railway to Luton, for example, brought with it large numbers of navvies to lay the line and with it a resurgence of the fear of 'outsiders' coming to the town and bringing offensive behaviour with them. Once the railway was established, this fear again manifested itself in the dread of the mobile criminal: a rash of burglaries in 1860 was attributed (without evidence) to thieves arriving in Luton by train, committing the crime and escaping the same way. This unsubstantiated concern was specifically referred to in a petition raised soon after the opening of the Luton – Hatfield link in 1858: '. . . thieves have much greater facility in disposing of their plunder by taking an early morning Train to London in little more than an hour and before the Police are aware of the Transaction'. There was also a spate of vandalism (damage to carriages, stones on the line, and so on) which coincided with the novelty of the railway.[73]

Acknowledging all these influences, there is nonetheless some broad agreement regarding the general trend in crime during the nineteenth century into which context it is possible to place Luton, albeit tentatively. Growing towns, with an unstable, youthful population have been acknowledged as being particularly prone to higher levels of crime. Nationally, the levels of crime rose after 1815 until the 1850s when a combination of criminal and social legislation, together with greater social stability, brought the rate down. Crimes became less violent and were committed less frequently by juveniles from this period. Tobias put this in perspective by stating 'we are not concerned to argue that all was well in England after 1850, but that things were a little better than they had been.'[74] In Luton the rate of crime could be expected to increase proportionally with the town's rapid urbanisation. The available data is not up to all the questions which are posed since there are only comprehensive and reliable returns from Luton's police court for the years 1855–63 and from 1866 onwards. A broad sketch only is possible.

Most studies of provincial crime tend to focus upon the big cities, and Luton is certainly not in this category. It was not a town with a definable 'criminal class' or rookeries which were impervious to the law, and containing a network of 'flash-houses'. Luton's crime was mostly small, though frequent – petty theft, poaching and drunkenness. Certain individuals appear again and again before the bench – Obadiah Worsley, James Adams, William Adams and John Day ('one of the worst characters in the town'). They are four examples of men who were frequently involved in trouble, including theft, assault and riot. Levi Welch made a considerable personal contribution to Luton's criminal statistics in a career which developed from poaching through to assault, then shooting, and finally to murder. He avoided the rope only by turning Queen's evidence against a confederate, William Worsley, thereby condemning him to the gallows. Solomon King was another 'old offender' who reappeared before Luton's police court, usually as a result of being the worse for drink, although theft and assault were also amongst his sins. Even when thrown into the workhouse, King, who had a family in Houghton Regis, could not avoid trouble: in 1851 he was sentenced to 21 days in gaol for scaling the wall to the women's section of the workhouse where he spent two happy hours before capture.[75] Solomon King was an exception in being someone seemingly incapable of employment. Even the likes of Adams and Day, notorious individuals that they were, at worst were semi-criminal, that is to say labourers who were frequently in trouble. Their sheer notoriety indicates that such men were rare and that in reality, whatever the fears of the timid, there did not exist a purely criminal class in Luton. Most who appeared before the bench were able to give some occupation, reinforcing a point already made by David Jones that the bulk of crime was committed by people in casual or full-time employment.[76] Certain streets became known for trouble, Chase Street probably being the outstanding example of this type. There the application of the law was consistently flouted and occasionally resisted. An attempt by PC Taylor to break up a cacophony of 'rough music' in July 1867 resulted in a minor riot in which Taylor was seriously injured.[77] Bad though elements within it undoubtedly were, there is no evidence that the local constabulary regarded even Chase Street as wholly impenetrable, and their beat was able to cover it both by day and night.

From another perspective, Luton's crime rate rose out of proportion to its population in the country as a whole.[78] A rapidly growing town, with a fluid population, Luton acquired the hallmarks of an immature and unstable society. Bedfordshire's period of greatest social upheaval came in the twenty years after Waterloo with an intense depression in agriculture characterised by low wages, migration and riot. By 1840 affairs became more settled in the county, whilst in contrast Luton's accelerating growth was just commencing. For the respectable, law-abiding inhabitants of the town this sudden social upheaval was viewed with great alarm – a familiar, national and age-old feeling. In 1846 'An Old Inhabitant' wrote to the *Beds Times* complaining about the darkness of streets and absence of police: '... lazy fellows fill up the pavements, and annoy all passengers whom they think they can insult with impunity. It has long been a fact that no lady dares walk the streets alone after dark...'.[79] Molestation by the *hoi polloi* touched a deep dread amongst many: 'idle young men' it was alleged, gathered in groups (especially in George Street) and would then 'behave themselves in such a manner as to be disgusting'.[80] Both the above allegations were made towards the latter part of the busy season when unemployment would be minimal. Once again the arrival of the railway provided a new angle: April 1869 saw letters in the local press concerning gangs of youths lurking under one of the newly constructed Midland Railway bridges. Whether their intentions were nefarious is irrelevant; their very presence being sufficient to induce fear.[81]

All in all, fear of crime, particularly as expressed by those from the 'middling orders', far exceeded the reality. Although 'crime' as defined by statute was usually committed by those in employment, it was also usually committed by and to the working class, taking the form of neighbourhood quarrels, drunken brawls and acts of theft from market stalls. Riot, an offence which could be directed specifically at middle class targets, was rare. There was one instance in 1847 when scandal-mongers spread rumours concerning the relationship between Dr E.O. Woakes and his niece, who died from taking poison. An excited mob assembled outside his house in Wellington Street and special constables were sworn in to disperse them. Besides the 1854 riot there were a further series of street brawls surrounding the general election in May 1859. Obadiah Worsley, who otherwise showed no inclination for political activity, was in the thick of it. Mob violence was so remote from the experience of middle class Lutonians that the *Luton Times* actually went so far as to condone the practice of 'rough music', an activity which could very easily degenerate into a mini-riot.[82]

Burglary at the homes of the better-off was also very rare, a spate occurring in 1855, 1860 and 1862.[83] Most thefts were, other than poaching, very minor cases, involving activities such as the stealing of straw plait or turnip tops. Murder, manslaughter and the more serious cases of assault were also exceedingly uncommon. The extent of infanticide in Victorian society remains one of the great unknowns: the body of a murdered baby was found in the River Lea in 1860 but the culprit was never traced. Neither found was the attacker of George Wing and his wife (who subsequently died). This assault took place whilst they were walking in daylight in Chapel Street. Besides these cases there were just nine indictments for murder or manslaughter between 1855 and 1875, although that does not necessarily mean that there were no deaths which would have aroused the suspicion of the authorities today. Similarly, instances of attempted murder or serious assault were rare before the courts. A policemen guarding a prisoner,

John Congreve (accused of embezzling money as Assistant Overseer), was stabbed in February 1872. Five months earlier an attempt was made to poison an open-air bible reader, Miss Wand, on Market Hill by offering her a piece of cake laced with aconite. Although taken seriously ill, Miss Wand survived.[84] To repeat, most crimes of violence involved the labouring classes but they aroused middle class concern on occasions. One such case concerned a vicious assault upon a sewer, Mabel Gray, 'a woman not of good character', by two men, Henry Holyoak and William Waller. This attack received much attention in the local press as it took place in broad daylight watched by a large crowd from which only one person attempted to intervene. The concern was particularly strong as it took the police three quarters of an hour to arrive to rescue the girl.[85]

The copycat crime was of more serious concern. The murder of his wife in 1859 by Joseph Castle gave rise to apparently imitative attacks by husbands upon their wives: one stabbing and several assaults, one with a bottle.[86] During a period of high bread prices, arson attacks were made upon the granary of William Drewett. Almost immediately afterwards there was another attack on a corn store at Turners Hall Farm.[87]

It was highly unlikely for a man to be successfully prosecuted for rape or sexual assault. Women were understandably reluctant to come forward in the face of an unsympathetic system and magistrates and police preferred not to become involved in domestic disputes. This was a feature which Luton shared with the rest of the country, but to what extent Luton women, with greater degrees of economic self-reliance, were able to escape the attentions of drunken, cruel and violent husbands is difficult to gauge. Only when the case went as far as blatant murder, as with the Castles, was there any real chance of official redress. In May 1855, Ann Bush died after her husband, Thomas, a jobbing carpenter, had repeatedly assaulted her, flinging her against a cupboard on the final occasion. Presented with this evidence the inquest jury found, however, that death was accelerated by depression and anxiety following the sale of her house. In February 1871 Joseph Andrews of New Town Street was indicted for the manslaughter of his wife for which he received six months in gaol. He had repeatedly beaten her, the last assault proving fatal.[88] Discrepancies in sentencing, in which attacks on property were clearly rated as more serious than attacks on people, especially poor female ones, caused the odd tremor of disquiet to emanate from the *Luton Times*. The principal concern of the liberal leading citizens of the town, however, lay more in the local control and efficiency of the administration of justice, issues with political ramifications.

There appears to be a high incidence of juvenile crime, a factor commensurate with Luton's levels of growth and social immaturity. The precise proportion of this is difficult to ascertain not least of all because some culprits would lie about their ages and their true names. Then, as now, the principal of working mothers, in this instance in the straw plait and hat trade, was thought by some to be harmful to the morals of children. 'We fear the bonnet-work engrosses more attention than the necessary attendance of their children' frowned the *Luton Times* in 1861. There is, however, no decisive evidence which can be supplied to support the contention that the hat industry specifically contributed to juvenile crime through its labour structure. Whether a different economic system would have helped Thomas Fleckney is open to question. Described by a court reporter as one of 'Les Miserables' of Luton, he was often in trouble, being convicted in 1875 of theft. William Fleckney, (who may have been related), was convicted of murdering another youth in a fight in 1868 when he was sixteen. Twelve year old Alfred Eames presented a pathetic spectacle when he appeared before the bench charged with the theft of toys in November 1862. In mitigation, Superintendent Pope said that the boy was 'appallingly' treated by his parents and turned out on to the streets to make a living 'as best he could'. Eames received one month in prison and four months in a reformatory, the magistrates clearly feeling that he was in better care there than at home. Luton was a fast growing and youthful town. It had a high proportion of young people who were provided with few recreational outlets and little else other than their own imagination for stimulation.[89]

Although detailed analysis of criminal cycles in Luton is problematic, some concluding pointers towards broad trends can be made. In general terms it is evident that there was an escalating incidence of criminal cases in certain categories that were brought before the Luton bench in the 1860s.[90] Analysis of seasonal and, in particular, monthly cycles of crime are difficult because they are susceptive to distortion due to a number of factors. The absence of sufficient magistrates for the dispensation of justice during a two week period, for example, could lead to a backlog of cases which would then exaggerate the number of cases heard the following month. Temporary surges such as this occurred frequently. A breakdown of offences over the period 1855–75 made on a monthly basis show an even pattern of offences brought before the bench. On a seasonal basis the late summer/autumn period accounts for the highest proportion of recorded crimes, a period when the town was beginning to fill with migrants seeking work and lodgings. This period also included the 'Stattie' and Guy Fawkes' Night. The peak of the hat trade's busy season, from December through to March, was a time when levels of recorded crime dropped appreciably although Luton's population was at its peak. Taking all factors into consideration, the tentative conclusion is that Luton's incidence of crime fell slightly during periods of most intense economic activity and rose (with the puzzling exception of July) during the subsequent lull and during the unsettled period when the town began to swell with migrants.

Yearly analysis for the twenty years leading up to 1875 presents, however, something of a paradox. The absence of sufficient returns to compile totals for 1864 and 1865 leaves an awkward void but the patchy returns which are available indicate that the crime levels were steadily rising in these years, at a time when the hat industry was active (see graph below). In contrast with the monthly patterns, the annual number of crimes rose during periods of greatest economic activity, falling away during the depression of 1867–71 and rising again once the staple trade had pulled out of the trough. It must be appreciated that these are actual returns, not percentages based upon Luton's population, which overall was also rising in the middle of the century. During the late 1860s, however, the resident population may have remained static, and possibly even fell. Luton's police force, strengthening belatedly in this decade would presumably also have contributed to the number of persons who were apprehended.

The Police

Contemporary discussion of policing was dominated by the issue of local control, spilling over into the field of politics. The difficulties which arose from the construction of the new police station in Dunstable Place epitomised the problem (see chapter four). There were sporadic accusations levelled at the police – that they were in cahoots with local criminals (unsubstantiated); that they were absent where they were thought to be needed most. One example of this was the complaint that the constabulary neglected to police High Town Road 'where the most disreputable scum of Donkey Hall' congregated causing a nuisance by throwing stones and committing acts of petty vandalism. There was one published complaint concerning the officiousness and calibre of the police. In this case, a constable threatened to lock up a tradesman he saw standing talking on 'at least seven foot of open path' and who refused to move on. The complainant concluded: 'I regret to say what is too generally known in this town, that the staff of policemen . . . are men entirely ignorant of not only their duty as men and officers, but of common civility.'[91] Criticisms of the performance of the police were so few, however, and so occasional, that it can only be concluded that in the opinion of the middle classes at least, there was not great dissatisfaction with their efforts. Superintendent Pope seems to have been especially well thought of, although on the issue of satisfaction with the police, as in others, the views of the poorest sectors of society were not documented.[92]

The strength of the police force rose steadily during mid-century. Two police constables were appointed to cover the whole of the Luton Parish in 1840 following government legislation empowering the Quarter Sessions to do so. These two officers replaced the watchmen who had patrolled the township alone (one in the day and two at night).

Following a swiftly raised petition by the Lighting and Watching Committee two policemen were assigned to the township alone and a superintendent with four other constables covering the remainder of the parish.[93] The Committee's priorities were clear: '... the present force is far from adequate to the protection of the vast property contained in the Warehouses and other Buildings ... totally unprotected from Fire and Robbery'.

Four more constables for the parish were added in 1855 but yet another petition was raised around 1860. This compared Luton (approximately 16,000 inhabitants and six constables, two of whom were based in the hamlets), with Bedford (12,000 according to the 1851 census and 12 constables). It sought to emphasise the thinness of the blue line, citing the desperate struggle to apprehend two men found with burglary equipment in the vestry of St. Mary's.[94] A further petition was received, signed by Colonel Ames and 100 inhabitants of Luton at the Easter Quarter Sessions in 1864, appealing for more policemen to cover the urban core specifically. When this was met the complement of men stood at fifteen constables for the township of Luton and a further six for the hamlets.[95]

Temperance

Surviving mid-nineteenth century opinions as to the causes of crime come overwhelmingly from one sector of society. There was, however, an impressive unanimity between contemporaries as to where the main cause of criminal activity in Luton lay. Economic factors did not enter into the reckoning. Lodging houses, which in a town with such a large transient population might have been expected to be a major area of concern, received some attention. Three in particular were noted for being 'crowded' with beggars and one owner was brought before the magistrates accused of allowing different sexes to sleep in the same room.[96] For the most part, however, lodging houses were regarded as a public health problem rather than one associated with crime and morals, their control lying with an inspector of the local Board of Health. The dread of outsiders entering the town and committing offences, a fear which might be expected to be expressed in a town with such a strong reliance upon seasonal employment, is only infrequently referred to in the period as a whole. For example, a large number of tramps were reported to be wandering around the Luton and Dunstable district in the autumn and winter of 1862.[97] Recurring though this particular fear may have been it was the public house, above any other factor, which in the minds of many in Luton was associated with crime and was to provide the impetus for the temperance movement. To understand the imperative by which temperance developed it is important to remember that many public houses had very bad reputations. A couple were ancient inns situated in the heart

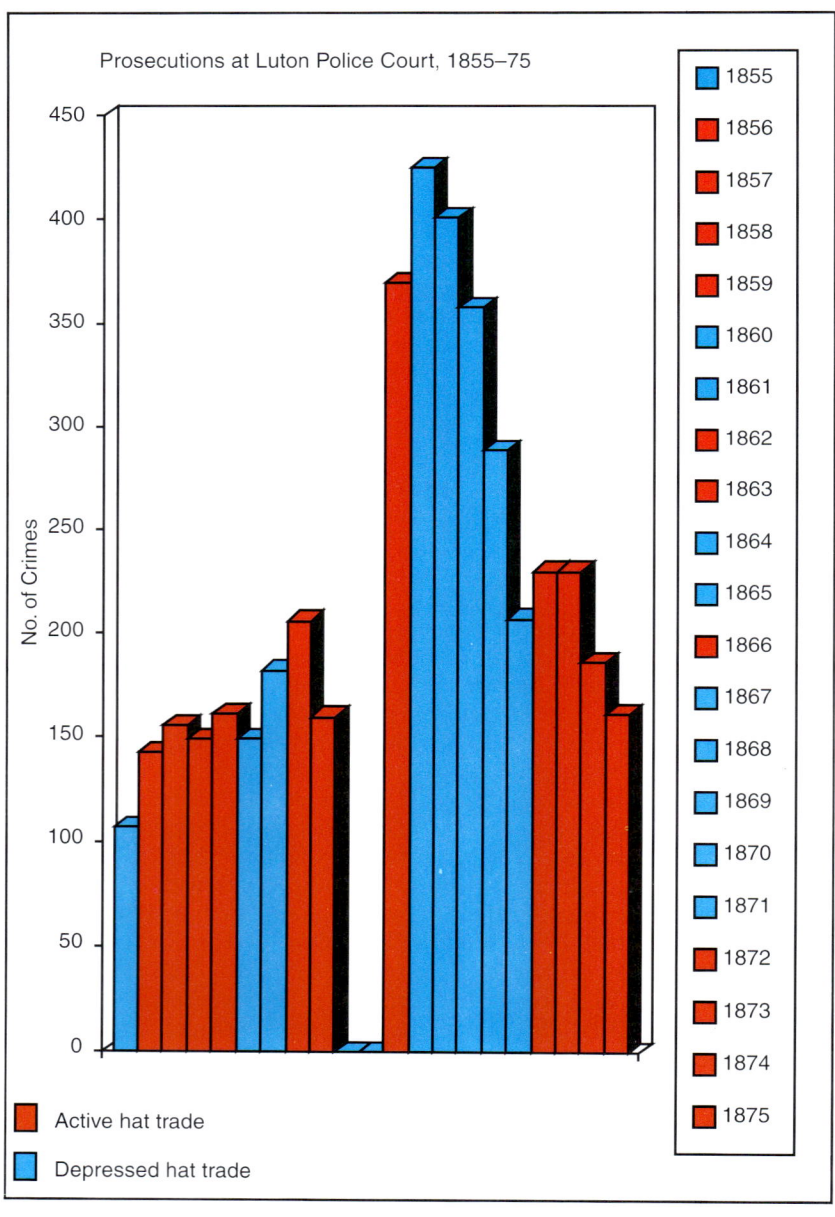

of town, one being the *White Hart* where landlord James Burgess was prosecuted in 1848 for keeping a disorderly house.[98] In 1856, a successor landlord was convicted of keeping the *White Hart* open beyond licensing hours, the police planting a plain clothes officer in the public house to circumnavigate the landlord's system of lookouts.[99]

Most problem beer houses and public houses, however, lay beyond the central area in the new streets within New Town and High Town. Most offences directly connected with licensed premises were of disorderly conduct or keeping open beyond licensing hours. Some houses, however, were recognised by the police as being merely fronts for criminal activity. These included the *Wrestlers* in Wellington Street which appeared to be little more than a brothel with public bar attached. In August 1863 two burglars were followed directly with their booty from the scene of a crime to a back room of the *Wrestlers*. The landlords of the *Freeholder, Mother Redcap, Eagle, Stag, Masons Arms, Fortune of War, Rising Sun* and *Robin Hood* all appeared before the Luton magistrates in the late 1850s for varying offences, the last two being serious enough to warrant a three month suspension of their licence.[100] The *Nelson* in Duke Street was recognised as 'a regular resort for thieves, prostitutes and other bad characters,' and the *Roebuck Inn* in Albert Road had its problems with clientele exacerbated by the violent conduct of the former landlord towards his estranged wife who had taken over the tenancy. In addition to cases such as these, there was a steady stream of offences committed under the influence of alcohol – including vandalism, assault, threatening behaviour, disorderliness and dangerous driving. Although the landlord could not be directly held responsible for these acts, they further tarnished the image of the public house.[101] To repeat Austin's estimate, there were a staggering 226 licensed premises by 1869.

Running parallel with the rise in the number of public houses, and soon to clash with it, was the burgeoning temperance movement. When this first became established in the town is not precisely known. A Temperance Society was in existence by 1846 with William Willis as one of its leading lights, and 'Sign the Pledge' meetings were being held by 1849.[102] It did not immediately find sympathy from the nonconformist churches: John Everitt was an early convert (in 1853) but was obliged to resign his membership of the Park Street Old Meeting a year later because of his refusal to partake of the communion wine which then contained alcohol.[103]

The early years of the Temperance Movement in Luton were marked by an evangelical campaigning style. Until the late 1850s lectures, rallies, tea meetings, galas and letters to the press were the order of the day. The first recorded gala, the forerunner to the excursion and holiday which were to be organised later in the century, was in August 1853.

A procession went to Park Meadow (Popes Meadow) where in the afternoon there were games followed by speeches, fireworks and an illuminated balloon in the evening.[104] A temperance tea meeting attracted 250 in 1854 and 2000 braved bad weather to attend the annual temperance gala in 1856.[105] How many of those who attended the galas were serious sympathisers with the cause is open to question. The same may be said of those who subsequently signed the pledge. At this point the movement was concentrated upon a combination of moral persuasion and attractive social events rather than political activity. Willis and Everitt apart, Robert How and Hiram Higgins were the leading figures at this time but interestingly there were no local ministers prominent. No number of galas and tea meetings, however, could halt the relentless increase in the number of licensed premises which were springing up in the town. Unlike the temperance movement they could offer attractions on a daily (and nightly) basis.

Lacking records of the local movement, its constituency is not known. Examples of Harrison's archetypal working class supporter – family oriented, Liberal, smart, self-educated, Mechanics Institute supporting, chapel attending – were numerous in the town. The schisms which afflicted the national movement between the moderate British and Foreign Temperance Society and the more radical teetotal movement did not affect the Luton organisation. This remained a broad church incorporating many strands of opinion, even those who had nothing else in common. Compared with another market town which has been studied, Banbury, Luton's temperance campaigners were able to avoid a number of pitfalls which could crucially weaken their impact. Never during the mid-nineteenth century did it veer toward teetotalism, although there were strong teetotallers within its ranks. The sabbatarianism element that was strong in Banbury, and which served to narrow the movement's appeal there, was not prominent in Luton. At the latter, perhaps because there was a measure of fluid social mobility, inter-class strife did not cause damaging internal divisions.[106] Luton was a politically neutered town, controlled (nominally at least) by county government and isolated from the national debates. If the Luton temperance movement was to make any impression it would have to do so on a local basis. The Board of Health, however, the nearest which Luton possessed to a local authority, had no jurisdiction over public houses. The Luton temperance movement comprised people who were used to finding their own solutions to problems and they chose to strike at the heart of the matter. In doing so, the local movement demonstrated a degree of sharp political awareness. The first sign of a change in tactics came in 1857. A meeting at the Town Hall heard a speaker estimate that Luton spent £24,637. 10s. 0d. annually on 'intoxicating liquor'. For the first time the town heard a recommendation from the platform of prohibition (the 'Maine Law'). This, according to the speaker, would mean that instead of money being wasted upon drink, it would be possible to buy (amongst other things) 500 women's shawls, ten almshouses, 4000 loaves and wedding portions for 25 women of good repute who had been teetotal Sunday School teachers for seven years![107] From this point the strategy followed a distinctive course, uniting all manner and shades of opinion and stifling any potential opposition. A meeting in September 1857 passed a resolution calling for magistrates to reduce the number of public houses in the town and the following autumn a memorial was submitted to the Luton bench, which at that time was considering the licence application of a number of premises. Part of it read '... this rising town being very seriously compromised and corrupted by a torrent of vice and ungodliness, let loose on it not least through the operation of its lower class of public houses...,'[108] As a result of this application, the *Bedford Arms* in Stuart Street, by no means the worst public house in the town, had its licence temporarily suspended. The local architect of this tactic is unknown but this memorial attracted the signatures not only of the usual radical supporters, but also of the Rev Peile of St. Mary's and a number of the main dissenting ministers in the town.

The tea meetings and festivals continued, attracting attendances measured in hundreds but now with nonconformist ministers to the fore, reflecting a broad denominational base. A meeting held at the Town Hall in January 1860 attracted 400 including Rev J. Phillips of High Town Primitive Methodist Church, Rev T. Hands of Park Street Old Meeting, Gustavus Jordan, a leading Wesleyan, and Henry Brown. The *Luton Times*, in carrying a report of the proceedings, noted 'the greater portion being from the middle class of society'.[109] It cannot be known whether this was a true reflection of the depth of temperance support in Luton. The meeting was held at the height of the busy season and it was, therefore, possible that many working people were unable to attend. Had the Primitive Methodist Church been the venue then it is possible that the social mix would have been different.

With a powerful appeal to the children of the working class, and also to the illiterate, was the magic lantern. The first recorded example of this being used for temperance purposes was in April 1862, at the Ceylon Baptist Church, Wellington Street. There, the wondrous show treated its audience to a tale depicting a 'drunkard's progress' (presumably downward). In adopting this approach the class divisions once again became evident as Aubrey Darby's perceptive, if slightly jaundiced eye, bears witness:[110]

> The Methodist Church on top of the hill overlooking the railway sidings stood four square, no spike, no ornamental masonry, symbolising a narrowness personified from within that only the poor needed saving the rich being blessed by the Lord. Inside the hall, gaslit and shabby, sat rows of children gazing at a white screen

from which light and colour would soon emerge. As the minutes ticked by from a large clock on the wall, a restlessness became apparent breaking out into loud cheers with the appearance of the Pastor on the platform. Did he know our cheers were for the imminent showing of the pictures heralded by his entry, if not we left him in no doubt when halfway through his address, the cry, 'Show the pictures', led to the exit of a chastened cleric. The hall darkened and the first slide appeared upside down, accompanied by screams of laughter and catcalls. There was Mafeking everywhere. Right way up the picture, in magnificent colour, depicted a filthy attic, the occupants a repulsive woman in rags and two scarecrows, barefoot, almost naked, presumably her children, peering at a crust of bread reposing on the rickety table, the scene highlighted by a candle stuck in a beer bottle, seemed to us who had experience of this kind of illumination remarkably bright, for every detail of the sordid room stood out clearly.

The story teller interpreting the scene told us the family were waiting for the father to come home with his pay, but the demon strong drink had waylaid him. The slide changed showing the drunken father, red choker round his neck, in the act of bashing the wife, whilst the kids cowered in a corner. The compere, warming up to his job, carried the cackle a bit too far, so we shouted for the next picture, the excitement of the imminent bashing fired our imagination, the plight of the victims worried us not. So the story unfolded, the droning voice of the story-teller lulling many of us to sleep, some even lost interest in something all so true to life in this age of pub and pulpit. Those who watched to the bitter end, saw the drunken swine repent, but only after his only son had been knocked over by a runaway horse and cart. The final scene, a beautiful room, the son between snow-white sheets, well-dressed father, wife and daughter smiling down upon the happy boy and in the background the pastor kneeling in act of prayer. In some strange way we wondered why the runaway horse received no credit for the happy ending.

In our world of reality, neither the magic lantern nor the religious man convinced us that strong drink or total abstinence would change our existence. Religion was alien to our environment, for what purpose we lived no one cared. Living was enough, mysticism had no abode in our attics. We had no education and believed those who craved after it were cranks. Nevertheless after the Lantern Show we were content, the herd instinct of being together, a free bun, a warm hall, and the joy of the upside down picture had satisfied our expectations. Our fathers would still visit the pubs and for this fact we said 'Amen'.

Homeward bound, more subdued with the cold night than the Magic Lantern, we passed some of the 90 pubs in the town. Tonight the soft murmur of voices, denoted peace in the pubs. There were no raucous brawls and we wondered who could have done this thing. We looked into the starlit sky, shivered, and scampered home.

The main thrust of the movement, however, formally known as the Luton Temperance Society by 1870, was now focused upon the magistrates bench. The 1858 memorial was followed up the following autumn (on 5 September) by a petition containing 600 names: '... your memorialists feel assured that intemperance is the principal cause of misery, crime, prostitution and pauperism that exists in the town of Luton...'. Once again, the *Rising Sun*, *Freeholder* and the *Robin Hood* fell foul and received licence suspensions, as did the *Oxford Arms* and the *Railway Hotel*. The latter had been associated with a recent assault case and, although it was often the haunt of prostitutes seeking travelling clients, the suspension could be viewed as somewhat harsh since the landlord was not directly culpable. This decision points to a spontaneous, knee-jerk response by the magistrates when confronted by a delegation from the temperance movement. There is little evidence of deep empathy between the bench and the memorialists; the bench wished to appease the temperance campaigners. Luton's magistrates needed pressure applied at licensing time before they would take action.[111] And so this tactic progressed throughout the 1860s, the emphasis of the temperance movement being the general one of the morally corruptive powers of the public house. This shrewd approach, concentrating the attack on the association between drink and the evils of crime and poverty, meant that it was not necessary to be an ardent advocate of temperance, let alone a teetotaller, to support this attack. The town's brewers, outflanked by a campaign that was directed at vices associated with some of their houses rather than the brewery itself, kept their profile low, making no attempt to counter the onslaught. Pressure applied via the courts began to tell upon the landlords: offences connected with refusal to leave a public house became a notable feature of the petty sessions reports from the mid-1860s.

The high point of temperance influence came in 1869 when the attack upon the public houses reached a crescendo. This coincided with the first fruits of parliamentary pressure upon the Liberal government resulting in legislation which began to reverse the free trade spirit which had produced the 1830 Beer Act. Tighter control over the operation of beer shops was to be exercised by local magistrates, a move which some in Luton may have regarded as literally a godsend. 'The pruning knife is to be applied without favour or affection, to the beershops... its end draws nigh' gloated the *Luton Times*, an enthusiastic supporter of the assault upon them.[112] In persuading the magistrates to apply the 'pruning knife' the temperance movement appears to have co-ordinated their action with Superintendent Pope who saw this movement as an opportunity to rid his area of jurisdiction of some of the worst concentrations of trouble. The emphasis also underwent subtle change: no longer was the case presented in moral terms. Instead, by linking with the police, they presented the licensed premises, in particular the beer shops, as sources of specific criminal activity. The association between the public house and the activities of the poacher, guaranteed to concentrate the minds of Luton's rural estate based magistrates, was repeatedly made. The autumn hearing took two whole sessions at the beginning of which a memorial headed by all the Anglican and nonconformist ministers was heard, their target conspicuously being the beer houses.[113]

For every licence application, Superintendent Pope rose to make an objection: the *Dudley Arms* (recently convicted for keeping a brothel); *The Black Boy*, Burr Street (landlord a 'bad character'); *The Tiger* (thieves and poachers); *The Blockers Arms*; *The George IV* (three small cottages – a haunt of prostitutes); *Lord Nelson* (poachers and thieves the 'principal class of customers'), *The World's End*, New Town (thieves and poachers); *Noah's Ark*, Church Street; *The Elephant and Castle*, (Inspector James 'had never seen a respectable person in it'); *The Railway Hotel* (thieves and prostitutes); *The Fortune of War* and *The Kings Arms*, (both High Town); *The Oxford Arms* and *The Pheasant*. All of these premises had their applications for licence renewal refused: only *The Butchers Arms, Welcome Stranger* and *Duke of Cambridge* got through. Although the occasional public house was refused a licence in the years which followed, 1869 was the most intense period of pressure upon the licensed premises in Luton.

Almost immediately after the 1869 Licensing Sessions, temperance supporters were claiming a drop in crime which was directly attributable to this move.[114] In February 1872, Luton magistrates, Rev Smyth and Colonel Ames presented a report to the Bedfordshire (Michaelmas) Quarter Sessions claiming a 75% drop in criminal activity in Luton: whereas the twelve cells at Luton police station were regularly filled in the late 1860s, only three were needed now. One thousand copies of this report were printed and interest was claimed to be shown from local authorities in Brighton, Scarborough, Gloucester and Lancashire. Austin went as far as to claim that this was known as the 'Luton System'.[115] For Superintendent Pope this parallel decrease in public houses and crime in Luton represented a rewarding end to his working career. He retired in October 1875 with the praises of the local press and magistrates ringing in his ears. With the attack on beer houses seeming to have had its effect, the local consensus broke up leaving the temperance movement to pursue once again its particular goals of suppressing and curbing the partaking of alcohol. By 1874 the United Kingdom Alliance, the national temperance movement, organised a meeting at the Plait Hall; its discussions carrying a more prohibitive, teetotalist tone. Representations were made towards later sittings of the licensing bench but these were notably smaller and ineffective.[116] The Luton Temperance

Society continued to fight the good fight into the twentieth century, sometimes attracting huge crowds for magic lantern shows, but they possessed a narrower appeal. Never again were they so effective as they had been in 1869.

Assessing the effectiveness of the temperance movement
There is seems little doubt that the incidence of crime dropped in the period coinciding with the local campaign against the beer houses. Certainly these places were a refuge and source of criminal activity with some run by appropriately disreputable landlords. It would be misleading, however, to attribute the fall in crime entirely to this beer shop cull and to portray them as the sole source of evil, to the neglect of other factors. The crime rate was already ebbing in the months before September 1869, a factor probably attributable to the deepening recession in the hat industry which was probably depopulating the town. This would have most affected the migratory, labouring classes who, forming the poorest sector of society, were particularly prone to fall foul of certain aspects of the law – drunkenness, vagrancy, petty theft and assault. It is also noticeable that there was a coincidental temporary recovery in the crime rate when the hat industry began to pull out of depression. The worst of Luton's criminals were hardly likely to reform overnight and join a chapel just because their regular haunt was now closed to them. They would seek other outlets. Public houses were by no means the only venue for the disposal of stolen goods and in November 1870 the Luton bench warned marine store dealers not to deal in items which were suspect.[117]

The report produced by Smythe and Ames for the Bedfordshire Quarter Sessions in 1872 estimated that there were 226 licensed houses in 1870 and 188 in 1871. By September 1872, according to official statistics, this figure stood at 132 with beer houses appearing to be the main casualty; just 38 were left in the town.[118] This is a puzzling return: had there been a major reduction in the number of beer shops after 1869 then this surely would have been reported. It is inconceivable that vast numbers operated without a licence but possible that Smyth and Ames were over estimating the numbers involved. No list of licensed premises exists before 1872 but in 1873 there were 129, in 1874 there were 134 and in 1875 the total was 136. The opposite to the temperance movement's assertions was taking place: the number of licensed premises was actually increasing whilst the crime rate was falling. Interestingly, the Chief Constable of Bedfordshire did not echo Smyth and Ames' enthusiasm, making only a passing reference to the decreasing number of beershops in his annual reports.[119]

The turnover of ale houses became very slow again after 1869. There were just five refusals in the years between 1871 and 1875 with a similar number not renewing their licences (the fee was 8*s.* 6*d.* for ale houses and 6s. for beer houses). There were, however, a number of new licences issued and old ones reinstated. Of those that went down in 1869, four – *The Tiger*, *The Blockers Arms*, *The Railway Hotel* and *The Dudley Arms* – had all resumed business by 1875. *The George IV* re-opened some time afterwards and after several changes of name still (at the end of the twentieth century) operates. Other public houses which had been suspended were soon operating again: *The Freeholder, Gardeners Call, Mother Redcap, The Grapes, Fortune of War* (re-named *The Britannia*), *The Harrow* and *Bedford Arms*. Many of the above premises are still (1999) open for business. The public house referred to as *The King's Arms*, High Town (in 1869) was probably, in fact, *The King's Head* (there was a *King's Arms* in Chapel Street, probably a transfer of licence from the Middle Row establishment of the same name), and this re-appeared as *The King Henry VIII*. The magistrates also demonstrated a willingness to grant a limited number of new licences to beer shops which carried no name – fourteen between 1873 and 1875. Most identifiable public houses in the 1860s were still operating in the 1870s and it is difficult to believe that more than fifty nameless beer houses would close between 1871 and 1872 when it was obvious that the pressure from their tormentors was easing. The only possible explanation for the apparent discrepancy between the licensed returns and the Smyth/Ames estimate could be that the latter incorporated off-licences in their figures (*The World's End* re-emerged as one). Whatever the precise figure the era of the beer house was passing and their numbers were declining steadily. This was more due to economics and changing patterns of leisure than sustained pressure from temperance campaigners. An irony of these changes was the strengthening of the larger breweries. In the Luton area this meant that Thomas Sworder and J. W. Green were able to increase their empires of tied houses, adding licensed premises as the independent landlords and victuallers sold up.

None of the above qualifications is in any way an attempt to decry the efforts of those who genuinely desired to halt an apparently inexorable rise in social misery, and who believed after 1869 that they had effectively blunted it. Contemporary perceptions, however, can be modified by the small advantage that is afforded by hindsight. Whilst few Lutonians in the 1860s would be so foolish as to believe that the love of alcohol was absolutely the cause of all sinfulness, the preoccupation with the pursuit of the beer houses led to a failure to acknowledge adequately that rising crime could be influenced by other factors. Consequently, they did not perceive that the fall in crime after 1868 could also be attributable to other influences. These included the decline and subsequent disappearance of the 'Stattie', the greater control over the 5 November celebrations, improved street lighting and, more contentiously, local control over the police and administration of justice after 1876. It is also possible to point to the development of large engineering firms (Hayward Tyler and Balmforths were amongst the first); they provided more secure male employment and consequently improved standards of living. This was reflected in the improvement in housing and the diminution of slums. There were also alternative outlets in which to spend spare time and money, such as swimming and cycling, and the development of mass audience entertainment: bands, choirs, the Grand Theatre, (opened in 1898), Luton Town Football Club, formed in 1885. The significance of these developments was not fully appreciated at the time but each contributed, to varying degrees, to the decrease in crime, as well as to the lessening of the attractiveness of the public house and the churches. The contribution made by one other factor, education, to the reduction of squalor, poverty, disease and anti-social behaviour has been questioned.[120] During the middle of the nineteenth century, however, there were undoubtedly people in Luton who set great store by its benefits.

Part Four. The Gospel of Education

'Such a town as Luton, cannot be expected to boast of much literature' jibed Sir Richard Phillips, with justification, in 1828.[121] Had he returned to the much enlarged town 45 years later, he would not have needed to revise his original indictment. W.B. Stephens' excellent chapter in *Literacy and Society 1830-70* on literacy in the South Midlands succinctly described the region as a whole: 'The picture of the area in mid-century is of a predominantly poor rural working class culture, inward looking, often resentful, and ... lacking a substantial middle- and upper-class leavening. And change was very slow ...'.[122] The reasons for this state of backwardness were many: early marriage; a high proportion of women and children in domestic industry; surplus male labour; low wages; poor communications; few resident gentry but those who were, such as the clergy, not active supporters of education. There was an especially high concentration of illiteracy in the lace and straw plait areas. These, of course, were especially found in Bedfordshire, the worst county in a backward area. Within Bedfordshire, Stephens noted that Luton, the fastest growing town in the region, shared a number of features with other towns which were dominated by the cottage economy: a reliance upon the Sunday School to provide education and a particularly poor education for girls – there was no National school for girls in Luton, Dunstable or Leighton Buzzard during the mid-nineteenth century.

Given these factors it is, therefore, not difficult to see why Luton's standard of literacy was so low. Many, perhaps the majority, of those migrating to Luton were those who were seeking success and employment – rural labourers, plait sewers, the poor and the unemployed. They were moving because they had not attained a level of achievement in the locality from whence they came. Luton's middle class, best placed to support an adequate level of educational provision, remained small, and for those who had 'made-it' – owners of small workshops, shopkeepers and the like – the prevailing ethos in the town to a significant degree mitigated against philanthropic gestures. Independent methods of production may generate independent thought but it can also lead to selfish motivation. 'Fortunes were made by the people who had no education or culture' recalled one local Methodist.[123] Such people might well reason that they had made their 'fortunes' without the benefits of schooling, and what had been good enough for them would be good enough for others. They would not present their philosophy in the correspondence columns of the local press, nor would they articulate their prejudices in the form of handbills or pamphlets. They would, however, remain sullen or hostile to any local initiative that would cost them money, and some (as with the 1848 Health of Towns Act) would seek to subvert national legislation which was pressed upon them. This was to be Luton's experience; attempts to promote literacy and education were restricted to small-scale examples of middle class patronage and philanthropy.

Luton in the mid-century was a town which displayed at times chronic levels of illiteracy and ignorance. H.O. Williams recalled that the warehouses in George Street contained notices with 'very incorrect spelling' and a letter to the *Beds Times* in 1847 complained that 'bad grammar, bad rhyme and bad taste are simultaneously perpetrated' upon Luton's gravestones.[124] For the literate middle class there existed a tiny fringe of educational and literacy provision beyond their own homes. A Literary Institute foundered in October 1847 but was revived the following spring.[125] It possibly had originated as an attempt to promote literacy amongst the working class but lost what working men it had as members to the Mechanics Institute. It was regarded by some as elitist. The revived body was comprised entirely of the upper echelons of Luton's middle class: John Jones, Alfred Heale, C.S. Benning, John Waller, Henry and Kitt Tomson, E.C. Williamson, Charles Waller, C.A. and T.S. Austin, Richard Vyse, James Muir, William Phillips, Rev T. Sikes, Thomas Sworder, William Bigg, Frederick Brown, William Willis and E.O. Williams. All other sectors of society were excluded. The patronage of Leigh, Crawley and Ames was sought but if they agreed they never extended this in any active way within the society, and the three men never pushed for their involvement within its affairs. The above company of men were the principal subscribers and the books purchased reflected their interests – mainly history and travel, but with some literature and biography. There was also a range of periodicals and newspapers – *Illustrated London News, Punch, Edinburgh Review, Quarterly*

Review, Morning News and *The Times* amongst others.[126] From time to time these were sold off to subscribers. The Institute's female counterpart was the Women's Literary Institution formed in March 1859.[127] This organisation also held evening lectures and by 1862 had fifty members. William Bigg's daughter, Louisa, was one of the leading members.[128]

The smallness of Luton's bourgeoisie and the proximity of the Bedford public schools, in particular, mitigated against the need for the establishment of private schools in the town. The former home of William Hunt in New Bedford Road was converted into the Villa School run by E. Parsons during the latter part of 1848. Upon his death in 1856 this passed into the hands of Henry Wright who had run the New Hall Academy (probably located near to the junction of Wellington Street and Stuart Street) close by another private school (for girls) in Upper Wellington Street. The New Hall Academy included evening classes for adults on Tuesdays and Fridays at 8.00 pm but details of the curriculum and the students are not known.[129] During the 1840s and 1850s there were a small number of other minor, often short-lived, schools within the town, many of them in the vicinity of middle class Wellington Street. The Luton Academy in Church Street was run by a Mr Newland, and next door to Henry Wright's Wellington Street school was another 'Ladies' School'. Here, in a schoolroom claimed to be capable of accommodating 60 children, pupils received a basic education in writing, arithmetic and needlework. At the same time there also existed Alliance House (run by Madame Villenoxe) and the Misses Beeby's private school for ladies 'conducted on principals calculated to lay the foundation of a sound moral and religious character'.[130]

From 1841 Rev Henry Burgess and his wife ran the Luton Grammar School from his home at the Bury. Here there were three resident masters, one being a 'Professor of French, German and Italian'. The education administered there covered 'Every branch of learning except Music and Drawing'. In 1848 fees ranged from £30–40 per annum for boarders and £8 for day scholars. The main schoolroom was nearly sixty feet in length and in January 1847 there were between 30–40 pupils. Naturally, Burgess stamped his own personality upon the place. In advertisements he stressed that he and his wife treated pupils as their own sons, adding that 'experience of five years has taught that corporal punishment is not necessary'. The Grammar School disappeared with Rev Burgess in 1848.[131]

Rev Henry Burgess was also the key figure in the early days of the local Mechanics Institute. Self-help for the working class did not exist in the field of education and in Luton, as elsewhere, dedicated commitment on the part of members of the middle class was required, without which educational projects were unsustainable.[132] The Luton Mechanics Institute was imbued with a middle class character but for a while at least seems to have run successfully. In 1846 there were claimed to be 200 members. It had its own reading room and took *The Times* and *The Sun*. Vice-President to Burgess was James Waller; John Wiseman was the secretary and Robert Marsh the treasurer. One 'soiree' held in 1846 featured a small choir and 'a series of dissolving views exhibited in a first rate style'.[133] A series of lectures was given by Henry Vincent, probably the Chartist campaigner, each 'to a large and highly respectable audience', with proceeds going towards the establishment of a library. The proportion of working class members in this 'highly respectable' audience would be interesting to know. Even more overtly middle class was a tea meeting held in the Victoria Rooms to raise funds for the Mechanics Institute. Burgess, William Willis, Henry Brown, John Everitt, and Rev Robert Robinson were all present at a ticket only meeting at which 500 'ladies and gentlemen of all political and religious parties' were in attendance. Many more were turned away.[134]

The strength of the working class component within the Mechanics Institute is not precisely known but it is apparent that in the first flush of enthusiasm a number were attracted whose attitudes challenged those of Rev Burgess. This was the reason for his warning, at the 1847 Annual General Meeting, against the 'levelling tone' in some of the speeches which had been heard from the platform, and his reminder that rank and degrees of wealth and intellect were of 'divine appointment'.[135] An attempt to assert control over the Institute, based upon such attitudes, would inevitably have alienated many in a town such as Luton. Burgess was to quit in any case within two years, and it was perhaps due to both these reasons that the Mechanics Institute began to run out of steam. Tea meetings, soirees and concerts were periodically held at the Town Hall to raise money for the Institute's library, but although they were successful social events in themselves few 'mechanics' actually attended them.[136]

William Bigg became the driving force in the 1850s and the Mechanics Institute instigated a series of 'popular lectures' in imitation of the revived Harmonic Society's 'People's Concerts'. In 1857 an 'Exhibition of articles of vertu and curiosities of art and nature' was organised. The seven man exhibition committee comprised Henry Wright, Henry Brown, John Wiseman, William Alford, Joseph Hawkes (wheelwright and victualler), John Merrit (carpenter) and William Faunch (shopkeeper). The successful exhibition, Luton's foretaste of a museum, attracted 2230 adults and 660 children in two days. The visitors viewed paintings loaned by Cumberland, Ames, Austin, Williamson, Rev Bartlett and Mrs Burr, together with gas meters lent by William Phillips on behalf of The Luton Gas Company. There were also two aquaria, books, medals, insects, minerals, stuffed birds, seaweed, a printing press and archaeological specimens lent by Dr Nicholson of St. Albans.[137] The Exhibition raised £51 10*s*. 3*d*. The Mechanics Institute was run at this time by a committee of eighteen men. An occupation can be attributed to thirteen of these with a fair degree of certainty, comprising one bank manager, one carpenter, one wheelwright and victualler, two who ran hat factories, one who owned a warehouse and seven who were shopkeepers. It was the bank manager, William Bigg, who was the leading light on this unwieldy, lower middle class committee. The reading room and library was situated in the Town Hall and took evening papers and periodicals in addition to the dailies. The charge for use was 2s. 6d. per quarter for daily readers and 1s. 6d. for evening readers. Women were admitted at 1s. per quarter. The library of 500 volumes made 600 issues per annum.[138]

The problem for the Mechanics Institute was that its support did not penetrate far into the working class. Lectures on general themes such as 'Anatomy' or 'French' (the country's topography not its politics), would attract reasonable audiences, but topics aimed specifically at enlightening the working class, such as E.C. Williamson's 'The Art of Reading', received only 'scanty support'.[139] By 1861 expenditure was exceeding income by £12 per annum. The library was clearly under utilised and was castigated as being 'shockingly bad ... (it) consists of books that do not add anything to the majority of the members'.[140] Saddled with a library which was just a repository for useless books which no-one had the heart to throw away, attracting the active support of just one member of the bourgeoisie and with no popular base amongst the working class, the Mechanics Institute had run out of steam. It limped on until it lapsed completely some time after 1872.

The Mechanics Institute's revival in 1875 was at the initiative of a group of High Town workmen. At the inaugural meeting repeated reference was made to the cause of past failures. Although it was acknowledged that the irregular, often late, working hours of many would weaken commitment, the fundamental reason for failure – lack of support from the working men of the town – was also emphasised. Nonetheless, once again the well-intentioned from the middle class took control: Elliot Howard, a manager of Hayward Tyler, William Bigg, Henry Wright, A.T. Webster and Revs Adams, Tuckwell and Billian. Once again the inaugural meetings were tea meetings and soirees held not in working class districts, but within the grander architecture of the Town Hall. Once again it failed. After initial enthusiasm (there were 130 members in December 1875), attendances at support meetings dropped dramatically and the Mechanics Institute made few inroads into the working class.[141]

It is useless to speculate whether the Mechanics Institute would have fared better or worse with greater control exercised by working men. It may have possessed greater relevance to that sector of society, but less resources and time on the part of those who would have had to shoulder the administration and programmes. With hindsight it seems more than a little naive for members of Luton's middle class to meddle with the aspirations of those of whom they had little understanding. Hindsight, however, ought to be accompanied by humility and an appreciation of the culture in which Luton's philanthropists worked, circumstances that were far from encouraging or helpful. At times the gulf between the different sectors of society must have seemed vast. Many working people would feel alienated in more affluent company, not by pure class antagonism, but for more prosaic reasons such as social awkwardness or embarrassment at inadequate literacy. Reluctant to admit their own deficiencies, many would simply stay away. 'What is needed in Luton... is a sincere desire on the part of the well-educated and thoughtful to raise the mental status of those beneath them' wrote one observer. There was much more to this than simply providing reading matter since this was merely 'an instrument or vehicle of wisdom and nothing more'.[142] Education was a means of enabling the working classes to enjoy middle class privileges and habits. In Luton, as in most Victorian towns and cities, an epitome of this was the tea meeting. 'The most popular form of entertainment in Luton is probably that which commences in a social cup of tea and finishes with a song, the intervals being well filled up with brief addresses.'[143] If the results of their attempts at patronage were disappointing, and they usually were, failure could be attributed to the lack of support from one's peers or any number of defects from those below. This in no way is intended to denigrate the voluntary efforts of those who became involved in attempts to promote popular education. After all, at least they made an effort and usually did so with genuine altruism. The problem was that they simply had so little understanding of those who they were trying to help.

The most serious indictment against middle class forays into the field of education, however, was not the dubious ideological base upon which they were established. Their primary weakness was that because they were voluntary they relied too often upon the commitment of a small number of individuals. Many attempts were simply half-hearted and short-lived, leaving the Sunday School organisation as the most consistent outlet for philanthropic work. Each church possessed its own Sunday School which combined a mixture of basic secular education with religious instruction. Accommodation was not always satisfactory and there is some evidence to suggest that discipline was not always of the highest order. The standard of teaching varied enormously: Joseph Hawkes, an active Methodist, later recalled that the small number of day school scholars were more than a match for their teachers.[144] There is also no doubt that secular education was provided out of a sense of obligation, Hawkes describing it as a 'drudgery' which was relieved by compulsory school attendance in the 1870s. Nonetheless, for up to a fifth of Luton's children (18% in the 1851 census) the Sunday School was the nearest they came to any form of instruction, this applying especially to girls. It also provided children with other benefits – teas, outings and in general a social life which removed them from the streets. Just 8% attended day school.

Although Rev Robert Robinson of the Union Chapel withdrew from active participation in the Mechanics Institute he did develop his own lecture series which were aimed at young people. The subjects included 'On Animal Instinct', 'The Philosophy of Common Things' and 'On the Importance and Means of Advancement in Knowledge'. In 1851 his Sunday School contained 810 persons (the age range is unknown), a massive burden upon those who possessed teaching abilities amongst the 330 members. This led to enormous pressure upon individuals to go straight into teaching once their own education was complete, no matter how rudimentary that happened to be.[145]

A case study is provided by Frederick Thurston, the outstanding photographer in Bedfordshire and north Hertfordshire during the late nineteenth and early twentieth centuries. The only son of a widowed straw plaiter he was raised in poverty in a street close to the Union Chapel. It is possible that he attended the nearby British Langley Street School, but more probably he received the bulk of his education from the Sunday School of the Union Chapel, a church of which he became a full member at the age of fifteen in 1869. Either way, his education would have been at best elementary and one which he augmented by attending 'Arts and Sciences' classes (at which he studied art) once he had gained full-time employment. It appears that Thurston graduated straight from the status of Sunday School pupil to Sunday School teacher. By the time he was twenty-four he was the Superintendent of the Sunday School at the village branch church in Caddington. The speed of his elevation was due as much to stretched personnel resources at Union Chapel as to any teaching gifts of his own.[146]

The Sunday Schools, and the various other educational programmes mounted by the churches, were vehicles which partly aimed to maintain what A.A. Maclaren defined as a 'church connection' with the working class.[147] A crucial element of this 'connection' was the personal bond between the teacher or officer on the one hand and the scholar on the other, a point which further emphasises the importance of gifted teachers. Sunday Schools were certainly not fertile recruiting grounds for church membership, a fact that was universally acknowledged at the time. Park Street Baptist Sunday School contained two sick visitors on its committee of nine, but an attempt (in 1863) to coax these scholars into the wider life of the church proved disastrous:

> We at school wanted more room to teach so we sent up to (sic) of our chief classes hoping they would prove a nucleus around which many others would gradually be drawn so as in time to

> include several adult classes . . . We thought that they would meet for an hour for studying the Bible and edifying conversation to Christian duty greatly neglected, at 3 O'clock the minister would come and close the service by giving a short address. We made rather a bad beginning. There was not sufficient distinctiveness of purpose in our plan and partial failure was the result. Two of the classes who with their Teachers had been used to the warmth, the kindliness, the coziness characteristic of our school felt the change to be far from beneficial – it seemed to them like leaving a family fireside and going out into a waste howling wilderness, it made them shudder to think of going there week after week – cold shudders came over them succeeded by a season of depression of spirits . . . [148]

The plan was aborted.

It is, however, a gross exaggeration to suggest that the educational ventures promoted by the religious or secular organisations, even the most glaringly middle class ones, were a means of exerting social control over the sectors of society beneath them. Naturally, education was used to impart virtues which, perhaps, some members of the middle classes regarded as distinctively associated with themselves. To espouse certain virtues, even to the extent of meddling in other people's lives, is not necessarily to control, an action which necessitates greater efficiency than was shown in Luton. Does '. . . the Importance and Means of Advancement in Knowledge' really lie squarely with social control? Luton provides no evidence that control was the purpose which motivated those who promoted education for children. 'Evangelicalism was the factor most responsible for moulding the Baptist conscience in the nineteenth century', argued David Bebbington, and for the Methodists, Congregationalists, and many Anglicans and even Quakers also, this spilled over into a host of unco-ordinated examples of social intervention.[149] Education was often at the heart of these efforts but evangelism was pursued for reasons of liberation – from ignorance, despair, sin and poverty – not control.

Indeed, far from a sense of confidence, the surviving Sunday School reports carry a tone of burdensome duty and humility. Park Street's annual report for 1869, laid this weary message before the church:

> Those of you have never been engaged in this work can have no conception of the disappointed hopes, the unavailing regrets . . . we are frequently obliged to experience.
>
> What a very chilling influence comes over us as we think of lost opportunities from our own neglect of duty – of the perverseness of human nature – of the folly that is boundless in the heart of a child – of prayers apparently unanswered – of the many instances we see of defeat, of the victories gained over is by the Devil, we feel disposed to lay down our arms to throw up our commission – to take our ease and leave the strife with evil to abler hands.[150]

Plate 13

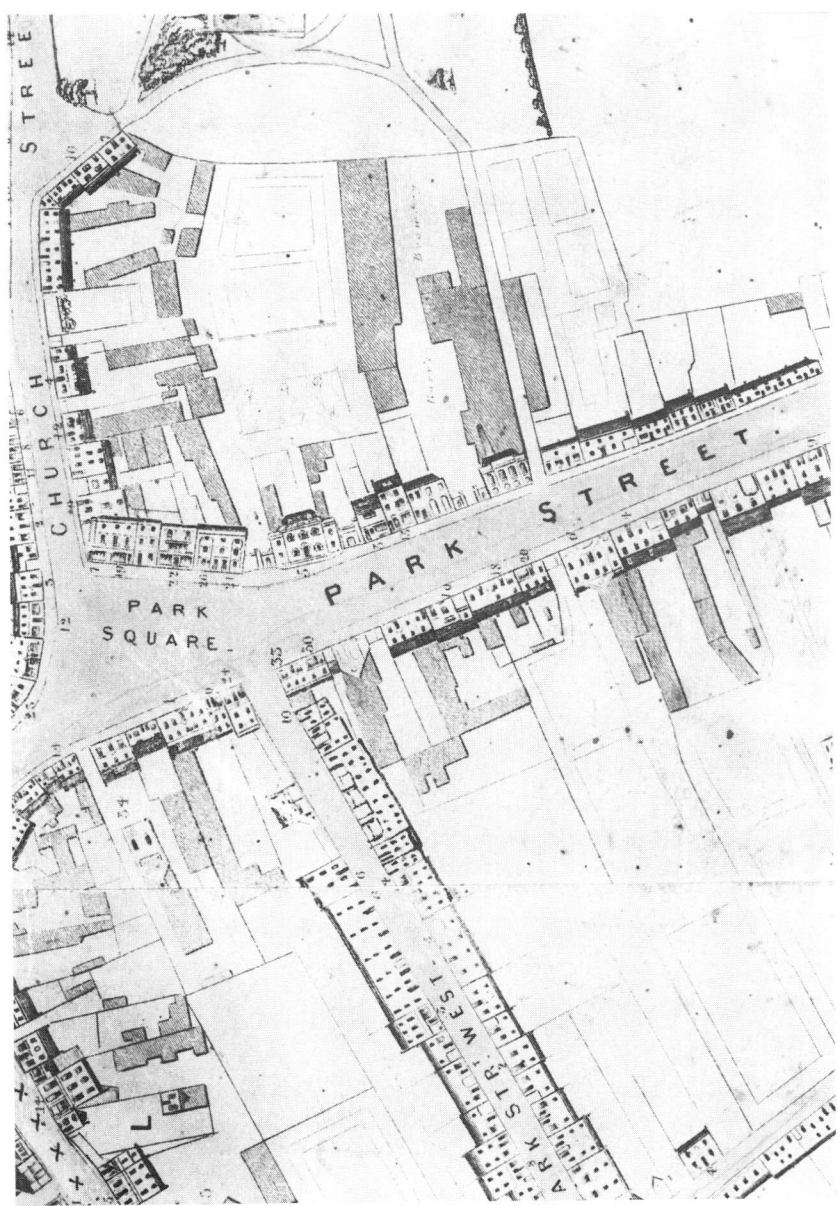

A section of Todd's map of Luton, 1862 (BRO).

Plate 14

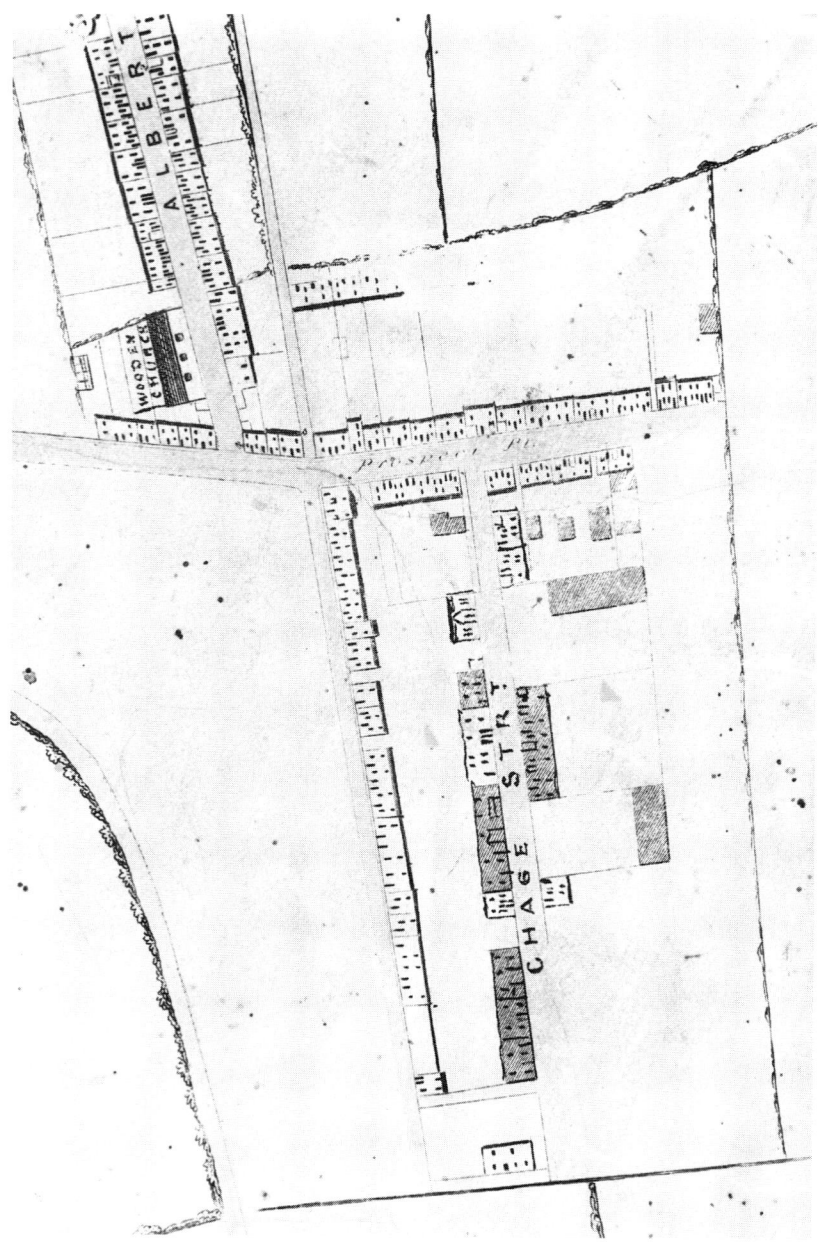

Chase Street and a section of Albert Road, showing the location of Harris' church, from Todd's pictorial map (BRO).

Plate 15

(a) The minister and deacons of King Street Congregational Church c. 1868. Rev J.H. Hitchens (seated centre) is flanked (clockwise from the left) by A.T. Webster, G.M. Johnson, Charles Robinson, W.T. Coates, Hugh Gunn and Charles Tomalin (LM).

(b) James Adams (BRO).

Plate 16

(b) Frederick Brown (LM).

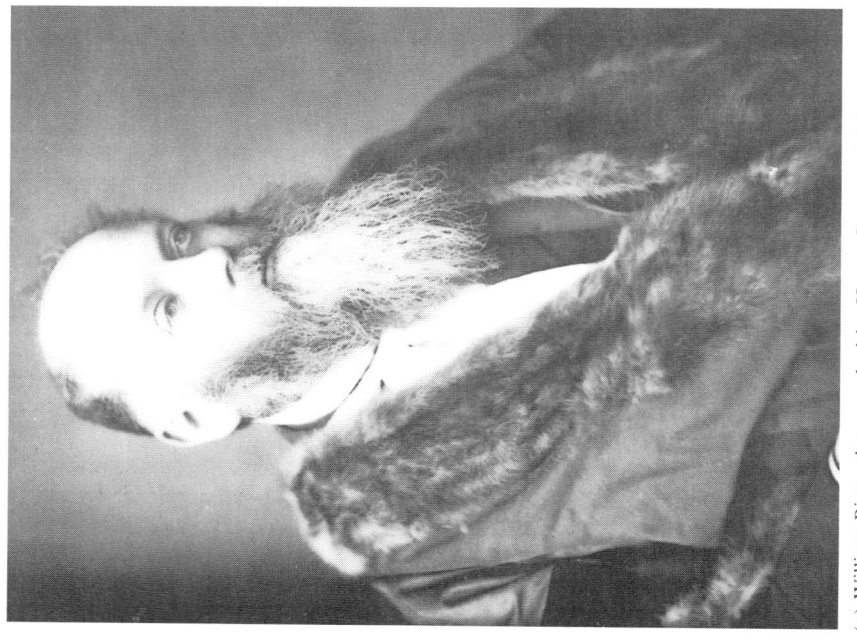

(a) William Bigg, photographed by Henry Gregson (LM).

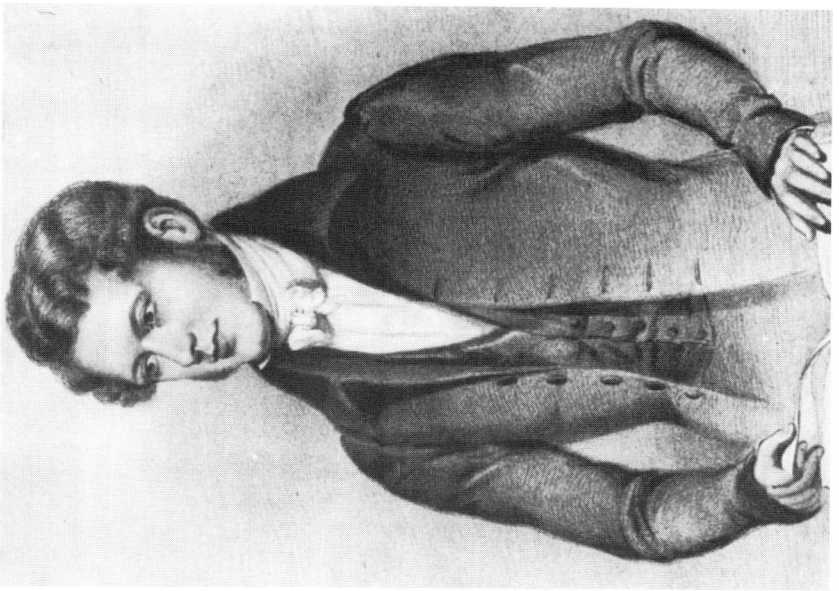

(a) Henry Brown (LM).

(b) Rev Henry Burgess (taken from *People of the Meeting House* by J.S. Fisher).

Plate 17

Plate 18

(a) John Cumberland, photographed by Henry Gregson. (LM).  (b) Hugh Gunn (LM)

Plate 19

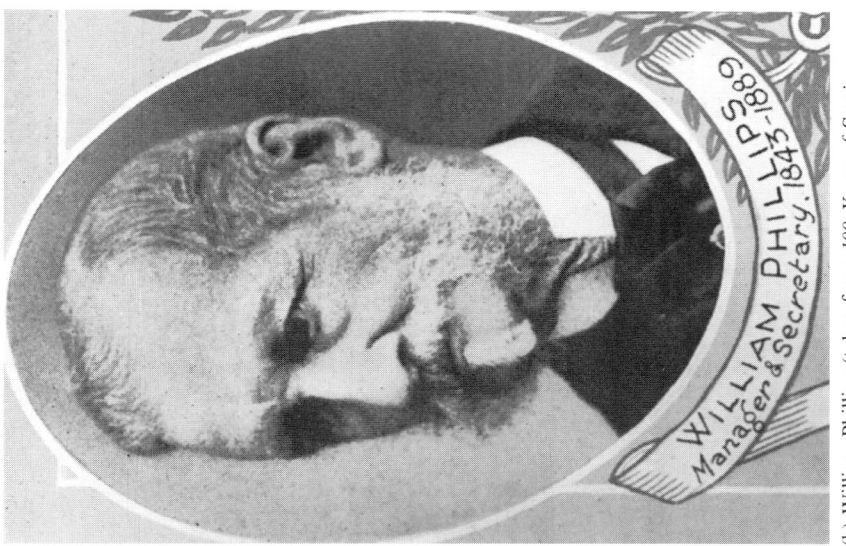

(b) William Phillips (taken from *100 Years of Service* published by the Luton Gas company, 1934, LM collection).

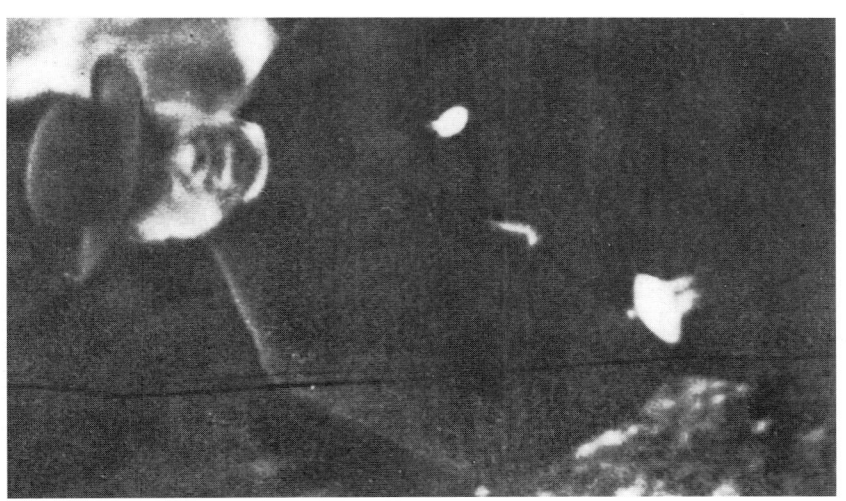

(a) Rev James O'Neill (LM/BI).

Plate 20

(a) John Webdale, photographed by Henry Gregson (LM).

(b) Levi Welch, from a photograph taken at the time of his imprisonment for the Round Green murder. Welch was aged 40, was 5'6" tall and was covered in sores from scurvy. Unable to read or write, Welch was a married man living at 83, Burr Street (BRO).

If the aim of the middle classes was to define the parameters of working class behaviour, then something a little more co-ordinated would have been forthcoming than the jumble of only partially successful ventures which Luton experienced until the 1870s. Indeed, it might be possible to argue that, if social control was a primary motive of the middle classes, they might not have bothered to attempt to impart the power of knowledge at all. In any case, the hat, retail and building trades did not require high standards of training in most of their branches.[149]

Until the advent of compulsory education the Sunday Schools were the most comprehensive, firmly founded and consistently financed institutions for the provision of education in Luton. Beyond them lay the philanthropic efforts of the middle class, initiating self-improvement amongst children and adults. The Gaitskell Terrace Evening School, situated in High Town, was one such effort. Formed in 1857, this establishment was presided over by Rev J.J. Davies and included the familiar roll-call of public spirited Lutonians amongst its committee and funders – William Stalker, Sworder, Bigg, C. Austin, the Burrs, the Browns, Tansley and Wootton. The first year's intake totalled 130 admissions with an average attendance of 40. Of the first batch, ten could read but not write and 43 could manage neither. The same number had not received any Sunday School instruction, emphasising that in creating the Gaitskell Terrace Evening School its promoters were aware of a constituency which was immune to the lure of the churches. The inevitable library was established (140 volumes after twelve months) which the organisers thought would be good for the students. A penny bank was also established but the 39 deposits totalling £46. 1s. 0d. was thought to be a 'disappointing' response.[151] The age and sex ratio of the pupils are not revealed but with its President dying shortly after the first AGM, the Gaitskell Terrace Evening School slipped into obscurity. There is little doubt that the School was a venture promoted from the Baptist Old Meeting by Rev J.J. Davies as a form of evangelism in High Town, an area in which the Baptists had no real presence, relying upon Davies' leadership for its continuation. It ran at the same time as the Mechanics Institute, an unnecessary duplication of limited resources, typifying the unco-ordinated nature of middle class effort. The absence of a local authority to act as a forum for debate and decision making pushed all the required initiative and commitment into the lap of a small number of individuals. This much was recognised by William Bigg who called in 1861 for Luton not to try and run numerous feeble self-help educational institutions (the Mechanics Institute was struggling at this time), but to have just one effective body.[152]

Having made this observation Bigg was then guilty of perpetuating the same error. The Luton Society of Friends, choosing to ignore Sunday School development, attempted to imitate the work of William White and Joseph Sturge in Birmingham by establishing an Adult

School in March 1862.[153] The aim of the school was 'the giving of instruction to young men and women of the more neglected class in Reading, Writing and the Holy Scripture'. To establish this school they made one major investment by purchasing the defunct National School in Church Street. In the schoolroom measuring 54'7" by 37'6" they erected wooden screens with men on one side and women on the other. Scholars (no one under the age of sixteen) were admitted upon recommendation after 'due enquiry' by the teacher. Initially, two lessons were run between nine and ten-fifteen in the morning, with the first half hour devoted to reading and writing and the latter part to scripture. The school was run by a Superintendent and a General Committee which met quarterly. Yet another library was established with 215 volumes by 1864 including 73 purchased from the Pure Literature Society. The Quakers, with their keen eye for business, were aware of past failure and consequently did not regard the school as a bottomless pit in which to pour their money. Income, during the initial period at least, was raised almost entirely from subscriptions. The total income quoted in the sixth annual report amounted to £52 17s. 7d. Of this figure £32 11s. 0d. was drawn from 26 subscribers, William Bigg, eight Browns and the names of Drewett, Lucas, Green, Marsh and Seebohm prominent amongst them.

Later plans for expansion, through the purchase of buildings in Melson Street to the rear of the school, were abandoned as only £150 of the £600 necessary was raised – the Quakers' caution was well-founded. Although the General Committee had agreed that the maximum membership should not exceed 40 of each sex, only three men turned up on the first day to be greeted by five teachers – Bigg, Richard and William Henry Brown, Benjamin Seebohm and Robert Marsh. Average attendances during 1862–3 was very low – approximately fourteen of each sex – from a total of 32 men and 42 women.

After a difficult first year matters improved, especially when evening classes were introduced in the late 1860s. William White was brought down to provide inspiration at the annual tea meeting in 1863 and a Mutual Improvement Society, Cottage Garden Society, Sick Benefit Club and Savings Bank were all formed during the first ten years. The savings of the scholars, meticulously recorded, would make an interesting area of separate study in their own right, not least to investigate the extent to which they reflected any patterns in disposable income during the yearly trade cycle. During the 1860s Mary Ann Haynott was one example of those who were able to make their strongest and most regular contributions from January through to the end of May.[154] The sixth annual report declared that due to '. . . the late distress in this town, owing to the extreme dullness of trade, there has been but little money either put into the Benevolent Box or laid by in the Savings Fund'. By the time of the second annual report the optimism was greater: 'In the reading and writing of the scholars generally an advance is perceptible. There is an increase of sympathy and attachment between the teachers and the taught, and the teachers are not without hope that some moral and religious benefit is derived'.

The numbers in attendance were prone to fluctuation, part of the reason for which was clearly understood. The drop in the summer months' attendance was attributed, in the 1866 annual report, to the 'fluctuating character of our population; many of the work people leave the town at the close of the busy season'. This is borne out by the numbers registered. In September 1865 there were 177 on the register (64 men and 113 women). By March of the following year, at the height of the busy season, the total stood at 239 (100 men, 139 women). By September of that year the figure had fallen back to 211 (84 men, 127 women). It appears that the number of long term pupils was relatively few.

There is also a clear realism, demonstrated in the pages of the Adult School records, as to the extent of its impact upon the recipients. 'We cannot point to any great results – but while there is much of sin and folly around us, still we may feel deeply thankful in seeing here and there the careless one becoming thoughtful . . .'. This realism was, furthermore, tempered with humility. In the eighth annual report (in 1870) Benjamin Seebohm, the secretary, considered the efforts of the staff – efforts which included home visiting. 'Whilst reviewing the past, many of the Teachers feel their deficiencies and short-comings . . .'. Two years later he concluded: 'How far their labours have been instrumental in elevating the moral character of their scholars . . . is known only to Him . . . but the Teachers feel that they need greater earnestness in the more serious part of their labours . . .'.

On a far less successful scale other self-help societies were formed or were spawned by churches. The Young Men's Mutual Improvement Society began at King Street Congregational Church in 1869 (at which there was already a Pleasant Sunday Afternoon meeting), although after a disagreement with the diaconate they began to meet at the Town Hall.[155] There was also an Elocution Society and, in 1873, 'evenings of instruction' for sewers at the Corn Exchange. As many as 60 apparently attended for activities which included needlework, singing and reading.[156]

Libraries

As with education generally, the provision of libraries depended upon individual promoters in the absence of collective organisation and popular support. Again, such ventures were short-lived. Wiseman operated a circulating library, although that presumably dissolved with his bankruptcy in April 1861. Joseph Tearle established a free reading room for the working class in Wellington Street (possibly in the same premises as his straw plait warehouse) in 1859. There was also a Workmen's

Reading Room which closed down in 1873 due to lack of support – the subscriptions did not even pay for the newspapers.[157]

It was William Bigg again who attempted to promote a Luton Library. On 29 January 1866 a soiree was held at the Town Hall to pursue this end. The core of the library was to be the 3000 volumes bequested by E.C. Williamson for this purpose (Williamson had been dead for nearly three years). The proposals foundered upon the question of money. Bigg suggested that shares be issued to raise approximately £2500 needed to erect a building. 'The proceedings were not very enthusiastic' commented the *Beds Times*.[158] Bigg tried again in 1872 and a public meeting was held at the Corn Exchange with a view to establishing a Free Library. Sadly, the meeting became over run with drunks and degenerated into a minor riot. With other educational matters to concern him, Bigg let the matter drop until after incorporation.[159]

The evolution of public education

It is little surprise that in such a highly individualistic town as Luton there should have been so little co-ordinated educational provision. The haphazard altruism of the local bourgeoisie, however laudable on an individual basis, produced no overall improvement in the standard of education for the majority of Luton's children. The nature of the local economy, and the prevailing ethos which resulted from it, mitigated against a popular ground swell in favour of the building of schools. The *Luton Times* declared that 'the duty of the people of Luton is no longer to leave the education of the poor in the irresponsible hands of sects and parties, but to take the management of the business in their own hands . . .'.[160] The people of Luton, however, showed no inclination to take matters of education into their hands in the way that the *Luton Times* would have wished. There were few, if any, plait schools within a town where only a small number of adults would have received more than a most rudimentary education. Parents may in all probability have decided that their children could manage well enough on what they themselves had received. People who were poor valued greatly, to the extent of reliance, the little extra income with which children could augment the domestic economy. The cogent rejoinder to the attitude articulated by such as the *Luton Times* and William Bigg came from Frederick Davis, a more typical Lutonian than the Quaker Bank Manager. Davis praised 'the industrious man', collectively ' . . . by their industry and the sweat of their brow have acquired a little money – they have invested it in freehold property – upon that property are put all local rates . . .'.[161] Davis was here opposing the proposals to establish a School Board and the inevitable rate which would follow. This attitude struck a chord amongst a sizeable part of Luton's citizens on almost any issue which required collective financial responsibility. The whole philosophy of the town was (and arguably remains), centred upon the individual and their home as a place of security and happiness, as a symbol of liberty and personal achievement. The opinions of the classes below Davis – the labourers who rented more humble dwellings, the migrant workers who crammed into lodgings – were never consulted, considered or recorded. Stephens' conclusion, that only the compulsion of central legislation and decline of domestic industry would improve the standard of literacy in the South Midlands as a whole, applied especially to Luton. He makes clear that the town's level of illiteracy fell slightly (from 44% in 1856 to 32% in 1871). He adds that its relative position compared with other registration districts within this backward region actually deteriorates from a ranking of 46 down to 60 out of 68 between the above dates. Slower growing towns such as Newmarket, St. Albans and Ely all superseded Luton in the fifteen year span. The position of schooling for girls was particularly abysmal with an estimated 36% being illiterate in 1871.[162] Those, therefore, who advocated a decent basic education for Luton's children faced formidable obstacles.

Accounts of educational developments in Luton have been also discussed by J. G. Dony and others, but a brief outline of developments up to the first election of a local School Board provides some context for what followed.[163] A school based upon Lancasterian principals opened in Park Square in 1809 and a Ragged School also existed in Park Street.[164] The local compromise between the nonconformists and the Church of England which allowed the Lancasterian School to operate disintegrated over the provision of grant, thereupon the two sides commenced a school building programme which was tightly affiliated to their respective wings of protestantism. The issue of grant was really the catalyst for change which was being brought about by a deepening division between them. The nonconformists in Luton were no doubt becoming increasingly dissatisfied with the no more than nominal contact with the successor body to the Royal Lancasterian Association, the British and Foreign School Society. The Luton Lancasterian School had succeeded the former Church School and remained largely in Anglican control. Once the split became imminent the two sides moved swiftly. The managers of the Lancasterian School applied to affiliate to the National Society taking up the grant from the Treasury (which was specifically for the construction of a new school), raising the rest by subscription. The Marquess of Bute provided the land plus more than £100 toward the £592. 18s. 4d. needed to build the first National School in Church Street in June 1835. Fourteen months later the nonconformists, affiliated to the British Society, were able to provide day education for between 200 and 300 boys with some girls being allowed to attend in the evening. In addition to this the Wesleyans established their own day school for between 250 and 300 children adjacent to their church in Chapel Street as well as the Crown and Anchor School at the rear of the public house of that name in New Bedford Road. The National

School in Church Street accommodated approximately 140 boys in what must have been extremely cramped conditions. The nonconformists could augment the minimal day school education with the Sunday Schools. The Church of England on the other hand, lacking the corresponding education provision on the Sabbath until probably the mid-1840s, needed to expand upon the tiny National School.

In attempting to do this the Anglicans were hampered by a lack of money from local sources to match central grants. The nonconformists had thwarted attempts by the Church to levy a church rate for school building in 1835 and so this option was no longer open. The departure of the Marquess of Bute in the following decade deprived them of a valuable source of support which J.S. Leigh did not show any inclination to replace. The Crawleys were notable omissions from the list of subscribers towards the first National School and remained that way, although they did give generous support to the building of schools on their estates in Stopsley, and probably also at Biscot. Powerful Anglican families diminished as farmers, such as Clarke and Kidman, left central Luton, and other supporters, such as the Burrs and Chases, departed. The manners of James O'Neill could not have helped. Church Street, therefore, was sold (becoming in time the Friends Adult School) in order to build a new one in Queen Square. This was still too small to meet the need, even allowing for its scholars' casual approach towards attendance.[165]

By 1870 the picture in Luton was of a disorganised assortment of educational facilities – sectarian, voluntary, charitable and private.[166] There were two British Schools, the purpose built Langley Street and the school operating at the Primitive Methodist Church in High Town. There were three National Schools, one of them purpose built. Considerable sympathy must be felt for the ill-resourced headmasters of Queen Square School, David Stalker (1863–72) and his successor, Edward Pegler, as they gamely battled on in the face of obstinate ignorance: '... many children are kept away on the most lame excuses by their parents ...' moaned Pegler in 1873.[167] Clearly, child labour in the straw trade and at harvest time was a principle reason for non-attendance but this problem was compounded by a consequent ill-discipline and, after an initial enthusiasm, a lack of resources. James O'Neill was a regular visitor, a mixed blessing perhaps, but support elsewhere was thin on the ground. The log book contains transcripts of the annual Inspectors' Reports and they make depressing reading. Assessment of the boys in 1866 revealed 'the want of Pupil Teachers ...' and two years later the Inspector made this terse comment: "It is to be regretted that greater efforts are not made by the supporters of this school to maintain its former efficiency". The headmasters were supported by usually no more than two pupil teachers, although by 1874 this had doubled and been further augmented by a full time teacher. The quality of the pupil teachers was unsatisfactory and there is little doubt that the overall standard of learning was abysmal. 'The children in this school do not appear to have had the care or instruction given to them which they ought. Many were kept back from examination and many more failed', concluded the Inspector in 1873. Infrequent attendance and a lack of books helped ensure a regular deduction of grant by the National Society: in 1865 Queen Square was threatened with complete severance.

The other two National schools were the Iron School in Church Street (opened in 1864) and Wellington Street (opened in 1868). Little is known about these, not even their exact location, although Wellington Street may have been an initiative of nearby Christ Church. It is difficult to believe that either were better resourced than Queen Square. The Methodists operated their Wesleyan Day School, now at their 'cathedral' in Chapel Street. Most schools were woefully inadequate for the pupils who attended and the majority of children remained untouched by them. The position was bad enough for boys but worse for girls. 'It is notorious how badly the female children of Luton have been educated in the past' complained the *Luton Times*.[168] By the early 1870s, a pedigree of foiled educational ventures and an inadequate British and National School system had left, in Henry Blundell's estimate, around 1200 children receiving no education at all.[169]

As Stephens correctly observed, it was national legislation, namely Forster's Education Act of 1870, which provided the opportunity for real improvement. Within the small bourgeoisie there were a majority in favour of the establishment of a Luton School Board to replace the voluntary system. These supporters included the usual phalanx of nonconformists plus the Liberal Vicar of Biscot, Rev E.R. Adams, and also J.S. Crawley. Opposed to a School Board scheme were, naturally, the other Anglican ministers and some of the Wesleyans such as Charles Mees, Gustavus Jordan and Rev P. Budd, who remained committed to the separate Wesleyan system. Amongst the ratepaying population in general, however, there was never any doubt that the School Board supporters were in a minority.

There is little reason to disagree with J.G. Dony's conclusion that the school building programme subsequently undertaken by the Established Church was little more than a desperate, not to say cynical, attempt to negate the need for a School Board to which it would have to surrender all its powers. Here at least we see an example of a desire to exert a form of social control through education. Rev O'Neill clearly wished to have the dominant say in what went into the minds of Luton children, although the Established Church's lacklustre record to date provided scant evidence that it rated education's varied benefits very highly. Rev T.J. Lee was actively raising funds for a new school building, having gathered approximately £1600 toward the total cost of £2500. It is not certain whether this was to augment or replace the Wellington Street

School but there was no doubt where he stood on the School Board issue:

> I will only observe on that part of the subject that we have opposed the School Board system as being dangerous, expensive, and despotic – dangerous, because its hold of religion is feeble – expensive, because every Scholar under its operation costs at least twice as much as under the Voluntary System – and despotic, because it already to a certain extent, and in the future threatens still more, to interfere with the right of a poor man to choose his own School for his own child.[170]

Echoes of the fight for a Board of Health thirty years before were heard again. Charles Robinson was ready to apply his own interpretation of recent history:

> 'Wait' is the old cry of the obstructers of public progress. The present time is never the right time for a reformation or a remedy, in the estimation of persons of this class. You will remember the cry was once 'Wait' for a railway, and so to us advantages were delayed which might have been earlier secured. Again 'Wait' for a Local government, which meant 'be satisfied with filth and fever, and hold cleanliness and comfort in abeyance .' Again, 'Wait for a Plait Hall,' – rain, mud and other evils notwithstanding. And yet again, your memory will recall other occasions when beneficial projects have been assailed in like manner. Have no faith, then, in a cry designed to deprive you of a great boon.[171]

For the pro-Board lobby, the arguments were simple: non-sectarianism, morality, egalitarianism, local control and more than a hint of anti-clericalism. One pro-Board poster counselled: '... do not allow the Interests of the Landlord and Clergy to Rob you of it'.[172] There were sentiments abroad even less measured than that. 'A Voluntary Sunday School Teacher' quoted John Bright in support of advice not to be 'bamboozled by the Parsons'. Warning of 'Popish tendencies... Church Rates, Tithes, Easter offerings, and other abominations', this rabid little diatribe concluded 'I implore you not to put the Education of your children under the control of any Sect. Follow the example of 8,000,000 of your countrymen, and free yourselves for ever from the trammels of PRIESTCRAFT!'[173]

A meeting in February 1871, billed as a Working Men's Meeting against the proposed School Board attracted, prominent labourers and mechanics such as Thomas Sworder, Frederick Davis and T.C. Johnson on to the platform. Frederick Brown was also present to deny rumours that his firm would dismiss any worker who opposed the idea of a Luton School Board. All speakers, for and against, were from the middle classes. A second working class meeting a week later at the National School in Queen Square attracted between 300–400 men, women and children. The instigation for this came from Rev Lee and

William Cammell, the owner of a small engineering factory in York Street.[174] In a published handbill Andrew A. Smith sought to address his 'Fellow Working Men' with an appeal to their duty and their higher nature (although he did not neglect to mention 'If you want better wages VOTE FOR A BOARD'). Smith called upon the working classes to 'display your love of country' and, through voting for a School Board, 'raise the standard of morality in your Town.' He finished with the rallying cry, 'let us . . . declare to the world that we will allow nothing sordid to stand between us and the attainment of our object, OUR JUST RIGHTS & THE EDUCATION OF OUR CHILDREN.'[175] Smith's credentials to speak on behalf of the working class are not clear but certainly there was an understanding that members of that sector of society formed a significant proportion of the electorate. Frederick Brown clearly thought so, addressing them directly in a handbill. 'Will the working classes, now they have the power in their own hands, vote for the voluntary system, which after long years of trial has proved to be *unequal* to the task?' he enquired.[176]

Mass Vestry meetings, with up to 3000 people, settled nothing, the second gathering generating into 'the most disgraceful meeting ever held in the town'.[177] Hecklers kept up a constant barrage against supporters of the School Board, unrestrained by O'Neill. Following the meeting Dr Woakes demanded a poll of the parish. The colours of yellow (pro-Board) and blue (anti-Board) were dusted off for a poll which was organised by central government. On 7 February 1871, Luton's male ratepayers voted not to pay more rates by an overwhelming majority (1796 against a School Board, 493 for). Apparently 500 of those endorsing the *status quo* were unable to sign their own names at the poll. On the day numbers of 'rough lads' lolled around in George Street and intimidation and heckling took place on both sides.

All of this, whilst increasing personal animosities, was irrelevant to the forces now at work. The School Board issue was to make it apparent to many that Luton was not a town with any control over its own destiny. In the eyes of central authority, school provision in Luton was inadequate. Successive memorandums, rowdy meetings, protests and frantic attempts at school building by the Church, made no difference to the outcome. Inspectors from the Education Department had made visits and recommendations and, as J.G. Dony records, the order for the formation of a School Board was finalised by the Department with crushing simplicity – 'Done 27/1/74'.[178]

As in 1850, those who opposed the formation of a local authority under compulsion from central government, then sought to subvert its aims when faced with its inevitability. There the parallels end. O'Neill, the leader of the anti-Board faction (later to be known as the Prayer Book Five), was no Brickwood or Chase. He wasted time and resources in trying to prevent the inevitable election from taking place, whilst the pro-Board faction, to become known as the Bible Five, prepared the ground. There were nine places on the Board and so whichever side could get five members returned would gain control. The Bible Five, demonstrating political shrewdness, chose their candidates with deliberate care, presenting a broad coalition in order to maximise their appeal. The list comprised a Quaker bank manager (William Bigg); an Anglican vicar (E.R. Adams); a Baptist shopkeeper (Peter Wootton); a Congregationalist straw hat manufacturer (Charles Robinson) and a Wesleyan shopkeeper. This was Henry Blundell, the owner of Luton's largest store.[179] Supporters of the Wesleyan Schools fielded two candidates and, therefore, Blundell's candidature served also to attract some votes away from them. The remaining votes for the Wesleyan Schools were sure to split the anti-School Board vote.

The election was the first to be held under secret ballot, voting taking place on 17 February 1874. There were many procedural difficulties. Only half who were entitled to vote did so and there were complaints by some that they were not allowed to vote due to lack of time. It was no surprise to see O'Neill at the top of the Poll, nor to see the Prayer Book Five secure more votes (but not many more) than the Bible Five. The result, however, came as a shock:

ELECTED

James O'Neill	Prayer Book Five	2485
William Bigg	Bible Five	2073
Henry Blundell	Bible Five	1848
A.P. Welch	Prayer Book Five	1682
John Higgins	Prayer Book Five	1678
E.R. Adams	Bible Five	1601
Thomas Sworder	Prayer Book Five	1522
Peter Wootton	Bible Five	1443
Charles Robinson	Bible Five	1425

NOT ELECTED

John F. Kershaw	Prayer Book Five	1325
Charles Mees	Wesleyan Voluntary Schools	1322
G.C.H Lockhart	Independent	467
John Webdale	Independent	341
William Shepheard	Independent	196
Gustavus Jordan	Wesleyan Voluntary Schools	192

Total Bible Five votes	8390
Total Prayer Book Five votes	8792

What would have happened if Mees in particular had withdrawn his candidature can only be speculation. The Bible Five had gone about the campaign with a sense of evangelistic zeal, carrying memories of past 'clean' party battles with them. Correctly anticipating bad weather they gave thought to the logistics of electioneering: taking the electors from Leagrave to the polls in a wagon yielded 105 votes throughout the day. At a celebratory victory meeting at the Town Hall an exultant Adams, who had faced most personal criticism, declared 'We have won it, gentlemen, in the face of ignorance; we have won it in the face of prejudice...'. There was also a measure of surprise, Henry Blundell confessing 'I little thought when I started from home, sir, this morning to see the ballot boxes opened and the papers counted, that I should have tonight the honour of standing next to my esteemed friend, Mr William Bigg'.[180]

After failing to get the election declared null and void, O'Neill and the other elected Prayer Book Five members attended the first meeting of the Board only to vote against Bigg and Robinson as Chairman and Vice-Chairman respectively, to hand in protests at the conduct of the election and, thereupon, to quit. Thomas Sworder was subsequently to play a more active part than his erstwhile allies, attending meetings more frequently. Of the others, O'Neill attended rarely, concentrating his efforts upon different tactics. The School Board itself made an active start with Adams naturally spearheading the development of schools in the hamlets. Of greater significance was the decision to pass a bye-law making school attendance compulsory up to the age of thirteen. This delivered a blow to the continuation of child labour. Although straw plaiting itself was in terminal decline, children were still a significant component of the cottage economy, busy in numerous tiny workshops and domestic premises.[181] A full-time visiting officer was appointed in June 1874 and parents who persistently refused to comply with the bye-law were brought before the local magistrates, the first case occurring in June 1875, and a second later in that year. Concern was expressed that the magistrates were less than supportive in assisting the School Board clampdown. Featuring amongst the Conservative magistrates were Colonel Ames, who had opposed the School Board, and Prayer Book Five member, A.P. Welch.

O'Neill meanwhile was busy raising a petition against the School Board plans for a much needed programme of school building in the town. He was successful in raising one of 2040 names. The proportion of those who were actually ratepayers is unknown.[182] In the face of this the Luton School Board turned to the Education Department for advice, which rather weakly suggested a 'conference' between the Board and the petitioners. Uncertain as to their popular support within the town the Board agreed at first to go along with what they should have known would be a pointless charade. Perhaps it was fortunate for the Board that they could not even agree with O'Neill upon how the meeting should be conducted. O'Neill attempted to constitute a majority of petitioners over Board members at the Conference and, therefore, give himself the chairmanship. Bigg, who rightly had no faith whatsoever in O'Neill's impartiality and integrity, turned his rival down.[183] The meeting did not take place, the school building programme continued and the Bible Five retained control at the 1877 elections. 'When the history of the first School Board for Luton shall be written, we fear there will be some passages which the faithful chronicler will have to record that will not shed much lustre upon certain members constituting the minority of the Board' concluded the *Luton Times*.[184]

A young man in his twenties who migrated to Luton in, say 1842, could have established himself in a shop and perhaps bought a couple of cottages. He could marry, have children and be a member of a local chapel. He would feel a bond of affinity with his fellow worshippers, his fellow shopkeepers in the same line of business, his local public house if he was a drinking man and, of course, his family and home. There does, however, seem to be a marked lack of collective spirit within the town as a whole. People came to Luton for the opportunities which it provided through work and, although local society evolved and matured, it retained a powerful sense of individualism. Improvements to the town were brought about by a small minority riding upon the backs of central legislation. Schools, public health and cemeteries all came about in this manner whilst most Lutonians remained either intransigent or indifferent. It was this same minority which capped these achievements through the acquisition of greater self-control and the symbols of self-government: incorporation as a Borough. Their fellow citizens, those who had really moulded the distinctive features of the town, stood by and watched.

NOTES

1. Briggs, Asa, 'Victorian Values' in Sigsworth, Eric M. *In Search of Victorian Values: Aspects of Nineteenth Century Thought and Society* (Manchester, 1988). Morris, R.J. *Class, Sect and Party. The Making of the Middle Class, Leeds 1820–1850* (Manchester, 1990).
2. Levine, David. *Reproducing Families. The Political Economy of English Population History* chapt. 3, 'The Industrialisation of the Cottage Economy', (Cambridge, 1987). Meller, H.E. *Leisure and the Changing City, 1870–1914* (1976).
3. PRO Kew, HO 129 184. There does not appear to have been great opposition to this census in Luton or comment about it. See also Bushby, D.W. *The Ecclesiastical Census, Bedfordshire, March 1851* (Bedfordshire Historical Record Society, vol. 54, 1975).
   St. Mary's
   The return made by Rev T. Sikes noted that the evening service was a recent innovation. He estimated that recent average attendances were between 1300 and 1400 and pointedly stressed that no attempt had been made to boost the figures for the purpose of the census.
   Old Wesleyan, Church Street
   The returns were supplied by John Waller.

Primitive Methodist Church, High Town
The average congregation was a little less than half the general congregation. Return by the minister, Henry Pope.
Society of Friends
The returns were made by Henry Brown, junior.
Old Meeting, Park Street
The returns were supplied by Robert How, Deacon. He remarked that the absence of an afternoon service and the lower than average overall figure was due to the anniversary service at Union Chapel.
Union Baptist Church
'Large numbers connected with the Sabbath schools are adults who after teaching are mixed with the general congregation'.
Ebenezer Baptist Church
This church contrived to make two contradictory returns – one each from deacons James Morris and Joseph Booth. The discrepancy between the two provides the clearest example of how often the returns were an approximation. The Ebenezer figures were really an average for the year. A remark was made concerning the low turnout in the evening – 'The Minister resides at a distance . . . Not any preaching in the evening consequently the attendance is less than other parts of the day'.

4. Cobbe, Henry. *Luton Church. Historical and Descriptive* (1899).
5. Ibid. p. 245. In 1832, for example, Sikes performed 118 baptisms, whilst two officiating ministers (A. Donald and Caleb Whitford) conducted a further 30 between them. MacDouall did none. Baptismal Register, Luton St. Mary's. BRO Mic 229/29.
6. *Beds Times* July 1849. Further detail on the dismal spiritual and physical state of St. Mary's is provided in Pickford, Chris *Bedfordshire Churches in the Nineteenth Century . Part II Parishes H to R.* (BHRS, vol. 77, 1998).
7. Sikes continued with at least some of his Luton duties whilst at Puttenham, continuing to baptise infants but with several visiting ministers conducting a larger proportion than before. The absence of Sikes prompted MacDouall to take his responsibilities as vicar more seriously and on 17 October 1841 he baptised four children. After this Herculean effort he rested awhile but returned a year later (16 October 1842) to baptise a further five. Autumn was clearly MacDouall's preferred time to pop into his parish: he certainly kept his distance for the rest of the year. Baptismal Register, Luton St. Mary's. BRO Mic 229/29. *Luton Times* 23.3.1861.
8. O'Neill was in trouble soon after commencing his duties. In July 1863 he appeared before the Arches Court to answer allegations of indecent assault upon a sixteen year old female pupil teacher whilst a curate at Blandford. Although the case was dismissed there was a strong hint of an improper relationship between the two which O'Neill had tried to hush up. *Luton Times* 1.6.1867, 23.11.1867.
9. Crawley contributed toward the restoration of the church in 1864–65. Leigh paid for a new screen in the Hoo chapel, the work being carried out by E. O. Williams at some point in the latter part of the decade. Quoted in Pickford, Chris *op. cit.*
10. *Beds Times* 28.7.1867 and 27.4.1867; *Luton Times* 8.6.1867.
11. Ibid. 28.7.1868; *Luton Times* 24.7.1867
12. McLeod, Hugh. *Religion and Society in England, 1850–1914* (1996). See p. 254.
13. Runciman, W.G. *Weber. Selections in Translation.* Section III chapt. 7, 'Protestant Asceticism and the Spirit of Capitalism' (Cambridge, 1978). Rubinstein, W.D. *Capitalism, Culture and Decline in Britain 1750–1990* (1993). Levine, David *op. cit.* Bradley, Ian. *The Call to Seriousness. The Evangelical Impact on the Victorians.* (1976).
14. *Beds Times* 4.3.1848; *Luton News* 14.12.1861.
15. Tearle, Douglas. *Chapel Street Methodist Church Centenary 1852–1952. 'Our Heritage'* (Luton,1952).
16. Longhurst, Liz. 'Memoir of a Victorian Quaker. William Drewett (1834–1900)'. Unpublished typescript, copy in LM.

17. Fisher, J.S. *People of the Meeting House. Tales of a Luton Church.* (1974).
18. *Luton Times* 1.4.1876.
19. Ibid. 10.4.1875.
20. 'Luton's First Circuit.' *The Christian Messenger*, no. 400, April 1899. Extract in LM.
21. *Beds Times* 1.5.1847.
22. Mahan, E.B. *The Congregational Church, Luton 1804–1914. Jubilee Memorials.* (1914).
23. Longhurst, Liz *op. cit.* Godber, Joyce. *Friends in Bedfordshire and West Hertfordshire.* (Published by the author, 1975).
24. *Beds Times* 29.8.1846. *Luton Times* 24.5.1851.
25. *Luton Times* 9.2.1867.
26. *Luton Times* 29.12.1855; 22.11.1856; 30.11.1867; 7.12.1867; *Beds Times* 11.1.1868.
27. *Luton Times* 17.11.1855.
28. Following a lecture by Henry Vincent on 'Civil and Religious Liberty', James Waller called for the formation of an Anti-State Church Association by local dissenters. This idea never gained support. *Beds Times* 16.5.1846. In 1869 a Luton Protestant Association commenced meeting (photographer Samuel Debenham was secretary) but this too gained little ground. *Luton Times* 11.9.1869.
29. *Luton Times* 1.9.1860. *Beds Times* 23.9.1854; 11.2.1854; 29.7.1854.
30. Briggs, J.H.Y. *The English Baptists of the Nineteenth Century* (1994). Mcleod, H. *op cit.* Church Book containing list of members for Ceylon Baptist Church, Wellington Street, 1871 (Luton Central Baptist Church). This list throws up a significant number of discrepancies with the corresponding census for that year.
31. *Luton Times* 3.9.1859
32. For an account of the timeless nature of these fears see, for example, Pearson, G. *Hooligan. A History of Respectable Fears* (1983).
33. 'A Journal of Home Mission Work in connection with the Congregational Church, Luton'. LM M/820. This Journal commences on 4 April 1872 and ends abruptly in January 1874.
34. *Luton Times* 17.7.1875.
35. Darby, Aubrey *A View From the Alley.* (Luton, 1974).
36. Allen, M.D. 'The Chase Street Mission'. *Bedfordshire Magazine.* Vol. 20, No. 153 pp. 16–19.
37. Collings, Harry. *History of Union Chapel, Luton.* (Luton, 1887).
38. Luton's First Circuit *op. cit.* Spedding, Robert: *'The Hill of the Lord . . . High Town Primitive Methodist Church 1838–1932.* (1932).
39. BRO G/DDA 151/5. Brief letter, dated 3.2.1842, addressed to Richard Marks Brown. The letter refers to a dinner recently held and the distribution of blankets for which the 'poor are feeling very grateful'. No other details appear but the society was apparently in a 'flourishing state', attracting numbers of 'young men'.
40. Beehagg, Clive. 'Secrecy, Ritual and Folk Violence: The Opacity of the Workplace in the First Half of the Nineteenth Century' in Storch, R. D. (ed.) *Popular Culture and Custom in Nineteenth Century England.* (New York).
41. Meller, H.E. *op. cit.* Morris, R.J. *op. cit.* Morris, R.J., 'Clubs, societies and associations' and Prochaska, F.K., 'Philanthropy' in Thompson, F.M.L. (ed.) *The Cambridge Social History of Britain 1750–1950. Volume 3. Social Agencies and Institutions* (Cambridge, 1990). Maclaren, A.A. *Religion and Social Class. The Disruption in Aberdeen.* (1974).
42. *Beds Times* 10.9.1853; *Luton Times* 16.7.1859.
43. *Glimpses of History.* A brief history of the Luton Foresters compiled by Samuel Pride and based upon a lecture given to the Luton Friendly Society Medical Institute in 1923. *Luton Times* 20.4.1861.
44. Ibid. 7.7.1860, 18.8.1860, *Luton News* 8.2.1862.
45. *Luton Times* 24.12.1859, 19.12.1859,
46. Allegation in letter to *Luton News* 17.8.1861.

47. *Beds Times* 23.9.1854, 15.2.1851. The Soaksters Club met weekly at *The Dog* having apparently been formed in the early 19th Century.
48. *Beds Times* 20.5.1848, 21.6.1851, 6.11.1852; *Luton Times* 3.11.1855, 29.11.1856.
49. Jones, S.G. *Sport, Politics and the Working Class.* (Manchester, 1988). Walvin, James *Leisure and Society 1830–1950* (1978).
50. *Beds Times* 12.7.1851. The attractively dressed Luton girls apparently turned a number of heads.
51. *Luton Times.* 13.11.1858.
52. Allen, M.D. 'World's End . . . The Story of Chase Street.' Unpublished typescript.
53. *Beds Times* 27.6.1846. *Luton News* 20.7.1862. *Luton Times* 24.4.1869, *Beds Times* 14.6.1873, *Luton Times* 25.7.1874. See also Board of Health chapter.
54. *Luton Times* 6.11.1875.
55. *Beds Times* 29.8.1846.
56. Ibid. 16.2.1850.
57. Walvin, James *op. cit.* Gatrell, V.A. 'Crime, authority and the policeman-state' in Thompson, F.M.L. (ed.) *op. cit.* See also Clark, Peter *The English Alehouse. A Social History 1200–1830.* (1983).
58. *Beds Times* 12.9.1846. Austin, William. *A History of Luton and its Hamlets.* (Isle of Wight, 1928) vol. II p.185.
59. 'Sewing and Sowing' was a popular lantern slide show written and presented by T.G. Hobbs in the 1890s. It illustrated the downfall (and eventual death), through drink, of 'Smyth' a relatively well-off straw hat manufacturer. It was set in the town of 'Strawopolis'.
60. Bradley, Ian. *The Call to Seriousness. The Evangelical Impact on the Victorians.* (Cape 1976).
61. *Luton Times* editorial. 3.9.1859.
62. *Beds Times* 25.11.1854, 2.12.1854, 9.12.1854.
63. *Luton Times* 2.10.1858.
64. *Beds Times* 23.9.1850.
65. Log book for Queen Square Boys' School, 1863–85. 18.4.1864. LM L/8/12/54. The fair decimated attendance over the whole week.
66. Darby, Aubrey *op. cit.* pp. 27–30.
67. Storch, Robert D. 'Please to Remember the Fifth of November; Conflict, Stability, Solidarity and Public Order in Southern England 1815–1900' in Storch, Robert D. (ed.) *op. cit.*
68. *Beds Times* 11.11.1862.
69. *Luton Times* 13.11.1858.
70. *Beds Times* 15.9.1868.
71. Emsley, Clive. 'Crime in 19th Century Britain', *History Today,* vol. 38, April 1988.
72. Bedfordshire's Chief Constable, for example, provided annual statistics on overall crime within the county accompanied by a report. His bland observations detail appointments and removals within the force but provide virtually no analysis. The reports give prominence to the issuing of certificates to peddlers and to incidents of foot and mouth disease, a reflection perhaps of county priorities. BRO QEV 4. Criminal statistics compiled by R.E. Roberts, Governor of Bedford Prison, for the period 1801–78 are filed at the BRO under QSS 4. Table 1 shows the different offences and the number of prisoners committed in each year tried at the assizes (breaking down the crimes according to category). Table 6 gives similar information for those tried at the county sessions.
73. Undated petition, BRO QEV 3. See also Cockman, F.G. *The Railway Age in Bedfordshire.* (BHRS Vol. 53, 1974).
74. Tobias, J.J. *Crime and Industrial Society in the Nineteenth Century* (1967). See also Foster, David, 'Victorian Concepts of Crime ' in Sigsworth, Eric M. *op. cit.* and Jones, David, *Crime, Protest, Community and Police in Nineteenth Century Britain* (1982).

75. *Beds Times.* 28.6.1851. Solomon King's portrait graces the frontispiece to the first edition of Brian Harrison's *Drink and the Victorians. The Temperance Question in England 1815–72.* (1971)
76. Jones, David *op. cit.*
77. *Luton Times* 27.7.1867.
78. Bedfordshire Quarter Sessions 1840–66. BRO, QSM 33–66. These figures are drawn from the list of indictments (one individual equals one indictment for which origin of prisoner can be made). Convictions filed, those referred to Assize and private cases (mostly poaching but including some assault, damage and drunkenness) are not included as they do not give the address of the defendant. From the late 1850s few locations are given.
79. *Beds Times* 28.3.1846.
80. Ibid. 25.3.1848.
81. *Luton Times* 24.4.1869
82. *Beds Times* 16.1.1847; Luton Petty Sessions report 23.5.1859; *Luton Times* 29.1.1876.
83. *Beds Times* 13.1.1855; *Luton Times* 15.8.1860
84. *Luton Times* 31.3.1860; *Beds Times* 7.1865; *Luton Times* 2.9.1871, 17.2.1872.
85. *Luton Times* 30.4.1870.
86. Petty Sessions reports in *Luton Times* 8.1859.
87. *Luton Times* 29.11.1856. William Drewett believed he knew the culprit claiming that he acted out of malice after being refused employment. He declined to prosecute. See Longhurst, Liz *op. cit.*
88. *Beds Times* 26.5.1855; *Luton Times* 18.2.1871.
89. Luton Petty Sessions reports, 17.11.1862, 23.3.1875. As ever there were complaints about the behaviour of young people and the crazes with which they were temporarily infatuated. Letters appeared in the *Luton Times* from those with nothing better to do which complained about slinging stones and 'hoop-trundlers' (i.e. 14.12.1858). In April 1861 there came a warning from the magistrates' bench concerning the dangers of catapults.
90. The crime assessment is based upon a compilation of offences brought before Luton's court of Petty Session (whether found guilty or not) in certain specified categories which remain fairly consistent throughout the year and the decades. Consequently, the result of periodic police clamp downs – deficient weights and measures, stray dogs, rate defaulters, poor control over horse drawn carts are not included. The sources for these statistics are the court of Petty Sessions Minutes at Bedfordshire County Record Office and the court reports in local newspapers.

    The specified categories are as follows:
    (a) Murder/Manslaughter.
    (b) Assault. This covers stabbing, wounding, shooting, some sexual offences (sometimes categorised under aggravated assault) as well as what today would popularly be defined as mugging.
    (c) Threatening behaviour.
    (d) Rape/Sexual Offence. Some within this category would have been counted under assault. This also includes homosexual offences.
    (e) Vagrancy. This covers a multitude of sins ranging from sleeping in unauthorised places to prostitution.
    (f) Theft. Includes attempted robbery and burglary, pickpocketing and petty theft (e.g. turnip tops).
    (g) Criminal damage. Vandalism and graffiti.
    (h) Bastardy.
    (i) Drunk/disorderly. Includes fighting (frequently alcohol induced), breach of peace and, from 1871, actions against those who refused to quit public houses.
    (j) Embezzlement. Fraud and counterfeiting.

SOCIETY: BELIEF AND BEHAVIOUR   199

      (k) Poaching. This included trespass as there is a problem with differentiation; in endeavouring to convict poachers the police would often use the more easily proved offence.
      (l) Licensing offence. Including disorderly house, opening beyond statutory hours and using a public house for unlawful purposes.
      A large number of offences are therefore not included in the crime returns. These include riot, misbehaving servant, unlicensed theatre/show, arson, highway offence, receiving (very difficult to prove), bye-law offences, loitering with intent to commit a crime, attempted suicide, neglecting/deserting family, failure to comply with certain legislation i.e. Factory Act, Vaccination Act, Education Act.

91. *Luton Times* 28.7.1855; *Beds Times* 4.5.1867; *Luton Times* 1.11.1856.
92. There was one case of assault brought against PC Taylor in 1870 but the case was dismissed.
93. The Watching and Lighting Committee comprised H.C. Brown, Charles Austin, Thomas Foster, Thomas Waller, A.J. Beale, William Phillips, Richard Vyse, Charles Burr and Daniel Goujon. The petitioners declared that even the old system was 'barely sufficient' but the new arrangement was worse, adding a request for a Luton based Superintendent with a house. BRO QEV 3. See also Madigan, T.J. *The Men Who Wore Straw Helmets. The Development and the Story of the Luton Borough Police Force 1876–1947.* (Book Castle, Dunstable, 1993).
94. BRO QEV 3. The undated petition was headed by Rev Peile.
95. *Luton Times* 1.12.1855, 23.7.1859; QSM. *op. cit.*. Easter Session 1864.
96. *Beds Times* 31.3.1849; Luton Petty Sessions report 16.7.1860.
97. *Beds Times* 4.11.1862.
98. *Beds Times* 30.9.1848. Burgess pleaded with the bench that refusal to renew his licence would drive him and his family into the workhouse. There was a new landlord by 1850.
99. Luton Petty Session report 13.10.1856
100. Ibid. September 1857, 2.11.1857, April–May 1858, 10.1858, (*Robin Hood* suspension), 8.1863.
101. For example see ibid. 5.9.1859, 12.12.1859; *Luton Times* 17.3.1860.
102. *Beds Times* 2.5.1846; 16.11.1850.
103. Fisher, J. *op. cit.* p. 60.
104. *Beds Times* 6.8.1853.
105. Ibid. 18.11. 1854; *Luton Times* 18.8.1855, 17.10.1955, 16.8.1856, 22.11.1856.
106. Harrison, Brian *op. cit.* This working class support was a crucial component of the temperance movement according to Harrison. Harrison, Brian and Trinder, Barrie, 'Drink and Sobriety in an Early Victorian Town: Banbury 1830–60'. *The English Historical Review.* Supplement 4 (1969).
107. *Luton Times* 9.5.1857
108. Ibid. 25.9.1857, 16.10.1858.
109. Ibid. 7.1.1860.
110. *Luton News* 16.4.1862. The *Luton News* gave prominence to events held at Baptist churches. Darby, Aubrey S. *op. cit.* pp. 23–24.
111. *Luton Times* 10.9.1859.
112. Dingle, A.E. *The Campaign for Prohibition in Victorian England 1872–1895* (New Jersey, 1980). *Luton Times* 18.9.1869.
113. *Luton Times* 25.9.1869, 2.10.1869.
114. *Luton Times* 20.11.1869.
115. Ibid. 3.2.1872, 18.5.1872. Austin, W. *op. cit.* p.185.
116. *Luton Times* 19.12.1874, 11.9.1875, 23.10.1875.
117. Ibid. 5.11.1870.
118. BRO PSL S/1. Register of Alehouse Licences.
119. BRO QEV 4.
120. See Tobias, J.J. *op. cit.*

121. Phillips, Sir Richard. *A Personal Tour through the United Kingdom Describing Living Objects of Contemporaneous Interests. No. 1 Bedfordshire, Northamptonshire, Leicestershire.* (1828).
122. Stephens, W.B. *Education, Literacy and Society 1830–70. The Geography of Diversity in Provincial England.* (Manchester, 1987).
123. Spedding, Robert K. *op. cit.*
124. *Luton News* 10.7.1930. *Beds Times* 19.6.1847. In the same year a rumour spread through 'certain classes' that the Queen had ordered all children under the age of five to be put to death 'if the scarcity of provisions continued . . .' A bemused *Beds Times* correspondent noted '. . . the march of intellect has left millions behind in its career'.
125. *Beds Times* 16.10.1847; 1.4.1847.
126. Minute Book of the Luton Literary Institution LM 295/32.
127. *Luton Times* 5.3.1859.
128. Ibid. 10.12.1859; *Beds Times* 4.11.1862; *Luton Times* 26.2.1870.
129. *Beds Times* 13.1.1849; *Luton Times* 14.7.1855; 4.11.1862; 26.2.1870.
130. *Luton Times* 7.7.1858, 27.12.1856; *Beds Times* 17.1.1846.
131. *Beds Times* 21.3.1846. 18.7.1846, 30.1.1847, 16.11.1847, 14.10.1848.
132. See Harrison, J. F. C. *Learning and Living 1760–1960. A Study in the History of the English Adult Education Movement.* (Routledge and Kegan Paul, 1961).
133. *Beds Times* 21.2.1846.
134. Ibid. 18.4.1846, 25.4.1846, 9.5.1846.
135. Ibid. 23.1.1847. The library contained 500 volumes and the Institute had organised nineteen lectures in the previous year.
136. Ibid. 12.11.1853, 21.4.1853.
137. *Luton Times* 23.2.1856, 15.11.1856, 17.1.1857. The printing press was presumably lent by Wiseman.
138. Ibid. 21.2.1857, 6.2.1858.
139. Ibid. 30.5.1857, 20.11.1858, 25.6.1859, 11.2.1860. An excursion to Woburn was also organised in 1859.
140. *Luton News* 17.8.1861, 13.9.1862.
141. *Luton Times* 27.2.1875, 8.5.1875, 12.6.1875,16.10.1875, 30.10.1875, 18.4.1876. The headquarters was 20 Park Street, Luton.
142. *Beds Times* 13.2.1847.
143. Mechanics Institute soiree at the Plait Hall, *Luton Times* 8.5.1875.
144. Hawkes, Joseph. *The Rise and Progress of Luton's Wesleyan Sunday Schools.* (Luton, 1885).
145. Collings, H. *op. cit.*
146. Bunker, Stephen *North Chilterns Camera 1863–1954. The Thurston Collection in Luton Museum.* (Dunstable, 1989). *Luton Times* 2.11.1872. It is not known under whose auspices the 'Arts and Sciences' classes were run. They seem to have been fairly short-lived.
147. Maclaren, A.A. *op. cit.* Sutherland, Gillian 'Education' in Thompson, F.M.L. *The Cambridge Social History of Britain 1750–1950. vol. 3.* (Cambridge, 1990).
148. Park Street Baptist Church Sunday School Committee. Teachers' Meetings 1864–1882. Luton Central Baptist Church. Rev J.P. Chown, a highly successful minister in Bradford and later at Bloomsbury, addressed the Yorkshire Conference of Sunday School Teachers on the theme of 'How to Retain Our Elder Scholars' on 18.4.1862. He was speaking of a problem which was already widely known. See Milner, D. 'J.P. Chown, 1821–1886' *Baptist Quarterly*, vol. 25, 1973–4, pp. 15–41.
149. Bebbington, D.W. 'The Baptist Conscience in the Nineteenth Century' *Baptist Quarterly* vol. 34, 1991–92. David Bebbington suggested that this evangelical imperative accounted for the effort of the Baptists in the Sunday School movement, disproportionate to their total numbers.

150. 'Park Street Baptist Sunday School Committee. Teachers Meetings 1864–1882'. Luton Central Baptist Church.
151. *Luton Times* 7.3.1857, 20.2.1858. The Secretary's name was Wardill, the local directories listing just one such surname, William Wardill a plumber, painter and decorator from Market Hill.
152. *Luton News* 17.8.1861.
153. Records of Luton Friend's Adult School, BRO X563. *Luton Adult School Jubilee Souvenir 1862–1912,* copy in LM.
154. BRO X563/12. Luton Friends' Adult School. Savings account book, 1864–77. William Andrews, for example, made regular deposits of 2*s*. 6*d*. between 28 February 1867 and 21 February 1868. The giving in other instances seems patchy. Phoebe Simmons made nine deposits between 24.4.1864 and 28.2.1866, varying between 3*d*. and 1*s*. 1*d*. Fanny Brown made more steady weekly deposits of 1*s*. between November 1868 and September 1870, although in December and January these savings halved.
155. *Luton Times* 30.1.1869, 11.9.1869. The advertised aim of the Luton Mutual Improvement Society was '. . . to provide the people, especially the young men and women of this town, with pleasant and harmless recreation, combined with instruction, and at such a price that all classes may be able to avail themselves of it'. The Society met on Tuesday evenings with subscriptions of 1*s*. per quarter. The secretary in 1869 was W.T. Coates, a Park Street draper.
156. Ibid. 9.12.1871, *Beds Times* 8.2.1873.
157. *Luton Times* 23.2.1856, 19.12.1859. *Beds Times* 24.5.1873.
158. *Beds Times* 13.1.1866, 3.2.1866.
159. *Luton Times* 16.11.1872, 23.11.1872. Baker, Lionel. *The Story of Luton and its Public Libraries.* (Bedfordshire, 1983).
160. *Luton Times* 4.2.1871.
161. Ibid. 28.1.1871.
162. Stephens, W. B. *op. cit.* Appendix F, pp. 332–3, Appendix G., pp. 342–5.
163. Dony, J.G. *A History of Education in Luton.* (Luton, 1970). Patterson, D. 'Nineteenth Century Elementary Education in Luton.' Dissertation, *Bedford College* (1969). Marshall, M.A. 'Elementary Education in Luton 1809–1874.' Dissertation, college unknown(1960). Parish, B. 'School Attendance in Rural Bedfordshire and Luton 1870–1903.' *Hertfordshire College of Higher Education* dissertation (1977).
164. The exact location of the Ragged School as well as its operation are not known. It had not been long established when the *Beds Times* carried a report of it on 30.11.1850.
165. Queen Square Boys' School Log Book, 1863–85. LM L/8/12/54. Almost anything going on in the town would disrupt school attendance. Fairs, fetes, processions by Foresters and Oddfellows, cricket matches, Sunday School teas (including chapels), Guy Fawkes night, rain: all at various times were held responsible. The period after public holidays did not elicit an immediate return. On 2 February 1864 David Stalker noted, rather forlornly, 'Slightly increased attendance I think'.
166. Dony, J.G. *op. cit.* p. 59.
167. Queen Square *op. cit.,* 14.3.1873. The Boys School had four rooms. These measured: 83' × 20'; 40' × 21'; 15' × 20'; 14' × 18'. There were two further rooms for the infants section: 53' × 22': 14' × 18'. Fees in 1869 were 2*d*./week.
168. *Luton Times* 21.1.1871.
169. A pro-School Board poster calculated that there were 3391 young people 'of the proper age to attend school' but only 2190 'on the books of the present schools'. From the 1200 remaining, however, this calculation also deducted a further 22 'who may be supposed to attend more expensive schools'. 'What Will A School Board Cost' LM 15/97/36.
170. Printed letter from T. J. Lee addressed to 'Fellow Ratepayers', 5.5.1873. LM 5/97/36.

171. 'Poll For A Luton School Board!' Published by Charles Robinson c. 1871. LM collection.
172. Pro-School Board poster (no date). It declared that he who neglected his children's welfare 'has no concern for anything beyond his own sensual pleasures.' LM 12/97/36.
173. 'Men and Women of Luton! Open Your Eyes & Judge For Yourselves . . .' LM collection.
174. Ibid. 4.2.1871, 11.2.1871.
175. 'To Be or Not To Be, That is the Question.' LM collection.
176. 'The Education Act.' Handbill published by Frederick Brown, 21.1.1871. Brown sought to allay working class fears over the loss of child labour. 'When trade is brisk, and all hands are wanted, the School Board of your own electing would be anxious to study your interests by making such arrangements as would enable you as far as possible to get the benefit of your children's labour'. It cannot be certain that Brown was representing the views of his fellow Board promoters and, of course, he was in no position to make such a promise.
177. *Beds Times* 31.1.1871.
178. Dony, J.G. *op. cit.* p. 24.
179. *Luton Times* 7.2.1874. At the selection meeting only two men supported Rev Tuckwell's and Rev Genders' opposition to Adams' candidature. Tuckwell wanted Henry Brown junior instead but the latter emphatically refused, supporting Adams. Frank C. Scargill declared the forthcoming election was a battle between modernity and old style conservatism.
180. *Luton Times* 21.2.1874.
181. Minute Book of the School Board of the United School District of Luton. LM M216.
182. *Luton Times* 6.11.1875.
183. Ibid. 12.2.1876. Bigg would not rely upon O'Neill's protection as Chairman of a meeting. During the debates on whether Luton should adopt a School Board in February 1874 a public meeting degenerated into what the *Luton Times* described as 'rampant rowdyism', with Bigg, Blundell and Rev Adams all shouted down by hecklers from the anti-Board majority. O'Neill made no attempt to intervene.
184. Ibid. 19.2.1876.

Chapter Four. Politics, Power and Self-Determination

> ... *I believe the heterogeneous character of the new streets of Luton, arose out of a dogged, pugnacious spirit of independence... The fact is, Luton is a complete nest of freeholders, as canvassing candidates find to their cost before an election.* (Letter from 'Edward' to 'Tom', Beds Times 23 September 1848).

Summarising the influence of various controllers of estates in England and Wales, David Cannadine wrote that '... generalising about Victorian landowners is almost as hazardous as generalising about Victorian cities: there is a constant need to do full justice to the local, the particular, the individual and the idiosyncratic'.[1] In Luton, a town shorn of the influence of concentrated estate and economic interests, the significance of the individual, even the idiosyncratic, was given sharper focus. No group or class controlled the town and consideration of the various factors which influenced Luton's internal politics must always bear in mind the absence of a manifested awareness of collective identity.

Only in relations with Bedfordshire, as represented by the Russells or the influence of the county through the magistracy, was there any sign of a desire to assert a collective or specifically Lutonian will, and even here there is doubt as to how far beyond the confines of a section of the upper middle class this motivation really went. The primary influence over the successive drives for borough status appears neither to be a desire for Luton to assert itself positively as a distinctive entity nor a desire on the part of a section of its society to assume control over the town. Instead negative feelings provided the imperative – dissatisfaction with the grip which Bedfordshire still held on a town with which it increasingly had little in common, and displeasure at the performance of the assortment of local boards which administered some aspects of Luton's affairs.

Part One. Internal Relations

The failure of institutions
The character, economy and social composition of the early market town had been shattered by a phenomenal transformation. An echo of the old rural links remained, such as the Corn Exchange, but its market town functions were swiftly diminishing. The new Corn Exchange served primarily as a meeting hall; the Plait Halls were to hold a decreasing

proportion of local plait as the twentieth century approached; manorial functions, such as the Court Leet, were already anachronisms. At the same time, by the mid-1870s many of the excesses of that period of change – unregulated property development, insanitary living conditions, crime ridden beer shops, child labour, unco-ordinated and poor provision of education – had been curbed or at least addressed. Still, however, Luton remained in many respects an immature society, one which had passed the pangs of adolescence but had not yet come of age: recreational facilities were few, secular societies established for personal development and social intercourse were puny and short-lived (other than the Oddfellows and the Foresters) and the town in general betrayed few signs of a developed sense of self-awareness or community. An ordinary market town until the urban explosion, few of the new Lutonians had any feeling for the town's heritage, such as it was. There was little to bind Lutonians together and their lives were governed by a mixture of public utility companies, unelected magistrates and local boards.

This latter group, the nearest which Luton possessed to self government, did not command deep respect and, the School Board apart, had ceased to be an attractive forum for public service for the town's social and economic elite. 'The Poor Law . . . is little else than a mockery in Luton' dismissed the *Luton Times* in 1867: independent relief funds were capable of alleviating suffering more effectively and swiftly, a reflection on the lack of confidence in the Guardians' ability.[2] Charles Maffey, the Relieving Officer, faced successive votes of censure for what the Secretary of the Board described as his 'harsh and oppressive treatment of the poor'. He finally resigned in 1870 but the disdainful manner in which he held out against his employers further damaged their credibility.[3]

The Board of Guardians did not possess men with the necessary calibre to conduct its affairs properly. In the absence of any replacement the seventy-two year old Henry Brown stayed on in 1869, although he had ceased to be an active member. There were additional complaints about the inadequacy of Luton's representation within a board representing the Union (seven out of twenty) even though the town contributed half the expenditure.[4] There were no cases of hotly contested elections nor of alleged ballot-rigging – few appeared to greatly care. The relative lack of importance which the Board of Guardians possessed in Luton's political life was also due to the unwieldy nature of the Luton Union, the Poor Law Amendment Act creating it out of no less than fifteen parishes, including Dunstable. The Luton component was thus diluted and the Guardians never became a focal point for parochial political machinations.

The Board of Health had similarly been abandoned. By 1876 its business had degenerated into petty personal squabbles between individual members and the clerk, George Bailey, with one complaining to him 'This Board has been overridden by you for too long'.[5] It is hard to imagine Bigg, Scargill or Sworder ever finding themselves in a position to make this complaint. The Board was held in particularly low esteem by the local press which expressed a degree of disillusionment, which may have been widely shared, when in 1875 it observed:

> It appears to be the fate of all public bodies to be afflicted with bores... Luton glories in rather more of them than most towns. On the School Board, when Mr. Adams is not present, she can fall back on half-a-dozen others who will calmly prose over a box of slate pencils for half-an-hour and then adjourn it to the next meeting. But on the Board of Health the public bore rises to a pitch of absolute perfection...

A suitable venue for the Board's meetings concluded the *Luton Times*, was 'The Mansion at Arlesey' (the Three Counties Asylum).[6]

The Vestry continued to operate, still the forum for public debate and as such a nominal decision making body, but it had declined from a position in the mid-1840s when most of the leading citizens of the town regarded it as necessary to attend its business. The deliberations of the Board of Health usurped much of its secular concerns so that by the 1870s its meetings were limited to little other than ecclesiastical affairs, such as the appointment of churchwardens. O'Neill rarely attended its infrequent meetings (there were, for example, none held between April 1876 and March 1877), leaving the chair to be often taken by men such as Peter Wootton and Frederick Davis, neither of whom was an Anglican.[7] Vestry decisions could still be overturned by the Justices of the Peace at Quarter Sessions. In 1845, for example, it had adopted the Lighting and Watching Act, appointing a local 'Board of Inspectors' which in turn selected a police superintendent and a number of paid constables; formal appointments, however, still had to be made by the Justices. Since the Vestry still controlled aspects of the work of the Guardians (such as the choosing of overseers) it was, however, vulnerable to raids by vested interests. In 1845 Edwin Brickwood opposed the appointment of an assistant overseer and, although he lost the vote at the meeting, was able to demand a poll of the parish. The fact that he lost this also (496 votes to 39) did not detract from the Vestry's unsuitability as an administrative body, a fact highlighted by Luton's growing sanitary problems.[8]

The office of churchwarden was still coveted, despite O'Neill's temporary devaluation of it in 1867 with the replacement of Samuel Oliver by Thomas Dunn. John Cumberland, George Bailey, Hugh Gunn and H.O. Williams were amongst later holders of the office. At no time during the nineteenth century was the office of churchwarden the subject of political in-fighting or indeed of personal rivalry. This was partly because the church rate, the main responsibility of the post holder, had been the ground upon which the political struggle had long been resolved. According to Austin, an attempt to build the National School by levying a church rate was thwarted by the nonconformists who organised a 'public demonstration' and who presumably refused to pay. Although no details are known this was successful to the degree that the Anglicans were unable to levy the rate, and made no attempt to raise any other.[9]

Thus, at this early stage, was Luton's nonconformist business elite able to flex its political muscle, forcing the Anglican and market town hierarchy into a retreat which financially they were not well-placed to afford. The cemetery dispute of the 1850s was another example of the stand-off between the two sides, but O'Neill wasted few opportunities, great or small, to try to assert Church of England control and marginalise all other elements. The School Board battle was the most vivid example of this but there were others: in April 1864 a vote of censure was passed against J.G. Shepheard, O' Neill's malleable churchwarden, for selling a set of standard weights presented by the Marquess of Bute to the vicar and churchwardens. Although technically allowed to do so, the meeting was crowded with dissenters objecting to the use of the money – for the restoration of the fabric of St. Mary's. Many of the nonconformists present, in particular Rev Thomas Hands, wished to know why the distribution of coal tickets for the poor had been kept exclusively in the hands of Anglican ministers, breaking the traditional cross-denominational allotment, and why dissenting ladies (including Mrs Hands) had been removed from the District Visiting Society without even notification.[10]

O'Neill enjoyed his high profile. Dissenting ministers came and went but the formidable Conservative vicar defiantly thundered on, very nearly to the end of the century.[11] His powerful personality should not be allowed to exaggerate the significance of religious rivalries. The School Board apart, most clashes were minor spats which merely served to highlight the limitations of Church power, despite its aggressive vicar. There were undoubtedly those in the town, however, who were not happy with the levers of power being pulled by those appointed to represent the 'parish'.

A middle class town

'Historians of the middle class lack the guidance and assurance which the labourist tradition has supplied to historians of the working class . . . Its historians have neither the excitement, guidance or distortions of any sense of historical mission'.[12] It is with R.J. Morris' rather depressing warning that the role of various classes of society within Luton's politics is addressed. The town, by the middle of the 1870s, was in a curious position with a plethora of authorities amounting to a vacuum of concentrated power. From its overall economic buoyancy there derived a curious social structure, distinctively a town of tradesmen and artisans wrapped around an unskilled labouring core and coated with a thin layer of professionals and large manufacturers. Just as the town's social functions and ethics reflected its economic base, so too did its politics. The fact that Luton grew as a decisively Liberal and nonconformist stronghold can obscure the very real divisions within the 'middling' classes. Fraser argued that the 'predominant endemic political rivalry in early Victorian cities was not the potentially explosive conflict between bourgeoisie and proletariat but a struggle for supremacy within the middle class itself'.[13]

This, however, tells only part of the story in a small town such as Luton, although it was true that the fight to wield effective power was held within the middle class. The aristocracy was absent and working class interest (distinctly female in many parts) was precluded from labour organisation by the small workshop and building site world of casual employment. It was unable to make any impact. As has been seen in the previous chapter, organisations such as the Mechanics Institute or the various working men's self-help societies had, in fact, a mixed social composition with the middle class prominent in the leadership (although such individuals are more readily identifiable). There is no example of local working class political organisation in this period.

This apparent middle class hegemony, overtly Liberal and nonconformist though it may have been, carried fluid divisions not only between those who are identifiable, in the inadequately simple historical sense, as members of the 'bourgeoisie' and 'petty bourgeoisie', but also within their respective ranks. These divisions were revealed most clearly in the fights for control of the Board of Health and the School Board. In the former case, Luton underwent in general terms what Hennock identified as the all too common experience for many towns: that is to say, a high spending and 'improving' interest, probably dominated by a professional and business elite, would be confronted by a ratepaying 'protection' interest drawn predominantly from the petty bourgeoisie of shopkeepers, small tradesmen and masters. This latter group frequently gained control at local elections, with a consequent decrease in both expenditure and quality of performance. Luton's experience, as with larger authorities such as Birmingham Corporation, was that this was a cyclical movement in which years of poor financial management on the part of those who advocated financial stringency would give way to a return of businessmen and professionals. The reason for this was always due not merely to a pro-improving surge amongst the electorate but also to other factors inherent within the lower middle classes which deserve further consideration.[14]

Even this view, however, is simplifying matters. The wealthier individuals in manufacturing and services were not a homogenous unit, dividing amongst themselves on each issue. United more or less on concerns such as the necessity of a Board of Health (although solicitors Chase and Brickwood led the opposition), they demonstrated a marked lack of cohesion during the 1840s and 1850s over the consideration of a railway for Luton; divided slightly on the issue of swimming baths in the early 1870s; split over the School Board question (denominational allegiance splitting former 'clean party' colleagues Sworder and Bigg), and over incorporation, with Scargill, Cumberland and Gunn representing hostility, indifference and enthusiasm towards the matter. Even when united, the political position of the bourgeoisie was hardly one of irresistible strength. Fraser suggested that 'the pace and direction of urban government would be determined by local tradition and practice and not by general legislation' with Briggs adding 'Many, indeed most, of the necessary improvements in a rapidly changing economy and society were made voluntarily in those times'. In Luton's context this certainly requires qualification. Advocates of improvement invariably did so without a firm popular base and were, therefore, dependent upon legislation from Westminster to provide the weight required to overcome opposition from a majority of ratepayers. The Board of Health and School Board issues are clear examples of this, but in different ways so, too, were the suppression of the 'Stattie' and the curtailment of beer houses.[15]

Middle class reformers were also weakened by Luton's unincorporated status, being shackled by legislation into a reliance upon property based rates as virtually the only source of finance for improvement. They did not have the scope to undertake enterprising schemes in order to diversify the revenue base as Birmingham Corporation was able to do by acquiring the local Gas Company. As Fraser observed, a 'thick skin' was required by those in local office to withstand the slings and arrows which continuously were pelted at them. Few were able to endure this for long. If not quite transient, many in the upper levels of the middle classes moved away from Luton having made their money there: Vyse, Brickwood, Everitt, Chase and Burr all quit the town before their death, and Scargill was one of those who abandoned public life relatively early, pursuing a social life centred upon his estate at Bramingham Shott. Naturally, nonconformist ministers, especially Methodists, regularly moved to other pulpits. Luton compares with Portsmouth (although for different reasons) in possessing a middle class who conspicuously were unable to exert any social control through the employment market. Whereas Portsmouth, like Luton isolated from other principal urban centres, had an economy dictated not by market forces but by central government expenditure, Luton's few large manufacturers found that the structure of the town's staple trade made them as dependent upon the workers as the workers were upon them. The inability of the big factory owners to force their operatives to start work early was frequently commented upon, being encapsulated in the *Children's Employment Commission Report* of 1862: 'the usual hours in factories, warehouses and sewing rooms are from 8 or 9 in the morning till 9 in the evening, or in the busy three months, till 10. But the workers are paid by the piece, and the demand for labour being great, and wages good, they are said to be very independent, both as to the hour of coming or going to or from work, and the time which they take for meals.' William Willis concurred: 'From 9 till 9 may be called their day: perhaps half are here by 9.30 am but they do not like coming early in the morning and would prefer coming from 10 till 10: whilst workers in the small manufacturing units could be kept at it until midnight, those in the larger factories would not normally stay until after 10 pm in the busy season, 10.30 at the latest.' The owners' view was reinforced by Charles Lutes, a blockmaker at Vyse's who had also worked at Gregory and Cubitt's: 'The females work by the piece and go to meals as they please ... If they do not like one place they can easily go to another.' Luton's upper middle class was small, lacking political or economic dominance. Amongst some at least, this served to diminish the incentive for a lifetime of commitment and investment within the town. This was reflected in a paucity of amenities and a functional dullness of architecture: a two-storey hat factory was a building of note in Luton.[16]

The limited power of the bourgeoisie was revealed in another sphere. The impact of the railway has been omitted from this discussion partly because Luton's pre-eminence as the centre of the straw hat trade did not depend upon the early establishment of a railway line. The reason for the late arrival of a line for Luton, however, was influenced in part by the social, political and economic structure of the town. There had been numerous abortive attempts from the 1840s which were not to see success until 1858 – later than smaller towns such as Dunstable, Leighton Buzzard or Hemel Hempstead. The reasons for failure in each instance were varied: opposition from the second Marquess of Bute to a railway line crossing his estate; failure of Luton and Dunstable businessmen to agree over which town should have the principal station and which town should be the branch in a scheme promoted by Robert Stephenson; inability amongst Luton businessmen to agree upon a suitable site for the station and the lack of local consensus on whether to dissect the Moor with a proposed line.[17] Even the scheme which finally proved successful, the formation of the Luton, Dunstable and Welwyn Junction Railway Company, was fraught with difficulty: at a shareholders' meeting in November 1855 it was reported that 3500 shares had not been sold and there was insufficient capital to complete the undertaking. Had it not been for the commitment of local banks, of which Lucas and Bigg were managers, there is serious doubt as to whether the work would have progressed further. Successive mergers were eventually deemed necessary with the line swiftly being absorbed into the Great Northern.[18] All this serves to illustrate that, although Luton was built upon an almost obsessive commitment to free enterprise, it is noticeable that the small-scale nature of individual economic activity provided few men within the town with the necessary capital and breadth of vision capable of investing in and promoting a railway undertaking. The fits and starts by which a railway line was acquired by Luton fittingly places the power of the bourgeoisie in its proper perspective, illustrating that many of Luton's social and business elite were not much more than big fish in a small pond.

Despite their greater numbers and their economic property owning position, Luton's petty bourgeoise blend of shopkeepers, cottage landlords, small manufacturers and masters was politically no stronger than those of slightly greater wealth or more enhanced social standing. Application of their collective power was used only in a negative manner on occasional issues. More financially vulnerable than the higher reaches of the bourgeoisie, their attitudes were primarily influenced by short-term monetary considerations. For example, the Small Tenements Act of 1850 increased both the size of the electorate and the political influence of the small property landlord, but was prevented from being applied to Luton by precisely this same group of people at a vestry meeting. The grounds were simple enough: they desired to prevent compounding between the overseers and the landlords for the payment of rates instead of the burden being carried by the occupier. In essence, therefore, they were choosing to sacrifice the potential for collective political power in preference for individual financial protection.[19]

This event revealed the specific weakness of what Cobden dubbed 'the shopocracy'. Larger and more diverse than the higher echelons of the middle classes, this group possessed no real sense of self-awareness and, therefore, no cohesion. In the words of Crossick it 'lacked . . . a vision of its past and an analysis of its future.'[20] Virtually all of Luton's small businessmen would regard themselves as 'self-made men'. Collectiveness was, therefore, alien to their experience, and to the very ethos which had made them successful independent commercial operators. Unsuited to the level of decision making required of senior public figures, the petty bourgeoisie was only sporadically 'pushed', as Hennock put it, into local politics by reactionary motives born of a timid financial self-preservation. Time and time again this self-preservation came back to property, with the Luton Ratepayers' Association being the most blatant example of this expression. As such there was no positive role for it to play, deriving no long-term benefit. The small ratepayers achieved greatest success in the first Board of Health elections of 1850, notably when in coalition with farmers, still powerful within the town (a fact reflected in the disproportionate numbers of

'Yellow' candidates from the farming interest), and led by two articulate and well-organised solicitors. On the School Board issue the leading activists on all sides were drawn mainly from large manufacturers, professionals, clergy and the gentry. Left to their own resources to exercise political influence, the efforts of the petty bourgeoisie were negative, disorganised, fractious, occasionally comic and arguably quite damaging. More mundane factors inhibited the lower middle classes: 252 out of the 773 voting papers (32%) at the annual Board of Health elections in March 1862 were declared invalid because of omitted signatures or other basic literacy errors. Illiteracy diminishes confidence and negates political influence.[21]

The most telling comment upon the degree of cohesiveness within the petty bourgeoisie is the fact that professionals and manufacturers with a recognised propensity for expenditure could, at various times, obtain seats upon Luton's public institutions. The upper middle class alone could not furnish enough votes to secure them places. Electoral support from part of the petty bourgeoisie, as well as an absence of hostility or interest from a greater part of it, were both significant factors. The degree of support for improvement programmes from sections of the petty bourgeoisie was evidence of a virtual absence of sustained class antagonism in Luton.

Arguably more than any other town, Luton's class system least resembled a rigid caste: its openness and fluidity defused potential for class conflict. There are numerous examples of the degrees of social mobility (both up and down) which were perfectly possible. Perhaps the disappearance of the town's old elite also eased the passage of social advancement, opening up positions in both old and new institutions. With the hat trade only starting to become mechanised during the 1860s and 1870s, Luton's small masters had not yet become squeezed by the capital intensive, factory-oriented mechanised production that became more of a feature of the industry at the turn of the century. Luton's class structure contrasts sharply with that of Birmingham where, in the early nineteenth century, the small masters were driven by mechanisation either to copy larger scales of production – as well as the labour organisation and discipline that went with it – or to remain as artisans. Whilst upward social mobility, according to Behagg, was becoming increasingly difficult in Birmingham, this was not yet the case in Luton where small workshops and seasonal piecework continued to dominate the main industry.[22]

This is not to paint a picture of cosy class harmony: many of those who migrated to Luton would have experienced the unhappy social relations of the 1820s and 1830s, especially those from the rural areas. These memories and experiences would have been brought with them. Luton was not a parvenu's paradise as there were few opportunities for the type of fortunes to be made which allowed for ostentatious displays of wealth, but with luck it was possible for many to achieve varying degrees of comfortable affluence. Whilst aspirations for advancement could be sustained there was no incentive for hostility from the petty bourgeoisie which could only serve to harden barriers between sectors of society. Lacking control of the property market the bourgeoisie did not possess the ability, even if it possessed the will, to build social barricades through clear demarcation in housing districts. The building of villas on land in New Bedford Road is the only clear example of this occurring in the mid-nineteenth century, and the impetus for this came from the Bute estate. To repeat the observation made in chapter one: at this time there remained many within the higher reaches of the small middle-classes, such as Bigg and Willis, who were content to live in the heart of town.

Women

The political strength of women within Luton during the mid-nineteenth century is, frustratingly, the most difficult to quantify. By the time of the first Borough Council elections in 1876, 650 of the 3960 ratepayers (16.41%) were women, this group being allowed to vote for the first time. This occurrence prompted little comment in Luton other than 'that the female portion of the constituency (the West Ward) polled a very large proportion of its number, thus disposing of one argument urged against the more extensive bestowal of women's suffrage, namely that if the extended franchise was given they would not avail themselves of it'.[23]

Overt campaigning for the enfranchisement of women was politely received. Lectures by a visiting speaker, Mrs Tracey, in November 1851 on the subject of 'bloomerism' attracted a good attendance on successive evenings and, according to a patronising *Bedford Times*, 'afforded much amusement'. More to the point was a meeting addressed by another visitor, Miss Beedy MA, at the Town Hall 21 years later. Chaired by William Bigg it passed a resolution in favour of the enfranchisement of women, with Bigg and Miss Beedy supported by (amongst others) Rev Adams, J.J. Willis, James Drewett, Henry Wright, A.T. Webster and John Cumberland.[24]

There was, however, no sustained organisation which pursued formal political recognition for women and, for all their various roles as independent producers, accumulators and investors of capital, landlords, ratepayers and ultimately voters, women remained beyond the confines of administrative power in Luton. This should come as little surprise if one accepts Patricia Hollis' assertion that early feminism and public life for women originated as a sphere of service (other than that of a governess) for 'surplus' middle class females.[25] Whilst undoubtedly there were local examples of such women, serving on various philanthropic committees and other social organisations, their numbers within a town containing such a social structure as Luton's were bound to be very small, fewer still if one subtracts the wives and daughters of the town's all too transitory clergymen.

Even within the Liberal dissenting churches the role of deaconess could be a short-lived affair (see chapter three). The extent to which bourgeoise women were content to fill this formal void through other spheres of influence within the chapels is extremely difficult to assess accurately given the highly domesticated orientation of Christian service in nineteenth century Britain and the absence of data, for which these same churches are notorious. Similarly, it is almost impossible to penetrate the homes and minds of those women who, through the economic opportunities afforded by the hat trade, were able to obtain a degree of financial independence, even in production units which were nominally controlled by their husbands. To what degree this was regarded as a satisfactory, even superior, alternative to a formal political role (at a time when there was simply no opportunity for it), is impossible to tell since, regrettably, Luton's women were even more prone to anonymity than the men.

Liberalism

Urban Liberalism was the predominant political force in Luton until after the First World War. Rooted in a commitment to free trade it was, therefore, most attractive to the vast majority of Luton's entrepreneurs, such as retailers or millers, who were reliant upon imports and also those who depended upon both imports and exports, most notably those involved in the straw hat trade. Engaged in a mutually supportive relationship with the nonconformist churches, the imbalance between Liberalism and any other political force was due not merely to the presence of a middle class free trade economy. The withdrawal of the landed and farming interest from Luton greatly weakened the power of Tory patronage. The absence of organised labour not only stunted the development of Socialism, but also held the petty bourgeoisie within the Liberal camp for much longer than elsewhere in Britain, where, in the face of organised labour, they began to drift into the waiting embrace of the Conservative Party.

There were a number of distinctive features to Lutonian Liberalism in the mid-nineteenth century. First, the town within which it was predominant was itself politically impotent in the sense that it was just a small part of a wider constituency. This factor served to blunt the edge of political competitiveness because neither party stood, in any real sense, to 'win' Luton. Simultaneously, it also served to weaken the commitment to Liberalism as a party political vehicle by bringing other elements into play, chiefly the desire for Luton to assert itself. Often this was focused in an expression of a desire for direct representation in Parliament and not continuing as a constituent part of a rural county returning two MPs, frequently at uncontested elections. The split within the ranks of the middle classes on many issues was given a further dimension by the schism in ideology and temperament between Luton's urban Liberals and the Whigs who dominated the County in the form of the Dukes of Bedford at Woburn. When Cobden referred to the Russells and others as the 'plundering aristocracy' there would have been many in Luton who would have nodded in affirmation. As will be seen, underlying all this was Luton's dissatisfaction at being under the thumb of county administration and its desire to establish a degree of self-determination.

There was a strong radical seam running through Luton's Liberalism, a letter to the *Beds Times* in February 1859 deplored this state of affairs:

> Luton is a very peculiar town. It confessedly has no aristocracy, and there are very few persons competent by education to edify their neighbour's by making a speech. It thus happens that only three or four persons volunteer to get on platforms, and they are always there, and always speak in the same strain. To rail against the aristocracy, to belabour a bishop. To exalt Richard Cobden and decry Lord Brougham; to survey Dissent with a telescope for the purpose of getting rid of its angularities and defects, and the Church with a microscope for the purpose of discovering them: these are the stock topics of our public meetings, and these are operating to bring together the lower classes and keep more respectable people away.

The correspondent had known Luton for 25 years, an experience which he felt entitled him to refer to himself as an 'Old Lutonian'. It was almost inevitable that one of the 'three or four persons' always to be found on Luton's platforms was William Willis, an irrepressible windbag and the most politically active person in the town. Others who were frequently alongside Willis were John Everitt, E.C. Williamson and the Browns. Although perceptive in many respects the letter misses one essential point. Luton's most radical and high-profile Liberals were drawn from the 'respectable persons'. Perhaps the 'lower classes' which the letter vaguely alluded to were less interested in the town's affairs. Certainly, the petty bourgeoisie were not in the vanguard of local radical Liberalism but whether this was due to personal philosophy or a lack of confidence at public gatherings is not easy to say.

Regrettably, there were no local newspapers to cover the effect that Chartism and the movement which culminated in the repeal of the Corn Laws had upon Luton or indeed its contribution to it. The 'shopocracy', prominent in the national Chartist movement, was only beginning to become a significant part of Luton's population at this time. The data available suggests that Chartism had little impact upon a town where the traditional class structure was beginning to disintegrate. Again, without evidence, it is difficult to establish clearly what was the ideology of

POLITICS AND POWER 215

Table 4.1. 1857 parliamentary election[27]

	County Votes	Luton votes
Hastings Russell (Whig)	1568	244
Colonel R.T. Gilpin (Con)	1379	88
Colonel W.B. Higgins (Whig)	1337	231
Captain W. Stuart (Con)	1253	80

Table 4.2. 1859 parliamentary election[28]

	County vote	Luton Resident vote
Colonel R.T. Gilpin (Con)	2027	132
F.C.H. Russell (Whig)	1837	287
Colonel W.B. Higgins (Whig)	1583	288

Identifiable occupational breakdown amongst Luton voters

	Whig	Con
Gentry	0	2
Farmers	2	2
Professions	8	7
Major manufacturers	8	2
Small/medium manufacturers	23	3
Building Trade	9	3
Retailers	37	6
Publicans	3	4
Others	4	9
Total	94	38

Table 4.3 1872 parliamentary election[29]

	County vote	Luton vote
F. Bassett (Lib)	2450	581 (65.43%)
W. Stuart (Con)	2250	307 (34.57%)

Identifiable occupations of Luton voters

	Lib vote	% of Lib supp.	% of trade vote	Cons vote	% of Con supp.	% of trade vote
Gentry	0	–	–	2	(2.08)	(100)
Clergy	2	(1.03)	(50)	2	(2.08)	(50)
Farmers	1	(0.51)	(12.5)	7	(7.29)	(87.5)
Professionals	8	(4.14)	(57.14)	6	(6.25)	(42.85)
Large business/manf.	20	(10.6)	(83.33)	4	(4.16)	(17.67)
Small/med hat manf.	56	(29.1)	(74.66)	19	(19.79)	(25.33)
Building trade	9	(4.66)	(64.28)	5	(5.20)	(35.71)
Retail	52	(26.94)	(68.42)	24	(25)	(31.57)
Publicans	3	(1.55)	(25)	9	(9.37)	(75)
Others	42	(21.76)	(70)	96	(18.75)	(30)
Total	193			96		

a class who, as a whole, were not distinguished by their literary output. Nonetheless, it is fair to assume that for the bulk of Luton's burgesses political ideology stemmed from personal or specifically economic experience – essentially a commitment to free trade and a desire for a high degree of individual autonomy. These were the principles which had brought them to their present situation in life. The aristocracy was an alien entity for most Lutonians and the backbone of urban liberalism, the independent manufacturers and retailers, were especially prominent in the town. It was this group, in particular the manufacturers, who delivered the Liberal votes. The petty bourgeoisie also provided the mainstay of the Tory vote, but in fewer numbers than for the Liberal Party.

There are a number of points to be made about the voting patterns of various occupational groups in the mid–nineteenth century. Both in 1859 and 1872 the various professionals in the town split more or less evenly, with only a slightly greater number supporting the Whigs/Liberals. The surgeons, Woakes, Beale and Kit Tomson, all voted Tory. Of the other smaller groups, the farmers form a diminishing presence within the township itself. Publicans become increasingly associated with the Conservative cause from a fairly even split in the 1850s. This was probably as much a reaction to the temperance cause associated with the nonconformist churches and the Liberal Party as a reflection of their brewers' beliefs. Whilst Thomas Sworder was a lifelong Tory, J.W. Green had not yet completely abandoned his roots and was still voting Liberal in the 1870s.

Clearly, public improvement and reform issues were in no way reflected in the party political divide. Of the gentry, J.S. Crawley, a supporter of the proposals for a School Board, was a Tory, whilst Colonel Ames, an opponent of it, voted Whig in 1857 and 1859. Determined advocates of 'economy' such as Frederick Davis, Samuel Toyer and Joseph Bailey could be consistently found on the Liberal list alongside the consistent advocates of public works such as J.S. Tansley, Peter Wootton and John Everitt. William Phillips always voted Tory as did one of the Quaker Browns, Richard Marks Brown of The Brache, at a time when virtually all his Quaker contemporaries were voting Whig/Liberal. As the pendulum swung nationally between the two main political forces so too were several men prepared to switch allegiance on at least one occasion. These included Samuel Oliver, Henry and Joseph King Blundell and Gustavus Jordan.

The petty bourgeoisie were the decisive difference. In 1841, during the first pangs of Luton's development and in a period of Conservative ascendancy, two Tories were returned unopposed for Bedfordshire, Viscount Alford and William Astell. With an election anticipated, however, the poll book drawn up shows the voting intentions of the electorate. Of those resident in Luton, 70 declared support for the Whigs and 54 for the Tories.[30] By 1857 the gap between the two stood at three to one in favour of the Liberals and two years later 215 Luton voters declared for the Whig candidates, Russell and Higgins, with just 79 for the lone Tory, Colonel Gilpin. Like 1841, 1859 marked a high tide of Tory support nationally. This was also the case in 1872 when locally other factors came into consideration which further eroded Liberal support, resulting in a pro-Liberal voting ratio of less than two to one in Luton. These reasons will be examined later in detail.

Overall, however, the Liberal Party enjoyed a political dominance which evolved with the town. The bitter party strife which was fought around control of the Board of Guardians, its appointees and the post of churchwarden in Leeds and Manchester was not seen in Luton, even before the spiking of the church rate in 1835.[31] The old, largely Tory, elite physically moved from the town rather than being removed in a political battle. As new political institutions were established men who were Liberals immediately assumed a predominant position upon them. Contests were not, however, markedly party political. Liberal dominance was assumed, allowing parochial issues to come to the fore. This also meant a preponderance of middle class Liberals on public bodies. Many self-styled 'working men', even those who today would be regarded as integral parts of the petty bourgeoisie (clerks, small manufacturers, publicans and the 'shopocracy'), would be excluded from civic duties by the sheer logistics of its functions. Public service was unpaid and frequently meetings would be held during the day or early evening. Many men simply could not afford or spare the time to be away from their work, and it is noticeable that attendance at meetings of the Board of Health was poorest when it possessed a strong petty bourgeoisie element upon it.

Formal party organisation in the town came late in the day, coinciding with the introduction of the secret ballot in 1872. Without parliamentary status there was little impetus for local organisation. The Luton Liberals in particular were uncertain as to their purpose and, for all their greater numbers, were beaten off the mark by the Conservatives in forming a local party structure. A Conservative Association meeting was held in November 1874 (at which reporters from the Liberal *Luton Times* were excluded), a few weeks ahead of the Liberals who formed their Association at a meeting at the Town Hall. The Liberals formed an unwieldy executive committee (forty men) and the next step for each Party was to hold a banquet, the Conservatives again organising theirs first.[32]

The Liberals were caught between the two issues which had dominated the town's politics for the previous 35 years. Were they in existence to promote the cause of Liberalism generally (Scargill's view)? Was their task to promote Luton in particular, preferably through parliamentary status returning a Luton Liberal? Failing that, were they there to return Liberal candidates for Bedfordshire (Bigg's and Rev Adams' view)? The first quarterly meeting, which was not well attended, failed to resolve this with Scargill sniping at Bigg, from whom he was already divided over the issue of incorporation. The meeting was adjourned to the following week, when only 40 turned up, and still nothing was decided other than resolving to link up with the Bedford Liberal Association. A cynic might be forgiven for believing that this was so that Luton could receive some guidance.[33] The problem for the Liberals was caused by the town's lack of political independence which some felt that they, as the dominant party within the town, ought to attempt to address. This was an uncertainty that was not shared by the Conservatives amongst whom there was no great desire for Luton to become a separate parliamentary constituency. They were no doubt aware that were it to happen then they stood to lose every election for the foreseeable future. They were correct in drawing this conclusion – no Conservative won any parliamentary election in Luton until 1922.

Part Two. External Relations

Nineteenth century Liberalism best suited the prevailing economic and ideological spirit which was building the town, but it was not the only manifestation of this spirit. Underlying all Luton's political activities was a desire, regularly articulated by some, for the town to establish itself as a distinctive entity. This desire was often undefined and when exposed was in many respects the antithesis of the busy spirit of individualism which had spawned the belief that authority should be kept to the (cheapest) minimum. Running parallel with this was a deep dissatisfaction with Luton's affairs being controlled to the degree that they were by outsiders from rural, sleepy Bedfordshire. Lurking just beneath the surface these feelings were so strong that, in the early 1870s, they very nearly overturned the Liberal hegemony in the town.

Luton and the County

The issue of self-determination, the all too evident lack of which led to great frustration in Luton, focused upon the critical relationship with the rural county of Bedfordshire. Within it Luton was growing like a cuckoo in an alien nest, increasingly outweighing its siblings and swelling disproportionately to the nest itself. Unlike the cuckoo, however, Luton served notice very early in its development that it also could do without motherly help as well. In 1820, 38 of Luton's leading citizens sent a petition to the Quarter Sessions appealing against the county rate. Rates were a vexatious issue at any time but, as Joyce Godber correctly surmised, this was not merely protest at the level of local taxation, but rather an early example of muscle flexing on the part of the town. Complaining that they were 'excessively aggrieved by the enormous County Rates that have been levied in the last three years' the petitioners specified a 'Bridewell' which they asserted had been paid for by the town but 'ought to have been defrayed out of County Rates'. There were also general complaints about the level of taxation, poor relief and the agricultural depression. Expressing the hope that there would be no 'further bother' the petitioners ended with the hint of a threat: they were 'fully convinced that if the present rates should be continued, we shall in the present exigencies of the Times be quite unable to meet them.'[34]

Of all the problems which affected relations between town and county, it was the administration of law and order and the dispensation of justice which caused most difficulties, especially since they also served to highlight Luton's subservience. The 'Bridewell' referred to in the petition was, in fact, a lock-up in Park Street – 'a genuine English cage, so marked with the spirit of liberty that a strong man could easily make his exit....'.[35] In a state of perpetual disrepair it was eventually replaced in 1849 by a police station and cottage on the corner of Peel Street and Dunstable Place. Immediately, it showed itself to be inadequate:

> The Police Station House at Luton is unfit for occupation. The stench from the main sewer, and two privies, (which are both four yards from the house door) is so great as to be injurious to health. The Superintendent's family are now lying ill with fever caused no doubt by the above. The wet penetrates through the walls, and daylight is visible beneath the window frames of the bedroom. The water from the well is unfit for drinking, caused by the cesspools in the neighbourhood drawing into it.[36]

Whilst entirely consistent with the prevailing building standards in Luton at the time, another building was necessary. By 1856 Jackson, the County Surveyor, was inviting tenders for a new court house and station, the latter containing six cells, each with basin and WC, this to be built on the corner of Dunstable Place and Stuart Street.[37] This also proved to have been constructed with inherent problems: there were allegations made of 'scamping' directed at the work which was undertaken by the contractors chosen by the Surveyor. These were Freshwater of Bedford and Haynes of Sandy, the appointment of whom would no doubt have been to the chagrin of Luton builders who did not need outsiders to show them how to throw up a bad building. Superintendent Pope complained to the magistrates and they ordered E.O. Williams to inspect the station. The dispute was carried to the Autumn Quarter Sessions where allegations of 'serious fraud' with the brickwork and cavities 'stuffed with rubbish' were made by Jackson who himself was being criticised in Luton for failing to monitor the work properly.[38] The new Court House, opened in 1858, proved to be a very uncomfortable sitting for all: by December 1859 rain was getting into every part of the building with not only walls but seats also being saturated.[39] The heart of the criticism was not merely that the building was so poor in quality, but rather that the whole manner in which it was constructed served as an analogy for the way that Luton was maladministered by an authority based in Bedford.

The magistracy itself, responsible for more than dealing with alleged criminals, presented a rancorous problem and one which the *Luton Times* described as 'degrading' for the town. It was not until 1868 that A.P. Welch became the first magistrate resident within the urban area. His fellow justices (with their dates of qualification) comprised Daniel Goodson Adey of The Cell, Markyate (1830); Rev Miles Bland, by then residing at Ramsgate (1839); Colonel Lionel Ames of The Hyde (1845); Richard Oakley of Lawrence End (1851); J.S. Crawley of Stockwood (1851); Arthur Macnamara of Caddington (1853); Rev T.W. Adey, also of Markyate Cell (1851); J.G. Leigh of Luton Hoo (1856); Rev Hugh Blagg Smyth of Houghton Regis (1858); Gerard Wolf Lydekker of Harpenden Lodge (1859); and Captain Francis William Sullivan of Kimpton vicarage (1865). Of these only Ames was a regular attender, and he alone seems to have been regarded with any degree of respect within Luton. Most on the magistrates' list rarely attended, some having duties as justices of the peace elsewhere within the area. At least one (J.G. Leigh) never attended. The preponderance of gentry against the absence of Lutonians caused considerable irritation, the inadequacy of the system being thrown into sharper relief when, as regularly occurred, only one magistrate attended and the sitting had to be suspended. From the late 1850s the *Luton Times* was suggesting the introduction of a stipend for magistrates in order to ensure a more professional commitment as well as to weed out those who were not prepared to fulfil their duties.[40] The issue, however, was not really a philosophical one of undemocratic administration or simply dissatisfaction with irresponsible absentees in positions of authority – the local Board of Health regularly had very poor attendance for which it received no censure from the local press. It was rather that Luton resented being subject to county control, and the failure of the system only served to intensify this resentment.

The reasons for this displeasure with control from Bedford lay at a number of levels. At one it was simply that a number of Lutonians believed that they possessed sufficient wisdom and ability to assume control of day-to-day functions such as basic dispensation of justice, maintenance of roads and the licensing of places of recreation. In another respect, there was a genuine dissatisfaction at the undemocratic nature of county administration as represented by the magistracy and the Quarter Sessions, as well as the perceived failure of its officers. There was also a frequently expressed antipathy towards the feeble institutions which Luton did possess. At a deeper level may also have existed a residue of a social antagonism imported from the rural districts by migrants seeking to escape harsh economic circumstances and even political oppression. Having achieved a measure of success in Luton which they could never have hoped to see from whence they came, such people understandably did not relish interference from members of the same class who embodied the very antithesis of the virtues which Lutonians saw as embodied within their town: freedom of trade, freedom of opinion, freedom of religion, hard work and adaptability. The feeling of not wholly belonging to the rest of Bedfordshire was a reciprocal one: during the cholera crisis of November 1853, a Dunstable member on the Board of Guardians registered his objection that his town was obliged to pay for Luton's self-inflicted disease.[41]

Luton and the Russells

Possessing an immense influence within Bedfordshire, the Russell family, Dukes of Bedford, with their seat at Woburn in the west of the county, remained the dominant force in Bedfordshire politics throughout most of the nineteenth century. Their land holding and influence, however, did not extend into the Luton area and there was decreasing common cause between the Whig landed estate and the Liberal manufacturing centre. Enthusiasm for the Russells had never been great in Luton, Hastings Russell reciprocating by rarely visiting the town, even to canvas votes. In 1859 the second Whig candidate, Higgins, polled just one vote less than Russell at Luton, proportionately his best showing in the whole of Bedfordshire, where he usually trailed his successful colleague on average by approximately fifty votes.

When Hastings Russell failed to support Luton's attempt to become a parliamentary borough under Disraeli's Reform Act in 1867, the town vented its frustration neither on any of the vested interests which had scuppered the move on the floor of the House nor on any of the horse-trading which went on behind the scenes. Instead it turned on Hastings to whom, however unenthusiastically, Luton had delivered up a sizeable proportion of the total Russell vote. Comparing Hastings unfavourably with Colonel Gilpin (who as a Conservative MP had even less common ground with Luton but at least had done his duty by his constituency), the *Luton Times* dismissed him as a 'weak-kneed Liberal'. The enormity of the gulf between the urban Liberals and rural Whigs became apparent. The paper snorted:

> For ourselves, Liberal though we be, we would infinitely prefer a gentleman of Colonel Gilpin's political creed with Colonel Gilpin's fidelity and pluck than a member of the house of Russell who could sit until 4 o'clock in the morning to vote in favour of the game laws which are a disgrace to the Nation, but could not find it convenient to be in his place to give his vote when the interests of Luton and Dunstable were under consideration in connection with the Reform Bill of 1867.[42]

The Reform Act added 419 voters to the electoral list in Luton and there was clearly a desire on the part of the Luton electorate for another Liberal in addition to, or preferably instead of, a Russell. At a public meeting William Willis had to defend his decision to support Hastings Russell at the 1868 hustings (when there was again an uncontested election) as the only way to prevent the return of two Conservatives.[43]

Until Luton and district received separate parliamentary representation its Liberal Association could only play a limited role and, until that time, it would continue to have a Russell foisted upon it. When Francis Bassett resigned as MP in 1875, the Marquess of Tavistock was selected to take his place. Although elected unopposed on 28 April there were a number of Luton Liberals who were not satisfied with him. Of his speech at the selection meeting the *Luton Times* wrote: 'It is absolutely colourless... Liberals had a right to expect an honest statement of intentions instead of the amiable enunciation of a set of trite truisms.' This assessment was supported by a correspondent who was at the meeting and who was similarly sceptical about the Marquess' abilities and commitment – 'he might as well stay at home'.[44] The Marquess of Tavistock paid a visit to Frank Scargill's offices and, in case he was in any doubt as to what was expected of him, had the pleasure of receiving a temperance delegation from William Drewett, Rev Gray (of Wellington Street Baptist Church), Johnson Willis and Matthew Judge.[45]

Self-determination: the Second Reform Act, 1867

'The town of Luton is something more than a collection of cottages, owned in part by men whose object in life is to make money' asserted the *Luton Times* in 1874. It was specifically referring to the issue of whether Luton's new swimming baths should be a profitable enterprise (on the one hand), or whether they should be regarded as an adornment to a mature, orderly town replete with the facilities needed to enjoy a civilised life.[46] It is possible that the writer was in fact precisely describing Luton, even if he desired something quite different. There were certainly contrasts between Luton and Bedfordshire, and Luton and the Russells. The varying experiences and outlook within Luton's social groupings, however, meant that there only ever existed a united sense of what sort of town Luton had become, and what it aspired to be, on the narrowest of parochial grounds: when it regarded itself as inadequately represented at county level or felt slighted by outsiders. When assessment is made of the representations made to the county, and to Parliament, by Luton's upper middle class on behalf of the town, questions must be raised as to how positive was this expression of self-awareness. It is no exaggeration to say that it was largely for negative reasons that Luton became a borough.

The background to the agitation for parliamentary status can be traced back to 1849. Luton's closest parallel with the political unions of bigger cities such as Birmingham and Leeds, the Luton Reform Association, was meeting as early as March 1849. William Willis, A.J. Tansley, James Waller, Robert How, James Muir and John Everitt featured amongst its members.[47] The Association was more than just a parlour debating society. Four hundred people attended a meeting at the Town Hall which passed the following resolution in May 1849:

> That believing the House of Commons does not at present represent the mind and industry of the country, and that the unequal and exorbitant burdens imposed by the present system of taxation may be regarded as effects of class legislation, this meeting is of an opinion that such an extension of the franchise as will secure a full and fair representation of the people in the Commons House of Parliament is necessary, both for the vindication of justice and the attainment of economy in the regulation of public expenditure.

This resolution was supporting a criticism of the taxation system which was deemed to be in the favour of the farming interest. It was also specifically encapsulating a call, repeatedly made at the meeting, for Luton to somehow seek representation in Parliament. This drew support from Edwin Brickwood (who served as solicitor to the Bedfordshire Conservative Association) expressing dissatisfaction with Lord Alford, one of Bedfordshire's sitting MPs, whom he felt was not representing 'their interest'.[48]

The Luton Reform Association, although acting as a vehicle for promoting Luton's aspirations, was, on paper at least, a branch of the Bedfordshire Reform and Registration Association. Its aim was simple: 'advancing the Liberal interest'. It endeavoured to ensure that every possible Liberal voter was registered and the revision of the register in Luton regularly showed a greater number of additions to the Liberal list than the Conservative. The chief target for the Luton Liberals was Colonel R.T. Gilpin, Conservative MP for Bedfordshire from 1851 until his retirement in 1874. With the nomination and election of any Russell who chose to stand as a parliamentary candidate virtually assured, Luton Liberals saw no reason why he should not be accompanied to the House by one who more closely represented their interests. Colonel Gilpin, in the early years of his tenure as MP, most certainly did not. At the nomination of MPs on the hustings outside Bedford's Shire Hall in 1852, Gilpin found himself under fire from the Luton radicals, notably Willis and Everitt on his attitudes toward taxation and protection. There were a number present from Luton clearly hoping that a second Liberal candidate (in addition to Russell) would declare himself, thereby forcing an election. They were disappointed as Russell and Gilpin were both elected unopposed. In 1857 Luton Liberals were amongst those who were successful in obtaining a contested election but the heavy Luton Liberal vote narrowly failed to unseat Gilpin. Aware of the source of the pressure, Gilpin blamed a coalition of radicals and gentry in his acceptance speech, specifically naming Willis, Everitt and Samuel Whitbread for having caused the voters the trouble of a contested election.[49] The National Parliamentary and Financial Reform Association published a weekly record in the local papers of the attendance of the Bedfordshire MPs in the House of Commons, revealing that Gilpin was not particularly assiduous in this respect.[50]

This remained very much the pattern for the 1850s. Successive meetings at the Town Hall called for an extension of the franchise as the means by which Lutonians could obtain greater electoral power and, ultimately, achieve direct parliamentary representation. The 1859 attempt to return two Liberals failed badly in Bedfordshire against a national swing to the Tories and Gilpin topped the county poll. Luton witnessed brawling around the polling booth in Park Square and windows were smashed at the Conservative Committee's meeting place at the George Hotel. Perhaps because of a growing awareness of Luton's impotence, the meetings had fizzled out by 1865. Little canvassing was reported at the election in which Gilpin and Russell were elected unopposed.[51]

The ebb in national campaigning was in part due to a growing emphasis upon the more parochial goals which ran parallel with it. In April 1851, a crowded meeting in the Town Hall (at which temporary galleries were erected) was held to pursue a dual purpose: to promote the Freehold Land Society and to explore ways of increasing a better representation for Luton voters. John Bright addressed the meeting although Richard Cobden was prevented from attending by his wife's illness. It was in the latter's written apology (read by Bright) that he described Luton as 'the Manchester of Bedfordshire', a centre of industry which ought not to need to go 'cap in hand' to the gentry and aristocracy in order to wield political power. William Willis also addressed the meeting criticising the snug electoral arrangement between the Whigs and the Tories which protected each other from total loss. He claimed that in twenty years as an elector he had never had a chance to register his vote at a parliamentary election. In fact, two months earlier he would have had the opportunity at the by-election which sent Colonel Gilpin to the House to take the place of the recently deceased Viscount Alford. Prior to that there had not been a contested election since 1832. Richard Vyse also criticised the 'rotten' electoral system in Bedfordshire claiming that there remained 500 deceased people with their names still upon the register.

The purpose of the Freehold Land Society was not merely to promote property development. It was also hoped to provide a vote for the would-be investor. As we have seen, however, in chapter one, the

Society also opened the door to those who were already enfranchised property speculators and never realised the hopes of its planners.[52] By 1858 the *Luton Times* was advocating borough status, at the same time publishing letters calling for Luton to return its own MP.[53]

Thus it was that the Reform Bill, drafted in late 1866 by the minority Derby administration, excited a level of expectancy in Luton. It appeared that the town would benefit both from an extension of the franchise and the conferring of status as a parliamentary constituency. Indeed, as late as 4 June 1867, this remained a strong possibility. A Committee of Enquiry was formed (chaired by Willis) and a public meeting called. In the absence of Everitt through illness, this was chaired by W.T. Pledge of the Board of Health (in its self-adopted capacity of shadow town council). Local clergymen, Rev J.R. Stevenson and Rev Thomas Hands, attended this meeting in support (at this stage they did not hold the vote). The public meeting also attracted a large number of 'working men', one of whom (Parker) proposed a motion, seconded by Rev Stevenson. The motion stated that the Bill, whilst falling short of their requirements for full enfranchisement, was at least a step in the right direction. This was duly carried.[54]

A year earlier, in May 1866, the Board of Health sent a petition to Earl Russell (Prime Minister from October 1865 to June of the following year) stating Luton's claims for parliamentary representation. Its eight point case rested upon Luton's growing size and the extent of its hat trade – 60,000 people were claimed to be involved in a manufacture which amounted to a value of £1,500,000 per annum. Point six emphasised the town's sense of detachment from the rest of Bedfordshire – '... the claim of Luton to direct representation is also based on the fact that it is purely a Manufacturing District, having little identity of interest with the greater part of the County'. A Luton branch of the Reform League was duly formed with William Willis as President and Henry Brown (junior) as Vice-President.[55]

As Disraeli piloted the Reform Bill through the Commons expectancy rose in Luton, transcending far beyond the usual minority of male middle class political activists. Charles Bradlaugh came to speak, increasing still further the feeling that Luton was a town which was acquiring national recognition. Nevertheless, the Luton branch of the Reform League was disappointed in being unable to acquire a cheap excursion train from the Great Northern Railway to carry upwards of 200 people to a major demonstration in London. By the beginning of June the excitement had reached a high pitch with Everitt or Ames being touted as Luton's first member of Parliament.[56]

The sense of deflation was, therefore, massive when Disraeli accepted an amendment to his bill, passed on 4 June, and moved by T.B. Horsfall. Horsfall was from Liverpool, a commercial and political contemporary of John Shaw Leigh, and sitting as a Conservative MP for that city. His amendment gave one extra MP to Liverpool, Manchester, Birmingham and Leeds, sacrificing in the process the proposed conferring of an MP on the towns of Keighley, St. Helens, Barnsley and Luton. Bright opposed this amendment, suggesting instead that four of the smallest boroughs should be the ones to lose an MP. Colonel Gilpin spoke for Luton, describing it as 'one of the largest and most improving towns in the South of England'. He reminded the House that this was not the first time that Luton had been considered for parliamentary status: during the Aberdeen administration Earl Russell had proposed that a third MP be granted to Bedfordshire 'on account of the various interests to be represented'.[57]

With Horsfall's amendment accepted, Gilpin gave notice of his intention to move his own. This was debated on 8 July when Gilpin moved 'that the four parliamentary Boroughs next above ten thousand inhabitants, according to the Census of 1861 now returning two members each, shall only return one member, and that Luton, Keighley, Barnsley and St. Helens shall each return one Member to serve'. The MPs for the four smaller towns in question – Tiverton, Tamworth, Barnstaple and Warwick – naturally came out fighting in a debate which divided party colleagues along constituency lines. Stuart and Whitbread, the Bedford MPs, both supported Gilpin.[58] A.W. Peel, MP for threatened Warwick, moved that instead Arundel, Ashburton, Honiton and Lyme Regis (all constituencies with fewer than 4,000 people at the time of the 1861 Census) should be completely disenfranchised. This was something which had already been agreed would not occur, and it was left to his nephew, Sir Robert Peel, MP for Tamworth, to pour invective upon the four candidates for representation. Of Luton he mockingly declared: 'I venture to say that there are not twenty people in this House who have ever heard of the town of Luton. I understand it is in the County of Bedford. I have seen straw bonnets which have been made there, but to tell me that Luton is worthy to return a Member to this House is what no one can understand but the Hon. and gallant Gentleman opposite (Colonel Gilpin).' Furthermore, according to Sir Robert, the very fact that there were more women than men in Luton devalued its claim, as in all likelihood the morals of the place would not be that commensurate with the standards expected of a parliamentary constituency. When reference was made to the number of new houses built within the town, Peel heckled that they were 'all built of straw'.

Although Gladstone spoke in favour of Gilpin's amendment, stating that the Government should stand by its original proposals, the proposed clause was defeated by 195 votes to 224. Having been pushed aside in favour of the big cities, ridiculed and rejected, Luton was finally patted on the head and told to run along. Referring to Gilpin's warning of great disappointment being expressed in the town, Disraeli concluded: 'I trust, therefore, that the philosophic temperament of the people of Luton will lead them to forbear from meditating any such assault on the Constitution or the tranquillity of the Empire.'

The motives and conduct of Colonel Gilpin are interesting. Although a Conservative, he clearly did not have a high regard for the slippery Disraeli and was quite prepared to vote against the Government, referring to himself as an 'independent'. Naturally, the creation of a separate Luton constituency would remove a sizeable slice of the Liberal vote, thereby strengthening his own position in the rest of Bedfordshire, but to assert that political opportunism was his guiding motive is to do him less justice than he deserves. At the time of the passing of the Reform Act Gilpin had not faced a contested election for eight years and it had been ten years since he had been under any serious threat of defeat. In the meantime he had assiduously cultivated the Luton part of his constituency and now, in his sixties, was nearing the end of his political career. Gilpin's home was at Hockliffe (near Dunstable), a village which would be close to the edge of the proposed Luton parliamentary constituency. With the early Luton Liberal antipathy towards him evaporating by the mid-1860s, Gilpin was increasingly able to draw upon a personal support which transcended party lines.

Self-determination: the threat to the Liberal hegemony

In 1872, the succession of Hastings Russell as 9th Duke of Bedford necessitated a by-election in the Bedfordshire constituency which the Conservatives decided to contest. They were hoping to give their party a second MP to serve alongside Colonel Gilpin. By this stage Gilpin was able to rely upon considerable personal popularity in Luton, not to mention the solidly Conservative areas in the county, in order to maintain his seat. This posed a dilemma for the local Liberals, particularly in Luton, as with one of the county seats securely Gilpin's, the competition had effectively been reduced for just one seat. Gladstone's first Liberal government was facing difficulties on a number of fronts and in Bedfordshire it became apparent that the choice of candidate for each party would be decisive. A fortnight before the election it suddenly became possible that Luton's voters would have the choice between a Russell (for the Liberals) and a Luton candidate (for the Conservatives). The county Liberals were proposing to approach Hastings' brother, Arthur, the current MP for the Russells' seat at Tavistock, to become the candidate for the Bedfordshire seat. At the same time it grew increasingly possible that John Gerard Leigh, a man who had hitherto played no active part in public life, would be nominated as the Conservative candidate. There was every probability that should these two men become the prospective candidates then Luton would have taken its revenge on the Russells by dumping Arthur in favour of the closest that they could get to a Luton MP. Parochial self-assertion was clearly outweighing party allegiance and perhaps economic interest.

As it transpired, the Conservatives fluffed their chance. J.G. Leigh travelled to the Party's selection meeting at Bedford only to be rejected in favour of Captain Stuart. This was a rebuff not only for Leigh, but for Luton also, and at the hands of the county. Meanwhile, Bedfordshire's Liberals, to the almost audible relief of their Luton colleagues, selected Francis Bassett, a Quaker banker from Leighton Buzzard, whose candidature carried the support of the Whitbreads and the Russells. Bassett was a reluctant candidate but Luton could now retain loyalty to the Liberals, as represented by a candidate of sympathetic background, and vent upon the traditional foe their displeasure at being snubbed. Captain Stuart was a relative of the Marquess of Bute.[59]

The result of the election held on 25 June 1872, and the last open election before the introduction of the secret ballot, was very close. Bassett received 2446 votes against Stuart's 2248, an overall majority of just 198 votes. Luton's proportion was most interesting, with Bassett gaining 626 (65.89%) and Stuart 324 (34.11%). Within this, the township figures were Bassett 581 (65.43%) and Stuart 307 (34.57%). At a time when nearly half its electorate were voting for the first time, the Luton Liberal vote was almost twice as great as for the Conservative. It was, however, still proportionately well-down on the level of support recorded in the late 1850s. Conservative canvassing was criticised as being ineffectual, which should have been a cause of great regret for them, since it required a further switch of Luton votes to their candidate from the Liberals on only a modest scale for Stuart to have been successful. Had J.G. Leigh been the candidate there is little doubt that the Luton result would have been closer, even if the Liberals had still nominated Bassett. By losing Luton, the Conservatives lost the county.[60]

Self-determination: borough status

Having failed with his amendment to the Representation of the People Act, Colonel Gilpin gave Luton a prod. At his instigation a committee was formed, following a meeting at the Board of Health offices, to pursue parliamentary borough status. To this was added another vast committee, under the presidency of William Bigg, which spanned all shades of the political spectrum. At Gilpin's suggestion approaches were made to Dunstable, as he felt that Luton would stand a greater chance of success if a joint application covering both towns (and the village of Houghton Regis) was submitted.[61] The Mayor of Dunstable expressed his support but added just two men, Alderman Gutteridge and E. Lockhart, to Luton's 31 strong committee.[62]

The movement carried overwhelming support within Luton, at least amongst those whose opinions were taken note of. So strong was the conviction that the cause was a right one and that success was assured, the town felt that it could ignore Gilpin's advice and dispense with its smaller neighbours. At a public meeting (chaired by Bigg) at the Plait

Hall in June 1870, A.P. Welch proposed and W. Jardine seconded, the following motion: 'The towns of Luton and Dunstable, and the Districts of the Straw Hat and Bonnet Manufacture are entitled, from their population and commercial importance, to direct representation in the Commons House of Parliament.' At this George Gilder rose and to 'loud cheering' moved that Dunstable and district be omitted from the resolution. Seconded by Henry Wright, this was carried by an overwhelming majority with only a few (including Rev J.R. Stevenson) standing out against. With Gilpin absent it was left to Cook, the Houghton Regis representative, to remind the meeting (to no avail) that it would tactically be better to submit an application on behalf of the entire district. Having experienced Lutonian hospitality, the Dunstable representatives then left the platform. Subsequently, Dunstable was to send a separate application for borough status (covering 'Dunstable, Luton and District').[63]

Cook's warning proved correct. Bigg was unhappy with the decision to leave out Dunstable (but said it was too late to change), and so too were F.C. Scargill and Frederick Davis. Henry Wright appears to have also changed his mind, feeling that rival claims would damage Luton's chances and the movement began to founder, with Toyer already squabbling over expenses. Although Hastings Russell informed the Board of Health that he was willing to introduce a delegation to Gladstone, details of events, after a committee meeting in early July, are unknown. No delegation appears to have approached Gladstone and no proposals, from either Luton or Dunstable, ever reached the floor of the House.[64]

It was in the disappointing context of failure to achieve national recognition for its economic progress that Luton hesitatingly moved towards accepting second best – incorporation as a borough (minus parliamentary status). It was William Bigg and William Shepheard who promoted a movement which, this time, remained confined during the crucial stages to the upper reaches of the middle class. Practical considerations were subservient to collective dignity and assertiveness, in particular a desire on the part of Luton to free itself from a county from which it considered it was growing apart. The *Luton Times*, ever the mouthpiece for urban middle-class Liberalism, stated the case:

> ... for a great overgrown young man to be clinging to the apron strings of his foster mother is not more absurd or degrading than for a town of twenty thousand inhabitants to be dependent for the administration of its public business on two or three county gentlemen and clergymen residing in more or less distant villages.[65]

By circulating selected citizens within the town, Bigg and Shepheard were able to gather together an initial meeting at the Town Hall, chaired by the former. Echoing the sentiment of the *Luton Times*, Bigg declared that incorporation was a logical consequence of the economic and physical growth of the town. It was 'due to our dignity and to our manhood ... we should rely upon ourselves to do the duties which become us as citizens'. Bigg was supported by A.T. Webster, Frederick Brown, Henry Wren, Henry Wright, Gustavus Jordan, Rev Adams and, less enthusiastically, John Cumberland. F.C. Scargill came out in opposition, bluntly stating that Luton would gain nothing by incorporation.

On a practical level Scargill had a point as, other than freeing Luton from the embrace of the county judiciary, there were few discernible benefits. The Board of Guardians and the School Board would remain outside borough control, and the Gas and Water Companies would continue to undertake their functions independently. The council, therefore, would be little more than a beefed-up Board of Health, which itself would give way to the new body. Subjection to the Bedfordshire judiciary might be irksome, but in reality it was rarely seen to meddle in Luton's affairs. Few people present supported Scargill, but ominously a third of those at the meeting did not vote at all. The majority (the hall was full) resolved to form a committee to prepare preliminary costings for incorporation. Like Scargill, Robert How remained unconvinced of the need to seek incorporation when, in his view, the town had progressed satisfactorily without the empty pomp of a Charter, and could continue to do so. It was How's opinion that at 'Luton Jack was as good as his master' and would not care to be lorded over by a Mayor. How was, however, missing the point – 'Jack' was not being asked for his opinion.[66]

The committee did its homework and reported back to a meeting three months later that the estimated total annual salaries bill would be £1370, and the cost of running a borough police force approximately £1400. Luton at the time was contributing £1580 towards the maintenance of the Bedfordshire Police. Scargill cast doubt upon the accuracy of these figures asking what precisely St. Albans and Dunstable had gained from incorporation. In his view, nothing. John Higgins suggested to the meeting that the debate should now be widened to a public meeting to which Bigg agreed. It is possible that Higgins, who was moving to a position opposing the necessity for a council, was calculating that the majority of townsmen, fearing consequential additional rates, would oppose the idea, just as they had attempted to suffocate past attempts at reform. Bigg could hardly refuse Higgins' request but was possibly confident that, with the crucial support of the majority of his peers, it would take a vast army of well-organised protesters to prevent what was, in effect, a private petition, albeit on behalf of the town.[67]

Before the petition was submitted to Parliament the potential obstacle of a public meeting, to be held in the Plait Hall in December 1874, still had to be surmounted.[68] The danger, however, was limited by the fact that most at the meeting (E.O. Williams estimated that there were approximately 500 present) appeared to accept that incorporation would not result in a greatly increased financial burden. With the argument, therefore, resting upon such nebulous concepts as 'dignity' and 'progress', the opposition was extremely muted. Rev O'Neill was swiftly to his feet to question the necessity of a town council since the Board of Health was doing an excellent job and the magistracy was respected 'throughout the Kingdom' (a reference to the beer house cull). Supported by Joseph Cox, O'Neill challenged William Bigg, as the architect of the movement, to state precisely why he supposed that Luton would benefit from borough status.

Hugh Gunn had already put the resolution 'that this meeting considers it desirable that a petition be presented to the Queen in Council for a Charter of Incorporation for the town of Luton' (seconded by Shepheard), when Bigg rose to speak. Picking his way through the minefield, Bigg made a long diplomatic speech, worthy of a man soon to become Mayor. Citing municipal government as 'one of the most valuable principles of this country and at the very base of our Constitution', he evoked Trafalgar, German 'Fatherland', English 'fair play' and the fact that little Dunstable had already been incorporated in order to support his case. Bigg echoed O'Neill's praise of the Board of Health, claiming that its success was attributable to the fact that its members were elected by the town, a principle which should apply in other areas. Pointedly reminding the meeting of past humiliations and failures, Bigg emphasised that if Luton were to approach Disraeli (now Prime Minister) again, desiring status as a parliamentary borough, it would greatly assist the case if representations were made by a town council. In such circumstances, a council would be responsible for many aspects of Luton life and preferable to a hotch-potch of private citizens, chairmen of local Boards and various committee members. Incorporation, he concluded, was necessary for the 'interest and dignity' of Luton, serving to 'increase the prosperity and promote the honour of the town'. The last point, in fact, was an honest statement of intent. One of Bigg's actions as Mayor in 1877 was to initiate the creation of the Chamber of Commerce. At the end of the century it was to act jointly with the Council in establishing the New Industries Committee, a deliberate and highly successful attempt to diversify Luton's industrial base, which was to be the progenitor of its twentieth century expansion.

All this was unforeseen to those who sat listening to Bigg in the Plait Hall. Against his lofty rhetoric there was little precise argument that could be made. Thomas Huckle made a silly, pointless speech and Higgins characteristically queried the cost, but it was left to F.C. Scargill to settle the matter in favour of incorporation with a vituperative attack upon Bigg. For reasons unknown, Scargill appeared to have developed a personal animosity towards a man whom he sneeringly referred to as a 'retired bank clerk'. He dismissed Bigg's speech as 'ingenious bunkem', before going further. The election of mayor was bad, he claimed, because 'it would be an encouragement for the holding of public meetings, which he did not believe in, as the oratory of the young men of Luton was not good'. This was greeted by hisses but Scargill went on to remind the hall that his position as Clerk to the Justices 'was secured to him by law' and that he was 'absolutely immovable' unless compensated out of borough funds. Scargill's invective rebounded upon him and he was forced to sit down amidst 'continued uproar'. Henry Wright weighed in to support Bigg, accusing Scargill of using his position for one of personal profit and claiming that incorporation would benefit all Luton's ratepayers by reducing their county obligations which he felt were iniquitous. Wright compared the rateable assessment for Woburn Abbey, which he claimed amounted to £26.14$s.$, contrasting this with his 'comparatively insignificant residence' from which 'the sum of £6.2$s.$ was extracted'. No more than 50 people supported Robert How's amendment to adjourn the matter for six months, and the original amendment was carried with 'only a few dissidents making a show of hands'. Lastly Williams, in his capacity as chairman, informed the meeting that the expenses towards incorporation would be covered by subscription, to be reimbursed from the first borough rate. Under the clauses of the 1835 Municipal Corporation Act (by which the application was being made) the costs of the process would fall upon the petitioners, so Williams' statement reveals a confidence in the degree of support amongst Luton's ratepayers for the movement towards incorporation.

The original committee (minus Higgins and Scargill, who were replaced by Peter Wootton and Henry Wren) then submitted an application for incorporation on behalf of the 'Inhabitant Householders of the Town of Luton', 1427 men lending their names to the petition.[69] This was dealt with by the Government's Sciences and Arts Department, which announced its intention to hold a public enquiry chaired by Major Donnelly RE on 24 June 1875. This local enquiry was scheduled to be held at the Corn Exchange.[70]

The enquiry presented Frank Scargill with a last forlorn chance to articulate the grounds upon which he opposed incorporation. It was clearly a hopeless struggle as it became apparent that there was a ground swell of support for incorporation which went beyond the ranks of the petitioners. A.T. Webster supported the move but had not been an original signatory to the petition: in his opinion most of the large manufacturers felt as he did. George Bailey confessed an oversight – a whole section of Luton's ratepayers had not yet been canvassed for their support. Had he known that it was advisable, he would have approached the 650 female ratepayers and expected that all but 100 of them would have been prepared to sign the petition. Most of the evidence submitted in favour of Luton's case for borough status followed the familiar argument of economic development and how borough status would assist further growth.

Marshalling what forces he possessed, Scargill declared he was representing Thomas Sworder, Rev James O'Neill, Robert Smith, A.P. Welch, Dr Woakes, Dr Heale, William Clarke, Thomas Smith and William Drewett. A difficult task was made harder by the poor acoustics of the hall and the evident lack of sympathy with which the audience viewed Scargill's cause, Major Donnelly several times having to call for order. The arguments against were a long way short of convincing. After protesting against the short notice allowed for preparing his case and following the equally well-trod path of heaping adulation upon the magistracy and the Board of Health (which was never in its history so praised as when it was about to be extinguished), Scargill turned his attention to the character of Luton. It was, he declared, 'a town of very peculiar description, its trade being of a very fluctuating kind'. He compared it with the county town – 'Bedford . . . a quiet town, populated with quiet well-to-do people who came there for the sake of the schools while Luton was a town inhabited by a different sort of people altogether'. Fortunately, for the sake of his personal safety, Scargill did not attempt to specify what this 'different sort' were, but the essence of his argument was that Lutonians were less amenable to social control than Bedfordians and, therefore, ought not to be entrusted with self-government. Incorporation, Scargill declared, would be to the benefit only of the middle classes (which was highly debatable) and that would serve only to sow discord between them and the working classes (which it did not).

Those who were brought along by Scargill to give evidence did the case little good. Chief Constable Warner and Superintendent Pope both felt that a separately controlled Luton police force would prove to be less efficient in fighting crime, a statement derided by counsel for the petitioners. Pope had little else that he could add except to recall that when he first arrived, in what he also described as ' a very peculiar town' in 1854, 'the population was very rough' and Luton 'was then a notorious place for rioting', a counter-productive exaggeration as it carried with it the unintentional subtext that the lately civilised town was ready to wear the mantle of a borough. Robert Smith was so decrepit that he barely could be understood, whilst Robert How contradicted himself in his evidence and was laughed out. Gustavus Jordan had 'primed himself for an hour's speech on the Constitution of England' and even Scargill had to ask him to retire. With the absence of effective opposition laid bare, it only remained for the Privy Council to announce draft notice of approval of incorporation in October. Approaches had been made by George Bailey (to become the first Town Clerk) to other towns and cities for advice on making initial arrangements on establishing an elected council. It was decided that Luton would be divided into three electoral wards, returning eighteen councillors in total. From these councillors six aldermen would be chosen, the resulting vacancies as councillors being filled initially by an immediate by-election.

Although it was true that most of Luton's ratepayers supported incorporation and were probably pushed further into this support by Scargill's intemperate language, the endorsement did not go far beyond thinking that in general terms borough status was a good thing to have. There were few stirrings of interest in the town as a whole. Upon hearing the notification of approval, a working men's meeting was organised, the venue being the New Hall in Wellington Street and the objective being to gather together 'those interested in obtaining a proper representation of the working class interest in the new municipality of the town of Luton . . . '.[71] A committee was formed to pursue this but, as ever, there were few labouring men or artisans amongst it – the 'shopocracy' being very much to the fore. This body metamorphosed into the Luton Working Men's Representation Association which subsequently adopted the rather self-defeating aim of obtaining councillors 'irrespective of class or position . . . to act as Representatives of their wants and interest.'[72] The Licensed Victuallers' Association were also preparing for the election: the recently bankrupted T.C. Johnson led the call for the Association to ensure that it was represented in some form upon the new corporation, presumably in case the ascendant temperance movement sought to use this as another vehicle for the pursuit of its aims.[73]

Clearly, one of the reasons behind the lack of euphoria and excitement at the approval granted by the Privy Council was that incorporation did not mark the opening of floodgates which brought certain sectors of Luton's social structure appreciable political power. There was no build up of pressure upon old institutions nor a concentrated battle for power which acted as a benchmark for a new era. Luton had developed new agencies in a piecemeal fashion as the town evolved. The town council was not replacing a corrupt corporation as existed earlier in the century in larger towns and cities, such as Liverpool, Leeds, Newcastle and Leicester. As such there was no need for anyone in Luton to adopt the role of a Cobden or an Attwood: there was no rallying cry, no barricades to storm. The town had evolved from market town to manufacturing centre, barely pausing for breath. In the process the old ways, old ethics and old institutions had either disappeared or fallen into irrelevance. Hennock assessed the changing administrative structure in Leeds as a means by which outsiders got onto the inside. In Luton they were there from the outset.

Thus it was that the Charter of Incorporation formalised the process of social evolution. The Charter itself, dated 25 February 1876, was proclaimed at a meeting at the Town Hall on 2 March 1876. George Bailey read out the Charter to the assembled gathering and Austin records that he was so nervous that he 'dropped the document, smashing the great seal'.[74] The brief celebrations over, there then followed a long embarrassed silence which stretched all the way to the first elections scheduled for 18 May 1876. It was one thing to create a council for the 'dignity' and 'honour' of the town, but besides superseding the Board of Health, controlling a tiny police force and appointing a handful of magistrates, the question remained: what were councillors to do that was not being done by the Board of Health, a body which had long ceased to attract Luton's business and social elite? Furthermore, who were councillors representing: localities, political parties or interest groups?

This element of uncertainty led to an absence of interest which pervaded the period of election. It was not until 23 March that the first ward meeting was organised by Thomas Huckle to clarify the above dilemmas. The North Ward, predominantly covered High Town but also took in the hat manufacturing district on the south-eastern side of George Street, the villas strung out along the New Bedford Road and the rural hamlet of Round Green on its eastern edge. The meeting, chaired by Charles Worboys, had a distinctly lower middle class character about it.[75] Huckle's view, which carried considerable support, was that two candidates ought to be selected for the North Ward who were distinctively High Town men and who would represent the interests of that district. He coupled this with a warning against approaches from 'some George Street gentlemen of the most philanthropic character and full of good promises ' who might offer to stand in the Ward. 'Past experience, however, had taught them that the less they had to do with George Street gentlemen the better', this latter observation being greeted by a chorus of approval. All other considerations were consciously excluded – 'it was nothing to do with either Church or Chapel or politics, for they were all at union on town matters'. High Town was seeking more than just 'mud and rates' from incorporation, an indication of what many believed that it had so far received from 25 years of the Board of Health. This parochialism went as far as to force the resignation of Matthew Judge from the Committee formed to co-ordinate the selection of candidates, as he did not come from the North Ward.

High Town was a distinctive community cut off from the rest of the town by the two railway lines, and with a high proportion of poor housing it is no surprise that a sense of locality should be so powerful in that ward where churches were few and political organisation in its infancy. Elsewhere in the town, without even this collective sense of locality, attempts at selecting candidates stuttered. A selection committee was assembled for the East Ward, an area which covered those streets between Castle Street and Park Street (incorporating those formerly within Hyde parish, known as Brown Brick), Park Square, the eastern side of Church Street and Hitchin Road and Hart Hill. At most only twenty people attended the third attempt to convene a general meeting at the Town Hall.[76]

An attempt to hold a similar meeting on 9 April for the West Ward was made by the relatively unknown Adam Cuthbertson, at the New Hall, Wellington Street. Just six people turned up, even after Cuthbertson had stood on a chair outside the hall and proceeded to 'harangue a small gathering'. This meeting fell through but a second West Ward meeting (the Ward was the most populous with over 7000 inhabitants covering New Town north of Castle Street, Stuart Street and the area either side of Dunstable Road) two days later was more successful 'but at no time was it (the New Hall) anything like filled and the proceedings were almost devoid of enthusiasm'. Thirteen men were nominated for the Ward at the meeting with again an underlying tone of parochialism: the nomination of Peter Wootton by Johnson Willis found no seconder, the chief objection being that he neither resided nor did business in the Ward. This was the case with all candidates who were nominated in the West and North Wards. Summarising this, the *Luton Reporter* concluded that 'there is a larger amount of mutual suspicion in Luton than is desirable...' The East Ward was the last to secure a list of candidates.[77] There is no indication that the Friendly Societies campaigned in any organised sense, even though Thomas Puddephat, an Oddfellows' Trustee, was a candidate.

The only issue which excited any debate during the whole of the campaign was instigated by William Bigg. He was clearly dubious as to the contribution by the local police in the recent decrease in reported crimes in Luton and, one suspects, doubtful as to the extent of the correlation between that and the reduction in beer houses. Bigg's view, expressed at the incorporation enquiry at the Corn Exchange, was that this was due to an increase in trade and an 'advance in civilisation'. However vague and inaccurate that view may have been, Bigg went further – not only were the county controlled police not particularly efficient but they were also under 'a temptation...to wink at crime'. In other words, a less than conscientious police force was making little real effort to apprehend wrong-doers and bring them before the Bench, helping, therefore, to reduce the crime statistics. Bigg stopped just short of accusing the police of colluding with criminals. This touched a raw nerve with the Conservative *Luton Reporter* and two magistrates, A.P. Welch and Rev H.B. Smyth, who took this as not only a criticism of the police but also as a 'slur' upon the local judiciary as a whole. Bigg wasted no opportunity to cite occasions when magistrates failed to attend, but provided no evidence to back up his allegations concerning the police. Despite this, few came forward to criticise him and evidently there were a number who sympathised with some, if not all, of his allegations.[78]

Other than this spat there was nothing apart from personal motivation and rivalry which animated the election. Those who had advocated incorporation, including Bigg, failed to inspire the electorate in any way. 'The bashfulness shown by aspirants to municipal honours in Luton may be creditable, but it is scarcely fair to those whom they intend to be their constituents . . . ' noted the *Luton Reporter*.[79] Eventually, a total of 37 candidates allowed themselves to be nominated, twelve each for the North and West wards and thirteen for the East. All the members of the Board of Health and five of the six Luton Guardians were amongst those who stood. There were also some notable omissions from the list: no Brown could be induced to stand, nor William Phillips, Kit Tomson, Dr Woakes, Thomas Sworder, J.W. Green (although he was elected in November), A.P. Welch, Alfred Toyer, J.J. Kershaw or Gustavus Jordan. Of the 37 candidates, John Higgins was the only identifiable opponent of incorporation. Eleven were associated with the hat trade. E.O. Williams was to be the Returning Officer.[80]

The election itself, like the campaign as a whole, was an extremely muted affair with only 1700 out of 3700 voters exercising their right to vote, some not bothering to go to the polls 'even when offered a carriage to ride in' by a candidate. The *Luton Reporter* concluded that 'apathy . . . reigned supreme throughout the day' and the candidates themselves were accused of going about the business of seeking election in a 'half-hearted manner'. In the North Ward seven candidates did not address election meetings, the six unsuccessful men all coming from that number.[81] A second round of voting was required on 6 June by the election of six aldermen at the first council meeting, at which William Bigg was unanimously elected as mayor.[82]

Overall the result of the election produced a council which represented a broad cross-section of the various religious, political and occupational background of Luton's male, middle class ratepayers (see appendices). Generally speaking, those candidates with good organisation, and who produced the most publicity, greatly increased their chance of success in the face of a largely indifferent electorate. 'The results prove, beyond question, that owing to the apathy and carelessness of the burgesses, almost any candidate with good organisation might win a place on the Council' noted Scargill's paper, the *Luton Advertiser*. George Wilcox Gilder was one such candidate who, backed by an enthusiastic support committee, topped the poll in West Ward leaving three more experienced public servants, A.T. Webster, John Higgins and William Bigg, in his wake. The top five candidates came within 35 votes of each other.[83] The East Ward, where the Working Men's Representation Association had apparently concentrated their greatest efforts, saw the return of two candidates sympathetic to their cause, Peter Wootton and Charles Mees, although neither could remotely be described as working class and possibly would have been elected in any case. Another Association candidate, Henry Wren, failed in that Ward. Henry Wright, long associated with the welfare of the working classes, was successful in the North Ward.

Localism was the most potent factor in a low key contest. The runaway success of William Clarke, the 'kindly' farmer at the Brache, can be attributed to the desire on the part of the voters of Brown Brick to ensure that their district was properly represented on the town's governing forum. In the North Ward the two 'High Town' candidates were spectacularly successful, their organisation being very thorough and the overall turnout, 600 out of 1100, being the best out of the three wards. Peter Wootton, who narrowly squeezed home in sixth place in the East Ward, had his lowly position attributed not only to the fact that he was a member of the School Board, but specifically that he did not reside in the ward. His saving grace was apparently his work with Park Street Baptist Church, situated in the heart of the ward.[84]

Two of the three Board of Health candidates in the North Ward were defeated, although one of them, W. Shepheard, the original co-promoter of the movement which led to incorporation, was successful at the subsequent June election. Board member George Chambers finished at the bottom of North Ward poll, a full 330 votes behind the winner, a verdict perhaps from High Town on its 'mud and rates' experience. William Drewett, the other Board of Health member, and Hugh Gunn, whom Thomas Huckle might have described as a 'New Bedford Road gentleman', both obtained places on the Council but polled a long way behind Wright, the two 'High Town' candidates (Huckle and Conisbee) and William Farr, landlord of the *North Star* in Dudley Street, the latter representing the interests of the Licensed Victuallers' Association. Elsewhere, amongst those who were not elected were the Smart brothers, Henry Blundell (who did not canvass for votes and failed again in June, but became Mayor ten years later) and William Thompson Pledge who, with 48 votes, came bottom of the West Ward poll. The latter served as town postmaster and his vote may have been a reflection on the efficiency of the local post office, which was not held in high regard in Luton.

By June, eight out of the nine Board of Health members had secured election to the Town Council, as had all those from the Board of Guardians who chose to place themselves before the electorate. To stand as a serving member of the School Board, however, was seemingly no commendation in the eyes of the Luton voters. Of the 24 councillors and aldermen, ten had voted on at least one occasion for a Conservative candidate at previous parliamentary elections. At first glance this was a high figure for such a staunchly Liberal town although it must be added that party allegiance played no part in the elections. Two 'gentlemen' were elected, plus two who were retired. A quarter of Council members were involved in the hat trade and a further five in retail or wholesale. There were two Thomas Smiths.

It was entirely apposite that the results of Luton's first borough council election should produce a group of councillors so varied in experience of public office, occupation and ability, but all were drawn from the middling sectors of local society. At face value, no political, religious, occupational or social group was, therefore, in a position to dominate the council, something which had been a feature of Luton's political life as a whole for the previous forty years. This council was possibly the most representative of the population of Luton as a whole that the town was to experience until after the First World War and the expansion of the electorate. The initial meeting of the council, however, carried the first sign of what was to change.[85] At the election of aldermen, which was carried out by the full council, the High Town candidates, most overtly parochial, lower middle class and sympathetic to working men, were frozen out. The other councillors voted to select the aldermen to serve specific wards not from those specifically elected for that ward, but from the council as a whole. Despite the protests of Wright and Conisbee, who were both unsuccessful in their bids, only Hugh Gunn from the North Ward was elected to serve as an alderman. Wright described it as a 'conspiracy'.

Similarly, the composition of the most powerful of the council committees, Finance, was dominated by the more affluent councillors (see appendix). The formation of the council had been promoted by men from the higher reaches of the middle classes, and, however uncertain they were as to its intended function, they were not about to surrender its control to the likes of Huckle. The dominance of individuals from this indeterminate sector would not become apparent until the latter quarter of the nineteenth century as gradually the 'shopocracy' and dead wood, which had comprised a substantial part of the old boards of the town, were whittled away. These people had been able to take advantage of the hesitancy of others to successfully jump ship. The gradual dwindling of men such as Conisbee, Farr, Dawson and the Smiths, during the 1880s and 1890s, represented the change in the socio-economic structure of Luton with the steady increase in the number of larger factories, engineering as well as hats. The mayoralty and key council positions became concentrated in the hands of the bigger businessmen – Hucklesby, Wilkinson, Warren, H.O. Williams, the Oakley brothers and Staddon, most of them active Liberals. Few from the less affluent ranks of business life could spare the time or bear the personal costs of the office of mayor. Some of these men were radical in their politics, sympathetic towards, even popular with, the working class. The year of incorporation, however, marked a watershed in Luton's political and social life – from then until after World War I, the shopkeepers, small masters and publicans, the groups which more than any other (amongst the men) had provided Luton with its distinctive characteristics, would be squeezed from power. Social divisions became more rigid, opportunities for social advancement were more curtailed. Luton had become a mature industrial society.

NOTES

1. Cannadine, David (ed.) *Patricians, Power and Politics in Nineteenth Century Towns.* (Leicester, 1982).
2. *Luton Times* 30.11.1867.
3. Ibid. 20.11.1869. *Luton Advertiser* 29.1.1870; 12.2.1870.
4. Minute Book of the Luton Board of Guardians P.U.L.M. 22, BRO. Robert Marsh, William Shepheard and J. K. Blundell were amongst the other Luton members. *Luton Times 28.8.1869; 9.4.1870.*
5. *Luton Times* 20.5.1876. This complaint was made by Lockhart.
6. Ibid. 8.5.1875; 27.11.1875.
7. BRO. Luton Vestry Minute book 1844–80, p. 85/8/1.
8. Austin, William. *History of Luton and its Hamlets.* (Isle of Wight, 1928). Vol. II, p. 146.
9. Cobbe, Henry. *Luton Church. Historical and Descriptive.* (1899). List of churchwardens on pp. 266–8 . Austin, William Ibid. p. 135.
10. Supplement to the *Luton Times*, 2.4.1864.
11. The *Beds Mercury* carried details of a Conservative meeting on 30.1.1875. Rev O'Neill delighted his audience with a speech at which he poked fun at an assortment of nonconformists, including Rev C.H. Spurgeon.
12. Morris, R. J. *Class, Sect and Party. The Making of the British Middle Class, Leeds 1820–1850.* (Manchester, 1990).
13. Fraser, Derek. *Urban Politics in Victorian England.* Chapt. 6. (Leicester, 1976).
14. Hennock, E.P. 'Finance and Politics' in Urban Local Government in England, 1835–1900. *The Historical Journal* II, 2 (1963) pp. 212–25.
15. Fraser, Derek. *Power and Authority in the Victorian City.* (Oxford, 1979). Briggs, Asa. 'Victorian Values' in Sigsworth, Eric M. (ed.) *In Search of Victorian Values. Aspects of 19th Century Thought and Society* (Manchester, 1988). See also Hennock, E. P. *Fit and Proper Persons. Ideal and Reality in 19th Century Urban Government.* (1973).
16. Field, John. 'Wealth, styles of life and social tone amongst Portsmouth's middle class, 1800–75', in Morris, R.J. (ed.). *Class, Power and Social Structure in British Nineteenth Century Towns.* (Leicester, 1986). *Children's Employment Commission* 2nd Report 1862. Evidence submitted by J.E. White and those involved in hat manufacture.
17. For some of the various schemes see *Beds Times* 18.10.1845; 14.2.1846 – this featured a 130 name petition to Parliament signed by 'the principal persons resident in the Town and neighbourhood' to be part of the London to Manchester railway; 7.3.1846; 21.3. 1846; 16.5.1856; 4.7.1846; 14.11.1846; 12.6.1847; 2.10.1847. Other records relating to the railway at Luton are held at the PRO, Kew. For the Stephenson *debacle* see Austin, William *op. cit.* vol. II, p. 142.; Dyer, J. and Dony, J.G. *The Story of Luton* p. 123; *Beds Times* 8.7.1848, copy of a letter sent to Robert Stephenson from Rev Henry Burgess.
18. Cockman, F.G. *The Railway Age in Bedfordshire* (BHRS vol. 53, 1974). *Luton Times* 17.11.1855; 21.6.1856; 6.2.1856; 12.12.1857; 30.1.1860; 24.11.1860.
19. Austin, W. *op. cit.* p. 157. The resistance was led by Brickwood and Robert How, and, according to Austin, the Act remained 'a dead letter' until 1868.

20. Crossick, Geoffrey. 'Urban Society and the Petty Bourgeoisie in Nineteenth Century Britain' in Fraser, Derek and Sutcliffe, Anthony (eds.) *The Pursuit of Urban History* (1983).
21. Hennock, *op. cit. Luton News* 29.3.1862.
22. Behagg, Clive. *Politics and Production in the Early Nineteenth Century.* (1990).
23. *Luton Reporter* 20.5.1876.
24. *Beds Times* 8.11.1851 and *Luton Times* 30.11.1872.
25. Hollis, Patricia. *Ladies Elect. Women in English Local Government 1865–1914.* (1987).
26. Letter from 'Q in the Corner'. *Beds Times* 16.2.1850. The letter was refuted the following week.
27. BRO, RV 224, 1857 Poll Book; *Luton Times* 4.4.1857.
28. BRO, RV 25, 1859 Poll Book; *Luton Times* 7.5.1859. The Luton returns omit those voters who are identifiable as not being resident in Luton. The division between 'major' and 'small/medium' manufacturers is entirely impressionistic. As such there may be a certain injustice in downgrading the scale of operation of one or two businessmen. This also applies to the 1872 returns in Table 4.3.
29. BRO RV 26, 1872 Poll Book.
30. BRO RV 903, 1841 Poll Book. This election was the only case of two candidates from the same party being returned unopposed, although this was balanced upon the death of Astell in 1847 with Lord Charles Russell being returned unopposed for the Whigs.
31. Fraser, Derek. *Urban Politics in Victorian England.* Chapters 2 and 3. (Leicester, 1976).
32. *Luton Times* 14.11.1874, 5.12.1874, 30.1.1874, 6.2.1875.
33. Ibid. 6.3.1875; 13.3.1875. 'We are not sure the Luton Liberal Association really knows what it wants' concluded the *Luton Times*.
34. BRO QSR. 24 1820/457. The petition was signed by (amongst others) Richard Marks Brown, Henry Brown, Charles Tomson, James Gutteridge, Thomas Partridge, William Adams, William Burr, John Chase, Thomas Smith, Edward Sell, James Waller, John Waller, William Sibley and Matthew Dancer. Godber, Joyce. *History of Bedfordshire* p. 449. (Bedfordshire, 1969).
35. Letter from 'Edward' to the *Beds Times* 16.9.1848. A petition was submitted to the Quarter Sessions in September 1847, the 83 signatories being headed by Rev Sikes, John Brett (churchwarden), Benjamin Bolton and E.J. Beale (both overseers). Revealing perhaps a surprising concern for the welfare of those incarcerated there, it referred to the 'unhealthy damp cold state of the present cage . . .'. The petition added '. . . that the present Cage is vested in Trustees and also claimed by the county which has occasioned considerable difficulty and disputes'. BRO QEE 1/1a.
36. *Beds Times* 20.10.1849. Quoted in Madigan, J. *The Men Who Wore Straw Helmets. Policing Luton 1840–1974.* (Dunstable, 1993).
37. *Luton Times* 20.9.1856.
38. Ibid. 17.10.1857; 31.10.1857; BRO QEE 1/1 Miscellaneous papers re the courthouse and police station.
39. *Luton Times* 4.12.1858; 10.12.1859.
40. Ibid 11.12.1858; 11.6.1859. In October 1874, for example, only one magistrate (Welch) turned up, and he was late. Someone was sent into Hertfordshire to try and find one.
41. BRO P.U.L.M. 18.11.1853.
42. *Luton Times* 27.4.1867; 4.5.1867; 6.7.1867; 13.7.1867.
43. Ibid. 22.9.1868; 17.11. 1868.
44. Ibid. 24.4.1875. Other Luton Liberals who went to Bedford (including Gilder and Wootton) declared themselves satisfied with the Marquess.
45. Ibid. 1.5.1875.
46. *Luton Times* 25.7.1874.

47. *Beds Times* 17.3.1849. This meeting featured a debate on the subject of who paid the greater proportion of taxes, the working classes (Willis), or the aristocracy (How), the result of which is not known. A.J. Tansley was Secretary of the Association.
48. Ibid. 2.6.1849.
49. Ibid. 8.3.1851; 24.7.1852; *Luton Times* 4.4.1857; 13.3.1857.
50. For example see *Beds Times* 7.5.1853. The Association's weekly tally was published regularly at this time.
51. *Luton Times* 7.5.1859; *Beds Times* 18.7.1865.
52. *Beds Times* 12.4.1851.
53. *Luton Times* 18.12.1858.
54. *Beds Times* 31.3.1866; 7.4. 1866.
55. Ibid. 19.5.1866,;LM 9/55; *Beds Times* 23.10.1866.
56. *Luton Times* 2.2.1867; 9.2.1867; 22.6.1867.
57. *Hansards parliamentary Debates 30 & 31 Victoria, 1867* Vol. CLXXXVII 6.5.1867–17.6.1867.
58. Ibid. Vol. CLXXXVIII, 18.6.1867–23.7.1867, July 8. Cowling, Maurice. *1867 Disraeli, Gladstone and Revolution. The Passing of the Second Reform Bill.* (Cambridge, 1967).
59. Brown, Maureen and Masters, June. *The Bassetts. Leighton Buzzard's First Family.* (Leighton Linslade, 1989).
60. Ibid 1.6.1872; 8.6.1872; 15.6.1872; 29.6.1872; 6.7.1872. 1872 Poll Book RV 26, BRO J.G. Leigh slipped back into as much anonymity as his ownership of Luton Hoo would allow. His death in February 1875 elicited only a brief notice in the *Luton Times*.
61. Ibid. 21.5.1870. In addition to Bigg, the amorphous committee comprised: Revs O'Neill, Stevenson and H.B. Smyth, Messrs. Lucas, Welch, Scargill, Bailey, Cooke, Wright, James and Henry Blundell, Kinder, Henry and Frederick Brown, Partridge, James Higgins, Webdale, Gunn, Kershaw, Seebohm (jun.), Cumberland, J.G. Shepheard, W.T. Pledge, G. Sell (Secretary). William Willis wished to take no part. Support was sought from Sowerby and Ames.
62. Ibid. 28.5.1870.
63. Ibid. 18.6.1870, 25.6.1870.
64. *Luton Advertiser* 9.7.1870.
65. *Luton Times* 10.10.1874.
66. Ibid 31.10.1874. This Committee comprised, Bigg, William Shepheard, J.G. Shepheard, Rev Adams, Williams, Cotchin, Cumberland, Lockhart, Walsh, John Higgins, Edward Taylor, Frederick Brown and A.T. Webster.
67. Ibid. 21.11.1874.
68. *Luton Advertiser* 12.12.1874. The meeting was chaired by E.O. Williams.
69. A copy of the petition requesting incorporation (minus the signatories) can be found with miscellaneous papers re incorporation in BRO QEE 1/3. These deal mostly with minor matters including the clarification of borough boundaries, plus some correspondence.
70. *Luton Advertiser* 26.7.1875. BRO QEE. 1/3, miscellaneous papers re Incorporation. Regrettably no details of the petition are known.
71. *Luton Times* 9.10.1875. A committee was formed comprising Henry Wren, Henry Wright, Frederick Lawford, G. Long, Samuel Tutt, Matthew Judge and Messrs Johnson, Chamberlain, Dixon, Gailer and Cox.
72. Ibid. 13.11.1875.
73. Ibid. 22.1. 1876.
74. Austin, W. *op. cit.* p 189. *Luton Times* 4.3.1876.
75. *Luton Advertiser* 25.3.1876.
76. *Luton Times* 15.4.1876.

77. *Luton Reporter* 15.4.1876; *Luton Advertiser* 22.4.1876. Cuthbertson may have been Adam Cuthbertson, one of the leading lights in the Working Men's Representation Association.
78. *Luton Advertiser* 26.7.1875; 22.4.1876; *Luton Times* 6.5.1876; *Luton Reporter* 29.4.1876.
79. *Luton Reporter* 1.4.1876.
80. Ibid. 13.5.1876; *Luton Times* 13.5.1876
81. *Luton Times* 20.5.1876, *Luton Advertiser* 26.5.1876.
82. *Luton Advertiser* 27.5.1876.
83. At the May election this Ward also saw a tie for sixth and last place between William Walsh and Edward Taylor, both receiving 213 votes. Taylor's magnanimous decision to withdraw in favour of Walsh saved E.O. Williams the onerous task of declaring a casting vote. Taylor was deservedly elected in the subsequent June election.
84. *Luton Advertiser* 26.5.1876.
85. Ibid.

Appendix 1. Results of Council Elections May 1876

NORTH WARD

Elected		Not Elected	
Conisbee, Frederick	374	Shepheard, William	125
Wright, Henry	357	Smart, Arthur	90
Huckle, Thomas	348	Smart, Thomas	75
Farr, William	231	Cawdell, William J.	51
Drewett, William	136	Rosson, Charles	46
Gunn, Hugh	128	Chambers, George	34

EAST WARD

Elected		Not Elected	
Clarke, William	249	Dawson, John	122
Smith, Thomas (builder)	187	Lockhart, G.C.H.	118
Mees, Charles	175	Drewett, Charles	116
Cumberland, John	155	Oliver, Samuel	113
Smith, Thomas ('gentleman')	137	Blundell, Henry	110
Wootton, Peter	125	Wren, Henry	104
		Dancer, Joseph	43

WEST WARD

Elected		Not Elected	
Gilder, George Wilcox	408	Taylor, William	213
Webster, A.T.	402	Puddephatt, Thomas	181
Higgins, John	402	Haselgrove, T.W.	166
Bigg, William	382	Higgins, William Hiram	121
Cotchin, John	379	Crouch, Edward	103
Walsh, William	213	Pledge, William Thompson	48

Appendix 2. Luton's first Borough Council at 31 December 1876

Councillor	Trade	Politics	Interests
Bigg, Wm.	Banking	Lib	School Board; Guardians; Water Co.; magistrate; Gas Co.; All C'tees
Conisbee, Fdk.	Retailer	Con	High Town candidate; Tolls & Municipal Buildings C'tee
Wright, Hy.	Headmaster	Lib	Working Men's Rep. Assoc.; Highways & Lighting C'tee
Huckle, Thos.	Hat trade	Lib	High Town candidate; Highways & Lighting C'tee
Farr, Wm.	Publican	Con	Lic. Vic. Assoc.
Drewett, Wm.	Miller	Lib	Board of Health; Tolls & Municipal Buildings C'tee; Sanitary & Deodorising C'tee
*Gunn, Hugh	Hat trade	Lib	Guardians; Finance C'tee; Sanitary & Deodorising C'tee
*Clarke, Wm.	Farmer	Con	Highways & Lighting C'tee; Sanitary & Deodorising C'tee
Smith, Thos.	Builder	Con	Board of Health; GP & Fire Brigade C'tee
*Mees, Chas	Hat trade	Con	Board of Health; Working Men's Rep. Assoc.; Tolls & Municipal Buildings C'tee; GP & Fire Brigade C'tee
*Cumberland, Jn.	Est. Agent	Con	Highways & Lighting C'tee; GP & Fire Brigade C'tee
Smith, Thos	Gentleman	Lib	Guardian; Tolls & Municipal Buildings C'tee; Highways & Lighting C'tee

Wootton, Peter	Chemist	Lib	School Board; Working Mens Rep. Assoc.
Gilder, G.W.	Hat trade	Lib	Tolls & Municipal Buildings C'tee; Finance C'tee
Webster, A.T.	Hat trade	Lib	Guardians; Finance C'tee
*Higgins, Jn.	Painter	Con	School Board; Finance C'tee; Board of Health; Sanitary & Deodorising C'tee
*Cotchin, Jn.	Merchant	Lib	Finance C'tee
Walsh, Wm. (elected in June)	Hat trade	Lib	Finance C'tee
Puddephat, Thos.	Retailer	Lib	Tolls & Municipal Buildings C'tee; GP & Fire Brigade C'tee
Shepheard, Wm.	Gentleman	Lib	Board of Health; Tolls & Municipal Buildings C'tee
Oliver, S.	Retailer (retired)	Lib/Con	Highways & Lighting C'tee; Sanitary & Deodorising C'tee
Lockhart, G.C.H.	Coal merch.	Con	Board of Health; Tolls & Municipal Buildings C'tee; Finance C'tee
Dawson, Jn.	Retailer	Lib	Sanitary & Deodorising C'tee; GP & Fire Brigade C'tee
Taylor, Edw.	Undertaker	Con	Board of Health; (elected in November) Tolls & Municipal Buildings C'tee; GP & Fire Brigade C'tee
Green, J.W.	Brewer	Lib	Finance C'tee

* Denotes Alderman

Epilogue

The town of 'Strawopolis' appeared as a thinly disguised Luton in a slide illustrated temperance lecture written by a local campaigner, T.G. Hobbs, during the 1890s. Hobbs may have conceived of the title himself or he may have lifted it from an earlier designation. Either way, the label was apt and this 'nest of freeholders' had experienced a remarkable transformation during the middle part of the nineteenth century. This wholesale change embraced Luton's economy, its social composition and its institutions. The landscape of the town was a testimony to the small speculators who had laid out the streets that were teeming with small enterprises. Although the town's powerful association with Liberalism and nonconformity would fade in the first half of the twentieth century, Luton's defining characteristic – as a place of plentiful work and affordable homes – was set in the middle of the nineteenth century, and would last until the end of the next.

In other respects, Sir Robert Peel's sneer that its houses were 'all built of straw' was also well-suited. All that flourished in the town was dependent upon the good fortune of a seasonal trade, subject to fluctuations in fashion, disruptions in the supply of plait and even changes in the weather. It also required, in the main, female labour. At the time that Hobbs was first delivering 'Strawopolis', Asher Hucklesby, as Mayor of Luton, was referring darkly to 'the hundreds of boys and men who wandered listlessly about the town for most of the year'. Thus, it was from the last decade of the nineteenth century that the second phase of Luton's transformation was set in place. Between this time and the end of the Great War, the town's dependence upon the straw hat trade was deliberately broken, and this was achieved in a very Lutonian manner. This conscious change involved the Borough Council and the Chamber of Commerce (the twin creations of William Bigg), bridged by a New Industries Committee. It also absorbed local public utilities, private landowners and syndicates created in order to speculate upon land. At no time, however, was there an all-encompassing strategy formulated and driven on by an over-arching single authority, or through a federation of interested parties. Instead, this metamorphosis was brought about, typically, through an amalgam of individuals and organisations each pursuing their own goals of public good and private profit. The negotiations which realised the switch from a devotion to straw to a dependence upon the internal combustion engine were remarkable in themselves for being conducted on a personal level, in secret and on the cheap: a campaign expenditure of £350 spread over twenty years secured Luton's new industries.

Amongst the new firms to arrive in the town at the beginning of the twentieth century were Kent Meters, SKF, Electrolux, the Davis Gas

Stove Company, the Omnia Works (aircraft manufacturers), the Co-operative Wholesale Society's Cocoa Works and the British Gelatine Company. Important though all of these undoubtedly were, they were over-shadowed by just one firm. Sufficient land was the inducement for the Vauxhall Ironworks to relocate from south London in 1905, at a time when the company was experimenting in the production of motor cars as a sideline to its main product of marine engines. Here was the final irony. By the time of the outbreak of the Second World War, dependence upon one industry was replaced by reliance upon a single company as Vauxhall Motors came to dominate the town, even to the extent of determining the timing of school holidays. The dangers implicit within such a relationship became apparent in the last two decades of the twentieth century when Luton's engineering firms in general, and Vauxhall in particular, begun to reduce their workforce significantly. In sharp contrast with late Victorian Luton, however, the scope for a locally formulated political and economic initiative in order to address this challenge had become greatly diminished.

Biographical Notes

This is by no means an exhaustive 'Who Was Who' of mid-nineteenth century Luton, as will be immediately evident by the few women listed. Instead it is a series of notes which draw together various threads of information, some of which appears in the preceding chapters. The entries highlight (where known) basic data such as occupation, religious denomination, family connections, politics and public life. Some 280 individuals, of the thousands of people who made the town in the mid-nineteenth century, are mentioned here.

ADAMS, REV EDWARD RICHARDS. Vicar of Biscot, 1869–75 after which he went to live in Great Yarmouth; Liberal; Bible Five member of the first School Board; Freemason; supporter of the Mechanics Institute and Gymnastic Society.

ADAMS, JAMES. Frequent offender, twice branded with a 'D'.

ADAMS, WILLIAM. Regular offender, not known if related to the above.

ALFORD, WALTER. George Street grocer, also owned a beer house; supporter of the Mechanics Institute and a Freemason.

ALLEN, JOSEPH or JAMES. George Street draper; developed sewing machine capable of 600 stitches per minute, 1856; Liberal; Vice-President of the Mechanics Institute in the 1850s and member of the Luton Reform Registration Association. Father-in-law of Samuel Debenham.

AMES, COL. LIONEL. (1809–73); lived at the Hyde, to the south-west of Luton; Liberal and according to the *Luton Times*, 'a model magistrate'; backer of the proposed Water Company in 1850; promoter of the railways in the 1840s and 1850s; opponent of the plans for a School Board.

ANSTEE, JOSEPH. Registrar of Births and Deaths and Relieving Officer for the Luton district of the Luton Union; official of the Luton Reform Registration Association; owner of property in Spring Place and New Street.

ATTWOOD, DANIEL. (1810–1902); shoemaker; secretary of court 'Benevolence' of the Foresters until obliged by 'economic circumstances' to emigrate to the United States in 1858.

ATTWOOD, ARTHUR BENNETT. (d. 1921); son of William Henry (jun.); builder, retired from business early; later became a Conservative Mayor of Luton.

ATTWOOD, WILLIAM H. Builder and owner of a number of cottages in High Town; occasionally fell foul of the Board of Health and went bankrupt with debts and liabilities of £2572 in 1865.

ATTWOOD, WILLIAM HENRY (jun.). (b. 1837); probably son of William H.; carpenter, builder and property owner; went bankrupt, 1873; had twelve sons plus daughters; charged with assault, 1874.

AUSTIN, CHARLES. (d. 1842); father of Charles Addington; solicitor; co-founder of the Luton lodge of Freemasons; promoter of early railway schemes; member of Lighting and Watching Committee, 1840.

AUSTIN, CHARLES ADDINGTON. (d. 1872); son of above; solicitor (partner of Williamson), Liberal; Freemason; member of Oddfellows and Literary Institute; gave financial assistance to Gaitskell Terrace Evening School; supporter of the railway propositions in the 1840s; related to T.E. Austin.

AUSTIN, THOMAS ERSKINE. Father of William, (the author of the *History of Luton*); solicitor; clerk to the Board of Guardians; Freemason; Literary Institute member; secretary to the Luton, Dunstable and Welwyn Junction Railway Company; secretary to George Stephenson's abortive scheme in the 1840s; backer of proposed Water Company, 1860.

BAILEY, C. Member of Luton Co-operative Company.

BAILEY, GEORGE. Solicitor; his mother died from cholera in 1854; served his articles with Frederick Chase; founder member of Luton Liberal Association; clerk to the Board of Health 1851–76 and subsequently the first Town Clerk of Luton; first secretary of the original branch of the Foresters; speculated in property through Luton Freehold Land Society, owning several cottages in Albert Road.

BAILEY, JOSEPH. 'Farmer and manufacturer'; Liberal; elected to Board of Health in 1858 but was unsuccessful when he stood as a 'Yellow' candidate in 1872; owned several properties in Wellington Street.

BAISLEY, EDMUND. Director of South Beds and North Herts Permanent Building Society, 1850s; appointed toll collector by Board of Health in 1866 at a salary of £40 per annum.

BARRETT, ALFRED. Director of South Beds and North Herts Permanent Building Society, 1850s.

BARRETT, THOMAS. Builder; chaired first meeting of the Luton Ratepayers' Protection Society in 1856; owned 35 properties in New Town by 1871.

BARRETT, WILLIAM. Park Street ironmonger; substantial property owner; member of the Board of Health.

BARTLETT, REV THOMAS. Vicar of Saint Mary's 1854–7; supporter of Mechanics Institute.

BEALE, DR A.J. Conservative; member of Lighting and Watching Committee in 1840 and serving as overseer in 1847; gave evidence to Cresy in 1850.

BELL, G.A. Shopkeeper and member of Co-operative Company.

BENSON, DR PATRICK. (d. 1872); surgeon; lived Wellington Street; Conservative; Freemason.

BERRY, REV ROBERT. Minister of Congregational Church appointed in August, 1874; temperance supporter; a 'simple, forceful' speaker.

BIGG, LOUISA. Daughter of William; founder of Womens' Literary Association.

BIGG, WILLIAM. (1814–78); born Swansea; manager of the London and County Bank at Witney, Oxfordshire and transferred to Luton branch c. 1848, becoming the manager soon after; member of Society of Friends but also attended the services of other denominations; Liberal; used his position as bank manager to promote various schemes in the town; elected to Board of Health, 1853 and was the first Chairman of the School Board, 1874; promoter of the Water Company, becoming a Director and shareholder; also on the Board of the Gas Company; promoted the railway developments of the 1850s; on the committee of the Gaitskell Terrace Evening School; leader of the Mechanics Institute; Superintendent of the Friends Adult School; member of the Literary Institute; elected to the first Town council and was unanimously elected Mayor to serve for 1876 and 1877; behind the establishment of a Chamber of Commerce in Luton in 1877; a keen walker, he often strolled from his home in Castle Street to the General Cemetery which was apparently laid out by his nephew, a Mr Atkins; chose the plot in which he wished to be buried in an unobtrusive corner of the cemetery; his long funeral cortege commenced from the Corn Exchange and the shops in Luton closed out of a mark of respect; personal estate of under £16,000 at death.

BLUNDELL, HENRY. Draper, by the 1870s being the leading retailer in the town; son of Joseph K. Blundell; Liberal; Wesleyan Methodist; Bible Five member of the School Board; unsuccessful in seeking election to the Town Council, in 1876, but was later elected, serving as Mayor in 1886.

BLUNDELL, JOSEPH KING. Hat manufacturer; father of Henry; Wesleyan Methodist; Conservative; served on the Board of Guardians; unsuccessful 'Blue' candidate in the first Board of Health elections, 1850; promoted railway development in the 1850s.

BOLTON, BENJAMIN. Overseer in 1847.

BOUTWOOD, J. (1821–73); Wesleyan; officer of the Mechanics Institute, 1850s.

BRETT, JOHN. Tenant farmer of the Marquess of Bute in George Street until his farm was demolished in 1818 to make way for Wellington Street; removed to the Bury Farm; Liberal; Board of Guardians; Board of Health; churchwarden 1814–29, 1845–50, 1853–7.

BRICKWOOD, EDWIN LATHOM. Solicitor, 'keen-witted . . . waspish'; solicitor to the Beds Conservative Association; owned Bull Court hovels; appointed Clerk to the Board of Health, 1851 but moved to Putney in the same year; consistent upholder of individual rights and opponent of any social reform that intruded upon them.

BROWN, DANIEL. Miller; Quaker; one of the richest men in the town; financed the British School built in Langley Street in 1835.

BROWN, FREDERICK. (1817–92); son of Richard Marks Brown; nephew of Henry and cousin of Henry (junior); partner in Brown and Green's iron foundry; Quaker; unsuccessful 'Blue' candidate in 1850s but later elected; promoter of Water Company, 1865, and campaigner for a School Board; financial supporter of Gaitskell Terrace Evening School and the Mechanics Institute; member of the Literary Institute.

BROWN, FREDERICK. (d. 1890); hat manufacturer at 11, Inkerman Street; Wesleyan; personal estate of £249. 8s. at death.

BROWN, HENRY. (1797–1880); cousin of Richard Marks Brown; timber merchant, a business he established on the corner of Chapel Street in 1820; Quaker, but would attend services at Baptist and Primitive Methodist chapels; member of Lighting and Watching committee in 1840; unsuccessful 'Blue' candidate for the Board of Health in 1850 but was elected in 1852 on the same ticket; member of the Board of Guardians; promoter of the Water Company; financial supporter of the Gaitskell Terrace Evening School; a convert to the temperance movement he discharged several men from his timber yard, ostensibly because of their drinking, although he had recently purchased an 8 h.p. machine to cut timber; personal estate of under £30,000 at death.

BROWN, HENRY (jun.) (1823–92); son of Henry, cousin of Frederick; lived Highfield House; miller; Quaker; Liberal; chaired public meeting in April 1864 that called for the building of a corn exchange and market hall; financial supporter of the Gaitskell Terrace Evening School; supporter of the Mechanics Institute and later Chairman of the School Board; became a J.P. but according to Samuel Drewett 'he rather failed in the expectation we had of him in that position. Whether it was he got mixed up with County families or what, I can't say but he had not back bone enough to stand up for the oppressed'.

BROWN, J.R. Builder; son of New Town Street grocer who also bought additional property; owned 29 properties by 1869; Director of the South Beds and North Herts Permanent Building Society, 1850s.

BROWN, LYDIA. (d. 1879); second wife of Daniel, cousin of Richard Marks Brown; shareholder in Water Company.

BROWN, RICHARD. (1826–72). Son of Henry, brother of Henry (jun.); lived at Whitehill; partner in Brown and Green; Liberal; Quaker; teacher in the Friends' Adult School.

BROWN, RICHARD. Timber merchant; lived Cromwell Road; shareholder in Water Company.

BROWN, RICHARD MARKS. (d. 1858); a small man, married three times and father of Frederick; miller at the Brache who got on well with the Marquess of Bute, but less well with John Shaw Leigh; Quaker; Tory; member of Board of Guardians from 1835 and into the 1840s.

BROWN, ROBERT J. Builder, brother of J.R.; married daughter of John Cumberland; father of Henry Cumberland Brown (a solicitor who later became a manager of Balmforths engineering works in Luton); built also in Harpenden to which he moved in later years, living with his unmarried daughter in 'increasing parsimony and discomfort'; kept a pet pig which followed him to the railway station before he embarked on his various journeys.

BROWN, WILLIAM HENRY. (1840–1915); son of Henry Coles Brown and grandson of Richard Marks Brown from his first marriage; Quaker; Treasurer of Friends' Adult School.

BURGE, JAMES. Publican; member of Board of Health, being one of the original signatories calling for its establishment; member of Luton Fire Brigade, 1858.

BURGESS, REV HENRY. (1808–86); an ultimately disastrous minister of Park Street Baptist Meeting House 1830–48; ordained into Church of England, 1850; vicar of St. Andrew, Whittlesey, Cambridgeshire, 1861–86; closely involved with the campaign for a railway line in the 1840s; ran Luton

Grammar School and published a monthly newspaper. Burgess' entry in the *Dictionary of National Biography* glosses over his nonconformist career.

BURR, CHARLES. (1806–92); partner in family brewery which he sold to Thomas Sworder in 1857 but still retained property in Park Square area; member of Lighting and Watching Committee, 1840; financial supporter of the Gaitskell Terrace Evening School; promoter of railway line in the 1850s; lived in Paddington at the time of his death.

BURR, FREDERICK. (1811–56); land owner and senior member of family brewing business; lived Park Square; member of the first Board of Guardians, 1835; supported Luton Horticultural Society, Church of England, church schools and Church Cemetery; churchwarden 1838–41.

BURR, WILLIAM. (d. 1830). Son of Thomas Godfrey, father of Frederick and Charles; brewer.

BUTLIN, ELIZABETH. Innkeeper; signatory to pro-Board of Health petition, 1849.

BUTTERFIELD, FRANCIS. Farmer; signed original petition calling for a Board of Health, later member.

CAMMELL, WILLIAM HENRY. Engineer and kitchen range manufacturer, York Street; opponent of the School Board.

CAWDELL, WILLIAM JAMES. George Street hat manufacturer; defeated candidate in first Borough Council elections.

CHAMBERS, GEORGE HENRY. Market Hill shopkeeper; Board of Health member but failed to secure seat on Borough Council in 1876, polling just 34 votes.

CHASE, EDWARD. (b. 1792); landowner, brother of Frederick.

CHASE, FREDERICK. (b. 1797). Brother of Edward; solicitor and landowner; Conservative; successfully master-minded 'Yellow' control of Board of Health serving as its Clerk from August 1850 until March 1851 when he left the district.

CLARK, JOHN. Farmer; 'Yellow' Board of Health member, elected in 1850.

CLARKE, DR FREDERICK J. Surgeon, Park Street.; supporter of establishment of Board of Health; served as Medical Officer to the Board of Health; treasurer of Gaitskell Terrace Evening School; member of Oddfellows.

CLARKE, JOSEPH. Director of South Beds and North Herts Permanent Building Society.

CLARKE, WILLIAM. (There were two, or possibly three William Clarke's which frustratingly are most difficult to tell apart). There are references to: landlord (and owner ?) of the *Cock Inn* from which he ran a coach service to London; 'kindly' farmer at the Brache; churchwarden, 1833–52; successful 'Yellow' candidate, 1850; owned a number of cottages around the southern side of town; successful candidate on the first Town Council; at least one William Clarke was a Conservative.

COATES, W.T. Park Street draper; Congregationalist; secretary of Luton Mutual Improvement Society.

COLLINGDON, THOMAS. (1791–1884); steward of Luton Hoo from 1834; officially resided there but was often away in London.

CONGREVE, JOHN. Assistant Overseer who was captured by police, 1872, after embezzling £12 and £15.9s.

CONISBEE, FREDERICK. Grandfather of L.R. Conisbee (ed. of *Bedfordshire Bibliography*); butcher; Conservative; owner of three properties in Burr Street; elected to Town Council, 1876 and retired 1878.

COOK(E), FRANCIS. Grocer, Park Square; St. Mary's churchwarden, 1858–9, 1860–2, 1868–75; listed as a member of the Fire Brigade, 1858; shareholder in Water Company.

COOK(E), JAMES. Maltster, brewer; member of Board of Health, 1858.

COTCHIN, JOHN. (1829–1904); hat manufacturer; Liberal; Freemason; elected to the Board of Health in 1861; official of the Luton Reform Registration Association; elected to the Town council in 1876 and became Mayor in 1880.

COTCHIN, R. Shopkeeper; Liberal; supporter of the Mechanics Institute.

COX, JOSEPH. Coal merchant; Wesleyan Methodist; member of the Board of Health.

CRAWLEY, JOHN SAMBROOK. (1823–95); inherited Stockwood estate in 1852 which he enlarged and improved; member of Board of Health, 1853; magistrate (although he rarely attended); churchwarden, 1864–6 but became involved in rows with O'Neill; supported the School Board and gave financial support to National schools, parish churches in Stopsley, Biscot and West Hyde, and the cottage hospital; President of the South Beds Conservative Association; estate totalled £71,594 and resworn £61,425 at death.

CRAWLEY, SAMUEL. (1790–1852); father of John Sambrook; owner of Stockwood estate; pursued a political career as a Whig MP first for Honiton, then for Bedford until defeated in 1837 by Tories Polhill and Stuart; enlarged estate 1839–42; died Naples.

CUMBERLAND, JOHN. Surveyor and auctioneer; Conservative; Freemason and owner of small number of cottages in New Town; churchwarden 1858, 1868–74; member of the Board of Health and successful 'Blue' candidate, 1872; lukewarm toward incorporation but was elected to the first Town Council and succeeded Bigg as Mayor, 1877.

CUTHBERTSON, ADAM. Member of Mechanics Institute and co-promoter of Working Men's Representation Association.

DANCER, JOSEPH. Butcher and farmer, Park Street; member of Luton Fire Brigade, 1858; owned 35 properties in New Town and High Town by 1871.

DANCER, MATTHEW. Butcher, Park Street; ally of Brickwood in opposing reform.

DANCER, WILLIAM. (1793–1863); successful grocer, Stuart Street but committed suicide soon after retirement in 1863; personal estate of £249.8s.

DANIELS, SAMUEL. Unsuccessful 'Blue' candidate, 1850.

DAVIES, DANIEL. Beer retailer; successful 'Yellow' candidate, 1850.

DAVIES, REV J. JORDAN. (1806–1858); minister of Park Street Baptist Meeting House, 1849–57, which he rebuilt after Burgess' ministry; President of the Gaitskell Terrace Evening School; often in delicate health.

DAVIS, FREDERICK. (d. 1874); Market Hill shoemaker; born in Luton, educated there and then in Towcester; apprenticed to a draper for eleven years; lived Stuart Street, married but many of his children died when still young; Liberal; Methodist lay preacher; signed original petition calling for a board of Health, 1849; churchwarden and member of the Board of Health, being first elected, 1859 and serving a total of twelve years; speculated in property in mid 1840s ultimately owning several around the town; amateur historian, publishing a *History of Luton* in thirteen parts in 1855 and re-published, 1874; opposed the School Board; of his public service the *Luton Times* wrote 'He was always ready to spring up to move a resolution which a majority supported ... lacking originality, he has been put forward by men who are in the background ... through a long public career we cannot call to mind one single project originated by him; he is not a leader, never was, but always a follower'; personal estate valued at less than £2000 at death.

DAWSON, JOHN. Shopkeeper; Liberal; unsuccessful candidate for Town Council in May 1876, but was elected in June; Mayor in 1882.

DAY, JOHN. Notorious figure; by late 1860s known as 'one of the worst characters in this town'.

DEBENHAM, SAMUEL. (d. 1887); occupied as a confectioner originally in Bury St. Edmunds; photographer, King Street, having moved to Luton from Bedford at some point in the mid-1860s; married Martha Mary Allen (daughter of Joseph) in 1867; secretary of Luton Protestant Association; business purchased by Henry Gregson by 1870; (see letter from Dr Turley, October 1991, in LM Local History correspondence file).

DORRINGTON, WILLIAM. Fire Brigade member, 1858.

DREWETT, WILLIAM. (1834–1900); miller at the Biscot Mill; Quaker; Liberal; opposed incorporation but was elected to the Town Council in May 1876.

DUNN, THOMAS. Gardener to James O'Neill and appointed by him to post of churchwarden, 1867.

ELLIS, CHARLES. Saddler and harness maker, Manchester Street; member of the Oddfellows.

EVERITT, JOHN. Straw hat manufacturer; an energetic man with a high sense of public duty; active Liberal; member of the Luton Reform Association, 1840s; a member of Park Street Baptist Meeting House at which he suggested the office of deaconess, adopted by Rev Davies; worked with youth of the church; worked for Edmund Waller in early career; served on both the Board of Health and Board of Guardians, 1850s, distinguishing himself during the cholera epidemic; an early convert to teetotalism, which was the cause of his resignation from Park Street; joined King Street Congregational Church; speculated (successfully) in land in King Street, early 1860s; promoted the various railway schemes, and the water company in 1860 and 1865; Everitt later moved to London.

FARR, WILLIAM. Landlord in Dudley Street; owner of cottages in Windmill Lane, High Town; elected to the Town Council in May 1876 representing the interests of the Licensed Victuallers' Association.

FAUNCH, WILLIAM. Shopkeeper; officer of Mechanics Institute.

FOSTER, JOHN. (d. 1864); Quaker minister; a small, wiry man; very careful in business, earning the nickname 'old pinch-plum'.

FOSTER, THOMAS. Cooper and seedsman, Chapel Street where he also owned a number of cottages, plus others in a yard bearing his name in Upper George Street; member of Lighting and Watching Committee, 1840; member of the Fire Brigade, 1858.

FOUNTAIN, ABRAHAM. Carpenter, New Town owner occupier; frequently in trouble.

GARDNER, JOSEPH. Church Street grocer; speculated in property through the Luton Freehold Land Society.

GARDNER, WILLIAM. (d. 1847); master of the Workhouse with his wife Elizabeth as matron; died from an outbreak of fever in the workhouse.

GEE, FREDERICK. Hat manufacturer; speculating in property, mid 1840s.

GENDERS, REV JOHN WILLIAM. Minister of Park Street Baptist Church, 1870–6; left for Portsea due to ill-health of his family; supported School Board.

GIBBON, RICHARD. Manager of Sworder's brewery; cleared of embezzlement, 1853.

GILDER, GEORGE WILCOX. Hat manufacturer; Liberal; Wesleyan; committee member of the Owners' and Ratepayers' Association, formed 1871; elected to Town Council, 1876 and Mayor in 1884.

GODWIN, JOHN. Director of the South Beds and North Herts Permanent Building Society.

GOUJON, DANIEL. High Town hat manufacturer; descended from Hugenot family; member of Lighting and Watching Committee, 1840.

GRACE, DANIEL. Park Square confectioner; shareholder in Water Company.

GRAY, JOHN. Owner of Crown and Anchor brewery in New Bedford Road which he sold to Thomas Sworder, 1849 at the same time also disposing of land and property in Wellington Street; afterwards described as one of the 'many spirited builders', being responsible for the building the *Eagle Tavern* in Wellington Street; before the building was completed the eagle statue on top of the public house was vandalised by someone who climbed up Gray's scaffolding and knocked its head off!

GREEN, EDWARD FOSTER. Brother of J.W. and son of Joseph; partner in Brown and Green; Freemason.

GREEN, JOSEPH. Father of Edward. F. and J.W.; iron founder; Quaker; Liberal.

GREEN, J.W. Brewer, acquiring the businesses of amongst others, Pearman and Sworder, in 1897; dominant brewer in the area by the 20th century; Freemason; Quaker, but later Church of England; initially Liberal but later Conservative.

GREEN, SAMUEL. Liberal; Board of Health.

GREGORY, ELIZABETH. Owned cottages in Old Bedford Road; operated brick kiln in Dunstable Lane.

GREGORY, GEORGE. Husband or son of Elizabeth; lived in Dunstable Street.; operated brick kiln in Dunstable Lane, late 1840s and early 1850s; owned property in Old Bedford Road; financial supporter of the Mechanics Institute.

GUNN, HUGH. Hat manufacturer; Liberal; Congregationalist; Freemason; member of the Co-operative Society and elected to the first Town Council, 1876; Mayor, 1879.

GUTTERIDGE, JAMES. The last prominent member of a family which established itself in the Luton area in the 16th century and which had built up a considerable stock of land; Baptist; possessed a volcanic temper – 'He had many good qualities, but he was a man of war' was the recollection of one contemporary; obliged his workmen from Sundon village to walk the several miles round journey each Sunday to Eaton Green, a hamlet on the eastern side of Luton, in order to collect their wages; John Waller was one of the executors of his estate.

GUTTERIDGE, RICHARD. Member of the Board of Guardians, 1840s.

HANDS, REV THOMAS. (1818–70); successful minister at Park Street Baptist Meeting House; Liberal – 'an ardent friend of the true elevation of the people and of Liberalism and of true reform' (his funeral address); did not extend this ardour to the role of women in the church, suppressing their right to vote and abolishing the office of deaconess.

HARRIS, REV CHARLES BUTLER. Leader of the Wooden Church in New Town, falling foul of O'Neill; ran private school in Stuart Street; Freemason.

HASELGROVE, RICHARD. Minor property owner; Liberal.

HASELGROVE, THOMAS W. Stonemason; Liberal; Freemason; owned scattering of properties; unsuccessful 'Yellow' candidate, 1872 and unsuccessful candidate in May 1876.

HAWKES, JAMES. Registrar of Marriages; member of Board of Health.

HAWKES, JOSEPH. Wheelwright and victualler; Liberal; supporter of the Mechanics Institute; official of the Luton Reform Registration Association.

HEALE, DR ALFRED. Surgeon; gave evidence to Cresy; member of the Literary Institute; opposed the School Board and incorporation.

HIGGINS, JAMES. Hat trade; Conservative; Freemason; opponent of School Board.

HIGGINS, JOHN. Painter and Plumber; Conservative; opponent of incorporation; member of the first Borough Council and the first School Board (Prayer Book Five); member of the Board of Health and the Board of Guardians.

HIGGINS, WALTER. Temperance sympathiser; Liberal.

HIGGINS, WILLIAM HIRAM. Hat manufacturer, Upper George Street; signatory to original pro-Board petition, 1849; temperance supporter; unsuccessful Council candidate, May 1876; owner of scattered cottages.

HITCHENS, REV J. HILES. Congregational Minister, 1866–70; excellent preacher and church builder; advocate of School Board.

HOBBS, ABRAHAM. (1816–87); father of T.G. Hobbs; carpenter, migrated from village of Bow Brickill to Luton; built up property holding in the town.

HOLYOAK, HENRY. Surveyor; Conservative.

HOPKINS, JAMES. Builder; Liberal.

HORNE, FREDERICK E. Plait dealer; promoter of waterworks, 1864–5.

HOW, ROBERT. Hat dealer; Baptist; Liberal; member of Luton Reform and Registration Association; temperance supporter; unsuccessful 'Blue' candidate, 1850; opposed incorporation; built Bramingham Villa which he then sold to Scargill.

HOW, THOMAS. Opponent of the proposed Board of Health; Liberal.

HOWARD, ELLIOT. Owner and manager of Hayward Tyler; Quaker; Liberal.

HUBBARD, ?. Secretary of New Building Society, 1851.

HUCKLE, THOMAS. Hat manufacturer; Primitive Methodist; owner of property in High Town, including beer house; member of first town council.

HUNT, GEORGE. Hat manufacturer, Chapel Street; Wesleyan; Superintendent of Sunday School; temperance supporter.

HUNT, GEORGE. Hat manufacturer, Upper George Street; shareholder in Water Company.

HUNT, JOHN. Hat trade; officer of Mechanics Institute, 1850s.

HUNT, WILLIAM. Solicitor, Stuart Street; originally from Leeds; lived at the Villa in New Bedford Road but quit in 1847 and appears to have gone bankrupt – his home contents were auctioned; solicitor to the New Building Society, 1851; cricketer – took all ten wickets in an innings, August 1858; Freemason; Conservative. William Austin wrote: 'His alcoholic joviality was notorious and notwithstanding that he was the subject of many a practical joke, his manners never degenerated into vulgarity or quarrelling. Many still recall the pomposity of manner, the faultlessness of dress, the spotless linen and glossy hat of "Squire" Hunt.'

JAMES, GEORGE. Inspector in Luton Police; left in 1870 to be Superintendent at Ampthill.

JAQUEST, DAVID. (1831–1901); first Chief Constable of Luton Police, 1876, having initially refused the post.

JOHNSON, G.M. Grocer; deacon of Congregational Church; Liberal; officer of the Mechanics Institute, 1850s.

JOHNSON, J.J. Hat manufacturer; Liberal; successful 'Yellow' candidate, 1850, after being one of the signatories to the pro-Board petition in 1849; member of Board of Guardians.

JOHNSON, T.C. Wine and spirit merchant, owning at least one public house; Freemason; member of Board of Health; School Board opponent; bankrupt, 1875 but still was a leading figure in the Licensed Victuallers' Association in preparation for the Town council elections of 1876.

JORDAN, GUSTAVUS. Born Cornwall; draper; Wesleyan; temperance supporter; signed petition calling for Board of Health in 1849; elected to the

Board of Health in 1859; opposed the School Board (and was an unsuccessful candidate) and opposed incorporation.

JORDAN, J. Joint manager of the Luton Savings Bank; official of the Luton Reform Registration Association.

JORDAN, J.J. Joint manager (with above) of Luton Savings Bank.

JUDGE, MATTHEW. Manchester Street watchmaker; Liberal.

KEELING, JOHN. Director of South Beds and North Herts Permanent Building Society; owned a number of properties, including twelve in Park Street West.

KERSHAW, J. JEFFERSON. Hat manufacturer, George Street.; father in law of Horace Sworder; led temperance delegation to magistrates, 1869; unsuccessful Prayer Book Five candidate, 1874.

KIDMAN, JAMES. Successful 'Yellow' candidate, 1850; tenant farmer of the Crawley's at Biscot and owned land in the Chapel Street area; Conservative.

KING, SOLOMON. An 'old offender' whose home was apparently in Houghton Regis, but who spent much of his time in various gaols and workhouses.

LANE, SAMUEL. (There were two, possibly three men living in Luton with this name; one was a butcher and another a builder (and wheelwright); one served on the Board of Health).

LAWFORD, CHARLES. Director of the South Beds and North Herts Permanent Building Society.

LAWFORD, FREDERICK. Accountant; Oddfellow; committee member of Owners' and Ratepayers' Association; promoter of Working Mens' Representation Association.

LAWFORD, SAMUEL. Plait dealer who went bankrupt in 1847 having traded 'heedlessly and recklessly'.

LEE, REV T.J. (d. 1875); Vicar of Christ Church 1857–75; opponent of School Board.

LEIGH, JOHN GERARD. (d. 1875); son of John Shaw Leigh; Conservative.

LEIGH, JOHN SHAW. (1791–1871); owner of Luton Hoo; former Mayor of Liverpool; played little active part in Luton's affairs; personal estate just short of £800,000 at death.

LOCKHART, G.C.H. Coal merchant; Conservative; member of the Board of Health and unsuccessful School Board candidate; failed to get elected to the Town Council in May 1876 but was successful in June.

LONG, G. Basket maker.

LOOT, CHARLES. (b. 1823); joined Foresters, 1849; served as secretary to court 'Benevolence', 1858–1901; recalled as being of 'genial manner, kindly disposition, and unvarying courtesy'; originally employed as a blocker at Vyse's, later establishing his own hat manufacturing business in Park Street.

LUCAS, EDWARD. Bank manager of Sharples and Company; Quaker; temperance supporter; promoter and Director of Water Company, 1875; promoter of railway in 1850s; lived Park Street.

LYE, THOMAS. (1820–98); originally from Yorkshire; dyer, New Bedford Road; Wesleyan; Liberal; cottage landlord; personal estate of £66,743 at death.

MACDOUALL, CANON WILLIAM. Relative of Marquess of Bute; vicar of St. Mary's 1827–49; Conservative; member of Board of Guardians, 1835.

MAFFEY, Charles. Relieving Officer; resigned in 1870 after vote of censure by Guardians because of his 'harsh and oppressive treatment of the poor'; secretary of a branch of the Foresters.

MAKEPEACE, REV J. Minister of Union Chapel 1855–63; organised mission work in town.

MARSH, ROBERT. Treasurer of Mechanics Institute in 1840s; Quaker; treasurer of Friends' Adult School; owned cottages.

MAYES, G. Member of fire brigade, 1858.

MEAD, JOSEPH. Grocer, Park Street; Board of Health.

MEES, CHARLES. George Street hat manufacturer; opposed School Board and was an unsuccessful candidate; elected to the first town council, his candidature being supported by the Working Mens' Representation Association.

MENLOVE, J. Baptist; served on Committee of Gaitskell Terrace Evening School.

MERRITT, JESSE. Carpenter; officer of the Mechanics Institute, 1850s.

MORTON, S.H. Temperance supporter.

MUGGLETON, ?. Store manager of Co-op Company on Market Hill; Baptist.

MUIR, JAMES. Hat manufacturer; unsuccessful 'Blue' candidate, 1850; member of Luton Reform Association; Literary Institute.

NEWLAND, ROBERT HENRY. Ran Luton Academy, Church Street, 1850s.

OLIVER, SAMUEL. Draper; promoted Water Company, 1864; St. Mary's churchwarden, 1866–7; elected to Town Council in June 1876 after failure in May.

O'NEILL, REV JAMES. Pugnacious Vicar of Luton, 1862–97; member of the Prayer Book Five faction on the School Board, and later its chairman, although he rarely attended.

ORDISH, C. Used Luton Freehold Land Society in order to speculate in property.

PADBURY, ?. Vice-President of New Building Society, 1851.

PARKER, WILLIAM. Shoemaker – 'working man'; promoter of Working Mens' Representation Association; Liberal.

PARKES, THOMAS. Solicitor.

PARSONS, E. (d. 1856); operated Villa School in New Bedford Road from at least 1849 until his death; school was then taken over by Henry Wright.

PARTRIDGE, THOMAS. Tenant farmer of Sir Edward Filmer at Leagrave; member of Board of Guardians from 1835.

PEARMAN, DANIEL. (d. 1857); father of Henry and Frederick; wine merchant; Quaker – dressed in traditional style of the Friends; signatory to petition calling for establishment of local Board of Health, 1849.

PEARMAN, FREDERICK. Wine and spirit merchant; Quaker, later Church of England; churchwarden, 1863–5; Board of Health and Fire Brigade; enjoyed the sporting life with John Waller (junior) and E.O. Williams.

PEARMAN, HENRY. Succeeded father Daniel in 1857 but proved to be a poor businessmen – expanded business 'regardless of expense' and was swallowed up by J.W. Green; Liberal; Quaker, but later Church of England.

PEGLER, EDWARD. Headmaster of Queen Square School from January, 1873.

PEILE, REV T.W. Ineffectual Vicar of Luton, 1857–60.

PHILLIPS, REV J. Primitive Methodist minister; temperance sympathiser.

PHILLIPS, WILLIAM. (d. 1889); originally from Kent; opened a chemist shop on Market Hill but became manager of the Gas Works being succeeded in that office by his son and subsequently his grandson; related to farmer and publican William Clarke; member of Lighting and Watching Committee, 1840; unsuccessful 'Blue' candidate, 1850; manager of fire brigade; member of the Literary Institute; officer in the Rifle Corps; Chairman of the Cottage Hospital; churchwarden, 1842–4, 1854–7; and Freemason; Conservative; personal estate of £33,979.15s. 10d. at death.

PLEDGE, WILLIAM THOMPSON. 1808–87; postmaster, having originally traded as a grocer; personally paid for much of the refurbishment of the new Post Office in King Street; Board of Health; unsuccessful in 1876 elections to Council; personal estate of £1975 at death.

POPE, SUPERINTENDENT. Head of Luton Police (officially Deputy Chief Constable of Bedfordshire) from 1850s.

POULTER, THOMAS. Liberal; Congregationalist.

PRESSEY, J.W. Secretary of the Luton Improved Building Society; accused of embezzlement, 1859.

PRIMETT, T. Shopkeeper; Co-operative Company

PUDDEPHAT, THOMAS. Shopkeeper; Liberal; trustee of Oddfellows; unsuccessful in May Council elections, 1876, but successful in following June.

RABAN, ?. Speculated in property through Luton Freehold Land Society.

RANDALL, A. Co-operative Company

READ, WILLIAM. Hat manufacturer; Co-operative Company.

ROBINSON, CHARLES. (1824–77); hat manufacturer and business partner of Tansley; Liberal; Congregationalist; member of the Board of Health and the School Board (Bible Five); supporter of the Gaitskell Terrace Evening School; promoter of the Water Company, 1865; personal estate of under £5000 at death.

ROBINSON, REV ROBERT. Minister of Union Baptist Church 1844–55; successful church builder, interested in education; signatory to 1849 petition calling for Board of Health for Luton; refused to marry non-believers to believers.

SANDOE, WILLIAM. Member of Gloucester family firm of estate agents; Board of Health Surveyor, 1861–9; leaving dinner described in *Luton Times* 3.4.1869; highly regarded by his employers; married to Alice Mayes (member of Stuart Street coach building family) and, therefore, also to Hobbs family – brother in law to T.G. Hobbs; Congregationalist.

SCARGILL, FRANK CHAPMAN. (d. 1919). Solicitor, with a practice in King Street. Built Bramingham Shott (later renamed Wardown and now present home of Luton Museum) in two stages 1867–77; Liberal; Freemason; travelled to the West Indies, summer of 1871; Clerk to the Justices; successful 'Blue' candidate for the Board of Health; owned *Luton Advertiser* (which he purchased in 1874) and small number of beer houses; supporter of School Board and leading opponent of incorporation; Keen cricketer, having his own team 'Scargill's XI' which played occasional friendlies at Bramingham Shott; purchased Biscot Mill from the Drewetts.

SEEBOHM, BENJAMIN. Quaker; Liberal; secretary of Friends' Adult School.

SHEPHEARD, J.G. A leading promoter of the campaign which culminated in incorporation; St. Mary's churchwarden, 1863.

SHEPHEARD, WILLIAM. 'Gentleman'; Liberal; unsuccessful School Board candidate; promoter of incorporation; elected to Town council in June 1876 after failure in May.

SIBLEY, HENRY. Farmer and slum landlord; lived Wellington Street, later Union Street; member of Foresters; 'Yellow' Board of Health member, 1850–51.

SIKES, REV THOMAS. Vicar of Luton, 1850–4, and Curate, 1828–50; Conservative; did much to revive the standing of the Church of England; married daughter of William Burr, therefore becoming brother-in-law to Frederick and Charles; promoter of establishment of Board of Health; member of the Literary Institute.

SIMPSON, FREDERICK. Hat? manufacturer; shareholder in Water Company; lived at Spa Cottage, Farley Hill.

SMART, ARTHUR. (1825–1903); builder, brother and partner of Thomas; Congregationalist; promoter of Water Company, 1864; defeated in May, 1876, but elected in 1878; both brothers owned property around the town; personal estate of £11,316. 6s. at death.

SMART, THOMAS. (1822–96); Luton builder, brother and partner of Arthur; firm built Corn Exchange, Plait Halls, Baths and the Baptist Chapel (which blew down, partially completed, in 1866); Congregationalist; unsuccessful in Council elections, May 1876; personal estate of £1978.15s. 1d. at death.

SMITH, H. Warehouseman; officer of the Mechanics Institute, 1876.

SMITH, ROBERT. Born at the end of the 18th century and claiming in 1875 to have lived in Luton for over 80 years; initially furniture dealer and builder, concentrating upon the latter from the 1840s; leased brick fields from Bute; substantial property owner, George Bailey jibing 'he has got a lot of old cottages about'; Board of Health and opponent of incorporation.

SMITH, THOMAS. Shopkeeper; successful 'Yellow' candidate, 1850.

SMITH, THOMAS. Builder; Conservative; elected to Town Council, May 1876; substantial property owner.

SMITH, THOMAS. Park Street 'gentleman'; Liberal; elected to Town Council, May 1876.

SMYTH, REV H.B. Vicar at Houghton Regis; Liberal; magistrate.

SOLE, GEORGE. (1811–78); shopkeeper; owner of cottages in High Town as well as the Tower Hill slums; elected to the Board of Health, 1858; personal estate of under £1000 at death.

SQUIRES, DR HENRY AUGUSTUS. 'Gentleman' living in Liverpool Road having moved there in 1866 buying 'considerable amount of property' in that road; Baptist theologian; Board of Health.

STALKER, DAVID. Head of Queen's Square School 1863–72.

STALKER, WILLIAM. Printer and Stationer; Baptist; Committee member of Gaitskell Terrace Evening School; published *Luton News* from 4, Wellington Street. from January 1861.

STANION, REV. Minister of Wellington Street Baptist Church; left in 1857, possibly under something of a cloud; still on committee of Gaitskell Terrace Evening School, 1858.

STEVENSON, REV J.R. Minister of Union Chapel, 1864–71; Liberal; supporter of School Board.

STRANGE, GEORGE. Lived and ran shop in Wellington Street; owned three houses in Farley Road, 1871; Liberal; Baptist.

STUART, JOHN CRICHTON, 2ND MARQUESS OF BUTE. (1793–1848); owner of Luton Hoo and Lord of the Manor but played little direct role in the affairs of the town; sold Hoo to C.T. Warde, before it was acquired by Leigh; first chairman of the Board of Guardians.

SWORDER, CHARLES. Brother of Thomas; appears to have been running the affairs of the brewery at the time of its financial difficulties in 1862.

SWORDER, DR HORACE. Son of Thomas, married Caroline, daughter of J.J. Kershaw in 1879; lived George Street in the last privately occupied house; after his death this was pulled down and taken by Sainsbury's site.

SWORDER, ROBERT. Partner of his brother, Thomas, in the brewery.

SWORDER, THOMAS. (1823–1910); solicitor, from Herts, came to Luton c. 1848; married the eldest daughter of Richard Vyse, 1851; became brewer out of 'necessity' not choice by purchasing businesses in Luton; purchased Crown and Anchor Brewery in Manchester Street, 1849, Burr's Brewery, 1857 and Burr and Crab in 1860; sold out to J.W. Green in 1897 for £139,000; Conservative; Anglican; gained election to the Board of Health as 'Blue' candidate in 1850s after being unsuccessful in 1850; churchwarden, 1851–3; backer of railway schemes; promoter of proposed Water Company, financial supporter of the Gaitskell Terrace Evening School; member of the Literary Institute; Prayer Book Five member of first School Board; organised Luton Industrial Exhibition and Bazaar, 1861, which he held at his brewery buildings; a great friend of T.J. Lee and James O'Neill, Sworder was a 'reserved' man and stayed awhile at the Bury before moving to Holly Lodge, where he lived until his death.

TANSLEY, A.J. (1819–63); hat manufacturer and business partner of Robinson; vigorous member of Board of Health and driving force behind the promotion of the Luton Freehold Land Society; Liberal; secretary of the Luton Reform and Registration Association; promoter of the Luton, Dunstable and Welwyn Junction Railway and supporter of the Gaitskell Terrace Evening School; personal estate of less than £5000 at death.

TAYLOR, EDWARD. (1836–90); undertaker and farmer; Conservative; served on Board of Health; promoter of incorporation; tied for sixth (and last) place in May Council elections in 1876, magnanimously withdrew and was rewarded with election in June; personal estate of £8625.8s. 5d. at death.

TEARLE, J. Operated a free reading room in Wellington Street, 1859.

TOMALIN, CHARLES. Baker in Park Street; Congregationalist deacon; owned several cottages in Lea Rd.

TOMSON, CHARLES. Father of Kit; Sundon farmer; vice-chairman of the Board of Guardians, 1840s.

TOMSON, HENRY. Promoted railway in the 1840s and 1850s; member of the Literary Institute; owner of property in Bute Street.

TOMSON, DR KIT. (1823–91); son of Charles; lived at Ivy Cottage, Langley Street; Medical Officer to the Board of Guardians and served a similar, temporary role for the Board of Health; founder member of the Luton Liberal Association; member of the Literary Institute; owner of five (1871) properties scattered around Luton; personal estate of £14,867.7s. at death.

TOWNROW, WILLIAM. (b. 1792); farmer; Baptist; successful 'Yellow' candidate, 1850; significant land holding in the centre of Luton.

TOYER, ALFRED. Born 1830 at Kinsbourne Green, between Luton and Harpenden; educated at plait school, never receiving any formal schooling and moved to Luton when in early teens; oilman and bleacher, High Town; Liberal; Baptist; committee member of Owners' and Ratepayers' Protection Association, formed 1871; at the time he owned seven cottages in Duke Street and one property in Brunswick Street; Mayor of Luton in 1890–1.

TOYER, SAMUEL. (1806–74); builder; Liberal; member of Wellington Street Baptist Church; member of the Board of Health; founder and President of Owners' and Ratepayers' Protection Association; President of the New Building Society (1850); owned 22 properties around Luton (1871), eighteen of which were in Wellington Street; promoter of Water Company in 1864; moved to Ramsgate; opposed the building of the Plait Halls and probably just about every improvement to the town; received just one kind notice from the *Luton Times* – his obituary; personal estate of less than £1500 at death.

TRANTER, WILLIAM. Member of the Mechanics Institute.

TUCKWELL, REV J. Baptist Minister of Union Church; supporter of School Board.

TWELLS, REV. Minister of Waller Street Methodist Church until 1874.

UNDERWOOD, JOHN. Shopkeeper; Wesleyan, involved with the Sunday School; member of the Mechanics Institute.

VYSE, EDMUND. Son of Richard; member of the Luton Reform and Registration Association; convicted of being drunk and disorderly in 1865.

VYSE, RICHARD. (d. 1855); father-in-law of Thomas Sworder; lived in Castle Street where he was recalled as a 'prince of hospitable entertainment' although also possessing a 'somewhat shy and retiring disposition'; hat manufacturer originating from London opening a Luton branch in 1826; employed between 300–500 men and women; Liberal, Freemason, Anglican but also supported dissenting causes; member of Lighting and Watching Committee, 1840; promoter of improvement and reform: member of Board of Guardians; campaigned for a Board of Health; promoter of railway, 1840s; member of the Literary Institute and Horticultural Society; keen cricketer and enjoyed shooting; died at Herne Hill.

VYSE, RICHARD. (d. 1867); son of Richard.

WADSWORTH, WILLIAM. Hotelier at the George Hotel; Freemason.

WALLER, EDMUND. (1783–1845); brother of Thomas, Robert, James and John; pioneer hat manufacturer and draper, George Street; associated with Baptists from 1812, providing the financial prop for the church during Burgess' ministry; Liberal; leading opponent of the church rate; promoter of railway schemes, 1840s and also the Gas Company; member of first Board of Guardians; from 1806 buying ground from Gutteridge; Joseph Hawkes recalled him as 'a very remarkable individual – personally tall and of a fine physical build, strong, energetic, doing with his might whatsoever his hand found to do. Mr Waller dressed in black, with pantaloons and hessian boots and tassels. His commercial walking pace was not less than four and half miles an hour. He was of very quick perception, and equally prompt in decision. When his judgement was once formed it was not easily changed . . .'

WALLER, JAMES. Brother of John, son of Thomas; hat manufacturer, George Street and succeeded father in the business; Liberal; member of the Board of Health, 1851; Vice-President of the Mechanics Institute; member of the Luton Reform and Registration Association; member of Freehold Land Society; promoter of the railway line, 1850s.

WALLER, JAMES. Brother of Thomas, Edmund, John and Robert; lived and traded on Market Hill.

WALLER, JOHN. (1792–1859); brother of Edmund, Thomas, James and Robert; wool stapler, draper; Wesleyan lay preacher; Liberal; successful 'Yellow' candidate, 1850; purchased Gutteridge's house in George Street with extensive gardens stretching down to the River Lea, these gardens being built upon after his death; left personal estate of less than £6000.

WALLER, JOHN. Son of Thomas and brother of James; hat manufacturer, working with his father; lived Wellington Street.

WALLER, ROBERT. Brother of Thomas, Edmund, James and John; hat manufacturer, but also employed by Edmund to operate around England as commercial traveller.

WALLER, THOMAS. (1795–1845); brother of Edmund, James, Robert and John; son of James, and father to James and John; pioneering hat manufacturer, developing the trade, concentrating in particular in the method of production of the plait and travelling to Tuscany in the process; Liberal; 'The intercourse of Mr Thomas Waller with the world, renders his house a very tasteful establishment, and he possesses a few good pictures' wrote Sir Richard Phillips in 1828; member of Lighting and Watching Committee, 1840; backer of railway; 1840s; died from a 'visitation of God'.

WALLER, DR THOMAS. Surgeon on Market Hill; originated from Yorkshire; Freemason.

WALSH, WILLIAM. Hat manufacturer; Liberal; member of first Town Council.

WARDE, C.T. Living in Warwickshire when he purchased Luton Hoo from Marquess of Bute; simultaneously separating from his wife; either was not able to complete the purchase or could not hold the property for long and it soon was purchased by Leigh.

WARDILL, ?. Secretary to Gaitskell Terrace Evening School.

WARR, JAMES. (1792–1853); farmer; member of the Board of Health, 1851.

WEBDALE, JOHN. (1817–87); warehouseman and retailer; Liberal; Congregationalist; owned twenty properties around the town (1871); successful 'Blue' candidate to the Board of Health, 1872 and unsuccessful School Board candidate, 1874; elected to town council, 1877 and Mayor of Luton in 1881.

WEBSTER, A.T. (1818–95); hat manufacturer employing approximately 150 in 1875; Liberal; Congregationalist deacon; supporter of the Mechanics Institute and incorporation, serving upon the first council; unsuccessful 'Blue' candidate in 1850 but was later to serve upon the Board of Health; member of Luton Reform and Registration Association; promoter of the Water Company in 1864; Mayor, 1878; personal estate of £1389. 16s. 7d. at death.

WELCH, A.P. Hat manufacturer; Liberal; first Luton based magistrate, 1868; signatory to petition calling for Board of Health, 1849; backer of the proposed water company, 1860 and Director of Water Company when established in 1865; financial supporter of the Mechanics Institute and the Prayer Book Five member of the School Board; moved to the south coast but retained contact with Luton through the Children's Hospital built in London Road in 1894 due to his financial support.

WELCH, LEVI. Pursued an escalating criminal career which culminated in his trial for murder in 1868; escaped the gallows by turning Queen's evidence; (see correspondence files at Luton Museum, 1998).

WILLIAMS, EVAN OWEN. (1822–86); son of John, father of Herbert Owen; builder, architect and surveyor; carried out much of the building on the north-eastern side of George Street; Freemason; Conservative; Anglican; St. Mary's churchwarden, 1859; member of the Literary Institute; served upon the Board of Health; performed the duty of Returning Officer at the first Council elections, after which he was appointed a J.P.; owned relatively few properties (eleven in 1871) for one in such an advantageous position; left personal estate of £4284.

WILLIAMS, HERBERT OWEN. (1855–1931); son of Evan O.; builder; Conservative; Mayor of Luton in 1929.

WILLIAMS, JOHN. (d.1851); father of Evan O.; corn merchant and builder, relinquishing the former trade from the 1840s in favour of the latter; owned and leased brick fields; original signatory to petition calling for Board of Health, 1849.

WILLIAMSON, EDWARD CHILWELL. (1786–1863); moved to Luton c. 1803; solicitor, partner in Williamson and Austin; Liberal; Freemason; very generous man and involved in many aspects of public life; Clerk to the Board of Guardians; promoter of attempt to acquire Improvement Bill, 1847; unsuccessful 'Blue' candidate, 1850; Registrar of the County Court; member of the Literary Institute, leaving 3000 volumes for the foundation of a town library; promoter of railway, 1840s and 1850s.

WILLIS, T.J. (d. 1888); hat manufacturer; Liberal, Baptist; temperance campaigner.

WILLIS, WILLIAM. Hat manufacturer; Liberal; member of Luton Reform and Registration Association; temperance campaigner; involved with all campaigns for improvement and reform but possessed an unfortunate propensity for long-windedness; involved with the Freehold Land Society and the various railway schemes; served upon the Board of Health; a member of the Literary Institute.

WISEMAN, JOHN. 'Printer, Book and Music Seller, Bookbinder, Stationer and News Agent. Dealer in Patent Medicines and Perfumery etc. etc.', 43, George Street; secretary to Mechanics Institute, 1846; operated a circulating library, 1856; supporter of the establishment of the Board of Health; published the *Luton Miscellany* (monthly) and then the *Luton Times* from 7 July, 1855; in the same year he published Davis' *History of Luton*; went bankrupt, March 1861 and was forced to sell the newspaper, but was able to start up again (in the same business) by 1862 in Bute Street.

WOAKES, DR E.O. Surgeon; lived Wellington Street in the 1840s; Conservative; Freemason; after the death of his niece (who was living in his house) in mysterious circumstances in January 1847, a mob had to be cleared from in front of his house by special police; set up the Luton Cottage Hospital (1872–82); supporter of sanitary reform; treasurer of the Luton branch of the British Schools Society; supporter of the School Board and opponent of incorporation; left Luton in 1876.

WONNACOTT, REV HENRY. (1851–77); Congregational minister, 1871–4; popular with the children.

WORSLEY, OBADIAH. Frequently bought before the magistrates bench for various breaches of the peace; also landlord of houses in Inkerman Street and High Town.

WOOTTON, PETER. Chemist in George Street; Baptist; an enterprising man who was interested in educational developments; Superintendent of the Park Street Sunday School; committee member of Gaitskell Terrace Evening School; Bible Five member of the School Board; signatory to petition calling for establishment of Board of Health; elected to first council, his candidature being supported by the Working Mens' Representation Association.

WREN, HENRY. Hat manufacturer – possibly employed originally by Willis; Liberal; Mechanics Institute official, 1850s; supporter of incorporation but was unsuccessful in two attempts to be elected in 1876 before finally succeeding in 1877.

WRIGHT, HENRY. (1829–85); ran New Hall Academy and subsequently Villa School; Liberal; Freemason; promoter of Water Company, 1864; supporter of the Gymnastic Society; Choral Society; pro-incorporation; elected to the first council and Mayor, 1883; Senior Sophister of Trinity College Dublin; churchwarden of Christ Church, Luton; promoter of the Working Mens' Representation Association; supporter of the Mechanics Institute; involved with the Agricultural Labourers Union, securing allotments for working men on the Duke of Bedford's estate through a personal interview with the Duke; out of gratitude for his various services, the Union presented him with a gold watch (worth £25) in 1876.

WRIGHT, JAMES. Coal merchant; member of the Co-operative Company.

Nineteenth Century Place Names in Luton with Modern Name of Street/Location or Nearest Equivalent

Adelaide Terrace	Eastern side of George Street
Bird End	In New Town Street
Blackwater Lane	Lea Road
Briden's/Bryden's Passage	Adjacent to New Town Street
Brown Brick/Brache	Park Town near to Park Street
'Cabbage St'	Local nickname for Strathmore Avenue
Cemetery Road	Rothesay Road
City Road	Early name for undeveloped end of New Town
Coney Hall	Old Bedford Road near to junction with Bridge Street.
Cross Hill	Site of Town Hall
Davis Field	Chase Street/New Town Street area
Donkey Hall	High Town
Dove Cottages	In High Town
Drop Short	New Town
Dunstable Lane	Upper George Street
Gaitskell Terrace	High Town/Hitchin Road
Gibb Square	In High Town (also known as Jebb Square)
Gutter Lane	Upper George Street
*High Street	George Street
*Hog Lane	Chapel Street
Jebb Square	In High Town (also Gibb Square)
Langley Road	Latimer Road
*Long Pond	Park Square
Kings Road	Kingsland Road
Mayes Lane	Stuart Street
Mount Pleasant	In High Town
North Street	George Street
Park Meadow	Popes Meadow
Park Road West	Strathmore Avenue
Pepper Hill	Peoples Park
Pondwicks Gardens	Land close to Crawley Green Road and Midland railway line
Prospect Place	Junction of Chase Street & New Town Street
Saffron Gardens	Near Pondwicks (sold 1859)
Seven Acres	Guildford Street & Waller Street vicinity
*Sheep Street	Park Street/Road
*South End	Park Street/Road
Tingewicke Cottages	Chase Street/New Town Street area
Tower Hill	Manchester Street
Townrow Close	Near to Chapel Street
Worlds End	Chase Street/New Town Street
Wren's Yard	Eastern side of George Street

*Abandoned in early 19th century

Bibliography

Agar, N.E. *Hitchin's Straw Plait Industry* (Hitchin Historical Society, 1982).
Agar, N.E. *The Bedfordshire Farm Worker in the Nineteenth Century* (BHRS vol. 60, 1981). Publication of a Ph.D thesis, University of East Anglia, 1979.
Allen, M.D. '"World's End..." The Story of Chase Street.' (Unpublished typescript, 1985, LM collection).
Allsobrook, David Ian. *Schools for the shires. The reform of middle-class education in mid-Victorian England* (Manchester University Press, 1986).
Ambler, R.W. 'The 1851 census of Religious Worship'. *The Local Historian* vol. II, no. 7, (1975), pp. 375–381.
Anderson, M. *Family Structure in Nineteenth Century Lancashire.* (Cambridge University Press, 1971).
Archer, A.J. 'A Study of Local Sanitary Administration 1830–1875.' MA thesis, *University College of North Wales* (1967).
Austin, T.G. *The Straw Plaiting and Straw Hat and Bonnet Trade with a Digest of the Recent Census for the Luton District...* (Patrick O'Doherty, Luton, 1871).
Austin, William. *A Short History of Freemasonry and of the Bedfordshire Lodge of St. John the Baptist... from 1841 to 1891* (Alfred Atkins, Luton, 1891).
Austin, William. *History of Luton and its Hamlets,* vol. II. (The County Press, Newport, Isle of Wight, 1928).
Austin, William. *The History of a Bedfordshire Family.* (Alston Rivers, 1911).
Baker, Lionel. *The Story of Luton and its Public Libraries* (Beds County Library, Luton District, and Luton Museum, 1983).
Balch, A. Ernest. *A Century of Methodism in Luton.* (Luton, 1908).
Bebbington, D.W. 'The Baptist conscience in the Nineteenth Century'. *Baptist Quarterly* vol. 34, (1991–2).
Bebbington, D.W. *The Nonconformist Conscience. Chapel and Politics 1870–1914* (Allen and Unwin, 1982).
Beehagg, Clive *Politics and Production in the Early Nineteenth Century.* (Routledge, 1990).
Bell, Patricia L. *Belief in Bedfordshire* (Belfry Press, Bedford, 1986).
Benson, Nigel. *Dunstable in Detail.* (The Book Castle, Dunstable, 1986).
Berg, Maxine, Hudson, Pat and Sonenscher, Michael. *Manufacture in Town and Country Before the Factory* (Cambridge University Press, 1983).
Bethel Baptist Church. *The Story of Bethel 1876–1976* (Luton, 1976).
Blundells of Luton. 1852–1952. Being some account of the history of the firm over the past one hundred years (Luton, 1952).
Bradley, Ian. *The Call to Seriousness. The Evangelical Impact on the Victorians* (Cape, 1976).
Briggs, Asa. *Victorian Cities* (Odhams Press, 1963; Pelican Books, 1968; reprinted by Penguin Books, 1990).
Briggs, J.H.Y. *The English Baptists of the Nineteenth Century* (The Baptist Historical Society, 1994).
Brown, Maureen and Masters, June. *The Bassetts. Leighton Buzzard's First Family* (Leighton Linslade and District Museum Project and the Leighton Linslade Local History Research Group, 1989).

The Builder vol. IV. pp. 155–9. (Details of invitation of tenders and Town Hall building committee).
Bunker, Stephen. *North Chilterns Camera. 1863–1954. The Thurston Collection in Luton Museum* (The Book Castle, Dunstable, 1989) .
Burgess, Keith. *The Origins of British Industrial Relations: the Nineteenth Century Experience* (Croom Helm, 1975).
Burnett, John. *A Social History of Housing. 1815–1985* (Methuen, 1986).
Burnett, John (ed.). *Destiny Obscure* (Routledge, 1982).
Bushby, D.W. *The Ecclesiastical Census, Bedfordshire, 1851* (BHRS vol. 54, 1975).
Cannadine, David & Reeder, David (eds.). *Exploring the Urban Past. Essays in Urban History by H. J. Dyos* (Cambridge University Press, 1982).
Cannadine, David. *Lords and Landlords: The Aristocracy and the Towns, 1774–1967* (Leicester University Press, 1980).
Cannadine, David (ed.). *Patricians, Power and Politics in Nineteenth Century Towns* (Leicester University Press, 1982).
Cannadine, David. 'Urban Development in England and America in the Nineteenth Century: Some Comparisons and Contrasts' *Economic History Review* 2nd series, vol. 33, no. 3, (1980).
Checkland, S.G. *The Rise of an Industrial Society in England 1815–1885* (Longmans, 1964).
Chinn, Carl. *Poverty amidst prosperity. The urban poor in England, 1834–1914* (Manchester University Press, 1995).
Christian Messenger (April 1899), no. 400 'Luton's First Circuit'.
Church, Roy. *Economic and Social Change in a Midland Town. Victorian Nottingham 1815–1900* (Cass, 1966).
Cirket, A.F. 'The 1830 Riots in Bedfordshire. Background and Events'. in *W.G. Smith and Other Studies* (BHRS vol. 57, presented to Joyce Godber, 1978)
Clark, Peter. *The English Alehouse. A Social History 1200–1830* (Longman, 1983).
Clark, Peter and Slack, Paul. *English Towns in Transition 1500–1700* (Oxford University Press, 1976).
Cobbe, Henry. *Luton Church. Historical and Descriptive* (George Bell and Sons, 1899).
Cockman, F.G. *The Railway Age in Bedfordshire* (BHRS vol. 53, 1974).
Collings, Harry. *History of Union Chapel, Luton* (Luton, 1887).
Cowling, Maurice. *1867. Disraeli, Gladstone and Revolution* (Cambridge University Press, 1967).
Cox, Alan. *Survey of Bedfordshire. Brickmaking. A History and Gazetteer* (Beds County Council, 1979).
Cox, Rev Thomas. *Magna Britannia et Hibernia. Bedfordshire* (1715).
Craig, F.W.S. (ed.). *British Parliamentary Results* (Macmillan, 1977).
Cresy, Edward. *Report to the General Board of Health on a Preliminary Inquiry into the sewage, drainage . . . of the town of Luton* (HMSO, 1850).
Darby, Aubrey. *A View from the Alley* (Luton Museum, 1974).
Daunton, Martin J. *House and Home in the Victorian City. Working Class Housing 1815–1914* Studies in Urban History no. 7. General Editor, the late H.J. Dyos, (Arnold, 1983).

Daunton, Martin J. *Progress and Poverty. An Economic and Social History of Britain 1700–1850* (Oxford University Press, 1995).
Davies, J. *Cardiff and the Marquesses of Bute.* Studies in Welsh History, (University of Wales Press, Cardiff, 1981).
Davis, Frederick. *Luton, Past and Present: its History and Antiquities* (Published by the author, 1874).
Davis, Frederick. *The History of Luton, with its Hamlets etc.* (Published by the author, 1855).
Derbyshire, W.H. *The History of Dunstable* (2nd edition, 1882).
Dingle, A.E. *The Campaign for Prohibition in Victorian England. The United Kingdom Alliance 1872–1895* (Rutgers University Press, New Brunswick, New Jersey, 1980).
Dodsley, R. & J. (printers). *England Illustrated, or a Compendium of Natural History, Topography and Antiquities, Ecclesiastical and Civil of England and Wales* (Bedfordshire section, 1764).
Dony, J.G. et al. *The Story of High Town* (Beds County Library Service, 1984).
Dony, J.G. *A History of the Straw Hat Industry* (Gibbs, Balmforth & Co., Luton, Ltd, 1942). Publication of Ph.D thesis, University of London, 1941.
Dony, J.G. *A History of Education in Luton* (Luton Museum, 1970).
Dony, J.G. 'How Luton Became a Borough'. *Bedfordshire Magazine* vol. 15, pp. 135–40.
Doyle, Barry. 'Temperance and Modernity: the Impact of Local Experience on Rank and File Liberal Attitudes to Alcohol.' *The Journal of Regional and Local Studies*, vol. 16, no. 2, (winter 1996), pp. 1–10.
Dyer, James. *The Story of Stopsley Schools* (Luton Museum, 1989).
Dyer, James & Dony, J.G. *The Story of Luton* (White Crescent Press, Luton. 1975).
Dyos, H.J. *The Study of Urban History* The proceedings of an international round table conference of the Urban History Group at Gilbert Murray Hall, University of Leicester, 22–29 September 1966, (Arnold, 1968).
Emsley, Clive. 'Crime in 19th Century Britain'. *History Today*, vol. 38, (April 1988).
Elliott, M.J. 'The Leicester Board of Health, 1849–1872. A Study of Progress in the Development of Local Government.' M.Phil *University of Nottingham*, (1971).
Englander, David. *Landlord and Tenant in Urban Britain 1838–1918* (Clarendon Press, Oxford, 1983).
Evans, R.H. 'The Biggs Family of Leicester' *The Leicestershire Archaeological and Historical Society Transactions* vol. XLVIII, (1972–3).
Evans, George Ewart. *Where Beards Wag All. The Relevance of the Oral Tradition* (Faber and Faber Ltd., 1970).
Finer, S.E. T*he Life and Times of Sir Edwin Chadwick* (Methuen, 1952).
Fisher, J.S. *People of the Meeting House. Tales of a Luton Church* (Luton, 1974).
Fraser, Derek & Sutcliffe, Anthony (eds.). *The Pursuit of Urban History* (Arnold, 1983).
Fraser, Derek. *Power and Authority in the Victorian City* (Blackwell, Oxford, 1979).
Fraser, Derek. *Urban Politics in Victorian England* (Leicester University Press, 1976).

Gaskell, S. Martin. *National Statutes and the Local Economy. Building Control. National Legislation and the Introduction of Local Bye-laws in Victorian England* (The British Association for Local History, 1983).
Gilbert, A.D. *Religion and Society in Industrial England. Church, Chapel and Social Change 1790–1914* (Longman, 1976).
Glass, D.V. *Numbering the People. The eighteenth century population controversy and the development of census and vital statistics in Britain* (Saxon House, Farnborough, 1973).
Godber, Joyce. *Friends in Bedfordshire and West Hertfordshire* (Published by the author, 1975).
Godber, Joyce. *History of Bedfordshire* (Beds County Council, 1969).
Goldthorpe, John H., Lockwood, D., Bechhofer, F. and Platt, Jennifer. *The Affluent Worker in the Class Structure* (Cambridge University Press, 1969).
Grundy, F. & Titmuss, R.M. *Report on Luton* (Borough of Luton, Luton, 1945).
Hambermehl, Rev K.C. *The Story of Christ Church, Luton* (Luton, 1956).
Harris, Jose. *Private Lives. Public Spirit. A Social History of Britain 1870–1914* (Oxford University Press, 1993).
Harrison, Brian. *Drink and the Victorians. The Temperance Question in England 1815–1872* (Faber and Faber, 1971).
Harrison, Brian and Trinder, Barrie. 'Drink and Sobriety in an Early Victorian Town: Banbury 1830–1860' *The English Historical Review* Supplement 4, (1969).
Harrison, F.M.W. 'The Nottinghamshire Baptists and Education'. *Baptist Quarterly* vol. 27, pp. 94–109.
Harrison, J.F.C. *Learning and Living. 1790–1960. A Study in the History of the English Adult Education Movement* (Routledge and Kegan Paul, 1961).
Harrison, R. & Zeitlin, Jonathan (eds.). *Divisions of Labour. Skilled Workers and Technical Change in 19th Century England* (Harvester, Brighton, 1985).
Hawkes, Joseph. 'Memory Sketches of Luton'. (Published in *Luton Reporter* between 1895 and 1897).
Hawkes, Joseph. *The Rise and Progress of the Wesleyan Sunday Schools* (Luton, 1885).
Hennock, E.P. 'Finance and Politics in Urban Local Government in England 1835–1900.' *The Historical Journal* VI, 2 (1963) pp. 212–25.
Hennock, E.P. *Fit and Proper Persons. Ideal and Reality in Nineteenth Century Urban Government* (Arnold, 1973).
Henriques, Ursula R.Q. *Before the Welfare State. Social Administration in Early Industrial Britain* (Longman, 1979).
Herrington, John Franklin. *The Merchants Miscellany and Travellers Complete Compendium . . . 1785* (Facsimile reprint, 1885).
Higgins, D. M. *Old Luton* (The Scientific Literary and Artistic Club, Luton, 1885).
Himmelfarb, Gertrude. *The De-moralisation of Society. From Victorian Virtues to Modern Values* (IEA Health and Welfare Unit, 1995).
Hine, Reginald. *Hitchin Worthies* (George Allen and Unwin, 1932).
Hine, Reginald. *The History of Hitchin* vol. II. (George Allen and Unwin, 1929).
Hobbs, T.G. *Recollections of Early Luton* (Luton News, 1933).
Hollis, Patricia. *Ladies Elect. Women in English Local Government 1865–1914* (Clarendon Press, 1987).

Horn, Pamela L.R. 'The Buckinghamshire Straw Plait Trade in Victorian England'. *Records of Buckinghamshire* vol. XIX, part 1, (1971).
Houfe, Simon. *Through Visitors Eyes. A Bedfordshire Anthology* (The Book Castle, Dunstable, 1990).
Hunt, E.M. *British Labour History, 1815–1914* (Weidenfeld and Nicolson, 1981).
Johnson, James H. & Pooley, Colin G (eds.). *The Structure of Nineteenth Century Cities* (Croom Helm, 1982).
Jones, David. *Crime, Protest, Community and Police in Nineteenth Century Britain* (Routledge and Kegan Paul, 1982).
Jones, Stephen G. *Sport, Politics and the Working Class* (Manchester University Press, 1988).
Jones, Tydfil Davies. 'Poor Law and Public Health Administration in the Area of Merthyr Tydfil Union 1834–1894' M.A. *University of Wales*, (1961).
Kellett, J.R. *The Impact of Railways on Victorian Cities* (Routledge and Kegan Paul, 1969).
King, J.F. 'The Heaton Local Board: A Victorian Local Authority' *Bradford Antiquary* 3rd series, vol. 1, (1985), pp. 31–7.
Lancaster, Bill. *Radicalism Cooperatism and Socialism. Leicester working-class politics 1860–1906* (Leicester University Press, 1987).
Law, C.M. 'The Straw Plait and Straw Hat Industries of the South Midlands. Luton and the Hat Industry'. *The East Midlands Geographer* vol. 4, part 6, no. 30, (1968).
Leigh's New Picture of England and Wales (c. 1820).
Leleux, Robin. *The East Midlands. A Regional History of the Railways of Great Britain. Vol. IX* (David and Charles, 1976).
Levine, David. *Reproducing Families. The Political Economy of English Population History* (Cambridge University Press, 1987).
Lewis, Jane (ed.). *Labour and Love. Women's Experience of Home and Family 1850–1940* (Blackwell, Oxford 1986).
Longhurst, Liz. 'Memoir of a Victorian Quaker: William Drewett 1834–1900'. (Unpublished typescript, copy in LM).
Lowerson, John & Myerscough, John. *Time to Spare in Victorian England* (Harvester Press, Hassocks, 1977).
Luton Adult School. *Jubilee Souvenir. 1862–1912* (Luton, 1912).
Luton Gas Company *100 Years of Service* (Luton, 1934).
Luton News (compiler). *Luton at War* (Home Counties Newspapers, Ltd., Luton, 1947).
Lysons, Rev Daniel & Lysons, Samuel. *Magna Britannia. Being a Concise Topographical Account of the Several Counties of Great Britain* (1806).
Madigan, T.J. *The Men Who Wore Straw Helmets. The Development and Story of Luton Borough Police Force 1876–1947* (The Book Castle, Dunstable, 1993).
Mahan, E.B. *The Congregational Church. 1864–1914. Jubilee Memorials* (Luton, 1914).
Maclaren, A. Allan. *Religion and Social Class. The Disruption Years in Aberdeen* (Routledge and Kegan Paul, 1974).
Malcolmson, Robert W. *Popular Recreations in English Society 1770–1850* (Cambridge University Press, 1973).

Marshall, M.A. 'Elementary Education in Luton 1809–1874'. (Dissertation, college unknown, copy in LM collection).
McLeod, Hugh. *Religion and Society in England, 1850–1914* (Longman, 1996).
McLeod, Hugh. *Religion and the Working Class in Nineteenth Century Britain* (Studies in Economic and Social History, Macmillan, 1984).
Meller, H.E. *Leisure and the Changing City, 1870–1914* (Routledge and Kegan Paul, 1976).
Metcalf, S. 'The Provision of Parks in 19th Century Britain.' (M.A. thesis, *University of London*).
Milner, D. 'J.P. Chown, 1821–1886'. *Baptist Quarterly* vol. 25, (1973–74), pp. 15–41).
Moore, Valerie J. 'The families of the Browns and Greens of Luton 1700–1950'. Unpublished dissertation, *Putteridge Bury College* (1970).
Morris, R.J. (ed.) *Class, Power and Social Structure in British Nineteenth Century Towns* (Themes in Urban History, General Editor, Derek Fraser, Leicester University Press, 1986).
Morris, R.J. *Class, sect and party. The making of the British middle class, Leeds 1820–1850* (Manchester University Press, 1990) .
New British Traveller. *Bedfordshire, General Description of the County* (1819).
Offer, Avner. *Property and Politics, 1870–1914* (Cambridge University Press, 1981).
Park Town Methodist Church, Luton. *One Hundred Glorious Years 1864–1964* (Luton, 1964).
Parish, B. 'School Attendance in Rural Bedfordshire and Luton 1870–1903'. Unpublished dissertation, *Hertfordshire College of Higher Education* (1977).
Parry, Rev I.D. *Select Illustrations, Historical and Topical of Bedfordshire* (1827).
Patterson, D. 'Nineteenth Century Elementary Education in Luton'. Dissertation, *Bedford College* (1969).
Pearson, Geoffrey. *Hooligan. A History of Respectable Fears* (Macmillan, 1983).
Pelling, Margaret. *Cholera, Fever and English Medicine 1825–1865* (Open University Press, 1978).
Pennant, Thomas. *The Journey from Chester to London* (1782).
Penny, R.I. 'The Board of Health in Victorian Stratford-upon-Avon. Aspects of Environmental Control.' *Warwickshire History* I no. 6, (1971) p. 11.
Phillips, Sir Richard. *A Personal Tour through the United Kingdom Describing Living Objects and Contemporaneous Interests. No. 1 Bedfordshire, Northamptonshire, Leicestershire* (1828).
Pickford, Chris. *Bedfordshire Churches in the Nineteenth Century. Part II, Parishes H to R* (BHRS vol. 77, 1998).
Pinder, D.A. 'The Luton Hat Industry.' Ph.D. *University of Southampton*, (1970).
Pride, Samuel (compiler). *Glimpses of History* (Luton, 1923).
Rose, Lionel. *Massacre of the Innocents. Infanticide in Great Britain 1800–1939* (Routledge, 1939).
Rose, Michael E. (ed.). *The Poor and the City: the English Poor Law in its Urban Context. 1834–1914* Themes in Urban History, Gen. ed. Derek Fraser (Leicester University Press, 1985).

Rose, S.O. 'Proto-industry, Womens Work and the Household Economy in the Transition to Industrial Capitalism.' *The Journal of Family History* vol. 13 pp. 181–193).

Rubinstein, W.D. *Britain's Century. A Political and Social History 1815–1905* (Arnold, 1998).

Rubinstein, W.D. *Capitalism, Culture and Decline in Britain 1750–1990* (Routledge, 1993).

Rubinstein, W.D. *Men of Property. The Very Wealthy in Britain Since the Industrial Revolution* (Croom Helm, 1981).

Runciman, W.G. *Max Weber. Selections in Translation* (Cambridge University Press, 1978).

Saul, S. B. 'House Building in England 1890–1914'. *Economic History Review* vol. 15, p. 119.

Sigsworth, Eric M (ed.). *In Search of Victorian Values. Aspects of Nineteenth Century Thought and Society* (Manchester University Press, 1988).

Smith, L.D. 'Industrial Organisation in the Kidderminster Carpet Trade 1780–1850.' *Textile History* vol. 15, (1984), pp. 75–100.

Spedding, Robert K. *'The Hill of the Lord...' High Town Primitive Methodist Church 1838–1932* (Luton, 1932).

Spencer, N. *Complete English Traveller. Bedfordshire* (1772).

Stephens, W.B. *Education, Literacy and Society 1830–1870. The Geography of Diversity in Provincial England* (Manchester University Press, 1987).

Storch, Robert D. (ed.). *Popular Culture and Custom in Nineteenth Century England* (St. Martin's Press, New York).

Taylor, Peter. *Popular Politics in Early Industrial Britain. Bolton 1825–1850* (Ryburn Publishing, Keele University Press, 1995).

Tearle, Douglas. *Chapel Street Methodist Church Centenary 1852–1952. 'Our Heritage'* (Luton, 1952).

Thomas, E. G. *'Chelmsford and the Board of Health Report of 1849.'* (Source of article unknown).

Thompson, F.M.L. 'Life After Death. How Successful Nineteenth Century Businessmen Disposed of their Fortunes'. *Economic History Review* (February 1990).

Thompson, F.M.L. (ed.) *The Cambridge Social History of Great Britain 1750–1950* Three vols. (Cambridge University Press, 1990).

Thompson, F.M.L. (ed.) *The Rise of Suburbia* (Leicester University Press, 1982).

Thorburn, D. 'Gender, Work and Schooling in the Plaiting Villages.' *The Local Historian*, (August 1989).

Tobias, J.J. *Crime and Industrial Society in the Nineteenth Century* (Batsford, 1967).

Tomlinson, Charles G. *Families in Trouble. An Enquiry into Problem Families in Luton* (Borough of Luton, undated but probably early 1950s).

Townley, William Edward. 'Urban Administration and Health: A Case Study of Hanley in the Mid Nineteenth Century.' M.A. thesis, *University of Keele*, (1969).

Vamplew, Wray. *Pay up and play the game. Professional Sport in Britain 1875–1914* (Cambridge University Press, 1988).

Walker, T.J. *The Depot for French Prisoners of War at Norman Cross, Huntingdonshire. 1796 to 1816* (Constable and Co. Ltd., 1913).

Waller, John. *Who's Who in the Town of Luton in 1842?* (Luton, 1842).
Waller, P.J. *Town City and Nation. England, 1850–1914* (Oxford University Press, 1983).
Walvin, James. *Leisure and Society, 1830–1950* (Longman, 1978).
Weiner, Martin J. *English Culture and the Decline of the Industrial Spirit 1850–1980* (Cambridge University Press, 1981).
Welch, Edwin. *Bedfordshire Chapels and Meeting Houses: Official Registration 1672–1901* (BHRS, vol. 75, 1996).
White, M. 'Family Migration in Victorian Britain. The Case of Grantham and Scunthorpe.' *Local Population Studies* vol. 41, pp. 41–50.
Williamson, Jeffrey G. *Coping with City Growth during the British Industrial Revolution* (Cambridge University Press, 1990).
Woods, Robert and Woodward, John (eds.). *Urban Disease and Mortality in Nineteenth-Century England* (Batsford, 1984).
Wrigley, E.A. (ed.). *Nineteenth-century Society. Essays in the Use of Quantitative Methods for the Study of Social Data* (Cambridge University Press, 1972).
Young, Arthur. *A Six Month Tour through the North of England* (1769).

Sources

Newspapers

The *Bedfordshire Times* was first published on 18 October 1845, initially as the *Bedford Times*. Produced at Bedford each edition included a trawl around the county's towns and villages for news. This is the best source of news for Luton until the advent of the *Luton Times*.

Rev Henry Burgess may have been responsible for the publication of the first newspaper based in Luton. This was a monthly newsheet and was possibly *The Wreath* to which the *Beds Times* referred on 28 August 1846.

The *Luton Times* was first published by John Wiseman on 7 July 1855. This superseded the *Luton Miscellany*, a monthly newspaper published by Wiseman since 1854. A bastion of urban Liberalism, the *Luton Times* highlighted social evils, including individual cases of hardship and injustice, was a consistent advocate of social reform and intervention. The town's chapels received extensive and sympathetic coverage. Wiseman continued to publish the *Luton Times* until his bankruptcy in March 1861.

On 28 July 1855 Wiseman made reference to a rival to the *Luton Times*, the *Luton Recorder*. Perhaps this was a new publication also, taking advantage of the lifting of stamp duty which had kept the cost of producing newspapers so prohibitively high. Little is known of the *Luton Recorder* except that it appears to have been short-lived.

The first edition of the *Luton News* appeared in January 1861. Like the *Luton Times* this was published in Wellington Street, the proprietor being William Stalker. The *Luton News* was a little more conservative than Wiseman's paper. Stalker was a Baptist and his paper gave prominence to events held at local churches from this denomination. *The Luton News* bore no relation to the current paper of the same name which was first published in 1891.

Two other newspapers were the *Luton Advertiser*, of which F. C. Scargill was the proprietor (see the *Luton Times* 17 January 1874), and the *Luton Reporter*. This latter paper, first published in 1874, was the only overtly Conservative paper in the town until its closure in 1926. Privately owned newscuttings state that Thomas Peer, the correspondent on the *Bedfordshire Mercury*, took over temporary management of the *Luton Reporter* from "that brilliant Irishman" J. Shanasy when the latter was ill. It was Peer who covered the incorporation meetings for the *Luton Reporter* in 1876, (PC Peer Newscuttings, vol. C, p. 78. Andrew Underwood's collection).

Directories

Directory for Bedfordshire, 1785 (1885 facsimile).
Pigot & Co.'s Commercial Directory 1823–24.
Pigot & Co.'s Commercial Directory 1826–27.
Pigot & Co.'s Commercial Directory, Bedfordshire section, 1830.
Pigot & Co.'s Commercial Directory 1832.
Pigot & Co.'s Commercial Directory 1839.
Pigot & Co.'s Commercial Directory, Bedfordshire section, 1839.
Slater's Directory, Bedfordshire section, 1850.
Kelly's Directory, Hertfordshire, 1850.

Craven & Co.'s Commercial Directory of the County of Bedford and the towns of Hitchin, Hertford and Baldock, 1853.
Craven & Co.'s Commercial Directory 1854.
Cassey's Bedfordshire and Huntingdonshire Directory 1862.
Kelly's Directory of Bedfordshire 1864
Kelly's Directory of Bedfordshire 1869.
Mercer and Crocker's Directory, (Luton extract), 1871.
Harrod's Royal Directory of Bedfordshire, Buckinghamshire, Berkshire, Oxfordshire, Huntingdonshire and Northamptonshire, 1876.
Kelly's Directory for Bedfordshire, Huntingdonshire and Northamptonshire, 1885.

Published Public Records
1841, 1857, 1859, 1872 Poll Books, Bedfordshire (BRO RV 903; RV 24, 27; RV 25; RV 26).
Census of England and Wales, 1841. Enumerator's return for Luton (Luton Central Library).
Census of England and Wales for the Year 1851. Vols. LXXXV; LXXXVIII; LXXXIX. (BL PP)
Census of England and Wales for the Year 1861. Population Tables. Volume II, Ages, Civil Condition, Occupations and Birth-Places of the People. (BL PP).
Census of England and Wales, 1871. Population Abstracts. Ages, Civil Condition, Occupation and Birth Places of the People (BL PP). Copies of enumerator's return for Luton in LM, Beds Central Library and Luton Central Library.
Hansard's Parliamentary Debates. 30 & 31 Victoriae, 1867. Vol. CLXXXVII 6 May 1867–17 June 1867 and Vol. CLXXXVIII 18 June 1867–23 July 1867 (BL PP).
Thirty-fifth Annual Report of the Registrar for Births and Deaths (Senate Library, University of London).
Children's Employment Commission (1862). 2nd Report of the Commissioners.
Provisional Order for dissolving the Local Government District of Luton 40–1 Vict. Ch xxii. (House of Lords Library).
Select Committee on Town Holdings, 1887. XIII. (Senate Library, University of London).

Unpublished Public Records
Miscellaneous Luton rate books (LM and BRO).
Petitioners appeal against level of county rates, 1820 (BRO QSR 24 1820/457).
Guardians of Luton Union minute books and accounts (BRO PULM; PULL).
Bedfordshire Quarter Sessions records 1840–1866 (BRO QSM 33–66).
Luton Vestry Minute Book, 1844 onwards (BRO P85/8).
Miscellaneous papers re. police station and incorporation (BRO QEE1).
Miscellaneous papers on policing and criminal statistics (BRO QEV3–4; QES 3A; QSS4).
Luton Board of Health minute books. 6 vols. (LM).
General Board of Health papers relating to Luton (PRO HO/45/OS 6006; MH 13/120; MH 13/230).
Ecclesiastical Census, 1851. Returns for Luton Poor Law Union (PRO HO 129 184).

Log book. Queens Square School Boys 1863–1885 (LM L/8/12/54).
Register of Alehouse Licenses (BRO PSL 5/1).
Minute books of Luton School Board (LM M/216).
Miscellaneous probate returns (Somerset House).
Borough of Luton housing clearance records, 1930s (BRO BOR L/EH 19/1–9).

Handbills, pamphlets etc.
Who's Who in the Town of Luton in 1842? The Question Answered by John Waller. (LM 117/43).
A Conversation between a Master and his workman upon the proceedings at the late Vestry held in Luton (LM 5/12/29).
Report of the Luton charities in the County of Bedford and the Proceedings of the Vestry in connection therewith, 1853. (LM 476/33).
In Chancery. The Attorney General and J. S. Leigh, Esq., versus Luton Local Board of Health. Judgement 1856 (LM).
Posters, pamphlets etc. re first Luton School Board (LM Education 1).

Estate, company and institutional papers and correspondence
Luton Hoo estate papers (BRO G/DDA; LHE; see also X312; X448; P85).
Misc. papers re. land in Luton (BRO DD BH).
Minute book of Luton Literary Institution, (LM 295/32).
Luton Water Company records (BRO, X739).
Records of Luton Friends Adult School, 1864 onwards (BRO X563).
'A Journal of Home Mission Work in connection with the Congregational Church Luton'. 1872–1874. (LM M/820).
Account book of Cooke and Sons (Cooke and Sons, solicitors, George St West).
Correspondence re first Luton School Board (LM Education 1).
Wellington Street Church and Sunday School records (Luton Central Baptist Church).
Park Street Baptist Church (Old Meeting) and Sunday School records (Luton Central Baptist church).

Maps, plans etc.
'Plan of the Township of Luton in the County of Bedford, 1839. Surveyed by E. Brown, Silsoe. (BRO C2264).
Plan of the Town of Luton, in the County of Bedford . . . Henry Davies, Surveyor, Kimpton Herts. 1842. (LM collection).
Luton Tithe Award map and register, 1844. (Later copy in LM collection).
Crawley estate map and register, c. 1844 (LM collection).
Map of Luton, 1855. (LM 297/32).
A Pictorial Map of Luton . . . by R. Todd. 1862. (BRO ME 37).
A Pictorial Map of Luton . . . by R. Todd. 1870. (BRO ME 38).
Map of the Borough of Luton, 1876. E. A. Cumberland, surveyor. (LM 262/65).

'Apportionment of the Rent Charge in lieu of Tithes in the Parish of Dunstable, in the County of Bedford'. (BRO MAT 12/1).
'Map of the Parish of Dunstable in the County of Bedford'. Surveyed by John Darnham in 1822 and revised by Joseph Mead for the Commutation of Tithes in 1840. (BRO MAT 12/1).

'Apportionment of the Rent Charge in lieu of Tithes in the Parish of Hitchin in the County of Hertford . . .', 1844. (Hertfordshire Record Office).
'Apportionment of the Rent charge in lieu of Tithes in the Parish of St. Albans . . . in the County of Hertford', 1847. (Hertfordshire Record Office).

See also Chambers, Betty *Printed Maps and Town Plans of Bedfordshire 1576–1900* (BHRS vol. 62, 1983).

Sale catalogues
Luton Hoo estate, 1844 (LM 238/81).
Misc. land, including Chapel St, 1845 (LM 7/93/28).
Building ground in George St & Chapel St (LM 45/31).
Misc. freehold estates, 1855 (LM 37/44).
Misc land around Luton, 1859 (LM M/353).
Misc. land including High Town, Brache, Hart Hill (BRO LHE33).
Bute estate, 1862 (LM M/354); 1865 (LM M356).
Land in Park St & Brown Brick, 1862 (LM colln.).
Lands belonging to Rev Lewis, 1855 (private collection, copy in LM).
Townrow estate, 1861 (LM 10/93/28).
Richard Vyse's estate, 1867 (LM M356).
Dunstable Rd, Mill St, Old Bedford Rd, 1869 (LM M/356).
Burr's brewery and other holdings in Dunstable, 1843. (BRO, DDBH 409).
Gutteridge land, Dunstable, 1862–1877. (BRO uncat. 355/4–8).

NAME INDEX

Illustrations are shown in bold type

Aberdeen, Lord, 226
Adelaide Street, 73
Adelaide Terrace, 43, 46, 49, 60, 85, 87, 91, 93, 98-100, 107, 125, 146, 269
Adey, Daniel Goodson, 124, 220; Rev. T.W., 220
Ainsworth Passage, 46, 128
Albert Road, 38, 68, 135, 148, 167, 250, **Plate 14**
Albert Terrace, 79
Alford, Viscount, 216, 223-4
Alford, William, 178, 249
Allen, 107; Joseph or James, 249; Martha Mary, 255; William, 58, 126
Alma Street, 58, 60, 66, 73
Amen Corner, 91, 146
America, United States of, 111-2, 127, 249
Ames, Colonel Lionel, 58, 108, 166, 172-4, 176, 178, 193, 216, 220, 225, 242, 249
Ampthill, 23, 258
Andrews, Joseph, 162; William, 201
Anstee, Joseph, 100, 104-5, 249
Antelope, The, 152
Arlesey, 205
Arundel, 226
Ashburton, 226
Astell, William, 216, 241
Atkins, Mr., 251
Attwood, 234; Arthur Bennett, 53, 249; William H., 107, 249; William Henry jr., 249
Austin, 178; Charles, 150, 199, 249; Charles Addington, 61, 89, 124, 176, 183, 250; Henry, 89, 101, 125; Thomas Erskine, 99, 108, 122, 250; T.G., 176, 178; T.S., 176, 178; William, 28, 33-5, 108, 114-5, 124, 154-5, 172, 206, 235, 258
Aylesbury, 120, 148
Ayrshire, 29
Axtell, Jane, 25

Back Street, 69-70, 80, 86, 91
Bailey, C., 250; George, 57, 59, 96, 100, 126, 150, 205, 232-4, 242, 250, 262; Joseph, 105, 114, 125-7, 216, 250
Bailey Hill, 35, 39, 41, 83; ——Cottages, 70; ——Street, 66, 122
Baisley, Edmund, 56, 250
Baldock, 10, 25
Balmforths Engineering Works, 175, 252
Bambray, Mr., 94
Banbury, 168
Baptist Meeting House, 138, 141
Barber, family, 22
Barbers Lane, 97
Barlow, Elizabeth, 26; Samuel, 25; daughters, 25
Barnsley, 226
Barnstable, 226
Barrett, Alfred, 56, 250; Thomas, 58, 103-4, 250; William, 58, 113, 250
Bartlett, Rev. Thomas, 134-5, 178, 250
Barton, 86
Bassett, Francis, 215, 222, 228
Beale, Dr. A.J., 89, 199, 216, 250; E.J., 241
Bedford, 2, 7, 21, 46, ,60, 88, 166, 177, 219-20, 223, 226, 233
Bedford, Duke of *see* Russell
Bedford Arms, The, 169, 174
Bedfordshire Mercury, 280
Bedfordshire Times/Bedford Times 8, 43, 49, 53, 85, 88, 92-4, 96-100, 102, 125, 135, 140, 154, 158, 161, 176, 186, 200, 212, 214, 280
Beeby, Misses, 177
Beedy, Miss, 212
Beeson, Thomas, 55
Bell, G.A., 250

Bellshaw, Ann, 73
Bennett, Mr., 154
Benning, C.S., 176
Benson, Dr. Patrick, 98, 124, 250
Berkhamsted, 27
Berry, Rev. Robert, 250
Bible Five, 192, 251, 261, 267
Bigg, Louisa, 177, 250; William, 56, 61, 97, 102, 104-5, 108, 130, 142, 176-9, 183-4, 186, 192-4, 202, 205, 208-9, 212, 217-8, 228-32, 236-7, 242, 244-5, 247, 250, 254, **Plate 16**
Biggleswade, 2
Billian, Rev., 179
Bird End, 269
Birden, Ann, 52
Birmingham, 1, 57, 184, 207-8, 211, 223, 226
Biscot, 35, 58, 66, 135, 188-9, 249, 254-5, 259, 262
Bishop Stortford, 10
Black Boy, The, 172
Blackwater Lane, 89, 93, 96, 269, **Plate 7**; - Field, 64
Bland, Rev. Miles, 220
Blandford, 195
Blenheim Palace, 29
Blockers Arms, The, 172, 174
Blundell, Henry, 111, 189, 192-3, 202, 216, 238, 242, 244, 251; James, 242; Joseph King, 64, 94, 216, 240, 251
Board of Guardians, 29-30, 84, 86-8, 98-9, 118, 204, 217, 221, 230, 237-8, 245-6, 250-3, 255, 257-8, 260, 263-5, 267
Board of Health, Luton, 13-4, 30, 40, 44-6, 50-1, 53-4, 57, 63, 68, 70, 84-6, 88-9, 91, 93-102, 104-5, 107-9, 111-3, 115, 118-22, 125-7, 153, 156, 166, 168, 190, 204-5, 207-8, 210-11, 217, 220, 225, 228-31, 233, 235, 237-8, 245-6, 249, 250-5, 257-67
Bolton, Benjamin, 241, 251
Bontems, Mr., 57
Booth, Joseph, 195
Boutwood, J., 251
Bow Brickhill, 258
Boyle Street, 67
Brache, The, 39, 216, 238, 252-3, 269; - Street, 122; - Mill, 103, 105
Bradlaugh, Charles, 225
Bradford, 1, 122, 200
Bramingham Shott, 152, 208, 262; - Villa, 258
Brett, John, 64, 87, 105, 241, 251
Brickwood, Edwin Lathom, 55, 63, 90-8, 100, 103, 108, 115, 124-5, 192, 205, 208, 223, 240, 251, 254
Briden [or Bryden], Peter, 69
Briden's/Bryden's Passage, 44, 48, 69, 81, 269
Bridge Street, 269
Bright, John, 190, 224, 226
Brighton, 115, 172
Bristol, 1, 149
British Gelatine Company, 248
Britannia, The, 174
Brown Brick, 122, 128, 137, 235, 238, 269
Brown, 13, 16, 50, 55, 105, 141, 183-4, 214, 237; Daniel, 251-2, E. [surveyor], 31, 33, 64; Fanny, 201; Frederick (died 1890), 62, 252; Frederick (died 1892), 94, 97-8, 105, 108, 126, 176, 242, 252, **Plate 16**; Henry 35, 51, 62, 67-8, 92, 94, 97-8, 100, 130, 169, 178-9, 184, 190-1, 202, 204, 230, 251-2, **Plate 17**; Henry jnr., 110, 195, 202, 225, 251-2; Henry Coles 55, 59, 66, 199, 252; Henry Cumberland, 252; Joseph, 65; J.R., 56, 252; Lancelot ['Capability'], 28; Lydia, 59, 252; Richard (died 1872), 252; Richard (publican) 64; Richard (timber merchant), 252; Richard Marks, 30, 87, 103, 196, 216, 241, 251-2; Robert J., 252; Thomas, 64; William (died

INDEX 283

1856) 55; William Frederick, 26; William Henry, 184, 252; two females, 59
Brunswick Street, 264
Buckinghamshire, 23
Budd, Rev. P., 189
Bull, Caroline, 25; George, 25; children, 25
Bull Court, 85, 93, 98, 125, 251
Burge, James, 252; William, 51
Burgess, Rev. Henry, 138-40, 177-8, 240, 252, 265, 280, **Plate 17**; James, 167, 199
Burr, 28, 32, 35-6, 38-9, 50, 64-5, 134, 151, 183, 188; Charles, 32, 35, 59, 71, 122, 199, 208, 253, 262; Edward, 26, 32, 34; Frederick, 30, 35, 39, 53, 64, 71, 253, 262; Thomas Godfrey, 253; William, 51, 241, 253, 262; Mrs. 178
Burr and Crab, 263
Burr Street, 49, 64-5, 124, 172, 254
Burton-upon-Trent, 62, 117-8, 120
Bury Farm, 31, 39, 251; The Bury, 138, 177, 263
Bury St. Edmunds, 254
Bush, Ann, 162; Thomas, 162
Butchers Arms, The, 172
Bute, Earls of/Marquesses of *see* Stuart
Bute, Isle of, 29
Bute Estate, 7, 13, 39, 47, 58, 64-5, 96, 212, 262
Bute Street, 39, 47, 65-6, 104, 125, 144, 264, 267, **Plate 10**
Bute Trustees, 40, 49-50, 60, 102
Butlin, Elizabeth, 253; Thomas, 51
Butt, Elizabeth, 73
Butterfield, Francis, 253
Buxton Road, 58; - Wood, 39

Cabbage Street, 269
Caddington, 30, 41, 68, 86, 122, 181, 220
Cambridge, 120; St. John's College, 135
Cambridgeshire, 23, 29
Cammell, William Henry, 191, 253
Cardiff, 31
Cardiff Road, 60, 67
Carnegie, Andrew, 17
Castle, Joseph, 162
Castle Street, 7, 32, 38, 47, 49, 60, 64-5, 137, 235-6, 251, 264
Cawdell, Ann, 58; William James, 244, 253
Cemetery Road, 60, 269
Ceylon, 135
Ceylon Baptist Church, 133, 169, 195, **Plate 12**
Chadwick, Sir Edwin, 116-7
Chamber of Commerce, 231, 247, 251
Chamberlain, Mr., 242
Chambers, George Henry, 238, 244, 253
Chapel Street, 35, 37-8, 64, 66, 133, 138, 144, 161, 174, 188, 251, 256, 258-9, 269
Chapel Street Wesleyan Church, 133, 138, 142, 170, 189
Chase, 34, 36, 38, 50, 64-5, 70, 188; Daniel, 65; Edward, 32, 253; Frederick, 30, 32, 35-7, 42, 55-6, 67, 91, 93-7, 103, 121, 191, 208, 250, 256; John, 32, 35, 241
Chase Street, 44, 70, 83, 145-7, 152, 160, 269, **Plates 4, 14**
Chatham, 46
Cheapside, 47, 66, 110-1, **Plate 11**
Chelmsford, 108, 117-8, 120
Chevening, 134
Chobham Street, 46, 55, 58
Chown, Rev. J.P., 200
Christ Church, 135-7, 189, 259, 268
Church Street, 7, 66, 87, 133, 146, 172, 177, 184, 187-9, 195, 236, 256, 260
City Road, 269
Clacks Yard, 91

Clark, 53, 71; James, 52; John, 94, 97, 253; Mary, 52; William, 124
Clarke, 112, 188; Dr. Frederick J., 64, 100, 124-5, 145, 150, 253; Joseph, 56, 253; William, 55, 68, 72, 87, 91-2, 94, 97, 124-5, 233, 238, 244-5, 253, 261
Coates, W.T., 144, 201, 253, **Plate 15**
Cobbe, Henry, 134
Cobden, Richard, 4, 214, 224, 234
Cock, The, 95, 124, 253
Cocoa Works, 248
Colchester, 46, 120
Cold Arbour, 68
Collingdon, Thomas, 29-30, 33, 36-7, 41-2, 49, 65, 253
Collingdon Street, 67
Conder, J.C., 67
Coney Hall, 40, 269; —Field, 69
Congreve, John, 112, 162, 254
Conisbee, Frederick 238-9, 244-5, 254; L.R., 254
Cook(e), 229, 242; Francis, 254; James, 254; Richard, 55, 67, 72
Cooke and Son, 55, 72
Co-operative (Wholesale) Society, 248, 257
Cooper, Messrs., 26
Copcutt, Prof. James, 115
Copt Hall, 134
Cornwall, 258
Cotchin, 242; John, 105, 107, 109, 244, 246, 254; R., 254; William, 140
Coupees, Francis, 65
Coventry, 1, 2, 120
Cox, Charles, 34-5, 65; Joseph, 231, 242, 254
Cranfield, 22
Crawley, 51, 61, 64, 112, 135, 188, 259; John Sambrook, 31, 34, 59, 72, 97-8, 102, 105, 113, 118, 136, 176, 189, 195, 216, 220, 254; Samuel, 33, 35, 254
Crawley Green Farm, 33; —Road, 269
Crescent Road, 60, 109, 126
Cresy, Edward, 46, 87-95, 99, 109, 112, 117-8, 120, 124, 250, 257
Crofts, Rev. John, 138
Cromwell Road, 252
Cross Hill, 7, 269
Crouch, Edward, 244
Crown, The, 110
Crown and Anchor, 188
Cumberland, John, 95, 97, 99, 105, 110-1, 114, 118-9, 178, 205, 208, 212, 230, 242, 244-5, 252-3, **Plate 18**
Cumberland Street, 72
Cutenhoe Closes, 34
Cuthbertson, Adam, 236, 243, 254

Dallow, 7, 35, 39; - Manor, 31, 34
Dancer, Joseph, 54, 61, 98, 100, 125, 244, 254; Matthew, 241, 254; William, 62, 254
Daniels, Samuel, 94, 254
Darby, Aubrey, 147, 156, 169
Darley Hall, 68
Davies, Daniel, 94, 125, 254; John, 29; Rev. John Jordan, 139, 183, 254-5
Davis, Frederick, 7-8, 37, 48, 58, 61, 105-7, 110-1, 113, 116, 119, 126, 186-7, 190, 205, 216, 229, 254, 267
Davis Field, 59, 269
Davis Gas Stove Company, 247
Dawson, John, 239, 244, 246, 255
Day, Frederick, 106; John, 54, 160, 255
Debenham, Samuel, 196, 249, 255, **Plates 8, 9**
Deodorising Committee, 112
Derby, Earl of, 225
Derby, 120

Derbyshire, 22, 62
Devon, 8, 135
Disraeli, Benjamin, 225-7, 231
District Visiting Society, 206
Dixon, Mr. 242
Dog, The, 197
Donald, Rev. A., 195
Donkey Hall, 164, 269
Donnelly, Major, 232-3
Dorrington, William, 255
Dove Cottages, 269
Drewett, 113, 262; Charles, 244; Samuel, 141, 252; William, 139, 141, 162, 184, 198, 212, 222, 233, 238, 244-5, 255
Drop Short, 269
Dublin, 268
Dudley Arms, The, 172, 174
Dudley Street, 67, 238, 255
Duke of Cambridge, The, 172
Duke Street, 49, 65, 167, 264
Dumfries Street, 200, 58, 65
Dunn, Thomas, 136, 205, 255
Dunstable, 2, 5, 7, 10, 12, 25-8, 32, 46, 63, 65, 86-7, 119-20, 152, 154, 166, 175, 204, 209, 221, 227-31; Brewers Hill Farm, 26
Dunstable Lane, 7, 257, 269
Dunstable Place, 66, 164, 219
Dunstable Road, 39, 41, 65, 67, 113, 236
Dunstable Street, 257
Durham, 29

Eagle, The, 167
Eagle Tavern, 256
Eames, Alfred, 163
Eaton Green, 257
Ebenezer Baptist Church, 134, 140, 148, 195, **Plate 2**
Edinburgh Review, 177
Edlesborough, 17
Edwards, Emma, 52
Electrolux, 247
Elephant and Castle, The, 172
Elizabeth Street, 65
Ellis, Charles, 255
Ely, 187
Essex, 8, 20, 23, 29
Evans, Thomas Lloyd, 101
Everitt, John, 5, 67, 97-9, 104-5, 139-40, 167-8, 178, 208, 214, 216, 223-5, 255; Joseph, 51, 102

Farley Hill, 60, 126, 262
Farley Road, 65, 263
Farr, William, 238-9, 244-5, 255
Faunch, William, 178, 256
Filmer, Sir Edward, 260
Finance Committee, 102, 111, 245-6
Fire Brigade, 112, 116, 252, 254-6, 260-1
Fish, R., 93
Fisher, Mary, 22
Fleckney, Thomas, 163; William, 163
Flower, William, 150
Foresters' Arms, The, 150
Fortune of War, The, 167, 172, 174
Foster, John ('Old Pinch Plum'), 141, 256; Thomas, 199, 256
Fountain, 53; Abraham, 52, 256; Kitty, 52; Mary, 52
Fox, The, 41, 156
Freeholder, The, 167, 171, 174
Freshwater's, 219

Gailer, Mr. 242
Gaitskill Terrace, 44, 49, 70, 87, 97, 145, 183, 250-4, 260-1, 263-4, 266-7, 269
Galloway, 29

Gardeners Call, The, 174
Gardiner, Mr. 128
Gardner, Elizabeth, 256; Joseph, 57, 256; William, 88, 256
Gates, Henry, 55
Gee, Frederick, 37, 256
Genders, Rev. John William, 139, 202, 256
General Board of Health, 87, 92, 94, 100-3, 107, 114, 117, 122, 125, 253; *See also* Board of Health, Luton
General Purposes and Fire Brigade Committee, 245-6
George IV, The, 172, 174
George Hotel, 39, 224, 265
George Inn, The 30
George Street, 5, 7-8, 24, 34-5, 37-40, 47, 55, 85, 88, 91, 107, 110-2, 144, 155, 157, 161, 176, 191, 235, 249, 251, 253, 259-60, 263, 265-7, 269, **Plates 10, 11**
George Street West, 34, 38, 44, 58
Gibb Square/Jebb Square, 269
Gibbon, Richard, 256
Gilder, George Wilcox, 229, 237, 241, 244, 246, 256
Gilpin, Colonel R.T., 215, 217, 221, 223-4, 226-9
Gladstone, W.E., 226-7, 229
Glamorgan, 29, 31
Gloucester, 172, 261
Godfrey, Edward, 101; Alderman S.H., 69
Godfrey_s Cordial, 12
Godwin, John, 56, 256
Goujon, 9, 28; Daniel, 199, 256; Samuel, 9
Gordon Street. 67
Grace, Daniel, 256
Grainger, R.D., 98-101
Grapes, The, 174
Gray, Rev., 222; John, 36-8, 65-6, 68, 256; Mabel, 162
Grays Yard, 87
Great Moor, 7
Great Yarmouth, 249
Green, 141; Edward Foster, 256; Frederick, 99; J.W., 141-2, 174, 184, 216, 237, 246, 256, 261, 263; Joseph, 110-1, 256; Samuel, 256
Gregory, Elizabeth, 41, 98, 256; George, 66, 87, 256; William, 41
Gregory, Cubitt and Co., 27, 209
Gregson, Henry, 255, **Plates 12, 20**
Grundy and Messenger, 111, 127
Guildford Street, 39, 66, 103, 169
Gunn, Hugh, 140, 144, 205, 208, 231, 238-9, 242, 244-5, 257, **Plates 15, 18**
Gutter Lane, 269
Gutteridge, 36, 65, 265; Alderman, 228; James, 32-5, 42, 64, 68, 241, 256, 257; Matthew, 26; Richard, 26, 87, 257

Hagdell Common, 65
Hall, Rev. Charles Henry, 134
Hands, Mrs., 206; Rev. Thomas, 139, 206, 225, 257
Hanley, 117, 120
Hanwell, Charles, 57
Harpenden, 60, 220, 252, 264
Harris, Rev. Charles Butler, 135, 147, 257, **Plate 14**
Harrison, Benjamin, 51
Harrow, The, 174
Hart Hill, 39, 60, 65, 108, 131, 236
Haselgrove, J.W., 114; Richard, 98, 100, 108, 257; Thomas W., 244, 257
Hastings Street, 25, 65-6
Hatfield, 10, 159
Havelock Road, 68
Hawkes, James, 257; Joseph, 106, 178, 180-1, 257, 265; Thomas, 71; William, 71

INDEX 285

Haydon, Samuel, 125
Haynes, Messrs., 219
Haynott, Mary Ann, 184
Hayward Tyler, 175, 179, 258
Heale, Dr. Alfred, 89, 124, 176, 233, 257
Heaton, 2, 122-3
Hemel Hempstead, 2, 20, 23, 25, 27, 57, 60, 106, 209
Henley, Robert, Lord, 33; Thomas, 10
Henry Street, 66
Hertford, 10, 20, 25, 39, 55, 103
Hertfordshire, 10, 23, 52
Hertfordshire County Chronicle, 32
Higgins, Ann, 59; James, 110-1, 242, 257; John, 109, 113, 115, 192, 230-2, 237, 242, 244, 246, 257; Rev. Henry, 148; Colonel W.B., 215, 217, 221; Walter, 257; William Hiram, 110-1, 168, 244
High Street, 269
High Town, 9, 20, 32, 34, 39, 53-4, 58, 64-5, 67-60, 80, 85, 87, 89, 91, 99, 109, 113, 125, 130, 133, 140, 144, 148, 167, 169, 172, 174, 179, 193, 188, 195, 235, 238-9, 245, 249, 254-6, 258, 263-4, 267, 269
High Town Road, 49, 58, 65, 104, 164
Highfield House, 252
Highways and Lighting Committee, 245
History of Luton, 254, 267
Hitchens, Rev. James Hiles, 141, 144, 257, **Plate 15**
Hitchin, 2, 10, 12, 21, 25-7, 32, 55, 60, 141
Hitchin Road, 65-6, 87, 91, 137, 236, 269
Hobbs, Abraham, 119, 258; T.G., 197, 247, 258, 262
Hockliffe, 227
Hoddesdon, 10
Hodge, George, 72
Hog Lane, 7, 269
Holly Lodge, 67, 263
Holly Street, 67
Holyoak, Henry, 162, 258
Honiton, 2, 226, 254
Hooper, George, 26
Hopkins, James, 40, 66, 258
Horne, Frederick, 258
Horninglow, 117
Horsfall, T.B., 225-6
Houghton Regis, 86, 160, 220, 228-9, 259, 263
How, Richard, 71; Robert, 64, 89, 94, 108, 168, 195, 223, 230, 232-3, 240, 242, 258; Thomas, 258
Howard, Elliot, 179, 258
Hubbard, Mr., 258
Huckle, Thomas, 231, 235, 238-9, 244-5, 258
Hucklesby, Asher, 5, 131, 239, 247
Hudson, William, 58
Hunt, George, 258; John, 258; William, 19, 37, 54, 56, 72, 177, 258
Hyde, Thomas, 65
Hyde, East and West, 31, 54, 65-6, 86, 122, 235, 254
Hyde, The, 220, 249

Illustrated London News, 177
Improvement Commission, 88
Inkerman Street, 67, 251, 267
Inskip, Mr. (photographer), 112
Ireland, 135

Jackson, Mr., 219
James, Inspector George, 172, 258
Jaquest, David, 258
Jardine, W., 229
Jebb Square, 269
Jennings and Gates, 43
John Street, 58, 66, 107
Johnson, G.M., 144, 258, **Plate 15**; John James, 87, 91, 94, 258; Reverdy, 111; T.C., 114, 190, 234, 242, 258

Jones, 33; Charles, 56; John, 23, 176; Richard, 23
Jones' Yard, 46, **Plate 8**
Jordan, Gustavus, 105-6, 126, 169, 189, 192, 216, 230, 233, 237, 258; J., 259; J.J., 259
Judge, Matthew, 222, 235, 242, 259

Keeling, John, 56, 66, 259
Keighley, 226
Kent, 261
Kent Meters, 247
Kerry, 135
Kershaw, Caroline, 263; J. Jefferson, 63, 121, 237, 242, 259, 263; John F., 192
Keyte, Joseph, 107-8
Kidderminster, 2, 21
Kidman, James, 58, 94, 188, 259; Thomas, 51
Kidman's Close, 38
Kidney Wood, 42
Kimpton, 220
Kinder, Mr., 242
King, Solomon, 160, 259
King Henry VIII, The, 174
King's Arms, The, 172, 174
King's Head, The, 174
Kingsland Road, 269
Kings Road, 66, 122, 269
King Street, 40, 61, 137, 139, 153, 255, 261-2, **Plate 6**
King Street Congregational Church, 137, 139-40, 144-5, 147, 185, 250, 255, 258, **Plate 15**
Kinsbourne Green, 264

Lake District, The, 8
Lancashire, 172
Lane, David, 64; John, 64; Samuel, 55, 59, 64, 72, 105-7, 126, 259
Langley Road, 269
Langley Street, 38, 64, 188, 251, 264
Langley Field, 55
Latimer Road, 269
Lawford, Charles, 55-6, 259; Frederick, 126, 242, 259; Samuel, 259
Lawford's Yard, 87
Lawrence End, 220
Lea, River, 7, 34, 66-7, 103, 108-9, 161, 265
Lea Valley Water Company, 126
Lea Road, 58, 66, 96, 264, 269, **Plate 7**
Leagrave, 31, 39, 58, 193, 260
Leagrave Road, 65
Lee, Rev. T. Jones, 136-7, 142, 190-1, 202, 259, 263
Leeds, 1, 130, 217, 223, 234, 258
Leghorn (Livorno), 8-9
Leicester, 2, 46, 115, 120, 234
Leigh, 31; John Gerard, 220, 227-8, 242, 259; John Shaw, 39, 47, 59, 66, 102-3, 105, 108, 110-1, 118, 126, 129, 136, 176, 188, 195, 225, 252, 259, 263, 266
Leighton Buzzard, 2, 21, 25, 27, 141, 175, 209, 228
Lewington, William, 52
Lewis, Rev. Mr., 39
Licensed Victuallers' Association, 234, 238, 245, 255, 258
Lighting and Watching Committee, 166, 199, 249-50, 253, 256, 261, 265
Limbury, 66, 135; - Farm, 33-4
Lincoln, President Abraham and Mrs., 112, 127
Literary Institute, 176, 249, 251, 257, 260-7
Liverpool, 1, 47, 61, 130, 225-6, 234, 259
Liverpool Road, 67, 72, 128, 262-3, **Plate 4**
Lockhart, E., 228, 240, 242, 244, 246, 259; G.C.H., 115, 192
London, 1, 6, 7, 10, 19-20, 27, 29, 116, 122, 225, 255, 265; Bloomsbury, 200; Herne Hill, 265; Paddington, 253; Putney, 96, 251; Westminster, 90; Whitehall, 111

London streets: Cheapside, 116; Goodge Street, 10; Grosvenor Square, 27
London Road, 34-5, 41, 43-4, 60, 266
Long, G., 242, 259
Long Pond, 7, 269
Loot/Lutes, Charles, 126, 150, 209, 259
Lord Nelson, The, 172
Lucas, 27, 39; Edward, 108, 184, 209, 242, 259
Lutes, Charles *see* Loot
Luton Advertiser, 116, 237, 262, 280
Luton Borough/Town Council, 41, 105, 166, 212, 247, 251, 253-262, 264, 266
Luton Co-operative Company, 150, 250, 260-1, 268
Luton Hoo, 7, 28-9, 31, 42, 51, 58, 103, 112, 129, 195, 220, 242, 253, 259, 263, 266
Luton Miscellany, 267, 280
Luton Museum, 17, 262
Luton News, 106, 157, 263, 280
Luton Protestant Association, 196, 255
Luton Recorder, 280
Luton Reporter, 236-7, 280
Luton Times, 101, 104, 107, 111, 114, 116, 122, 144, 146, 157, 161-3, 169, 171, 186, 194, 204-5, 217, 220-2, 225, 229, 249, 255, 261, 264, 267, 280
Luton Town Female Missionary Society, 142, 144
Luton Union Rural Sanitary Authority, 116
Luton Water Company, 108-9, 115, 230, 245, 249-52, 254, 256, 258-64, 266, 268
Luton Working Men's Representation Association, 234
Lydekker, Gerard Wolf, 220
Lye, Thomas, 54, 260
Lyme Regis, 226

Mabbot, Thomas, 58
Macdouall, Rev. Canon William, 30, 124, 134, 195, 260
Macnamara, Arthur, 220
Maffey, Charles, 150, 204, 260
Makepeace, Rev. J., 260
Maiden Common Farm, 31
Manchester, 1, 4, 26-7, 44, 150, 217, 224-5
Manchester Street, 39, 255, 259, 263, 269
Manor Path, 69
Market Hill, 7, 24, 58, 65, 111-2, 116, 144, 162, 201, 253-5, 260-1, 265-6, **Plates 8, 9**
Market Place, 68
Market Street, 65
Markyate, The Cell, 220
Marsh, 141; Robert, 178, 184, 240, 260
Masons Arms, The, 167
Mayes, Alice, 261; G., 260
Mayes Lane, 269
Mead, Joseph, 97, 105, 126, 260
Mechanics Institute, 93, 139, 176-9, 181, 183, 207, 249-52, 254, 256-8, 260, 262, 264-8
Mees, Charles, 189, 192-3, 237, 244-5, 260
Melsom Street, 66, 184
Menlove, J., 260
Merritt, Jesse, 260
Merrit, John, 178
Merthyr Tydvil, 117-8
Methodist Church (High Town), 86
Middle Row, 110, 174
Middlesex, 23; Finchley, 35
Mildmay, family, 118
Mill Street, 67
Millbrook, 62
Mills, Benjamin, 124
Moody and Sankey, 140
Moor, The, 209
Moor Committee, 113
Morning News, 177

Morris, Henry Bebb, 30; James, 195
Mortimore, Martha, 73
Morton, S.H., 260
Mother Redcap, The, 70, 167, 174
Mount Pleasant, 87, 269
Muggleton, Mr., 260
Muir, James, 64, 89, 94, 176, 223, 260
Munt, James, 16
Munt and Brown (Munt, Brown and Company), 13, 20, 27, 152

Napoleon III, 150
Naples, 254
Nelson, The, 167
New Industries Committee, 231, 247
New Bedford Road, 38, 54, 60, 67-8, 153, 177, 188, 212, 235, 238, 256, 258, 260
New Street, 52, 64, 68, 78, 249
New Town, 21, 24, 36, 38-9, 43, 49, 51-4, 64, 66, 68-70, 91, 96, 101, 135, 137, 144, 148, 167, 172, 236, 250, 252, 254, 256-7, 269
New Town Street, 22-5, 52, 58, 61, 65, 67-8, 79, 269, **Plate 5**
Newcastle, 1, 112, 234
Newland, Robert Henry, 177, 260
Newman, James, 86-7
Newmarket, 187
Nicholson, Dr., 179
Noah's Ark, The, 172
Norman Cross, 17
North, Lady Maria, 29
North Star, The, 238
North Street, 67, 269
Northampton, 120
Northamptonshire, 23
Nottingham, 1, 6, 28, 46, 118, 120-1

Oakley, brothers, 239; Richard, 220
Old Bedford Road, 32, 65-7, 87, 98, 256-7, 269
Old Dunstable Road, 32
Old Meeting, 133, 140, 142, 167, 169, 181-3, 195, 238, 252, 254-7
Old Yard, 85-7, 96
Old Wesleyan Church, 133, 195
Oliver, James Hopkins, 26; Samuel, 58, 70, 113, 136, 205, 216, 244, 246, 260
Omnia Works, 248
Ordish, C., 260
Orkneys, 8, 23
Osborne, Charles Haddon, 147
O'Neill, Rev. James, 105, 135-7, 140, 142, 148, 188-95, 202, 205-6, 231, 233, 240, 242, 254-5, 257, 260, 263, **Plate 19**
Oxford, 1, 2, 120
Oxford Arms, The, 171-2

Padbury, Mr., 260
Parker, William, 225, 260
Parkes, Alexander, 36, 65; Thomas, 260
Park Road, 7, 65-6
Park Road West, 269
Park Square, 65, 187, 235, 253, 256, 269
Park Street, 7, 32, 40, 47, 58, 64-5, 85, 91, 93, 96-7, 116, 122, 128, 133, 140-1, 144, 152, 167, 169, 187, 200-1, 219, 224, 235, 250, 253-4, 259-60, 262, 264, 269, **Plate 13**
Park Street West, 58, 65-6, 70, 72, 259
Park Town, 43, 269
Parkins, 53; Frances, 52; John, 52
Paris, 49
Parsons, E., 177, 260
Partridge, Thomas, 30, 58, 241-2, 260
Pashley, T.H., 72

INDEX 287

Payne, Charles, 125
Peach, Ann, 52-3, 61
Pearman, 141-2, 256; Daniel, 141, 260-1; Frederick, 109, 141, 260-1; Henry, 141-2, 260-1
Peddor, family, 22
Peel, A.W., 226; Sir Robert, 226, 247
Peel Street, 65, 219
Peer, Thomas, 280
Pegler, Edward, 188, 261
Peile, Rev. Dr. Thomas Williamson, 135, 169, 199, 261
Pepper Hill, 58, 269
Peterborough, 9-10, 46, 120
Pheasant, The, 172
Phillips, Rev. J., 169, 261; Sir Richard 175, 265; William, 89, 94, 108, 126, 176, 178, 199, 216, 237, 271, **Plate 19**
Phippen, Mr. 121
Pigg, Mr. 107
Piggott, Frederick, 68
Pledge, William Thompson, 107, 109-10, 225, 238, 242, 244, 261
Polhill, Mr., 254
Pondwicks, 269
Pondwicks Road, 66
Pope, Henry, 195; Superintendent Samuel, 101, 163-4, 172, 219, 233, 261
Portsea, 139, 256
Portsmouth, 208
Poulter, Thomas, 261
Prayer Book Five, 192, 257, 259-60, 263, 266
Pressey, J.W., 56, 261
Primett, T., 261
Primitive Baptist Church, 137
Primitive Methodist Church, 130, 133, 137, 140, 148, 169, 188, 195, 251
Prospect Place, 23, 25, 36, 38, 52, 65, 68, 269
Puddephat, Thomas, 58, 61, 236, 244, 246, 261
Punch, 177
Puttenham, 134, 195

Quarterly Review, 177
Queen Square, 65, 156, 188-9, 191, 201, 261, 263
Quirk, Rev. G., 135

Raban, Mr., 57, 261
Radcliffe, Frederick Delme, 26-7
Railway Hotel, The, 171-2, 174
Ramsgate, 220, 264
Randall, A., 261
Ransom, family, 27
Ratepayers Protection Association, also known as Owners and Ratepayers Association, 103-4, 114, 210, 256, 259, 264
Read, William, 261
Red Cow, The, 7
Red Lion, The, 33
Regent Street, 58, 66
Relief Committee, 155
Rising Sun, The, 167, 171
Roberts, R.E., 197
Robin Hood, The, 167, 171
Robinson, Charles, 11, 58, 61, 105, 108, 126, 140, 144, 190, 192-3, 261, 263, **Plate 15**; Rev. Robert, 178, 181, 261
Roebuck Inn, The, 152, 167
Rosson, Charles, 244
Rothesay Road, 47, 269
Round Green, 41, 235
Roy, Mr., 33-4
Royal Hotel, The, 67
Rudd, Miss, 143
Rural District Sanitary Authority, 116-127

Russell, 203, 214, 217, 221-3, 227-8, 268; Lord Charles, 241; Earl, 225; F.C.H., 215; Lady Frankland, 151; Hastings, 215, 221-2, 224, 227, 229; Lord John, 87. See also Bedford, Duke of; Tavistock, Marquess of
Rutland, George, 150

Saffron Gardens, 269
St. Albans, 7, 10, 12, 25-7, 60, 65, 141, 179, 187, 230
St. Anne's Hill, 66, 152
St. Anne's Lane, 59
St. Helens, 226
St. Mary's Church, 30, 34, 88, 91, 133-7, 140, 143, 166, 194, 206, 250, 253, 260, 262, 266
St. Matthew's Church, 135
St. Paul's Church, 135
Sandoe, William, 101, 108, 121, 140, 261, **Plate 10**
Sandy, 219
Sanitary and Deodorising Committee, 245-6
Saxony, 8
Scarborough, 172
Scholefield, William (M.P.), 57
School Board, 116, 153, 186, 189-91, 193, 201-2, 204-8, 211, 216, 230, 238, 245-6, 249-64, 266-7
Scotland, 1, 16, 23
Seebohm, Benjamin, 184-5, 262; jnr., 242
Sell, Edward, 241; G., 242
Seven Acres, 34, 36, 38-9, 41, 65, 269
Shanasy, J., 280
Sharples, Joshua, 27
Sharples and Company, 108, 259
Scargill, Frank Chapman, 72, 105, 114, 152, 202, 205, 208, 217-8, 222, 229, 230-4, 237, 242, 258, 262, 280
Sheep Street, 269
Shefford, 10, 25
Shelton, 117
Shepherd, J.G., 136, 206, 229, 231, 242, 262; William, 110, 192, 238, 240, 242, 244, 246, 262
Shovelton, Rev. Wright, 138
Sibley, 70; Henry, 54, 58, 65, 91, 93-4, 97-100, 107, 115, 125, 150, 262; William, 241
Sikes, Rev. Thomas, 30-1, 88, 96, 98, 124, 134, 143, 176, 194-5, 241, 262
Silsoe, 31, 64; Wrest Park, 64
Silver Street, 66
Simmons, Phoebe, 201
Simpson, Frederick, 262
SKF, 247
Smart, Arthur, 140, 244, 262; George, 140, Thomas, 244, 262
Smart Brothers (builders), 67, 111, 114, 238, 262
Smirke, Robert, 29
Smith, 59; Andrew A., 191; H., 262; Robert, 42-3, 55, 233, 262; Thomas (builder), 53, 94, 244-5, 262; Thomas (gentleman), 244-5, 262; Thomas (shop-keeper), 26; Thomas (tailor), 150; Thomas (unspecified) 233, 239, 241; Toulmin, 94; William, 24
Smyth, Rev. Hugh Blagg, 172-4, 220, 236, 242, 263
Sole, George, 58-9, 61, 73, 105, 263
Someries Farm, 31
South End, 269
Sowerby, Mr., 242
Spencer's Yard, 85, 107
Spring Place, 44-5, 60, 64, 66, 68-9, 73, 78, 249
Spurgeon, Charles Haddon, 142, 240
Squire, Charles, 64
Squires, Dr. Henry Augustus, 113, 128, 262
Staddon, Mr., 239
Stafford, 120
Stag, The, 167
Stalker, David, 156, 188, 201, 263; William, 183, 263, 280

288 STRAWOPOLIS

Stanion, Rev., 263
Stanton, Mr., 33
Steed, John, 55
Steel, John, 55
Stephenson, George, 250; Robert, 209, 240
Stevenson, Rev. J.R., 225, 229, 242, 263
Stockport, 120
Stockwood Park, 7, 35, 113, 220, 254
Stoke on Trent (inc. Hanley), 120
Stopsley, 32, 35, 41, 116, 188, 254
Strange, George, 263
Stratford-on-Avon, 117
Strathmore Avenue, 269
Stuart [Earls and Marquesses of Bute], John [3rd Earl], 28; John Crichton [2nd Marquess], 28-37, 41-2, 51, 65-6, 87, 134, 187-8, 206, 209, 228, 251-2, 260, 263, 266
Stuart, Capt. W., 215, 226, 228, 254
Stuart Street, 34-5, 37, 39-40, 58, 64-6, 80, 84, 96, 110, 121, 135, 169, 177, 219, 236, 255, 257-8, 262, 269
Sturge, Joseph, 184
Sullivan, Capt. Francis William, 220
Sun, The (newspaper), 178
Sun, The, 64
Sundon, 86-7, 257, 264
Surrey Street, 81
Swansea, 250
Switzerland, 8
Sworder, Charles, 263; Dr. Horace, 259, 263; Robert, 263; Thomas, 32, 53, 55, 61, 72, 94, 97-8, 104-5, 108, 119, 137, 174, 176, 183, 190, 192-3, 205, 208, 216, 233, 237, 253, 256, 263
Tamworth, 226
Tansley, A.J. (Alfred), 57, 61, 64, 102, 104-7, 118-9, 140, 147, 183, 223, 242, 261, 263; J.S., 216
Tavistock, Marquis of, 222, 241; also see Russell
Tavistock, 227
Taylor, 160, 199; Ephraim, 25; Edward, 242-3, 246, 264; Frances, 25; J., **Plate 10**; James, 57; Richard, 25; Robert senr., 25; jnr., 25; W., 115; William, 244
Taylor's Yard, 69, 82
Tearle, George, 24; Joseph, 186, 264
Thames, River, 103
Thurston, Frederick, 181, **Plate 8**
Tiger, The, 172, 174
Times, The, 177-8
Tingewick Cottages, 269
Tiverton, 226
Tolls and Municipal Buildings Committee, 112, 245-6
Tomalin, Charles, 140, 144, 264
Tomson, 33; Charles, 36-7; 41-2; 65, 241, 264; Henry, 87, 176, 264; Dr. Kit, 58, 87-9, 98-9, 105, 124, 176, 216, 237, 264
Torquay, 101
Tottenham, 103
Towcester, 255
Tower Hill, 7, 38, 58-9, 87, 89, 97, 145-6, 262, 269, **Plate 7**
Townrow, William, 35-6, 39, 64, 66, 91, 96-7, 264; Mrs., 66
Townrow Close, 269
Toyer, Alfred, 237, 264; Samuel, 56, 59, 105, 107, 110-1, 114-5, 119, 126-7, 216, 229, 264
Tracey, Mrs., 212
Tranter, William, 264
Trent, River, 117
Tring, 20, 25, 27
Tuckwell, Rev. J., 179, 202, 264
Tunbridge Wells, 46
Turner, Rev. Samuel, 148

Turner's Hall Farm, 162
Tuscany, 9-10, 265
Tutt, Samuel, 242
Twells, Rev., 264

Underwood, John, 264
Union Baptist Church, 134, 139, 195, 261, 264
Union Chapel, 140, 147, 181, 195, 260, 263
Union Street, 67, 262
Upper George Street, 39, 61, 66, 256-8, 269
Upper Pondwicks Gardens, 66
Urban Sanitary Authority, 116

Verulam, Earl of, 27
Victoria Rooms, 178
Victoria Street, 59, 104
Villa Road, 67
Villenoxe, Mde, 177
Vincent, Henry, 178
Vyse, 10, 13, 51; Edmund, 61, 264; Richard (died 1855) 16, 38, 54, 87-95, 122, 124, 176, 199, 208, 224, 263-4; Richard (died 1867), 40, 49-50, 67, 140, 265
Vyse and Sons, 10, 150, 209, 259

Wadsworth, William, 265
Wales, Prince of, 27
Wales, 16
Waller, 9-10, 13, 16, 28, 33, 35, 51, 54, 103; Charles, 176; Edmund, 5, 9, 16, 29, 30, 33-5, 65, 139, 255, 265; James senr., 9, 57, 91-2, 97, 109, 178, 196, 223, 241, 265, **Plate 11**; James Jnr., 9, 265; Jane, 34, 65; John, 9, 33-4, 36-7, 49-51, 66-7, 91-2, 94-5, 102, 176, 195, 257, 261, 265; Robert, 9, 265; Thomas, 9, 19, 30, 33-6, 64, 199, 265; Dr. Thomas, 30, 266; William, 162
Waller Street, 47, 66, 111, 113, 269
Waller Street Methodist, 264
Walsh, William, 242-4, 246, 266
Wand, Miss, 162
Warde, C.T., 31, 263, 266
Wardill, William, 201, 266
Wardown, 262
Waring, Richard, 72
Warner, Chief Constable, 233
Warr, James, 97, 266
Warren, Mr. 239
Warwick, 226
Warwickshire, 31
Watford, 48
Webdale, John, 114, 192, 242, 266, **Plate 20**
Webster, A.T., 54, 64, 94, 97, 109, 140, 144, 179, 212, 230, 232, 237, 242, 244, 246, 266, **Plate 15**
Welch, Alfred P., 63, 108, 121, 124, 192-3, 220, 229, 233, 236-7, 241-2, 266; Levi, 160, 266, **Plate 20**
Welch and Sons, 152
Welcome Stranger, The, 172
Wellington Street, 29, 47, 58, 65, 85, 110, 133, 144, 155, 161, 167, 169, 177, 186, 189-90, 234, 236, 250-1, 256, 262-5, 267, 280
Wellington Street Baptist Church, 139, 143, 222, 263, 264
Welwyn, 27
Wenlock Street, 67-8
West Indies, 262
Wheelwrights Arms, The, 150
Whitbread, 228; Samuel, 224, 226
White, 9; J.E., 240; William, 184
White Hart, The, 167
Whitehill, 252
White Hill Close, 41-2
White Hill Piece, 59
Whitford, Rev. Caleb, 195

INDEX 289

Whiting, John, 27
Whittlesey, 252
Wilkinson, Mr., 239
Williams, Evan Owen, 61, 109, 119, 176, 195, 219, 231-2, 237, 242-3, 261, 266; Herbert Owen, 176, 205, 239, 266; John, 36, 41-3. 53, 64, 84, 266
Williamson, Edward Chilwell, 38, 86-7, 93-4, 102, 105, 124-5, 176, 178-9, 186, 214, 250, 267
Williamson and Austin, 267
Williamson and Son (hat manufacturer), 50
Willis, Johnson (J.J.), 212, 222, 236; T.J., 267; William, 20, 57, 61, 63-4, 89, 97-8, 102, 105, 121, 126, 136, 167, 168, 176, 178, 209, 212, 214, 222-5, 242, 267
Wills family, 149
Wilshere, 26-7; Charles, 27; William (1, M.P.)27; William (2), 27
Wing, George, 161; Mrs., 161
Wingrave, Thomas, 115
Windmill Lane, 255
Windmill Road, 103
Windsor Street, 64-6, **Plate 6**
Winsdon Hill, 113
Wiseman, John, 178, 185, 200, 267, 280

Witney, 56, 250
Woakes, Dr. E.O., 124, 140, 161, 191, 216, 233, 237, 267
Woburn, 200, 214, 221; Abbey 232
Wonnacott, Rev. Henry, 139, 267
Wood Street, 66, 122
Wooden Church, 135, 257, **Plate 14**
Wootton, Peter, 183, 192, 205, 216, 232, 236-8, 241, 244, 246, 267
Worboys, Charles, 235
Worlds End, 269
World's End, The, 172, 174
Worsley, Obadiah, 160-1, 267; William, 160
Wreath, The, 280
Wrestlers' The, 167
Wren, Henry, 230, 232, 238, 242, 244, 267; John 87
Wren's Yard, 87, 269
Wright, Henry, 153, 177-9, 212, 229, 232, 238-9, 242, 244-5, 260, 268; James, 268; Josiah, 24

Yaxley, 9
Yorkshire, 260, 265
York Street, 65, 191, 253
Young, John, 58

SUBJECT INDEX

Agriculture: Organisations: Agricultural Labourers Union, 268; Agriculture Society, 151
Aristocracy and Gentry, 4, 18, 28-32, 50, 54-5, 58-60, 71, 129-30, 132-3, 137, 158, 175, 207, 210, 214, 216, 220-1, 224, 242, 245-6, 253-4, 259, 262-3

Banks, 183-4, 201; Friends Adult School Savings Account 201; London and County, 56; Luton Savings Bank, 49, 184-5, 259; Penny Bank 183
Bankruptcy, 53, 267, 280
Bonfire Night/Guy Fawkes Night, 23, 111, 157-8, 163, 174
Borough Status, 14, 105, 110, 114-6, 122, 129, 203, 208, 222-3, 225, 264, 266-7, 280; 1866-7, 221, 225-7; 1875-6, 50, 60, 228-235, 242, 245-6
Brewing, 38, 171, 216; Burr's Brewery, 32, 38, 53, 263; Crown and Anchor, 256, 263; Dunstable Brewery, 26-7; Fordhams Brewery, 154; Green's Brewery, 174; McMullen's Brewery, 154; Sworder's Brewery, 38, 53, 174, 256, 263
Brickmaking, 41-3, 49, 68, 256-7, 262
Building Societies: Luton Benefit, 56; Luton Equitable, 55-6; Luton Equitable Loan Association, 56; Luton Improved, 56, 261; Luton Permanent Benefit/Luton Permanent, 56, 72-3; New Building Society, 258, 260, 264; South Bedfordshire and North Hertfordshire Permanent, 55-6, 250, 252-3, 256, 259; Town and Country, 72

Cemeteries, 143, 206; General, 101-2, 152, 251; Church, 101-2, 263
Charities, 35, 64, 67, 147; Ashton, 39, 64, 66, 68; Dunstable, 26, 32, 34; Luton, 34
Common Lodging Houses, 101
Conservatism, 127, 141, 157, 193, 206, 213-8, 221, 223, 227-8, 240, 245-6, 249-54, 256-265, 267, 280
Corn Exchange, 110-2, 157, 185-6, 203, 232, 236, 251-2, 262, **Plate 9**

Crime, 157-164, 198, 267; Arson, 162, 199; Assault, 160-2, 167, 171, 173, 198; Burglary, 159-60; Drunkenness, 156-8, 160-1, 198, 264; Embezzlement,162, 198; Manslaughter and Murder, 160-3, 198, 266; Poaching, 159-60, 172, 198-9; Theft, 160, 163, 172, 198; Vagrancy, 198; Vandalism, 112, 159, 198

Death Rates, 120
Disease see Health

Education, 14, 149, 152-3, 175-185, 257, 267; Private: Alliance House, 177; Collegiate, 152; Luton Academy, 177, 260; Luton Grammar School, 138, 177, 253; New Hall Academy, 177, 268; Villa School, 152, 177, 260, 268; Ragged School, 187, 201; School Board Controversy, 105, 129, 136, 189-194, 201-2, 208; Sunday School - see Religion; Voluntary System, 180, 186, 188-9; Adult School (Friends), 183-5, 188, 251-2, 260, 262; British School, 181, 187-8, 192, 251, 267; Crown and Anchor School, 187; Gaitskill Terrace Evening School, 145, 183, 250-4, 260-1, 263-4, 266-7; Lancasterian School, 187; National School, 175, 184, 187-90, 201, 206, 261, 263; Wesleyan Day School, 189
Elections: Local, 106, 114, 116, 130, 235, 237, 241, 243-4, 261-2, 264, 266-8; Parliamentary, 161, 224, 227-8; Societies: Working Men's Representation Association, 237-8, 243, 244-6, 254, 259-60, 267-8
Exhibitions, 152, 178, 263

Fairs, 111, 150, 156-8, 201; Fox Fair, 156; Statute (Stattie) 21, 155-7, 163, 174, 208
Fire Brigade, 112, 116, 121
Friendly Societies, 149-50; Foresters, 150, 201, 204, 249-50, 259-60, 262; Manchester Unity, 150; Oddfellows, 149, 201, 204, 236, 250, 253, 255, 259, 261

Gas Supply: Gas Committee, 112; Gas Company, 64, 97, 104, 108, 112, 125, 127, 178, 230, 245, 251, 261, 265

Hat Trade, 8-12, 19-29, 48-9, 61, 70, 110, 163, 175, 247; Pay and Conditions, 9-12, 20-3, 63, 209, 225; Plaiting, 8-12, 20-2; Seasonal variations, 11-12; Sewing, 9-11; other branches, 9-10, 12, 20, 25
Health: Cholera, 43, 88, 98-100, 125, 221, 250, 255; Disease, 46, 86, 88-9, 98; Hospitals, 254, 261, 266-7; Profession, 51, 54, 58, 71, 73, 150, 250, 253, 257, 263-4, 266; see also Board of Health
Housing, 13, 24, 29, 40-1, 49, 54-5, 60, 64-70; Conditions, 41, 43-7, 85, 91-3, 107; Materials, 49, 68

Ironworks: Brown and Green Iron Foundry, 251-2, 256; Vauxhall, 1, 248

Justice: Courts, 86, 106, 159, 166, 172-3, 205, 218-20; Imprisonment: Bridewell, 219, 241;
Justices, 220; Policing, 158, 164-5, 167, 219, 230, 233, 235-6, 258, 261, 267; Police Station, 219-20

Lace Industry, 22, 175
Land, 12, 18, 52, 56-7, 64-7, 70, 122, 248; disposal, 19, 26, 31, 33-6, 39-40, 42, 49, 51; and housing, 16, 36-8, 40, 43-4, 46-50, 53; ownership, 18, 26-9, 31-2, 59-61, 113; Societies: Bedfordshire and Huntingdonshire Freehold Land Society, 57; British Land Company, 26; Luton Freehold Land Society, 57, 224, 250, 256, 260-1, 263, 265, 267
Liberalism, 118-9, 141, 168, 171, 207, 213-8, 221-4, 227-8, 239, 241, 245-6, 247, 249-52, 254-68, 280; Societies: Bedfordshire Reform and Registration Association 223; Luton Reform Association, 223, 249, 254-5, 257-60, 263-7
Libraries, 17, 149, 178-9, 183-6, 200, 267; Reading Room, 38, 179, 185-6, 264
Lighting, 97, 104, see also Gas Supply
Lord of the Manor, 30-1, 63, 110, 132; Manor Courts, 204

Markets, 30, 110-1; Market House, 7, 110-1, 113, 116, 252, **Plate 8**
Marriage, 19, 24-5, 175

Occupations: *passim* but see especially 71, 73, 215

Parks, 113, 168; East Ward Recreation Ground, 40; People's Park, 67, 152, 269; Pope's Meadow (formerly Parks Meadow), 168, 269; Working Men's Recreation Ground, 67
Paving, 106-8, 119, 123
Photography, 112, 181, 196, 255
Plait Hall(s), 38, 111-2, 173, 190, 203, 228, 230-1, 262, 264
Population, 23, 46, 49, 51, 85; Luton, 16
Post Office, 261; Postmaster, 71, 261
Poverty, 128, 131, 144-8, 155, 158, 204, 206; Poor Man's Club, 148; see also Board of Guardians
Public Houses, 24, 87, 154-5, 157-8, 164-5, 167-9, 171-5; Licensing, 199; see also individual premises
Public Slaughter House, 89

Railways, 14, 19, 39, 48, 67, 69, 109, 113, 115, 152, 161, 208-10, 225, 240, 249-50, 252-3, 259, 263-5, 267; and crime, 159-60
Rates, 119, 218-9; Church Rate, 188
Reading Room see Libraries
Refuse Collection, 98, 107
Religion, 71, 133-148, 172, 213-4; Baptist, 29, 32, 35, 137-9, 140-3, 145, 147-8, 167, 181, 183, 192, 200, 252, 257-8, 260-5, 267, 280; Church of England, 132-40, 142-3, 187, 252, 188-9, 192, 249-50, 252-7, 259-61, 263, 265-6; Congregationalist, 137-9, 141, 144-5, 147, 185, 192, 258, 261-2, 264, 266-7; Methodist, 29, 62, 137-8, 140-2, 145-6, 148, 169, 176, 180, 182, 187, 189, 192, 208, 254-6, 258, 260-1, 264-5; Mormons, 142; Roman Catholics, 142; Society of Friends (Quakers), 13, 27, 29, 35, 55, 59, 133, 137, 141-2, 182-4, 186, 192, 195, 216, 228, 250-2, 255-6, 258-62; Sunday Schools, 139, 169, 175, 180-1, 183-4, 188, 195, 200-1, 258, 264, 267; see also individual churches
Riots, 23, 156, 160-1, 199, 233; Peace Day, 14; *see also* Bonfire Night

Sanitation and Sewage, 40, 57, 86, 89-91, 96-7, 100, 102-6, 108-10, 115, 118-20, 124-5
Self Help: Freemasons, 249-50, 254, 256-8, 261-2, 265-8; Luton Mutual Improvement Society, 184, 201, 253; Sick Benefit Club, 184; Young Men's Mutual Improvement Society, 185
Slaughter Houses, 89, 97, 101, 107, 113, 120
Solicitors, 50-1, 54-5, 71, 91, 150, 211, 249-53, 258, 260, 262-3, 267
Societies: Choral Society, 268; Cottage Garden Society, 184; Elocution Society, 185; Harmonic Society, 139, 151, 178; Horticultural Society, 151, 253, 265; Rifle Volunteer Corps., 150-1, 261; Soaksters Club, 197; Women's Literary Institution/Association, 176, 250
Sport and Recreation: 151-2, 169, 175, 201, 261; Circuses, 152, 157; Concerts, 151, 178; Cricket, 152, 201, 258, 262, 265; Cycling, 175; Dances, 152; Football, 152, 175; Gymnastics, 153, 268; Horse racing, 152; Hunting, 27; Magic lantern, 169-71; Swimming Baths, 38, 113-4, 152-3, 175, 208, 222, 262; see also Parks; Theatre, 152-3, 175
Street Cleaning, 107, 125

Temperance Movement, 145, 149, 151, 154-5, 165-175, 199, 216, 252, 255, 257-261, 267
Timber Merchants, 23, 71, 251-2
Tories (see Conservatism)
Tower Hill Almshouses, 59, 87, 93
Town Hall, 8, 14, 17, 38, 67, 85, 89, 94, 97, 103, 108, 112, 114-5, 121, 124, 151, 153, 169, 178-9, 185-6, 193, 212, 217, 223-4, 229, 234, 236, 269

Voting, 216-7, 222-4, 228
Vestry, 84-86, 89-91, 102, 113, 127, 191, 205

Water Supply/Drainage, 89-90, 95, 99, 101-2, 108-9, 115, 258; Water Closets, 45, 70, 102
Weights, sale of, 206
Whigs (see Liberalism)
Wombwell's Menagerie, 153, 158
Workhouse, 30, 64, 88, 160, 199, 256, 259

About the Author

A Lutonian, Stephen Bunker read Politics and Modern History at the University of Manchester and was awarded the degree of Ph.D. from University College London for the thesis which forms the basis of this volume. He was Keeper of Local History at Luton Museum from 1982-93 and is currently Senior Lecturer in History at the University of Luton.